IOANNIS D. STEFANIDIS

ISLE OF DISCORD

NATIONALISM, IMPERIALISM AND THE
MAKING OF THE CYPRUS PROBLEM

HURST & COMPANY, LONDON

Τοις κεκοιμημένοις

Published in the United Kingdom by
C. Hurst & Co. (Publishers) Ltd.,
38 King Street, Covent Garden, London WC2E 8JZ
© Ioannis Stefanidis, 1999
All rights reserved.
Printed in Greece
ISBN 1-85065-415-8

CONTENTS

PREFACE

The present study is an attempt to inquire into the post-war origins
of the Cyprus question, which is commonly described as one of the
longest-standing and most intractable problems in contemporary
international politics. It focuses on the years 1949 to 1955, that is
from the inception of the drive towards what is generally called the
'internationalisation' of the problem up to the outbreak of armed
struggle against the British colonial regime. This period has been
selected for several reasons, being the time when the *Enosis* movement exceeded the narrow confines of Greece and Cyprus and
reached the international community, particularly through the UN;
the future of Cyprus ceased to be an Anglo-Greek issue and, without becoming an Anglo-Cypriot one, evolved into an international
problem; Turkey was practically admitted as the third party to the
dispute, alongside Britain and Greece; the United States was drawn
in by the parties involved; and last but not least, it was during this
period that the opportunity for a peaceful and gradual evolution of
Cypriot politics towards self-government and self-determination
was repeatedly and fatefully squandered.

A further reason for choosing this particular period is the relatively scant attention it has received in comparison to subsequent
phases of the Cyprus saga.[1] There are, however, a few notable exceptions. One is Professor François Crouzet's two-volume *Le conflit
de Chypre, 1946-1959* (1973), which covers the period in its first
volume. It remains an impressive piece of work of high scholarly
calibre, based on a wealth of material other than diplomatic records
– the latter, of course, being unavailable at the time it was written.
In *Countdown to Rebellion. British Policy in Cyprus, 1939-1955*

---

1. For an annotated bibliography on post-war Cypriot history and politics, see
Paschalis M. Kitromilides-Marios L. Evryviades, *World Bibliographical Series*,
vol. 28, *Cyprus*, revised edition, Oxford 1995.

(1990) former US Army intelligence officer George Horton Kelling devotes 63 out of 167 pages to the 1949-55 period. His work is based on British records and secondary sources in English. Perhaps inevitably, it touches upon the other parties to the problem – Greeks, Turks, Americans – only to a limited extent. Furthermore, it ignores certain aspects of British policy, particularly towards the Greek recourse to the UN. It also misses a number of important documents, such as the memorandum supporting a revision of British policy on 16 December 1949. A third study which needs to be mentioned is Robert Holland's article 'Never, Never Land: British Colonial Policy and the Roots of Violence in Cyprus, 1950-1954', in the *Journal of Imperial and Commonwealth History* (1993). As its title suggests, it is a penetrating inquiry into the attitude of British officialdom towards the question of Cyprus, on the basis of primarily Colonial Office material.

What is attempted here is a broader approach based on sources which to a considerable extent have not been utilised in the past, primarily British and US records but also some Greek material. The study ranges over the policies of *all* parties or 'actors' involved, the states and organised groups whose attitude contributed, in one way or another, to making the Cyprus problem an international one. Of course, there are obvious limits to this undertaking. Even in well documented cases, like the British or the US policy-making process, working methods – for example the unrecorded volume of telephone conversations – and record-keeping procedures leave out much that could have helped explain the 'whys and wherefores of decisions'.[2]

Part I of the study present a more or less straightforward narrative, telling the 'story' of the period on the basis of events and physical and verbal acts directed by one party to at least one other. This section reconstructs the succession of events which provide, so to speak, the external setting for the purpose of Part II. Chapters 4-8 analyse the policies of each actor individually. This concerns decision-making in the light of both external and internal circumstances as perceived by policy-makers on various levels. The intention is to identify the various forces, particularly the competing interests and

2. Adamthwaite 1988, 2-3.

pressures, that helped shape specific decisions; also to test the claims of ideological motivation behind the final attitude of the actors. A final assessment of this process and its outcome is attempted in the Epilogue.

In identifying the parties to the problem one might easily distinguish four national 'actors': Britain, Greece, Turkey and the United States. While each of these actors may appear unitary, a closer investigation reveals that several poles are at work when it comes to policy-making. The structure and processes of Western-type government assign important roles to bureaucratic agencies which sometimes appear as quasi-independent actors.[3] This was to a certain extent true in the British case, in which one may distinguish the roles played by various sets of actors: the 'diplomats' (the Foreign Office and its Southern Department in particular, the Ambassador in Athens, the British delegation to the UN, and, upon occasion, the Commonwealth Relations Office), the colonial apparatus (the Colonial Office and its Mediterranean Department, the Governor of Cyprus and the colony's bureaucracy), the military (the Chiefs of Staff). Bureaucratic politics were a more visible aspect of US policy-making, where the State Department and its various divisions, the delegation to the UN, diplomats and other 'men in the field', plus the Joint Chiefs of Staff played clearly identifiable parts. In both the British and the American cases various *ad hoc* committees or meetings chaired by the Foreign Secretary were often called to smooth out internal differences and impose a common stand. The role of Greek and particularly Turkish bureaucratic divisions was less easy to document.

As part of the domestic setting, parliamentary politics also attribute a special role to parliaments, opposition parties, pressure groups and the press. Again, their importance varies in each case. Certainly, the US Congress enjoyed a potentially greater margin of influence than the British House of Commons, as did the Greek-American lobby in comparison to British philhellenes. In Greece the pro-*Enosis* movement claimed an autonomous role, whereas its Turkish counterpart remained under effective government control

3. For the concept of bureaucratic politics as a 'paradigm' of decision-making theory, see Allison 1971, 144ff..

throughout. More problematic is the concept of public opinion, which, at best, is a malleable factor with a potential influence largely limited to pre-election periods. In cases, however, of circumscribed parliamentary regimes or under-developed civic societies like Turkey, Greece and colonial Cyprus, its role may be little more than a self-fulfilling prophecy.

At first sight, the two ethnic communities in Cyprus also emerge as 'actors' in their own right. As it turns out, however, this was only true of the Greek Cypriot political leadership, both nationalist and communist: even the former tended to act independently of the 'national centre', i.e. the Greek government, in a way that often predicated the policies of the latter. By way of contrast, the Turkish Cypriot leadership was neither willing nor able to dispute the leading role of the Turkish government in the course of the anti-*Enosis* struggle.

Finally, from the time that international 'parliamentary diplomacy' was co-opted by one of the contending parties, the United Nations and its organs, particularly the General Assembly, also became an important part of the external setting in which decisions had to be made.

While the preceding points and the structure of the present study may suggest a decision-making approach to the study of this particular topic, this is not a theory-orientated work. The tools of decision-making theories are primarily employed in the Epilogue with the specific aim to gauge the divergence of decisions taken during this period from the precepts of rationality.[4]

For those who may be taken aback by certain findings of this study, particularly regarding the role of venerable personalities or the use of national ideologies, I would recall Hedley Bull's remark, according to which 'inquiry has its own morality, and is necessarily subversive of political institutions and movements of all kinds, good as well as bad'.[5]

---

4. Of course, the concept of decision-making as 'the act (or the *art*?) of choosing among available alternatives about which uncertainty exists' is ever present in a study of an international problem. The quotation is from Dougherty-Pfaltzgraff 1981, 469.
5. Bull 1995, xviii.

This work has greatly benefited from the comments and suggestions of Professor Paschalis Kitromilides, Professor John S. Koliopoulos, Dr Costa Carras and Christopher Hurst, the publisher, who were kind enough to spend precious time reading the manuscript.

My research at the British Public Record Office and the British Library was partly facilitated by the generous support of the Institute of Balkan Studies and its Director, Professor Kaliopi Koufa, in the summer of 1991. My research at the United States National Archives and Library of Congress in the summer of 1995 was made possible thanks to a Mutual Exchange Grant under the auspices of the Fulbright Program, the staff of which in Thessaloniki, Athens and Washington DC kindly assisted me in every possible way. I also wish to thank the Board of the Catholic University, Washington D.C., for providing accommodation in their comfortable surroundings in July-August 1995.

This publication would not have been possible without the support of Christopher Hurst and the co-operation of his able colleague, Michael Dwyer. Special thanks to Klimis Mastoridis for his expert typographic job.

My greatest debt of gratitude is of course owed to my family, my mother Foteini in particular, and my friends who sustained me in various ways during the long months of writing.

Thessaloniki   I.D.S.
July 1998

CHRONOLOGY

1571	Ottoman conquest of Cyprus
1832	Greece becomes independent
1869	The Suez Canal opens
1878	Cyprus leased to Britain
1914	Britain annexes Cyprus
1922	Greek defeat in Anatolia; Mustafa Kemal abolishes the Ottoman monarchy
1923	Turkey recognises the British annexation of Cyprus by the Lausanne Treaty
1925	Cyprus becomes a Crown Colony
1931	Anti-British riots lead to the suspension of civic liberties
1941	Civic liberties partially restored; formation of the communist AKEL
1946	The Labour government announces constitutional and economic reform
1948	The 'Winster Constitution' is offered but rejected

1949
September   The Greek Civil War ends
November   AKEL launches the drive to internationalisation

1950
January   The Ethnarchy plebiscite
October   Election of Makarios III as Archbishop of Cyprus

1951
March   Greek Prime Minister Venizelos acknowledges the Greek claim on Cyprus

September	Greece and Turkey are accepted into NATO
October	The British Conservatives return to office

1952

July	Makarios denounces the Greek government for refusing recourse to the UN
November	Field Marshal Papagos becomes Greek Prime Minister
December	British decision to transfer the Middle East Headquarters to Cyprus

1953

September	The Papagos-Eden meeting
November	The Greek government indicates its decision to resort to the UN

1954

July	British offer of constitutional development for Cyprus combined with Hopkinson's 'Never'
August	The first Greek recourse on Cyprus to the UN
October	Anglo-Egyptian agreement on the evacuation of the Suez Zone
December	The UN General Assembly decides 'not to consider' the Greek item

1955

April	The EOKA armed struggle begins; Eden becomes Prime Minister; Britain joins the Turco-Iraqi ('Baghdad') Pact
August	Britain convenes Tripartite Conference with the participation of Greece and Turkey
September	Anti-Greek riots in Istanbul and Izmir
October	Papagos dies; Karamanlis becomes Prime Minister
December	AKEL is proscribed in Cyprus

1956

March	Five-month talks between Governor Harding and Makarios fail; the Archbishop is deported to the Seychelles
October	Anglo-French intervention in the Suez
December	The 'Radcliffe plan' of constitutional reform; the Turkish government adopts the partition of Cyprus as its goal

1957

January	Eden resigns; MacMillan becomes Prime Minister
March	Makarios is released from exile
December	A Resolution supporting self-determination in Cyprus musters a simple majority in the UN General Assembly

1958

Feb.-August   Violence reaches climax in Cyprus

July   The overthrow of the Iraqi monarchy imperils the Baghdad Pact

Sept.-August   The 'MacMillan plan' providing for tripartite condominium on Cyprus is rejected by Greece but accepted by Turkey; Makarios consents to independence

December   Greek-Turkish understanding on Cyprus

1959

February   The Zurich agreement between Greece and Turkey is followed by the tripartite London agreements on the establishment of a Republic of Cyprus

December   Archbishop Makarios is elected first President of Cyprus

1960

August   Cyprus becomes officially independent and member of the Commonwealth

1963

December   The Cyprus Constitution breaks down and intercommunal violence erupts

1964

May-June   President Johnson's intervention staves off a Turkish invasion; Greece sends troops to the island as the Turkish Cypriots withdraw to fortified enclaves

1967

November   After further violence, the Greek military regime withdraws the troops dispatched in 1964

December   A 'Provisional Cyprus-Turkish Administration' is set up in the Turkish Cypriot enclaves

1974

July-August   Following a coup against President Makarios instigated by the Greek military dictatorship, Turkey invades and *de facto* partitions Cyprus

ABBREVIATIONS

AKEL	*Anorthotiko Komma Ergazomenou Laou* (Progressive Working People's Party)
BIS	British Information Service
BMEO	British Middle East Office
CIA	Central Intellingence Agency
CO	Colonial Office
COS	Chiefs of Staff (British)
CRO	Commonwealth Relations Office
CTCA	Cyprus Turkish Cultural Association
EAM	*Ethniko Apeleftherotiko Metopo* (National Liberation Front)
EAS	*Ethnikos Apeleftherotikos Synaspismos* (National Liberation League)
EDA	*Eniea Dimokratiki Aristera* (United Democratic Left)
EOKA	*Ethniki Organosis Kyprion Agoniston* (National Organisation of Cypriot Fighters)
FO	Foreign Office (British)
FTA	Federation of Turkish Associations
GTI	(US State Department Bureau for) Greece, Turkey, Iran
GSEE	*Geniki Synomospondia Ergaton Ellados* (General Confederation of Greek Workers)
IDEA	*Ieros Desmos Ellinon Axiomatikon* (Sacred Bond of Greek Officers)
JCS	Joint Chiefs of Staff (USA)
KATAK	Cyprus Turkish Minority Association
KKE	*Kommounistiko Komma Elladas* (Communist Party of Greece)
MEDO	Middle East Defence Organisation
NAC	North Atlantic Council
NATO	North Atlantic Treaty Organisation
NEA	(State Department Office for) Near Eastern (South Asian, African) Affairs
NSC	National Security Council (USA)
OHEN	*Orthodoxos Hristianiki Enosis Neoleas* (Orthodox Christian Union of Youth)
PEAEK	*Panellinios Epitropi Agonos Enoseos Kyprou* (Panhellenic Committee of Struggle for the Union of Cyprus)
PEEK	*Panellinios Epitropi Enoseos Kyprou* (Panhellenic Committee for the Union of Cyprus)
PEK	*Panagrotiki Enosis Kyprou* (All-Farmers Union of Cyprus)

PEO	*Pankypria Ergatiki Omospondia* (Pancyprian Federation of La-bour)
PEON	*Pankyprios Ethniki Organosis Neoleas* (Pancyprian National Youth Organisation)
PPS	Policy Planning Staff (USA)
RPP	Republican People's Party
SEATO	South-East Asian Treaty Organisation
SEK	*Synomospondia Ergaton Kyprou* (Cyprus Workers Confedera-tion)

1

THE PRELUDE TO
INTERNATIONALISATION, 1945-1952

The Cyprus question is essentially a legacy of that celebrated subject of modern diplomatic history, the Eastern Question. After three
centuries of Ottoman rule, the island of Cyprus – strategically lo-
cated at the hub of three continents – did not follow the pattern of
the sultan's former territories in Europe, which for the most part
came under the control of successor nation states. Instead, it entered a colonial phase that ensured, long after the Ottoman Empire
had ceased to exist, the island's continuing role as a bone of contention between rival nationalisms – the Greek and the Turkish.

British rule in Cyprus began in June 1878, when Britain was
granted possession of the island in exchange for her support to the
Sublime Porte against further Russian encroachments. The Ottoman sultan retained a nominal suzerainty, which Britain unilaterally
abrogated during World War I. Kemalist Turkey, as successor to the
Porte, recognised the annexation of Cyprus to the British Empire
under the terms of the Lausanne Peace Treaty (1923) whereby she
also renounced all rights to former Ottoman territories outside her
frontiers.[1] In 1925, Cyprus became a Crown Colony. Hardly six
years had passed when economic grievances and the Greek irredentist cause of Enosis (union with Greece) were fused in an insur-
rection against the British authorities.[2] In reaction, representative
institutions, however 'rudimentary and distorted',[3] were abolished.
From then on, the island was ruled as a bureaucratic autocracy. The
Deportation Law of 1931 and the restrictive laws of 1937 on the
Orthodox Church ensured that the Greek nationalist movement
was bereft of both its ecclesiastical and lay leadership.[4] Significantly,

after the death of Cyril III in 1933, the all important throne of Archbishop and Ethnarch (spiritual and quasi-political leader of the Greek-
Orthodox) would remain vacant for fourteen years.[5]

In view of security considerations and pressing domestic issues,
pre-war Greek governments avoided making an issue out of the
situation in Cyprus and continued to adhere to a consistently pro-
British line. Turkey, on the other hand, showed little interest in the
Muslim community of the island, which had for the most part remained unaffected by Kemalist secularism.

The post-war thaw of Cypriot politics and Enosis

From 1941, the loss of Greece and the exigencies of the war effort
compelled the British to relax repression. As a result, Cypriot political life experienced a genuine revival. Undoubtedly, the most
important new element in the situation was the rise of a strong left-
wing party, the Progressive Working People's Party (AKEL), and a
militant labour movement led by the Pancyprian Federation of Labour (PEO). The party was formed in 1941 and soon came under
firm Communist control. In the 1943 municipal elections, AKEL
tried its hand with impressive results. The reaction of the Right,
which still suffered from the debilitating effects of the 1931 uprising, was bitter but ineffectual. In the next municipal elections, held
in 1946, AKEL's front tactics paid off, and its National Liberation
League (EAS) candidates swept all four major urban centres, including Nicosia. The advance of AKEL seemed irreversible, especially when, in the summer of 1947, its favourite, Leontios, was
elected Archbishop of Cyprus.[6]

This event, which coincided with the British effort to introduce
a constitution, led the right-wing nationalists grouped around
Makarios of Kyrenia, an aging deportee of 1931, to commence an
all out struggle to recover the ground lost. Leontios' sudden death,
within forty days of his election, provided the Right with the opportunity to recapture the archiepiscopal throne. From then on,
Church and Right were closely identified, the former taking the
lead as the traditional leader (Ethnarchy) of the Orthodox flock.
The Ethnarchy already controlled the strong Farmers' Union (PEK)
and also set up a 'national' Cyprus Workers Confederation (SEK) to

compete with the leftist PEO for labour support. From then on, the acute polarisation between Right and Left became a dominant feature of Greek Cypriot politics, leaving no space for a middle-of-the-road party.[7] There were political stirrings within the Turkish Cypriot community, too. In 1943, a group of nationalists established the Cyprus Turkish Minority Association (KATAK). A year later, a faction led by Dr Fazil Küçük broke away and set up the Cyprus National Turkish People's Party.[8]

Between 1945-9, the British colonial authorities had to deal with a tumultuous political situation, which owed more to the Left-Right division within the Greek Cypriot community than to nationalist passions. Anti-colonial feeling was nonetheless present, as manifested by the bloody mutinous incidents that marked the return and discharge of Cypriot army units in the second half of 1945. The end of the war also brought economic discontent, as military expenditure declined and markets for the predominantly agricultural Cypriot produce shrank. Industrial action became more frequent and violent, culminating in the drawn-out strikes of the miners and builders in early 1948. During the same period, the establishment of detention camps for illegal Jewish immigrants to Palestine became a further source of ill-feeling.[9] Again, discontent and repression were translated into more votes for AKEL rather than the nationalist Right.

Meanwhile, Cyprus had once more become a focus of Greek irredentism. The catalyst was provided by World War II. In March 1941, a month before the German invasion of Greece, Prime Minister Alexandros Koryzis asked Anthony Eden, the British Foreign Secretary, to consider the cession of Cyprus as a reward for the Greek war effort. Eden stated that he was not prepared to discuss that 'most delicate political question' at that time.[10] On the eve of the Greek collapse, Emmanouil Tsouderos, Koryzis' successor, pleaded for permission to establish King George in Cyprus, while the island would remain under British administration. The request was turned down by Churchill himself.[11] Tsouderos, as head of the Greek government in exile, included Cyprus in Greek post-war claims. The position of the British government was that it could not discuss such claims while the war lasted.[12]

Liberation found Greece enmeshed in bitter civil conflict. Successive governments were too dependent on British assistance for their survival to raise the Cyprus question. To be sure, the Greek Left, represented by the Communist Party (KKE) and its National Liberation Front (EAM), never ceased clamouring for the cession of the island.[13] The Greek Regent, Archbishop Damaskinos, also raised the question on his own initiative during his visit to London in September 1945. In return for Cyprus, Damaskinos offered bases not only on the island but anywhere on Greek soil – an offer that was to be repeated several times in the future.[14] The response of Ernest Bevin, the British Foreign Secretary, was non-committal. Shortly, however, the steadfast opposition of the Chiefs of Staff (COS) and the Colonial Office would tip the scales against the cession of Cyprus.[15]

At the same time, the Labour government realised that it was improper to go on ruling Cyprus as a bureaucratic autocracy. In October 1946, the newly appointed Colonial Secretary, Arthur Creech Jones, repealed the illiberal measures taken since 1931 and announced a programme of constitutional reform and economic development for the colony. The implementation of the new policy was entrusted to a new governor, Lord Winster of Witherslack, a man of good intentions but with no experience in colonial and, more particularly, Cypriot affairs.[16] Both the Greek Cypriot Ethnarchy and AKEL rejected the plan and reiterated the demand for Enosis. In November, a representative Greek Cypriot delegation, under the *locum tenens* Leontios, set out for Athens and London. In the British capital, Creech Jones told the delegates that, while self-government was on offer, no change in the status of Cyprus was contemplated.[17]

Governor Winster arrived at his post in March 1947. Enlisting the support of local political forces proved harder than anticipated. The Ethnarchy denied co-operation. AKEL, however, decided to take part in the constitutional process. Thus, unlike the Right, the Left was present at the Consultative Assembly, which the Governor convened in November in order to discuss the future constitutional proposals. The leftist representatives pressed for a wholly elected parliament and responsible government in domestic affairs, while accepting that external relations and defence should be reserved for Britain. A delegation was also despatched to London to press these views with the Labour government. Soon, however, the Communist leaders felt that the Ethnarchy's nationalist stand threatened to take the wind out of their sails in local politics. What was more, the British government finally refused to grant full internal self-government. The draft constitution, which London issued in May 1948, more than eighteen months after its announcement, provided for a very limited form of representative government, since the Governor concentrated all executive and a wide measure of legislative power in his own hands. This led AKEL to withdraw from the Consultative Assembly.[18] With the withdrawal of AKEL and the absence of the Ethnarchy, the Assembly was reduced to its *ex officio* members and the representatives of the Turkish Cypriot minority. Realising its futility as a legitimising instrument, Winster decided to dissolve it.[19]

As a matter of record, the constitutional offer of 1948 provided for a legislature with an elected majority and proportional representation of the Greek and Turkish Cypriot communities, an executive with an officially nominated majority of ministers, whereas defence, foreign affairs and minority rights rested firmly in British hands.[20] This was the only serious attempt by post-war Britain to move the island 'along the classic path of self-government'[21] and it failed ingloriously. The so-called 'Winster Constitution' technically remained on offer until 1954, without ever being taken up by its recipients. Its economic complement, however, the ten-year development programme announced in 1946, was put into effect with some positive results.[22]

In October 1948, Winster resigned a bitter man. Greek nationalist agitation intensified and, by January 1949, AKEL too reverted to unconditional support for Enosis. The line of self-government as a preliminary to full self-determination was condemned as a serious error, and the entire Central Committee was relieved of its post. In August, the Sixth Party Congress elected a new, staunchly pro-Soviet leadership. Ezekias Papaioannou, a veteran of the Spanish Civil War who had spent the war years in London, became the new Secretary-General.[23]

Meanwhile, Ronald Turnbull, the Acting Governor, took steps to reassert colonial authority. These were primarily directed against AKEL, whose growth had also provoked American concern. Penalties for seditious activity increased and several leftist activists were

sent to prison, occasionally on rather trivial charges; political activity was forbidden to civil servants; strict limitations were placed on
trade union fundraising and industrial action; electoral registers were
manipulated in view of the 1949 municipal elections.[24] The elections prompted the Americans – ever sensitive to the Communist
menace – to suggest that Greece and Turkey use their influence in
support of the anti-Communist candidates. This, in the eyes of the
colonial administration, was tantamount to inviting foreign intervention and was rejected.[25]

Relations between the colonial administration and the Right were
as frosty as ever and contacts between British officials and Ethnarchy
leaders were reported as 'practically non-existent'.[26] The appointment of Winster's successor, Sir Andrew Wright, was greeted by the
Church with encyclicals reaffirming commitment to the Enosis
struggle and calling on the faithful to boycott government functions.[27] In this atmosphere of estrangement the Enosis movement
took a new and decisive turn.

On 27 September 1949, as its sister party in Greece met defeat,
AKEL took the first step towards the path of internationalisation by
publicly offering the Ethnarchy its co-operation in promoting the
cause of Enosis before the United Nations. The next move came on
23 November, when the AKEL-controlled city councils addressed a
message to the UN Security Council denouncing British domination and declaring the ardent desire of the Greek Cypriot population for union with Greece. AKEL asked for a plebiscite under UN
auspices to ascertain the people's will. Shortly afterwards, it started
collecting signatures to support its proposal.[28]

The Ethnarchy rejected AKEL's overtures but endorsed the plebiscite idea in a somewhat modified form – instead of seeking UN
involvement and supervision, it decided to keep the process within
the domestic domain. The decision was taken by the Ethnarchy Bureau, chaired by Makarios, the young Bishop of Kition, and was
confirmed by the Ethnarchy Council on 5 December.[29] A week later,
Archbishop Makarios addressed a letter to the Governor, requesting that the authorities conduct the plebiscite themselves. Predictably, Wright turned down the request. He emphasised that there
could be no question of change in the sovereignty of Cyprus and
warned against any sign of disloyalty. He also disputed the validity

of the undertaking in advance,[30] yet did not attempt to prevent the Ethnarchy from going ahead with its plans. The proposed plebiscite was actually a collection of signatures for or against union with Greece, to be waged under ecclesiastic supervision in the churches of the island on 15 January 1950. Much to the embarrassment of the Ethnachy, AKEL announced that it was dropping its own campaign to join in the 'national' effort of the Church.[31] It also appealed to the Turkish Cypriots to support the anti-colonial struggle.[32]

It was no coincidence that, since autumn 1949, Enosis had suddenly attracted the attention of the Eastern-bloc media. To be sure, the 'Free Greece' radio transmitter of the KKE had never ceased attacking British rule in Cyprus and the acquiescence of the Greek governments.[33] Now it was joined by the entire Cominform propaganda apparatus, which undertook to lay the ground for AKEL's renewed drive for Enosis. Starting in September, the Greek language transmission of Radio Sofia urged the Cypriot Communists to intensify the anti-colonial struggle. The campaign intensified after AKEL's appeal to the UN and the announcement of the Ethnarchy plebiscite. The plebiscite was exalted as a 'solid anti-imperialist weapon in the hands of the Cypriot people', which would 'make the position of the British in Cyprus more difficult and [would] show even more the treacherous character of Greek monarchofascism'.[34] On the day of the plebiscite, 15 January, the Sofia station reminded its audience that it was taking place thanks to the AKEL initiative, which had forced the hand of the Ethnarchy. After the plebiscite, Soviet-bloc broadcasts continued their daily invective against the British, the Greek government and, occasionally, the Turks.[35]

'Friendly' persuasion

Quite predictably, once less dependent on British support, Greek governments would sooner or later feel freer to reassert their interest in Cyprus. Of course, with a war effort against the Communists and a diplomatic struggle at the United Nations on its hands, no government could possibly risk alienating its major allies. Still, in late 1946, Prime Minister Konstantinos Tsaldaris attempted to raise Cyprus as possible compensation for the rejection of Greece's

claims on Albanian and Bulgarian territory at the Peace Conference. This provoked Bevin's angry retort that Cyprus could not be
handed to a country that 'was on the point of going Communist'.[36]
Two months later, on 28 February 1947, the visit of the Cypriot
delegation to Athens prompted the Greek parliament to adopt a
unanimous resolution expressing the hope that Britain would accept friendly talks with Greece on the question of Enosis.[37] Even at
the height of fighting, in July 1948, King Paul himself reaffirmed
the claim on Cyprus. In an interview with Cyrus Sulzberger, the
influential foreign editor of the *New York Times*, the King repeated
the offer of strategic bases to Britain anywhere on Greek soil.[38] His
statement provoked the first in a long series of British *démarches*
on Cyprus. As a result, and after some American prodding, the aging Prime Minister Themistoklis Sofoulis issued a statement discouraging further public discussion of the issue.[39]

   Pro-Enosis manifestations in Greece did not fail to provoke the
reaction of the Turkish press, a section of which lashed out against
Enosis and criticised the Republican People's Party (RPP) government for neglecting the Turks of Cyprus. To be sure, President Ismet
Inönü did receive a Turkish Cypriot delegation in November 1948
and the Turkish Foreign Ministry sought British assurances that there
was no intention to hand the island over to Greece.[40] For the first
time, press polemics on account of Cyprus seemed to cast a cloud
over the Greek-Turkish *rapprochement*.[41]

   A similar situation arose in November 1949, when press reports
alleged that the Greek Prime Minister, Alexandros Diomidis, and
Queen Frederica had referred to the fulfilment of Greek national
aspirations in their contacts with Greek Cypriots.[42] This gave Wright
the opportunity to ask for a strong representation to Athens. A few
weeks later, he added a demand for the removal of the Greek Consul-General, Alexis Liatis, whom he suspected of encouraging the
plebiscite drive of the Ethnarchy.[43] Eventually, the Foreign Office
asked the Greek government to discourage the pro-Enosis clamour
in the same way the late Sofoulis had done a year earlier.[44] The
United States Ambassador, Henry Grady, also came to the assistance of Sir Clifford Norton, his British colleague, lecturing Tsaldaris
on the need to avoid 'agitation regarding boundaries and annexa-
tions at this time'.[45]

Yielding to combined pressure, the Greek government offered
not one but three statements. On 14 December, Tsaldaris denounced
as 'irresponsible' all public discussion of the Cyprus question and
stated in parliament that the government continued to adhere to
the line set forth by Sofoulis. The raising of the matter at that moment, he added, might well harm the Greek case. Then, replying to
one of the deputies supporting a motion in favour of Enosis, Tsaldaris
went as far as to warn that making statements 'about a people which
is not under Greek sovereignty' amounted 'to open intervention
which we ourselves always try to reject when it concerns us'.[46] On
the following day, Diomidis issued a press communiqué, in which
he emphasised the 'delicacy' of the circumstances and the 'necessity' for maintaining close collaboration with Britain and the United
States, on whose assistance 'the satisfactory solution of all national
problems depend[ed]'. Then, he asked for the cessation of public
excitement about Cyprus.[47] These statements, Tsaldaris' speech in
particular, provoked sharp criticism in the Greek press, which did
not fail to attribute them to British pressures. As a leading newspaper, *To Vima*, put it, 'anything discouraging which the Greeks might
say to the Cypriots would have no effect on them. On the contrary,
[…]'.[48]

The Greek statements satisfied the Foreign Office, all the more
so since they were coupled with the recall of Consul General Liatis.[49]
Still, on Wright's insistence, Kenneth Younger, the Minister of State,
summoned the Greek Ambassador in London and deplored Greek
nationalistic claims which, as with the 'clamour over Northern
Epirus',[50] caused embarrassment to Greece's allies.[51]

The announcement of the Ethnarchy plebiscite seemed to toll
the bell for the Turkish Cypriot leaders. The spectre of Enosis apparently prompted the existing two rival parties to bury their differences and merge into a single Federation of Turkish Associations
(FTA). The Turkish Cypriot press demanded that the Governor intervene and stop the process. Failing this, the FTA organised protest meetings against Enosis and dispatched a representation to Turkey,[52] where the ground had been prepared by student demonstrations and angry press comment. Eventually Foreign Minister Necmeddin Sadak came out and reassured the public that there was no
cause of worry since Britain was determined to retain her sover-

eignty and the Greek government displayed a 'prudent' attitude.[53] Sadak had already conveyed to the British Ambassador Turkey's interest as well as anxiety about Cyprus. On 21 December 1949, he told Sir Noel Charles that his government would keep calm about Cyprus so long as the British stood pat; if, however, things changed, then it would have to protect its own, mainly strategic, interests.[54]

British diplomacy used both the strategic importance of Cyprus and Turkish reactions in an effort to induce the Americans to openly support it on Cyprus.[55] On the eve of the Ethnarchy plebiscite, Lord Jellicoe, Second Secretary of the Embassy in Washington, proposed to the State Department a statement discouraging Enosis. The Americans explained that, although they did not consider the plebiscite to be properly conducted and, thus, accurately reflecting Cypriot opinion, they had no intention of issuing a statement. Instead, Leonard Cromie, the Desk Officer for Greece, made Jellicoe regret his attempt to use the Turkish card: United States diplomats at that point disapproved the expressions of Turkish interest in Cyprus.[56] Thus, Jellicoe was told that the British had better 'allay popular suspicions that [they were] encouraging the *ilhak* (annexation) agitation as [a] counterweight to Enosis and pursuant to [the] age-old policy of divide-and-rule'.[57]

The plebiscite mission

The Ethnarchy went ahead with its plans for the plebiscite almost unencumbered, while the authorities took only selective action. Pantelis Bistis, director of the nationalist *Ethnos*, and Sokratis Loizidis, the Secretary General of PEK, both Greek subjects, had their residence permits withdrawn and were forced to leave Cyprus; two more journalists were put on trial for inciting violence; and civil servants were barred from signing the plebiscite rolls.[58] The fact that there was no secret ballot but rather an open collection of signatures in churches meant that the project was inevitably limited to the Greek Orthodox.[59] Starting on 15 January 1950, the plebiscite resulted in a 96 per cent majority of the adult Greek Cypriot population in favour of Enosis. There were only a few isolated signs of dissension.[60] The Archbishop communicated the result to the Governor on 4 February and asked for the transfer of

sovereignty to Greece. Nearly three weeks later, the reply came
from the Secretary of State for the Colonies, who simply restated
that the question was closed.[61]

Meanwhile, as the plebiscite was being concluded, AKEL publicly invited the Ethnarchy to take the lead on a common programme
of action. This provided, among other things, for the formation of
an all-party delegation to proceed to Athens. Its task would be to
induce the Greek government to claim Cyprus, and, if Britain was
not forthcoming, to take the matter to the UN.[62] Once again, the
Ethnarchy declined co-operation but endorsed the essence of the
AKEL proposal, deciding to send an all-Ethnarchy representation
under Kyprianos, Bishop of Kyrenia, first to Athens and London and
then to the UN seat, in New York. There, it would deposit the rolls
of the plebiscite as evidence of the Greek Cypriot will for union
with Greece.[63] Barred from the Ethnarchy mission, AKEL decided
to dispatch its own 'People's National Delegation' to tour European
capitals, before attempting to reach the UN seat.[64]

In Athens, the newly-formed coalition government under General Nikolaos Plastiras was already under British pressure. The latter's aim was to have the impending visit of the Cypriot delegates
quietly discouraged and, failing this, to bar them from being received by high ranking Greek officials. Such a step, the British
warned, would be interpreted as 'interference in the affairs of the
United Kingdom'.[65] Plastiras professed embarrassment over the visit
and assured Norton, the British Ambassador, that his government
had no intention of making an issue out of Cyprus. According to the
British Ambassador, Georgios Papandreou, the Deputy Prime Minister, also appeared 'genuinely disturbed'.[66] Stepping up the pressure, Norton tried to impress upon the King that the reception of
'unruly subjects' of the British Crown would set a dangerous precedent, 'comparable to the attitude of the Bulgarian government to
dissident Greeks'. King Paul was evasive, entrenching himself behind the sensitivity of the public to the issue.[67]

Despite the assurances of the Greek government, the British took
the prospect of internationalisation quite seriously. From the outset, they tried to enlist American support on two accounts – to
restrain the Greeks and to avert an eventual discussion of the Cyprus question at the UN. The Americans proved more forthcoming

on the first score. The United States Embassy informally approached
Greek officials and advised against agitation. Yet the Americans were
not prepared to do more for fear of weakening the Plastiras government. The palace, the opposition, and Sofoklis Venizelos, leader of
the Liberal Party and reluctant partner of the Centre coalition, simply waited for an opportunity to bring it down.[68]

   With regard to internationalisation, the British had already waved
the danger of Eastern-bloc meddling at the UN. This, however, was
a double edged argument, since the State Department realised that
the continuation of colonial rule over Cyprus was itself a good propaganda issue. This was pointed out by William Rountree, the new
head of the Bureau for Greece, Turkey and Iran (GTI), to Lord
Jellicoe, in late May. Yet Rountree asked for British views before
formulating a clear United States position on the matter.[69] The British
realised that considerable counter influences were at work in Washington: traditional anti-colonialism was now coupled with Greek-
American lobbying activities.[70] From late May, petitions calling the
United States to take the initiative in submitting the Cyprus question to the UN started reaching the American delegation in New
York. Since these petitions were often sponsored by members of
Congress, the State Department was compelled to send replies. In
these, it took pains to explain that the United States was not 'directly involved' in the matter and, therefore, could not support such
action.[71]

   On 20 May 1950, the four-member Ethnarchy delegation arrived in Athens amid manifestations of popular support.[72] It soon
became evident that the Greek government had little choice but to
receive the Cypriot delegates. Apart from front-page publicity, their
arrival spurred a debate in parliament, during which several deputies from all sides voiced their support for Enosis. Yet, with the exception of the leftist spokesman Ioannis Sofianopoulos, all speakers
came out in favour of direct Anglo-Greek negotiations rather than a
recourse to the UN. At the conclusion of the debate, Prime Minister Plastiras simply expressed the hope that the 'universal Greek
desire for Enosis' be satisfied within the framework of traditional
Anglo-Greek friendship, which, he hastened to add, his government
wished to preserve undisturbed.[73] In the following days, the delegates completed their first round of calls on the palace and gov-

ernment leaders. To their plea for raising the question first with Britain and then with the UN, Plastiras reiterated that the issue could only be settled within the framework of Anglo-Greek relations when the time was ripe. The delegation got no more satisfaction from its meeting with Deputy Prime Minister Papandreou.[74]

Undeterred, the Ethnarchy delegation tried to fulfil its mandate by turning to its natural allies, the Church and nationalistic opinion at large. The press, for its part, kept the Cyprus question in the headlines, while student organisations could fill the streets of Athens at short notice. The right-wing General Confederation of Greek Workers (GSEE) also pledged its support. In fact, it took the initiative in giving the Enosis movement a more organised form under the aegis of the Church of Greece. Thus, in mid-June, a Panhellenic Committee of Struggle for the Union of Cyprus (PEAEK) was formed with Spyridon, the Archbishop of Athens, as chairman.[75] This organisation undertook to lobby members of parliament and to keep the public's interest in Cyprus alive. The delegates themselves toured Salonika and Patras steering considerable public feeling. Last but not least, the Greek parliament appeared as a promising source of support. Following a second abortive meeting with Plastiras, on 13 June, the delegation circulated a petition asking the parliament to accept the plebiscite volumes and declare its support for Enosis. Tsaldaris, who only six months earlier had condemned a similar motion as irresponsible, now, as leader of the opposition, undertook to sponsor it.[76]

At that point, the delegation's task was inadvertently facilitated by British ineptitude. In reply to a parliamentary question on 21 June, Colonial Under-Secretary John Dugdale not only reaffirmed that there was 'no change' on the Cyprus position but, adding insult to injury, he commented unfavourably on Greece's record of administering the recently acquired Dodecanese Islands.[77] This naturally provoked a wave of indignation in Greece. The recently-formed PEAEK announced mass demonstrations for 6 July. Suddenly, as the British Ambassador observed, the Enosis movement had achieved 'such momentum, that no public figure would dare to oppose it or try to put the brake on too openly'.[78] Both the British and the United States Embassy, which had earlier commented on the remarkable absence of anti-British feeling from public pronouncements on Cyprus,[79] reported that this was no more the case.[80]

To a certain extent, the Korean crisis saved the day for both the British and the Greek government. One of its side effects was to make the Americans much more forthcoming over British requests for support. Agitation about Cyprus coupled with the difficulties in the way of the Western-sponsored Greek-Yugoslav rapprochement, caused a sharp reaction from Secretary of State Dean Acheson. On 27 June 1950, the Embassy in Athens was asked to remind the Plastiras government that for Greece, which faced a problem of survival 'as a free country', nationalistic visions were an unacceptable luxury. The United States, Acheson implied, might suspend its assistance if the Greeks continued 'to exhaust themselves and embarrass us by heading for such distant shores as Cyprus'.[81]

Still, the State Department stopped short of satisfying the persistent British request for a public rebuke, nor was any American commitment against a discussion at the UN. The difference in views of the two powers centred on the competence of the Organisation to discuss an issue like Cyprus. The British insisted that this was a matter of domestic jurisdiction and, consequently, barred from discussion under Article 2(7) of the Charter. The Americans, however, had traditionally adhered to a wider interpretation, according to which 'any international question could be discussed in the appropriate UN forum'.[82] These differences were confirmed during the visit of Under-Secretary for Colonial Affairs, John Martin, to Washington on 10 July 1950. The State Department was mainly concerned with the prospect of the Soviet bloc exploiting the Cyprus question at the UN. As a way out, it proposed to induce the Greek delegation to state that a settlement should be sought by direct negotiations with Britain. This, of course, was something that the British wished to avoid.[83] Their efforts to swing the Americans continued throughout the summer without effect.[84]

At the same time, under the impact of the worsening international situation and American pressure, the Greek government moved to contain the pro-Enosis tide. Even before the North Korean invasion, an official of the Greek Foreign Ministry had attempted to explain to the Cypriot delegates the political and procedural difficulties inherent in a recourse to the UN. The Cypriots insisted that a discussion at the UN would exercise a great deal of moral pressure on Britain. A member of the delegation went as far as to hint at the possibility of asking a third, even Eastern-bloc, country to sponsor the Cypriot case.[85]

When, on 4 July, the plebiscite lists were finally presented to the Greek parliament, Plastiras paid lip service to national aspirations but firmly discouraged a public debate. Stressing the delicate international situation and the need for Western unity, he asked the deputies to allow the government to handle the matter as it saw fit. The chamber approved the Premier's request and voted in a resolution asking the Speaker to convey to the British parliament its endorsement of the plebiscite result.[86] The eventual message requested that 'Cyprus should not be deprived of what has been granted to so many other peoples under British rule' and there was no reference to internationalisation.[87] Following the parliamentary session, the government issued a communiqué calling attention to possible 'harmful developments' which might ensue, if 'irresponsible' discussion of the Cyprus question persisted.[88]

Shortly before the departure of the Ethnarchy delegation, PEAEK staged a public meeting at the Athens Stadium on 21 July. The government had been able to persuade the organisers to postpone the day by a fortnight and to abandon their plan for public demonstrations across the country.[89] Before a large crowd, Archbishop Spyridon declared the determination of the Church to take on the national struggle if the government continued to hesitate.[90] The presence at the meeting of several opposition leaders, including Tsaldaris and the allegedly pro-British Napoleon Zervas and Panayotis Kanellopoulos, seriously embarrassed the government.[91]

In late July, the Ethnarchy delegates left Athens for London. The party had been reduced to three, since its secretary, Georgios Rossidis, had chosen to return to Cyprus. There he stated that the delegation ought not to have pressed the matter further 'because of the general trend in international affairs'.[92] In London, his colleagues unsuccessfully tried to present their case at the highest possible level but were only able to meet with members of Parliament who could not be counted upon to influence the government's policy.[93]

The delegation pinned its hopes on its next destination, the United States, where Greek-American associations and sympathetic Congressmen had done some groundwork. Thanks to the intervention of Senator George Malone, the delegates were received by the Assistant Secretary for Congressional Relations, Jack McFall. The meeting took place at the State Department on 13 September. Wasting no time, the delegates asked for American mediation between the British and the people of Cyprus 'in order to avoid the necessity of raising the matter' in the UN. McFall replied that the question concerned the British government alone and, in any case, it was improper to raise it in such a time of crisis.[94] In the event, the delegation limited itself to depositing the plebiscite rolls at the UN headquarters. Although it realised that it could not get anywhere by appealing as a private petitioner, it did not seek the sponsorship of a member state. The deadline for putting items on the agenda of the 5th General Assembly would pass without the question of Cyprus being raised.[95]

The delegates returned to Cyprus via Athens,[96] their mission not having achieved much in terms of tangible results. Their main accomplishment, as an officer of the British Colonial Office observed, was that they had stimulated interest in the Cyprus question wherever they had been.[97] The Greek Cypriot press gave wide publicity to the delegation's activities in the United States, playing up its reception at the State Department. Its reports anxiously tried to project the Americans as sympathetic to the Greek cause, which annoyed the Governor who complained to the US Consul in Nicosia. The latter assured Wright that the Americans only desired 'to be helpful and avoid friction'.[98]

Finally AKEL also tried to publicise the results of its own mission abroad. Having been denied entry to the United States, its delegates limited their activity to London. There, like the Ethnarchy, they were refused access to the government. They also visited Paris, where they had a disappointing meeting with Plastiras, who happened to be there at the time. Then, they went on to various Eastern capitals, excluding Moscow. Upon his return to Cyprus, Secretary-General Papaioannou stated that the People's Republics had given assurances of support at the UN.[99] In the event, the only proof of such support was a reference to Enosis by the representative of Poland in the Second (Ad Hoc) Political Committee of the General Assembly, who criticised the Greek government for its failure to support the Cypriots.[100]

Enosis enters the Anglo-Greek agenda

Before the end of 1950, the Ethnarchy camp acquired a new and dynamic leadership. On 28 June, the aged Archbishop Makarios II died. The obvious contestants for St Barnabas' throne were Bishops Kyprianos of Kyrenia and Makarios of Kition, both in their thirties. Before long, the pro-Ethnarchy press came out in favour of Makarios and pressed for the withdrawal of Kyprianos, who was then leading the Ethnarchy mission abroad. AKEL was reported to be 'quietly' supporting Kyprianos with a view to splitting the vote. The *locum tenens*, Bishop of Paphos, saw to it that no 'disrespectful' left-wingers were present on the voting list. In the event, Makarios ran uncontested and, on 18 October 1950, was elected Archbishop of Cyprus.[101]

During the respite that followed the termination of Greek Cypriot activities abroad, the British resumed their effort to win American support in advance of future contingencies. This time, military as well as diplomatic channels were employed. In early October, Lord Tedder, Chief of the British Joint Services Mission to Washington, wrote to the Chairman of the American Joint Chiefs of Staff (JCS), General Omar Bradley, that the retention of Cyprus under full British sovereignty was indispensable to Western planning in the region.[102] Agreement on this score[103] was confirmed at the Malta conference of British and American area commanders in January 1951.[104] On the other hand, the policy of the State Department was to discourage the internationalisation of the Cyprus question and it did not share the British position that the matter was closed.[105] Thus, it submitted various ideas towards easing the problem, such as a renewed constitutional offer, and regularly expressed concern with British softness on AKEL. The Foreign Office countered that an expressed revival of the 1948 Constitution would suggest they were yielding to pressure and would encourage further agitation.[106]

For a moment, British policy seemed to harden as Whitehall gave in to Governor Wright's longstanding demand for the introduction of repressive measures. On 24 January 1951, the colonial administration published four amendments designed to strengthen the existing legislation against 'sedition'. Thus, the judiciary was empowered to take action against persons merely on suspicion that they were likely to commit an offence; the authorities could refuse the re-publication of suppressed newspapers or the importation of any newspaper containing 'seditious' material; and they could deport for 'unlawful association' persons who were born in Cyprus but had subsequently acquired foreign nationality.[107]

The publication of such draconian measures provoked indignation and defiance in Cyprus. The newly-elected Archbishop denounced them as proof of Britain's 'illiberal and undemocratic disposition'.[108] In Greece, press polemics and public excitement revived.[109] Furthermore, anti-sedition did not fail to touch the anti-colonial strings of American opinion.[110] In the event, Wright was not allowed to use his new legal armour in the way he had undoubtedly intended to do. In response to the public relations fiasco, London advised utmost leniency and the laws were left to lapse.[111]

On the heels of anti-sedition, another instance of British ineptitude helped keep the Cyprus question alive.[112] On 14 February 1951, Minister of State Kenneth Younger, when asked in parliament whether the government faced any prospect of ceding Cyprus to Greece, stated that no such demand had been received. In Athens, the opposition challenged Premier Venizelos, who headed a minority government, to answer Younger's contention. Under the circumstances, Venizelos affirmed that there existed 'a demand for the union of Cyprus with mother Greece'. Later, talking off the record to journalists, he did not exclude the possibility of pursuing the matter at the UN if the British persisted in their refusal to discuss it.[113]

Realising Younger's gaffe, the Foreign Office refrained from further public statements. The Greek government, however, after some prodding from the United States Embassy,[114] sought to explain its position. The Greek Ambassador in London, Leon Melas, was instructed to point out that the present government could not 'maintain silence once the question had been raised in the House of Commons'. Melas handed Sir William Strang, the Permanent Under-Secretary, a version of Venizelos' statement in parliament on 16 February, from which the crucial phrase containing the demand for Enosis was omitted. Strang made it clear that any expression of Greek interest in what was sovereign British territory was intolerable. Rather brusquely, he reminded the Ambassador of Greek sensitivity 'about references by foreign Governments to populations in Greek territory who were of another race and spoke another language'.[115] It was an obvious reference to Greek reactions against Yugoslav pronouncements on the position of the Slavic element in Greek Macedonia.

Subsequently, as Makarios was expected in Athens, Norton, in concert with his United States colleague, John Peurifoy, tried to obtain from Venizelos a statement discouraging agitation on Cyprus. Venizelos was unmoved, stating that no Greek government, and certainly not his minority one, could stand against public opinion on this matter. In his view, the only way was to put the problem 'in cold storage' if the British could find 'some soothing formula' such as a promise to discuss Cyprus in a number of years. Norton replied that his government would not admit that there was anything to discuss.[116]

The arrival of the young Archbishop in Athens was certain to arouse public emotion. Addressing large crowds in the centre of Athens on 15 March, Makarios openly invited the Greek government to raise the Cyprus question with the British, and, failing to get satisfaction, to resort to the UN. Venizelos, who was standing next to the Archbishop, was pressed by the crowds to speak. Though he chose his words carefully, his vague assertion that his government would perform its duty was widely interpreted as opening the door to internationalisation.[117]

Faced with conflicting pressures from Makarios and the Anglo-Americans, Venizelos convened a council of all party leaders on 21 March, in search of a broad consensus on Cyprus policy. The meeting essentially reaffirmed the line of seeking a solution within the framework of the 'ancestral Anglo-Greek friendship' and authorised the government to submit to the British a twofold proposition – the cession of Cyprus in return for bases anywhere in Greek territory, or, if the 'critical international circumstances' did not permit that, a British pledge to settle the issue in accordance with the right of the Cypriot people to self-determination. The prospect of a recourse to the UN was unanimously ruled out.[118]

For a time, it seemed that this approach, which allowed for a compromise solution, was acceptable to Makarios. This was the upshot of the Archbishop's meeting with the United States Ambassador. Profiting from Makarios' protestations of pro-American and anti-Communist feeling, Peurifoy suggested that the professed com-

munity of interest would be better served if agitation on controversial issues between allies was to be avoided. He also made it no
secret that the United States opposed the raising of the question of
Cyprus at the UN. Thereupon, the Archbishop appeared inclined to
discuss a compromise similar to that envisaged by the Greek party
leaders – agitation could cease, if the 'British stated that although
[the] international situation precluded any alteration [of the] island's
status at present, they would be willing to discuss [the] question at
some specific time in [the] future, perhaps within one or two
years'.[119] Makarios conveyed his conciliatory mood to the British
Ambassador when the two men met on 27 March. On that occasion, he remarked that it was one thing to refuse to discuss the matter 'in present circumstances' and quite another to say that the question was closed.[120] At the same time, however, he tended to dismiss
the Turkish reactions as 'relatively unimportant' and to overlook the
risks of internationalisation.[121]

Makarios' overtures attracted the interest of the State Department. Since January 1951, the Americans had expressed interest in
using air facilities on the island[122] and securing a training area for
the marines of the Sixth Fleet. Yet, to British dismay, the latter request was withdrawn out of fear of local reactions.[123] Since the introduction of the anti-seditious measures, the American preoccupation with British policy on Cyprus had grown. Not only the prospect of the matter being raised at the UN but also the reactions of
US public opinion were causing concern, a fact that the State Department did not hide from the British.[124] On 21 March, Democrat
Senator Pat McCarran introduced a motion inviting the Senate to
declare Cyprus an issue meriting the attention of the UN.[125] A few
days later, the State Department received a Greek note communicating the proposals of the Greek leaders' council.[126]

In early April, the officer in charge of the Greek desk, Norbert
Anschuetz, informally put a set of ideas to Jellicoe. These included
a general statement along the lines indicated by Makarios: a British
promise to discuss the possibility of a change in the status of Cyprus
in the future; a renewed constitutional offer in advance of the coming General Assembly; an offer of dual nationality; last and probably
on Anschuetz's own initiative, a 'bargain' between the British and
Greek governments, whereby the latter would undertake to dis-

courage Enosis agitation in return for support of Greece's admission into NATO.[127] The latter suggestion, however, when taken up by the British a few months later, would be repudiated by the State Department, thus raising doubts about the coherence of the American attitude to Cyprus.

However, before the Foreign Office had time to formulate its reply, Makarios publicly rejected any idea of a compromise. During a press conference on 6 April, he stated that a British promise to discuss Cyprus in a future time would be worthless, unless it was accompanied by a pledge to cede Cyprus to Greece 'within a reasonably short time'. The Archbishop went on to call upon the Greek government to 'make an immediate *démarche*' to the British and, failing this, to lodge an appeal with the forthcoming UN General Assembly. In any event, he declared, the Greek Cypriots were determined to follow the path of internationalisation.[128] Many responsible people in Athens and Washington must have felt the ground cut from under their feet on that day. The Foreign Office, for its part, was better able to reject the American proposals. It only agreed to consider a renewed constitutional offer, but saw no reason to hurry.[129]

Being unaware of the American initiative, the Greek government did not submit its twofold proposal until 2 May 1951. Yet Bevin's successor in the Foreign Office, Herbert Morrison, made it clear to Ambassador Melas that his government had no intention of discussing the Greek proposals and ruled out any change in the status of Cyprus for the foreseeable future. Instead he urged the Greek government to dampen agitation and avoid antagonising the Turks, who had already shown signs of anxiety.[130]

Indeed, the clamour about Cyprus had not failed to provoke exactly what Venizelos had wished to avoid – a Turkish reaction. Ankara had earlier used an informal occasion to deplore 'politely' the Greek claim.[131] Its views were more forcefully conveyed in an interview with Foreign Minister Fuad Köprülü by the daily *Hürriyet*, on 21 April 1951. Köprülü stated that Turkey was 'closely concerned' with the fate of Cyprus due to its geographic proximity, historical ties and Turkish minority. While seeing no reason for a change in the *status quo*, Köprülü declared that his government would 'not permit' this to happen in the future 'without our participation and due

regard for our rights'.[132] Subsequently, Turkish concern was officially conveyed to the British,[133] and, in July 1951, to the Americans
too. Citing a press report, whereby the United States supported an
eventual Anglo-Greek accommodation, the Turkish Ambassador in
Washington, Feridun Erkin, repeated to the State Department
Köprülü's line, stressing that his government expected to be party
to any future re-opening of the Cyprus question.[134]

Meanwhile, partly in response to persistent British requests, the
Americans did seek to discourage further Greek moves, above all a
possible recourse to the UN.[135] Venizelos was reminded that both
the State Department and the Pentagon opposed a change in the
status of Cyprus at that time and did not like all that fuss either.
Venizelos then accused the British of inspiring Turkish reactions. He
also stressed his difficulties with public opinion, particularly in view
of the forthcoming elections. He confirmed, however, that his government 'had no intention' of taking the matter to the UN. Finally,
he appealed for American mediation in order to extract 'even [a]
most vague and general sort of statement' indicating British willingness to discuss the question 'at some indefinite time in [the] future'.[136]

Having already tried its hand once, the State Department refused to grant Venizelos' request. Instead, it kept pressing its 'strong
objection' to the airing of the question, though the Ambassador in
Athens was authorised to point out that a solution satisfactory to 'all
parties' could be found in the future. The Turkish card was also
thrown in and Venizelos was told that the Department did not doubt
the sincerity of Turkish feeling on Cyprus.[137]

Faced with all this, the Greek Prime Minister beat a retreat with
some honour. While giving the assurances the Americans sought, he
added that he could not take Morrison's reply to the Greek note as
final.[138] Significantly, Venizelos chose not to disclose the Greek approach to London and its rejection. When asked by journalists later
in May, he merely stated that the Greek demand for the cession of
Cyprus still stood, although the international situation did not permit any further steps towards its fulfilment.[140] At the same time, he
asked Ambassador Norton whether any future Ethnarchy delegation 'could not be prevented from leaving Cyprus'.[140]

British gambits

Cyprus became a topic of the Anglo-American talks on colonial issues that were regularly held on the eve of each General Assembly. A preliminary meeting, which took place in Washington on 10 July, revealed a significant divergence of views.[141] Disturbed by what they saw as American 'flabbiness', the British sought to make their position clear in advance of further talks. In an *aide-mémoire*, dated 13 August, the Foreign Office emphasised the recently reaffirmed position of the COS supporting the retention of Cyprus on strategic grounds. In order to pre-empt further American prodding, it was argued that no 'palliative measures' could appease pro-Enosis feeling or discourage any 'trouble-maker' from raising the matter at the UN; rather, the United States should help to keep the matter out of the limelight and prevent it from reaching the UN floor. Finally, the document repeated the usual plea for a joint Anglo-American statement.[142]

Although both parties agreed that the airing of the question at the UN should be avoided, they held different views as to how to achieve this. Replying to the British *aide-mémoire*, the State Department insisted that 'certain helpful adjustments' were required in order to strengthen the common position in the General Assembly. Thus, the Americans kept talking of a renewed constitutional offer, the repeal of the anti-seditious measures and an offer of dual nationality. They also continued to resist the plea for a public statement on the grounds that they could do more if they did not become 'publicly identified' with either side – a position they maintained until the eventual Greek recourse of 1954.[143] The British reply proved that the Anglo-American exchange of views on Cyprus was hopelessly caught in a vicious circle. For the second time in a few months, the Foreign Office repeated the familiar objections: the 1948 Constitution was still on offer but its expressed renewal would invite unwelcome public discussion; dual nationality was bound to lead to 'divided allegiance'; finally, the anti-seditious legislation would help the administration of Cyprus 'to drive a wedge between the Communists and the nationalists' and deflate agitation – a bizarre statement in view of the fact that 'anti-sedition' had been left to lapse.[144]

The British also tried to exploit the entry of Greece and Turkey into NATO in order to extract an undertaking from both countries to respect British sovereignty over Cyprus.[145] The Americans, who sought the extension of NATO in earnest, firmly opposed this attempt.[146] Once the admission of the two countries was formally approved by the North Atlantic Council (NAC) on 20 September, the British renewed their effort. The North Atlantic Treaty had to be revised in order to provide for its new adherents. Thereupon, they proposed the expressed exclusion of Cyprus from the area of allied operational responsibility. The Americans, however, resisted this as an unnecessary provocation.[147] The NAC eventually agreed that Cyprus lay outside the NATO area, but this was not communicated to either Greece or Turkey.[148]

Greek stirrings

On the surface, all was quiet on the Cyprus front during the summer of 1951. In the island, Makarios was busy consolidating his own position within the Ethnarchy. Both Britain and Greece went to the polls. In October 1951, the Conservatives under Sir Winston Churchill were back in office with a small but working majority. Sir Anthony Eden, Churchill's heir apparent, became the new Foreign Secretary. In Greece, the elections of 20 September failed to return a clear winner. It was only in late October that a Plastiras-Venizelos coalition was formed with a slender majority. Significantly, the new government's statement of policy made no reference to Cyprus. For this omission the government was fired at in parliament even from within its own ranks. Loukis Akritas, a Plastiras supporter of Cypriot origin, asked the government how it intended to work for Enosis. Venizelos, now deputy Prime Minister and in charge of the Foreign Ministry, was non-committal. He also admitted that the delicacy of the matter and its effect on Anglo-Greek relations accounted for its exclusion from the statement of policy. All this hardly appeased the opposition press or the champions of Enosis – PEEK, the Church and the Ethnarchy Office in Athens – who did their best to stir up public feeling.[149]

By November, the Cyprus question was again in the foreground. Despite Anglo-American pressure, the Greek delegation broached the matter during the Fifth session of the General Assembly in Paris. The first indirect reference was made by Ioannis Politis, the head of the Greek delegation, during the general debate. Profiting from a discussion on certain discrepancies between the treatment of non-self-governing and trust territories in the Charter, Politis pointed out that the first category of territories included peoples who claimed a civilisation older than that of any European state. The Greek representative argued that the same principles should apply in both cases and asked for an official interpretation of the relevant text.[150]

This statement was criticised in Greece and Cyprus as vague and, on 22 November, Georgios Mavros, political member of the Greek delegation, undertook to be more explicit at the Fourth Committee dealing with non-governing territories. Mavros referred to the failure of certain administering powers to provide information on the state of political advancement in territories under their rule. Then, he specifically complained that Britain was withholding information from the UN regarding the 1950 plebiscite in Cyprus. He concluded by expressing the hope that the British government 'would satisfy the aspirations of the people of Cyprus', in conformity with the principles of the international organisation.[151]

Meanwhile, a British statement had helped raise false expectations and pressures in Greece. Talking to Greek journalists, the new Parliamentary Under-Secretary for Foreign Affairs, Anthony Nutting, stated that 'whatever may be the long-term thoughts or intentions of Greece or Great Britain' with regard to Cyprus, 'the immediate position must inevitably be influenced by the strategic situation on the Eastern Mediterranean'. The Greek press related this rather sibylline remark to Nutting's reply to an unrelated question, that his government 'was always prepared to discuss matters with friendly governments'.[152] Speculation about a change in British policy was accompanied by increased activity on the part of PEEK and its sponsors. On 22 November a pro-Enosis student demonstration in Athens resulted in clashes with the police and several wounded. In parliament, Minister of the Interior Konstantinos Rentis candidly stated that the course of foreign policy could not be determined in the streets, only to be assailed by the opposition for police brutality and insensitivity to the Panhellenic desire for Enosis.[153]

This was the context for Mavros' intervention at the Fourth Committee and a further Greek effort to approach the British on Cyprus. On 24 November, the Greek Deputy Minister for Foreign Affairs, Evangelos Averof, called on the new British Ambassador, Sir Charles Peake, and elaborated on the pressures facing his government on account of Enosis. Averof maintained that, if the opposition took the matter to parliament, the government might have to resign rather than face a vote of no-confidence. He also handed Peake an *aide-mémoire* reiterating the Greek views and requesting a fresh look into the matter.[154] According to Averof's own account, the British Ambassador suggested a meeting with the British Foreign Secretary in Rome, where Averof was to head the Greek team of observers to the NAC.[155] This meeting took place on 29 November but as soon as Averof raised the subject Eden interrupted to make clear that Cyprus was not a topic he was prepared to discuss. When Averof tried to explain the position of his government, the British Secretary of State remarked that he could not allow British policy to be influenced by the domestic difficulties of another government. According to Eden, the conversation 'ended coldly'.[156]

On the same day, Venizelos, who was with the Greek delegation to the UN, had a talk with the US Acting Secretary of State, James Webb. A fortnight earlier, the Greek Ambassador had spoken to the State Department of a Communist attempt to move a large number of weapons from Greece into Cyprus.[157] This was an unsubstantiated claim, but it gave Venizelos the opportunity to reiterate his favourite formula of a soothing British promise to consider Enosis when the international situation permitted. Webb's reaction was discouraging: the time was inopportune for opening the question, whereas a British statement of the kind envisaged by Venizelos would only encourage the Communists to stir up more trouble; above all, the airing of differences between allies was bound to undermine the 'badly needed' stability in the area to the benefit of the Soviets.[158]

This new bout of Greek interest in Cyprus provoked the first Turkish representation. The Greek Ambassador in Ankara was given a warning that the raising of the Cyprus question would be a 'dangerous' act.[159] Still, Greek-Turkish ties appeared to develop stronger than ever: both countries were officially admitted into NATO and the concept of a triple Balkan alliance, including Yugoslavia, began to materialise. 1952 was a year of high level exchanges: Venizelos visited Ankara in late January, Prime Minister Adnan Menderes and Köprülü reciprocated in April, the Greek royal couple embarked on a ten-day state visit in June, and President Celâl Bayar came to Athens in December. Cyprus did come up during Venizelos' visit, in January. The Greek deputy Premier stated that the issue was one for settlement between the Cypriot people and Britain, and reaffirmed that it should not be allowed to affect Greek-Turkish relations.[160] According to one account, Venizelos also briefly touched on the matter during his talks with Menderes, who replied that it could 'be settled in a friendly manner'.[161]

Makarios' 1952 campaign

Following its tidal pattern, the issue subsided in early 1952. In Cyprus, Makarios was still engaged on the domestic front. Apart from reorganising the Ethnarchy and its affiliated organisations, he took steps to meet the challenge from the Left on the labour and youth fronts. Then, on 25 April 1952, Makarios convened a Pancyprian National Assembly. Addressing 600 delegates, he declared his determination to step up the Enosis campaign. Once more, he rejected all co-operation with the colonial administration and threatened to start a campaign of civil disobedience. Above all, he proposed to resume the drive towards internationalisation. The meeting ended by approving a resolution that called on the Greek government to bring the Cyprus question before the next UN General Assembly.[162·]

Shortly afterwards, Makarios began his diplomatic campaign in earnest, which first took him to the adjacent Arab states – Lebanon, Syria and Egypt. This tour was indicative of the importance that those pursuing the internationalisation of the Cyprus question attached to the Arabs as an allegedly solid ally against colonialism. In fact, shortly before Makarios' visit, the Lebanese delegation to the UN Commission on Human Rights had tabled a resolution calling the British to report on the political situation in Cyprus. Still, Makarios' tour did not unduly upset the British, who noted with amusement that in Damascus he was even confronted with a Syrian claim on Cyprus.[163] The Archbishop, for his part, tried to cultivate the impression that he had secured Arab support for recourse to the UN.[164]

Meanwhile, Cyprus had become a recurrent theme in Anglo-Greek contacts. In February, while in London for the funeral of King George VI, King Paul asked Strang whether it was not possible to 'open up the possibility' of future talks. By way of reply, the Permanent Under-Secretary pointed to the difficulties facing Britain in Egypt and Iran, and the likely reaction of the British public.[165] A few months later, the issue came up on the occasion of Lord Halifax's visit to Athens. The King was gratified to hear Halifax, who spoke in no official capacity, remark that it was Britain's duty to get the Cypriots 'forward to self-government, after which stage they could no doubt choose for themselves'. The King then expanded on the importance of showing 'the donkey a carrot'.[166] Venizelos also pleaded for a British 'gesture'.[167]

The visits of British dignitaries such as Halifax and Field Marshal Montgomery in early May were an opportunity for PEEK to hot things up with petitions and demonstrations.[168] On 14 May, a group of deputies, including supporters of the government, attempted to introduce a resolution in parliament calling for a more active policy on the Cyprus question. Significantly, there was provision for recourse to the UN. Speaking for the main opposition party, the Greek Rally, Kanellopoulos suggested a meeting of government and opposition leaders to formulate a common line – something that Venizelos had done a year earlier.[169] However, the Rally leader, Field Marshal Alexandros Papagos, quickly repudiated his lieutenant's proposal, which he considered inconsistent with his tactics of non-cooperation with the government. Through his chief political adviser, Spyros Markezinis, the Field Marshal informed the British that he 'disagreed with the Government's policy of encouraging public agitation' and that he intended to handle the matter personally when he came to power; until that time, he had to ensure that no moves were made.[170] At the same time, he reassured Venizelos that the Rally would not seek to make capital out of the government's handling of the Cyprus question.[171]

Upon his arrival on 6 June, Makarios made it clear that he intended to press for 'the (government's) handling of the Cyprus question in a more determined manner'.[172] Unlike his previous visit, Makarios conspicuously avoided contact with either the United States or the British Embassy. Once again, his efforts were unwittingly assisted by another British statement. On 17 June, Nutting told Greek journalists that his government 'was not prepared to discuss' the question of self-determination for Cyprus on account of its strategic importance 'to Britain and indeed to the free world'.[173]

Nutting's statement added little to the well-known British position but its timing was unfortunate. The entire Greek press interpreted it as a confirmation of British intransigence and rose in support of a recourse to the UN. Averof publicly wondered about the reasoning behind Nutting's statement and pointed to the dangers for Anglo-Greek relations.[174] Venizelos felt justified to hand the British Ambassador a *mémoire* originally intended for Halifax. It was an informal text, in which, after restating the Greek position, Venizelos did strike a note of warning about Cyprus embroiling Anglo-Greek relations.[175] Peake's reply contained standard language save an interesting passage to the effect that the history of the British Commonwealth was 'proof in itself that the people of Cyprus would be free to work out their own destiny and determine their own form of government' without the 'intercession of a foreign power'.[176] This failed to have any appreciable effect. On 20 June, the Greek Ambassador in London submitted to the Foreign Office an amplified set of ideas, adding to the standard offer of base rights the idea of an Anglo-Greek condominium over the island. If none of these was acceptable, the Greek government could settle for the familiar formula of a British promise to re-examine the problem at a later date.

This Greek approach took place against a worsening climate in Anglo-Greek relations, as a result of the Greek government's decision to recognise Egyptian King Farouk's title to Sudan. Coming first from a NATO member, this step, taken out of concern for the numerous Greek community in Egypt, irritated London which was committed to promoting Sudanese independence. Thus, Strang gave Melas to understand that his approach on Cyprus was both 'ill-conceived and ill-timed'.[177] At the same time, Makarios' reception at the palace offered Peake the opportunity to take Venizelos to task. Faced with a strongly-worded *démarche*, the acting Premier professed anxiety 'to get the question of Enosis out of the limelight'. He added, however, that a 'very little formula' of the familiar sort would be needed in order to allay domestic pressure. Peake cat-

egorically ruled out any such prospect.[178] He went on to make a
more carefully worded representation to the King himself, dispel-
ling the latter's hopes that the British government could ever accept
his favourite 'donkey and carrot' formula.[179]

Following his abortive approaches to the British, Venizelos sought
an 'official' American reaction to the possibility of the Greek delegation airing the issue at the forthcoming General Assembly in
some way short of a formal appeal.[180] At the same time, the Greek
Permanent Representative to the UN, Alexis Kyrou, allegedly on
his own initiative, solicited the good offices of the United States
delegation in securing some relaxation of British attitude.[181] The
Americans, however, had no intention of offering Venizelos an alibi
for an unpopular decision. Peurifoy was instructed to stress the dangers inherent in a discussion at the UN, particularly for Greek-Turkish
relations and allied unity as a whole. This argument, it was hoped,
could have an effect on Venizelos, a known supporter of ever closer
Greek-Turkish co-operation.[182] Kyrou also got the message and,
when he returned to Greece in mid-July, advised the government
against a move at the UN.[183] Moreover, the Americans, despite their
reservations towards the British position, would shortly promise to
'work behind the scenes' in order to prevent colonial issues such as
Cyprus and Kenya from reaching the General Assembly.[184]

By that time, Greek public opinion habitually regarded the Americans as the key to the solution of the Cyprus question. It was no
mere chance that PEEK chose the 4th of July to stage a four-hour
'silent protest' across Greece. On that occasion, Archbishop Spyridon
appealed to the American people for support, while announcing a
new and more intense phase in the struggle for Enosis.[185]

Throughout Makarios' stay in Athens, government-inspired press
and radio comment sought to convince the public that the odds
were against a recourse to the UN.[186] Venizelos, while professing to
defy external pressures, confirmed press reports to the effect that
the United States and other Western powers were pressing against a
recourse to the UN.[187] Eventually, on 23 July, he informed Makarios
of the government's decision not to pursue the Cyprus question at
the UN. According to Venizelos' account, the Archbishop threatened to denounce the government before the Greek people, whereupon the acting Premier reminded him that it was not for Makarios

to direct the foreign policy of Greece.[188] The latter got no satisfaction from the opposition either.

On the day of his departure, Makarios did not hesitate to deplore the Greek political leaders' lack of 'patriotic courage' and accused the British for inspiring Turkish opposition to Enosis. He also reaffirmed his determination to continue the struggle in a more 'combative spirit'. Then, in his farewell broadcast to the Greek public, the Archbishop repeated his denunciation of both government and opposition in exceptionally strong terms. The country's leaders, he exclaimed, were deluding themselves as well as the Greek and Cypriot people 'when they talk of a door open to friendly talks [with Britain] and the like'; the only way to force this door open was by using the UN lever. Finally, Makarios appealed to the people to 'impose' on their leaders the demand for internationalisation.[189] Neither the Greek government nor the opposition reacted to this unprecedented expression of contempt.

The Plastiras-Venizelos coalition resigned on 10 October, before the opening of the 7th session of the UN General Assembly. The caretaker government that succeeded it simply lacked the authority to pursue any major issue of foreign policy. Thus, there was only 'a very moderate and oblique' reference to Cyprus, made before the Fourth Committee by the Greek delegate Konstantinos Triantafyllakos. Another delegate, Dimitrios Lambros, also referred to the political maturity of the Cypriots during a discussion on self-determination at the Third Committee. Significantly, Lambros' allusion to the prospect of self-determination in Cyprus provoked the reaction of the Turkish representative, who stressed that the Turkish Cypriots should be party to any future arrangement and that his country would support their rights to the full.[190]

Archbishop Makarios' long visit to the United States, from December 1952 to February 1953, came too late to have any serious impact on the fortunes of his cause at the UN. However, he scored some public relations successes, particularly when, on 10 February 1953, he appeared before the House of Representatives Foreign Affairs Committee.[191] He also met an old acquaintance, William Porter, former US Consul in Nicosia, who then served at the GTI. When the United States official reminded him of the talk they had had about a compromise solution some three years earlier, the Archbishop had little difficulty in reaffirming that he was still in favour, provided that the British were 'definite and clear' in the undertaking to hold a plebiscite after a number of years.[192] In short, the Archbishop's visit, like that of the Ethnarchy mission before him, succeeded in reviving the interest of the Greek American community in the Cyprus question and to cultivate a climate of false expectations in the Greek Cypriot press.[193] However, his absence from Cyprus helped dampen agitation and the third anniversary of the Ethnarchy plebiscite, a regular occasion for stirring nationalist passions, passed in remarkable calmness.[194]

NOTES

1. United States National Archives, Record Group 59, General Records of the Department of State, decimal file 747C.00/1-2555 (hereafter only the decimal file number is cited), 'The Cyprus Question at the Conference of Lausanne (1923)', office memo from Howard to Wood. For an account of the British attitude towards the Cyprus question on the eve and during the Lausanne Peace Conference, see Svolopoulos 1985, 233-241. It should be noted that the question was not specifically discussed at the Conference, save for the references in Articles 20-21 of the Treaty.
2. For developments in Cyprus during the governorship of Sir Ronald Storrs, which led to the 1931 events, see Georghallides 1985.
3. Kitromilides 1981, 451-452.
4. Mayes 1981, 20. For political and labour activities in Cyprus before World War II, see Attalides 1986, 123-144.
5. The *locum tenens*, Bishop Leontios of Paphos, was the only remaining prelate in Cyprus, the other two residing in exile.
6. For political developments during and immediately after World War II, see Attalides 1986, 144-147; Crouzet I 1973, 135-150. For the emergence of AKEL as successor to the pre-war Communist Party of Cyprus, see Adams 1971, 21-29.
7. More on Cypriot politics during this period see in Chapter 7.
8. Crawshaw 1978, 43; Crouzet I 1973, 173; Kyriakides 1968, 27-28.
9. The camps operated between 1946-1949. See Adams 1971, 28-29; Crawshaw 1978, 31-34; Crouzet I 1973, 150-159; Kelling 1990, 67-68, 86-87.
10. Memorandum by Alexandros Koryzis, Prime Minister and Minister for Foreign Affairs, Athens, 2 March 1941, in *GDR, 1940-41*, 124; cf. Svolopoulos 1982, 199-217.
11. Svolopoulos 1982, 199-217.
12. Crouzet 1973 I, 280-284; Kondis 1991, 309-313; Vlahos 1980, 14-15.
13. Kondis 1991, 315-316, 321.

14. Crouzet 1973 I, 186-187; Kelling 1990, 82-83; Kondis 1991, 314.
15. For a well-documented account of the interdepartmental debate on the future of Cyprus during the early years of the Labour government, see Louis 1984, 205ff. See also Chapter 4.
16. Crawshaw 1978, 35; Crouzet I 1973, 197-210; Kelling 1990, 71-72, 74; Louis 1984, 216-217.
17. Crawshaw 1978, 35; Kelling 1990, 72-73.
18. As Ezekias Papaioannou, future Secretary-General of AKEL, put it in his *Reminiscences*, 'the impression would be given to the outside world that a constitution functions in Cyprus, [whereas] the representatives of the people would shoulder responsibilities without being able to fulfil any [of their] promises to the people': Papaioannou 1988, 81-83.
19. Crawshaw 1978, 36-37; Kelling 1990, 74-78; Kyriakides 1968, 30-34.
20. Crawshaw 1978, 37-39; Crouzet 1973 I, 211-242; Kelling 1990, 76-78; Kranidiotis 1981, 23-27; Servas 1985, 127-132.
21. Louis 1984, 222.
22. Crawshaw 1978, 35; Crouzet 1973 I, 70-71; Kelling 1990, 78-79. See also Chapter IV.
23. UK Public Record Office, Foreign Office Papers, FO 371 series, file number 78421 (hereafter only the file number is cited), R2794, Cyprus Political Situation Report, January 1949; R2860, Government of Cyprus to FO, 8 March 1949; 849C.00/3-2349, Rankin to Acheson, desp. 224; Crawshaw 1978, 41; Crouzet I 1973, 254-260; Papageorgiou 1984, 236-242; Servas I 1985, 135.
24. 78422, R4849, Fisher, CO, to Peck, FO, 10 May 1949; 849C.00/3-2349, Rankin to Acheson, desp. 224.
25. 78421, R4088, minute by Peck, 8 April 1949; 849C.00/4-1849, Porter to State, A-35. In the 1949 elections, AKEL lost Nicosia but retained Limassol, Famagusta and Larnaca. Its total percentage of the votes cast was estimated by the colonial authorities at 44.6 per cent: 78424, R7700, Turnbull to CO, 22 July 1949. The results of the three electoral contests in the six major towns between 1946-53 are given by the US Consulate in Nicosia, in: 747C.00/7-3153, Wagner to State, desp. 11.
26. 849C.00/4-1849, Porter to State, A-35.
27. 849C.00/6-1049, Bartch to State, A-51; 78423, R7440, Turnbull to CO, 21 July 1949; Kranidiotis 1981, 36.
28. 87716, 1081/44, FO to H.M. Representatives, 13 Jan. 1950; Crawshaw 1978, 46-47; Crouzet I 1973, 265-267; Vlahos 1980, 20-22.
29. Crouzet I 1973, 266-267; Mayes 1981, 37; 849C.00/12-2449, Porter to State, desp. 102.
30. 78427, R11842, Wright to Creech Jones, 19 Dec. 1949; 849C.00/12-2449, Porter to State, desp. 102; Crouzet I 1973, 269-271; Mihalopoulos 1982, 573-574; Vlahos 1980, 22-24.
31. Crawshaw 1978, 46-47; Crouzet I 1973, 269.
32. Kelling 1990, 111.
33. Several transcripts of such broadcasts are to be found in files 78422-78427;

on reactions to Turkish involvement, see, for instance: 78422, R4849, BBC Monitoring Service, 5 May 1949.

34. 87717, 1081/65, BBC Monitoring Service, 14-18 Jan. 1950; cf.Vlahos 1980, 19.

35. 87717, 1081/65, BBC Monitoring Service, 14-18 Jan. 1950; 747C.00/1-2550, Porter to State, desp. 10.

36. Alexander 1982, 229; cf. Kelling 1990, 72; Pipinelis 1959, 9.

37. Crawshaw 1978, 35-36; Kelling 1990, 72-73.

38. See the part of the interview referring to Cyprus in Kyriakides 1968, 36.

39. 849C.00/3-2349, Rankin to Acheson, desp. 224.

40. 78420, R1187, Turnbull to CO, 16 Jan. 1949; R1097, British Embassy, Angora (*sic*), to FO, 29 Jan. 1949; Crawshaw 1978, 45.

41. 849C.00/3-2349, Rankin to Acheson, desp. 224; 78424, R7674, Chancery, Athens, to Southern Department, 4 Aug. 1949.

42. 78424, R10544, Norton to FO, 6 Nov. 1949; Rumbold to Norton, 14 Nov. 1949; 78425, R11187, Wright to Creech Jones, 25 Nov. 1949; 78426, R11668, Norton to FO, 16 Dec. 1949.

43. 78424, R10544, Rumbold to Norton, 14 Nov. 1949; 78425, R11375, Wright to Creech Jones, 1 Dec. 1949; R11540, Wright to Creech Jones, 10 Dec. 1949.

44. 78425, R11316, FO to Athens, 5 Dec. 1949; R11485, Norton to FO, 9 Dec. 1949.

45. 78425, R11617, Norton to FO, 13 Dec. 1949; 747C.00/1-350, Grady to Acheson, tel. 9.

46. 78425, R11654, Norton to FO, tel. 895, 15 Dec. 1949.

47. 78426, R11685, Norton to FO, 16 Dec. 1949.

48. 78426, R11666, Norton to FO, tel. 896, 15 Dec. 1949; R11667, Norton to FO, tel. 899, 15 Dec. 1949; R11706, Norton to FO, 17 Dec. 1949.

49. 78425, R11485, FO to Athens Embassy, 13 Dec. 1949; 87716, 1081/44, FO to H.M. Representatives, 13 Jan. 1950.

50. Younger apparently referred to the unsuccessful Anglo-American attempt to assist Albanian dissidents in overthrowing Enver Xoxha's regime. At that time, he could not possibly know the crucial role played by Kim Philby, the Foreign Office official and Soviet spy, in ensuring the failure of that enterprise.

51. 78427, R11866, Younger to Norton, 6 Jan. 1950.

52. 78425, R11553, tel. from Küçük to FO, 12 Dec. 1949; cf. Crawshaw 1978, 48; Mihalopoulos 1989, 21-24, who inaccurately dates the Turkish Cypriot appeal in March 1950.

53. 87716, 1081/45, Charles to McNeil, 30 Jan. 1950.

54. 78427, R11889, Charles to Bevin, 21 Dec. 1949; 747C.00/1-1250, memo of conversation between Cromie and Jellicoe.

55. 87715, 1081/10, minutes of meeting at the FO, 23 Dec. 1949.

56. *FRUS 1949*, VI, 171.

57. 747C.00/1-1250, memo of conversation between Cromie and Jellicoe.

58. These were Polykarpos Ioannidis and Giorgis Stavrinidis, editor and printer of *Efimeris*: 747C.00/1-2550, Porter to State, desp. 10; cf. Crawshaw 1978,

48-49; Crouzet I 1973, 270-271; Mihalopoulos 1982, 575.

59. There were instances, however, of Armenians and Turkish Cypriots signing in favour: Kelling 1990, 103, 115 n. 46; Mihalopoulos 1982, 576-577 and notes 22, 24. On the 'voting' process, see Crouzet I 1973, 273-274.

60. These came from wealthy businessmen: Mihalopoulos 1982, 575-576; cf. Crouzet I 1973, 274, who speaks of the 'moral pressure' exercised by the Church and concludes that, as the result was predictable, there had been 'much less enthusiasm and excitement than it is claimed by the nationalist side'; cf. Mayes 1981, 38.

61. 87719, 1081/90, 'The Greek Desire for Cyprus', FO memo, 24 April 1950; Crawshaw 1978, 49; Crouzet 1973 I, 275.

62. 747C.00/1-2550, Porter to State, desp. 10; Crouzet I 1973, 275.

63. Crouzet I 1973, 275-276; Vlahos 1980, 30.

64. The AKEL/EAS delegation consisted of Papaioannou, the Party Secretary-General, Evdoros Ioannides, Secretary of the AKEL organisation in London, and Adamos Adamantos, Mayor of Famagusta.

65. 87718, 1081/84, Norton to Bevin, 19 April 1950; 1081/89, FO to Athens, 8 May 1950.

66. 87719, 1081/95, Norton to FO, 10 May 1950.

67. 87719, 1081/98, Norton to FO, 17 May 1950. Norton's round of callings included the leader of the opposition, Tsaldaris, who also was non-committal: 87719, 1081/102, Norton to FO, 20 May 1950.

68. 87719, 1081/100, Norton to FO, 18 May 1950.

69. 87720, 1081/128, Stephens to Rumbold, 2 June 1950.

70. 87720, 1081/132, Chancery, Washington, to Southern Department, 13 June 1950.

71. 747C.00/6-250, office memo from Hare to McFall.

72. 747C.00/6-2150. Its members were Kyprianos of Kerynia, Nikolaos Lanitis, a wealthy businessman, Savvas Loizidis, lawyer and expatriate since the 1931 riots, and Georgios Rossidis, lawyer and secretary of the delegation.

73. 87719, 1081/107, Norton to FO, 24 May 1950; 87720, 1081/114, Norton to FO, 25 May 1950; 747C.00/6-2150, Memminger to State, desp. 976.

74. 87719, 1081/113, Norton to FO, 25 May 1950; 87720, 1081/116, Norton to FO, 27 May 1950; 747C.00/6-2150, Memminger to State, desp. 976.

75. Crawshaw 1978, 61, 63; Crouzet I 1973, 346-347. The organisation was later renamed the Panhellenic Committee for the Union of Cyprus (PEEK).

76. 87721, 1081/140, Norton to FO, 23 June 1950; 747C.00/6-2150, Memminger to State, desp. 976.

77. 747C.00/7-650, Memminger to State, desp. 27.

78. 87720, 1081/139, Norton to FO, 23 June 1950; 87721, 1081/152, Norton to Younger, 29 June 1950.

79. On 26 May, for instance, Norton reported that 'the press is perhaps more universally friendly to us than I remember': 87720, 1081/118, Norton to Rumbold, 26 May 1950; 747C.00/6-2150, Memminger to State, desp. 976.

80. 87721, 1081/152, Norton to Younger, 29 June 1950; 747C.00/7-650,

Memminger to State, desp. 27.
81. *FRUS 1950*, V, 378-379. The British were duly informed of this *démarche*: 87721, 1081/157, Norton to Rumbold, 6 July 1950.
82. 747C.00/7-2650, Acheson to American diplomatic officers, tel. 1225.
83. 87722, 1081/158, Hoyer Millar to Rumbold, Washington, 14 July 1950; *ibid.*, record of discussion on Cyprus held at the Department of State, 10 July 1950; cf. Kelling 1990, 106-107.
84. 87723, 1081/193, Franks to FO, Washington, 20 Sept. 1950; *ibid.*, FO to Washington, 25 Sept. 1950.
85. The official was Ambassador Alexandros Kontoumas: Vlahos 1980, 32.
86. 87721, 1081/156, *Greek Bulletin*, 7 July 1950; 747C.00/7-650; Vlahos 1980, 33.
87. 87722, 1081/163, resolution about Cyprus passed by the Greek Chamber of Deputies, 26 July 1950.
88. Vlahos 1980, 33.
89. 747C.00/7-1850, Minor to Acheson, tel. 213.
90. 87722, 1081/169, Crosthwaite to Bevin, 8 Aug. 1950; 747C.00/7-2750, Memminger to State desp. 155; Vlahos 1980, 34.
91. 747C.00/7-2750, Memminger to State, desp. 155.
92. 747C.00/7-2750, Memminger to State, desp. 155. Earlier, the US Embassy had reported divisions of opinion within the delegation: 747C.00/7-650, Memminger to State, desp. 27.
93. 747C.00/9-1450, Tibbetts, London, to State, desp. 1269; Crawshaw 1978, 59.
94. 747C.00/9-1350, memo of conversation between McFall and Cyprus Ethnarchy delegation; 87723, 1081/191, Franks to FO, Washington, 14 Sept. 1950.
95. 747C.00/10-650, letter from Hickerson to Wainhouse; Crawshaw 1978, 60.
96. The three delegates spent some eighteen days at the Greek capital, where they had a further round of contacts. According to the British Embassy, the Greek political leaders seemed 'to have succeeded in showing the delegation the maximum of goodwill without committing themselves to any definite course of action': 95132, 1081/3, Norton to Bevin, 2 Jan. 1951.
97. 747C.00/9-1450, Tibbetts, London, to State, desp. 1269.
98. 747C.00/9-1950, Porter to State, desp. 39.
99. 747C.00/9-650, Porter to State, desp. 30; /9-1150, Porter to State, desp. 35.
100. 747C.00/1-1452, office memo from Howard to Porter.
101. 747C.00/8-150; Crawshaw 1978, 50-51; Kranidiotis 1981, 44; Mayes 1981, 38-39.
102. 87723, 1081/195, Franks to FO, Washington, 4 Oct. 1950; 1081/199, letter from Lord Tedder to General Bradley; 747C.00/10-1650, letter from Lovett to Acheson.
103. *FRUS 1950*, III, 1688.
104. DEFE 5/31, COS (51) 245, COS Committee, 24 April 1951; 95133, 1081/61, note by the War Office, 24 April 1951; records of the United States Joint Chiefs of Staff, Record Group 218, Geographic File 1951-53, 381 EMMEA,

Section 4, JCS 1887/20, 175-185, memo by Chief Naval Operations, appendix D.
105. *FRUS 1950*,VI, 256, 260.
106. 87723, 1081/193, Franks to FO,Washington, 20 Sept. 1950; 95132, 1081/8, Jellicoe to Lord Talbot, 5 Feb. 1951.
107. Anti-sedition, as enacted by in January 1951, comprised the following pieces of legislation: 1. Law to make better provision for the preservation of peace and order and the prevention of crime; 2. amendment of the 1947 Press Law; 3. amendment of the 1949 and 1950 Aliens and Immigration Laws; 4. amendment of the 1949 Criminal Code Laws: 95115, 10113/5, Fisher, CO, to Mathieson, UKUN Del., 15 March 1951; 747C.34/1-3051; cf. Crawshaw 1978, 51.
108. Letter from Makarios to the Secretary-General of the UN and the Foreign Minister of member states (except those of the Soviet bloc), in *Eleftheria*, Athens daily, 11 Feb. 1951; 747C.00/2-1451, letter from Makarios to Acheson, Nicosia to State, desp. 135.
109. 95115, 10113/4, Chancery to Southern Department, 31 Jan. 1951.
110. 747C.00/3-1451, Bartch, Nicosia, to State, desp. 155; 95132, 1081/33, Washington Embassy, to Morrison, 15 March 1951.
111. DEFE 5, COS (51) 245; 747C.00/7-2451, Wagner to State, desp. 18.
112. Crawshaw 1978, 62.
113. 95132, 1081/10, Norton to FO, 16 Feb. 1951; 1081/18, Norton to Bevin, 21 Feb. 1951; *FRUS 1951*,V, 528-529; Linardatos I 1977, 186-187. Linardatos' series *From the Civil War to the Junta*, is a journalist's chronicle of political events from 1949-1974. Here, it is used to the extent that it is based on information from the contemporary press.
114. *FRUS 1950*,V, 528-529.
115. 95132, 1081/16, memo of conversation between Strang and Melas, 19 Feb. 1951.
116. 95132, 1081/29, Norton to Morrison, 14 March 1951; 1081/35, Norton to FO, 19 March 1951; 747C.00/3-1951, Peurifoy to Acheson, tel. 3074.
117. Vlahos 1980, 45-46.
118. *Ibid.*, 47-50.
119. *FRUS 1951*,V, 529-531.
120. 95133, 1081/39, Norton to Morrison, 28 March 1951.
121. *FRUS 1951*,V, 530-531.
122. DEFE 5/31, COS (51) 245, COS Committee, 24 April 1951; records of the US JCS, Record Group 218, Geographic File 1951-53, 381 EMMEA, Section 4, JCS 1887/20, 175-185, memo by Chief Naval Operations, appendix D.
123. 95147, 1214/1-3, 'abandoned proposal to allow US marines to train in Cyprus'.
124. 95132, 1081/33, Washington Embassy to Morrison, 15 March 1951.
125. 95133, 1081/45, Jellicoe to Lord Talbot, 3 April 1951; 747C.00/3-2251, McFall to Senator Connally, March 26, 1951; cf. Crawshaw 1978, 61; Kelling 1990, 106.

126. 747C.00/3-2950, note from the Greek Embassy to Anschuetz.

127. 95133, 1081/45, Jellicoe to Lord Talbot, 3 April 1951.

128. 95133, 1081/46, Norton to Morrison, 6 April 1951; 95133, 1081/47, Norton to Morrison, 18 April 1951; 747C.00/4-751, Peurifoy to Acheson, tel. 3345.

129. 95133, 1081/45, Barnes to Jellicoe, 28 April 1951; *FRUS 1951*, V, 534.

130. 95133, 1081/57, memo of conversation between Morrison and Melas, 2 May 1951.

131. 95132, 1081/24, Chancery to Southern Department, Ankara, 5 March 1951.

132. 95133, 1081/49, Norton to FO, 25 April 1951; 95133, 1081/60, Charles to Morrison, 1 May 1951; cf. Bahcheli 1990, 36.

133. 95133, 1081/55, Charles to Morrison, 23 April 1951.

134. *FRUS 1951*, V, 534-535.

135. 95132, 1081/32, FO minute from Barnes to Morrison, 30 March 1951; 781.022/5-151, memo of conversation between Dixon, Wagner and Jellicoe; *FRUS 1951*, V, 531.

136. *FRUS 1951*, V, 532-533.

137. *FRUS 1951*, V, 533-534, and n. 3; 95133, 1081/69, Jellicoe to Lord Talbot, 15 May 1951.

138. 95133, 1081/62, 63, Norton to FO, 11 May 1951; *FRUS 1951*, V, 534, n. 3.

139. 95133, 1081/72, Norton to FO, 23 May 1951.

140. 95133, 1081/62, 63, Norton to FO, 11 May 1951.

141. Kelling 1990, 106-107.

142. 95134, 1081/88, enclosure: British *aide-mémoire* to the State Department, 13 Aug. 1951; *FRUS 1951*, V, 535-536.

143. *FRUS 1951*, V, 539-540.

144. 95134, 1081/88, Burrows to Cheetham, 3 Oct. 1951; *FRUS 1951*, V, 537-539.

145. 95134, 1081/85, Norton to Cheetham, 1 Aug. 1951; *FRUS 1951*, V, 536-537.

146. 95134, 1081/80, Burrows to Cheetham, 6 July 1951; *FRUS 1951*, V, 537.

147. *FRUS, 1951*, III, 586-587, Webb to Spofford, 4 Oct. 1951; *ibid.*, 587, n. 3, Spofford to Webb, 4 Oct. 1951; *loc. cit.*, Spofford to Webb, 5 Oct. 1951; *loc. cit.*, Webb to Spofford, 6 Oct. 1951; *ibid.*, 593-594, Acheson to Athens, 12 Oct. 1951; *ibid.*, 600-601, Acheson to Spofford, 20 Oct. 1951.

148. 112882, 1081/1212, FO minute, 14 Dec. 1954.

149. 95134, 1081/91, Chancery to Southern Department, 18 Oct. 1951; 101793, 1011/1, 'Greece', annual report for 1951; Crawshaw 1978, 64; Vlahos, 54-55.

150. 747C.00/9-2353, 'Background of the Cyprus Problem Within the General Assembly', office memo by Howard; Linardatos I 1977, 354.

151. 747C.00/1-1452, office memo from Howard to Porter; /9-2353, 'Background of the Cyprus Problem Within the General Assembly', office memo by Howard; Linardatos I 1977, 355-357.

152. 95134, 1081/95, FO to Athens, 16 Nov. 1951.

153. Linardatos I 1977, 358-359; Vlahos 1980, 55.

154. 95134, 1081/103, Peake to FO, 24 Nov. 1951; 1081/109, Greek *aide-mémoire* in Galsworthy to Southern Department, 28 Nov. 1951.

155. Averof I 1982, 37.
156. 95128, 1023, Eden to FO, Rome, 29 Nov. 1951; Averof I 1982, 38-39.
157. *FRUS 1951*, V, 540, n. 2.
158. *FRUS 1951*, V, 524; 540-541.
159. 95134, 1081/105, FO minute, 26 Nov. 1951; 101811, 1081/37, Scott Fox to Cheetham, 23 June 1952.
160. Linardatos I 1977, 402-404.
161. Mostras ms, 15.
162. 101811, 1081/21, Wright to Lyttelton, 5 May 1952; Crawshaw 1978, 52.
163. CO 926/19, Political Situation Reports, April-June 1952; cf. Terlexis 1971, 92-93. Terlexis' *Anatomy of a Mistake* was probably the first scholarly attempt to approach Greek policy on Cyprus in a critical manner.
164. 747C.00/8-1452, Memminger to State, desp. 190.
165. 101808, 1052/1, minute of conversation between King Paul and Strang, 28 Feb. 1952.
166. 101807, 1051/2, notes by Lord Halifax, 9 May 1952.
167. 101807, 1051/2, notes by Lord Halifax, 10 May 1952; 747C.00/6-2452, Peurifoy to Acheson, tel. 5449.
168. 101810, 1081/19, Peake to FO, 9 May 1952; 747C.00/5-952, Peurifoy to Acheson, tel. 4802.
169. 101811, 1081/22, BBC Monitoring Service, 14 May 1952.
170. 101811, 1081/27, Peake to Strang, 31 May 1952.
171. 101811, 1081/39, Galsworthy to Western and Southern Departments, 1952; 747C.00/6-2452, Peurifoy to Acheson, tel. 5449.
172. 101811, 1081/30, Galsworthy to Southern and Western Departments, 11 June 1952.
173. 101811, 1081/36, FO minute by Nutting, 20 June 1952.
174. 101811, 1081/38, BBC Monitoring Service, World Broadcast Extract, 21 June 1952; Pipinelis 1959, 22.
175. 101811, 1081/33, Peake to Harrison, 17 June 1952; 747C.00/7-852, enclosure in Athens desp. 21; Terlexis 1971, 99.
176. 747C.00/6-2852, Peurifoy to Acheson, tel. 5512. This indirect admission of the Cypriots' right to decide for themselves in the future is not to be found in the British record: 101811, 1081/33, Peake to Harrison, 17 June 1952.
177. 101811, 1081/35, minute of conversation between Strang and Melas, 20 June 1952.
178. 101812, 1081/44, Peake to Eden, 7 July 1952.
179. 101812, 1081/46, Peake to Eden, 14 July 1952.
180. 747C.00/7-852, Peurifoy to Acheson, tel. 83.
181. 747C.00/7-952, Gross to State, tel. 29.
182. 747C.00/7-952, Acheson to USUN Delegation, tel. 28, July 11, 1952; 747C.00/7-1852, Acheson to Athens, tel. 236.
183. 101812, 1081/48, Galsworthy to Western and Southern Departments, 23 July 1952; 747C.00/8-1452, Memminger to State, desp. 190.
184. *FRUS 1952-54*, III, 1259-1260; cf. 747C.00/9-3052, Baxter to Popper.

185. 747C.00/7-552, Peurifoy to Acheson, tel. 51.
186. 101812, 1081/41, Galsworthy to Western and Southern Departments, 25 June 1952; 1081/50, Peake to Eden, 30 July 1952; 747C.00/8-1452, Memminger to State, desp. 190.
187. 101812, 1081/40, Galsworthy to Western and Southern Department, 14 July 1952; 747C.00/6-2452, Peurifoy to Acheson, tel. 5449.
188. Averof I 1982, 34; Linardatos I 1977, 463.
189. 101812, 1081/49, Galsworthy to Western and Southern Departments, 28 July 1952; 747C.00/8-1452, Memminger to State, desp. 190. See the Archbishop's farewell message of 25 July 1952 in *Makarios III*, 158-160; cf. Averof I 1982, 35-36; Mayes 1981, 48-49; Vlahos 1980, 57-58.
190. 101812, 1081/63, Crosthwaite to Barnes, 13 Nov. 1952; 747C.00/9-2353, 'Background of the Cyprus Problem within the General Assembly', Anschuetz to State, desp. 307.
191. 107501, 1081/23, 11 Feb. 1953.
192. 747C.00/2-1253, memo of conversation between Porter and Makarios. The Archbishop's statement became known to the British via the US Embassy in Athens: 107501, 1081/16, Embassy to Western Department, 9 March 1953.
193. 107485, 10110/3, Cyprus Political Situation Report, Feb. 1953; 107501, 1081/1, New York, 3 Jan. 1953; 747C.00/1-2153; 747C.00/2-1253. Apart from supporting his moves in the United States, the Greek-American Orthodox community presented Makarios with a Cadillac, the importation of which the colonial authorities of Cyprus refused.
194. 747C.00/1-2153, letter from Wagner to Porter.

2

TOWARDS THE UNITED NATIONS

The last months of the Plastiras-Venizelos coalition marked a low point in Anglo-Greek relations. The Cyprus question remained a constant irritant as new issues arose. The recognition of the Egyptian monarch's pretensions to Sudan continued to bedevil relations with London until Farouk was overthrown later that year.[1] A further complication related to the expropriation of British property as part of the Greek government's programme of land reform. During the lengthy negotiations over compensation rights, London repeatedly intervened on behalf of British interests, the sizeable Lake Copais Company in particular.[2] Even personal relations between the British Ambassador and government leaders, Venizelos in particular, went through an extremely strained period. In late August Peake felt it necessary to warn the Greek Deputy Prime Minister that 'certain trends' in Greek foreign policy 'antagonised' the policies of 'both the United States and Her Majesty's Government at one and the same moment'.[3] Lord Mountbatten's visit at the head of a contingent of the British Mediterranean Fleet was the only success story in this otherwise bleak Anglo-Greek summer.

Nor was there any love lost between the government and the American Embassy. The latter's intervention was instrumental in precipitating the elections of 16 November, which brought Field Marshal Papagos to power. Owing to the plurality electoral system, his party, the Greek Rally, won an overwhelming majority in parliament with 240 out of 300 seats. Shortly afterwards, Peake met the new Prime Minister, who professed readiness to see Anglo-Greek relations restored 'on the closest and most confident footing'. As the discussion turned to foreign affairs, Papagos was quick to raise the question of Cyprus, expressing the hope that Greece and Brit-

ain could one day reach an 'amicable solution'. This should be possible, he claimed, provided the issue was lifted 'out of the domain of
public emotion' and discreetly dealt with 'as between friends'. Peake
held out no hope that talks might take place 'in any foreseeable
future'. His suggestion was to shelve the question 'for the time being' and to concentrate on other issues.[4]

A few weeks later, in presenting his government's programme in
parliament, Papagos only briefly referred to the Cyprus question as
one dear to every Greek heart, which his government proposed to
handle 'within the framework of the present realities'. This, albeit
modest, reference was the first ever made by a Greek government
in an inaugural statement of policy.[5]

Papagos' coming to power coincided with shifts in British for-
tune in the Middle East, which were bound to affect Cyprus. After
long and fruitless efforts to obtain Egyptian consent to the prolongation of British military presence in the Suez zone, Churchill's cabinet agreed in principle to have the Joint British Middle East Headquarters transferred to Cyprus.[6] Thus, although the island still lacked
the capacity to host ground or naval forces of any size, its importance for British military planning steadily increased.[7]

Fanning the flames

The early spring once more brought a new bout of pro-Enosis activity. On 16 February 1953 Makarios reached London, where, according to the British, he was able to attract more local attention
than any other Cypriot visitor before him. He was received by the
Archbishop of Canterbury, the Liberal Party's leader Clement Davies,
and Labour MPs, and met the press.[8] King Paul, however, who was
visiting London privately, assured the British Foreign Office that he
would avoid Makarios 'like poison'.[9] The Archbishop's stay in London coincided with the Anglo-Egyptian agreement giving Sudan
independence in three years' time. This caused bitter comment in
Cyprus as well as speculation regarding ultimate British intentions.
Makarios, for one thing, had little difficulty in reassuring his flock
that Enosis was 'round the corner'.[10]

After London, Makarios embarked on a three week visit to Athens. The Archbishop met Papagos and the two men appeared to-

gether before the press. The Prime Minister maintained a facade of
reserve. Once more, the British were irritated by Makarios' royal
reception, this time by Queen Frederica. Peake was able to extract
a pledge from Foreign Minister Stefanos Stefanopoulos that the government would consult him prior to any future visit by Makarios.[11]
The Foreign Office also sent for the Greek Ambassador in London.[12] Makarios' visit was marked by the customary student demonstration, which, as usual, resulted in violent clashes with the police. Scores of demonstrators and policemen, including the Chief of
General Security, were injured. In the end, the Archbishop turned
up at the scene and exhorted the participants to dissolve in peace.[13]

Makarios returned to Cyprus on 21 March, having been absent
for more than three months. Addressing the usual crowd, he announced a new phase in the struggle for Enosis: first, as his predecessor had done in 1949, he would call the Governor to hold a
plebiscite; failing this, he would appeal for UN intervention, and to
that end he professed readiness 'to seek the support of every nation
and accept help from every hand, even from dirty hands'.[14]

In relaunching the plebiscite idea, Makarios was propelled by a
resolution of the Seventh General Assembly, which seemed to advance the principle of self-determination towards recognition as a
fundamental collective human right. Resolution 637A (VII) of 16
December 1952 recommended that member states 'shall support
the principle of self-determination of all peoples and nations' and
'shall recognise and promote the realisation of the right of self-determination of the peoples of the non-self-governing territories who
happened to be under their rule'; the ruling powers, the text went
on, should facilitate the exercise of this right, whereas the will of
the affected people could be ascertained 'through plebiscites or other
recognised democratic means'.[15] Armed with this text, Makarios
wrote to Governor Wright, on 27 April 1953, asking him to put the
latter recommendation into effect. London authorised a short and
sharp reply, reiterating the closed matter position.[16]

Until the end of the summer, the focus of attention remained on
Cyprus itself. Unlike in the past, the municipal elections of May
took place in conditions of calm. AKEL retained control of the three
main urban centres, except Nicosia where the nationalist
Themistoklis Dervis was re-elected, but its overall vote dropped.[17]

The colonial administration reported a decline in Communist influence, which it attributed to the Ethnarchy's clear lead over
Enosis.[18]

   Queen Elizabeth II's coronation in early June 1953 was an ideal
occasion to demonstrate the strength of pro-Enosis feeling. Apart
from the expected boycotting of festivities, the day was marred by
widespread disturbances, in which secondary school students played
the leading part. In Nicosia and Larnaca they disrupted the official
parade, while in Paphos, a town with a formidable record of violence, Greek youths tore down Union Jacks and clashed with the
police as well as Turkish Cypriots.[19] The authorities took discipli-
nary action against students and teachers. A few weeks later, they
outlawed and dissolved the Ethnarchy's youth organisation, despite
the latter's attempt to disassociate itself from the riots.[20] In protest,
the Ethnarchy sought to organise a mass meeting. Failing to get permission for the Nicosia stadium, Makarios invited the faithful to the
Faneromeni Church on 28 June. AKEL issued a call for unity and
actively contributed to the success of the gathering.[21] During the
impressive display of pro-Enosis sentiment, the Archbishop once
more denounced the official Greek position on the Cyprus question as illusory and demanded an immediate recourse to the UN. If
Athens continued to hesitate, he warned, then the Cypriots would
stretch out 'both right and left hands to accept help offered from
both East and West'.[22]

   Early in the following month, the colonial authorities amended
the secondary education laws, in an effort to gain more control
over the conduct and discipline of students and staff. In the light of
the recent disturbances, the measures were justified on grounds of
'public security and social order'. The Ethnarchy, however, was quick
to condemn them as part of a sinister design to dehellenise secondary education.[23] There were unfavourable Turkish reactions too.[24]

   In July the Ethnarchy announced its intention to send a delegation to the next UN General Assembly.[25] On 10 August, Makarios
addressed a petition to the new Secretary-General of the UN, Dag
Hammarskjöld, requesting him to bring the Cyprus question before the General Assembly. Evoking Resolution 637A (VII), the Archbishop framed his appeal as a 'complaint' of the Cypriot people
against Britain for obstructing the realisation of their right to self-

determination.[26] The reply from New York was in the negative as the Secretary-General did not deem it appropriate to place the issue on the agenda in the absence of a request from a member state.[27] Following that, Makarios publicly appealed to Papagos to take the matter in hand. Stressing that the Cypriots asked for neither self-government nor independence, but for union with Greece, the Archbishop reiterated his threat to 'turn to all member states' for support in the UN.[28]

Preliminaries

In Athens, hopes for a breakthrough in Anglo-Greek relations had been raised by the prospect of Eden's visit in April. Yet the overstressed Foreign Secretary fell seriously ill that month and remained out of office for half a year. At about the same time, John Foster Dulles' visit to Cyprus was also cancelled. The US Secretary of State had planned to spend a short holiday there, towards the end of his tour in the Near East in May. Clearly ignorant of the ground he was treading, he justified his choice as free of 'any political implications'. The Governor of Cyprus opposed it from the outset, while the US Embassy in London also expressed concern, lest the visit be exploited by Enosis supporters. Yet, despite their misgivings, the Foreign and Colonial Offices did not think it proper to discourage the visit. Eventually, second thoughts prevailed in Washington and Dulles changed his plans.[29]

Dulles did, however, come to Athens as part of his Near Eastern tour. There he met Papagos on 27 May, who briefly but earnestly referred to the Cyprus question in connection with the Greek interest to join the projected Middle East Defence Organisation (MEDO). His government, Papagos stated, was seeking a solution within the framework of Anglo-Greek friendship, but this was an issue which 'no Greek government [could] afford to ignore'. Dulles replied that the whole scheme was going slowly, but if it ever involved 'an area so historically important to Greece', her position would be 'carefully considered'. The US Secretary of State hardly seemed to realise what was really at stake.[30]

By the time he received Makarios' appeal in late August, Papagos had already decided to raise the Cyprus question with Eden, who was to spend part of his recovery in Greece. Stefanopoulos had so informed the American Chargé in Athens, Charles Yost, on 26 August, revealing the content of Papagos' approach: he would propose the immediate granting of self-government, to be followed by a plebiscite in two or three years; this would allow the Cypriots to choose between independence, union with Greece or some status within the Commonwealth. For some reason, Papagos intended to lead Eden to believe that he was speaking to him unknown to his own Cabinet.[31] Stefanopoulos also told Yost that, if the meeting was fruitless, the Field Marshal 'would feel obliged to support' Makarios' complaint in the UN.[32]

Pending the Papagos-Eden meeting, the Greek government sought to dissuade Makarios from flying to New York. The task was entrusted to Kyrou, who also confided to the Archbishop that there was to be a 'high level approach' to the British. Makarios was seemingly unimpressed and leaked the information to Cypriot newspapers. Stefanopoulos asked the Americans to lend a hand in changing the Archbishop's mind.[33] The State Department refused, estimating that the Greek government once more was in search of an alibi for a difficult decision. The Embassy was instructed to remind Stefanopoulos that, although the US did not wish to become party to the problem, it still did not think it useful for the Greeks to press it.[34]

In the event, Makarios neither visited the UN nor sought support for his petition from a third country. An earthquake, which hit Cyprus severely on 10 September, also contributed to his change of plans. More important, he knew that Kyrou intended to express Greece's interest in Cyprus and to let the door open for future action.[35] Already on 31 August, speaking during the Security Council debate on Morocco, the Greek permanent representative had made it clear that, in supporting the inscription of any item brought before the UN, his delegation upheld 'the special interests of Greece'. He had further explained that his country entertained the 'possibility of eventually bringing before the General Assembly, as a last resort, a cause dear to every Greek heart'.[36] On 21 September, during the general debate, Kyrou became more specific. Referring to the Archbishop's petition to Hammarskjöld, he pointed out that, despite heavy domestic pressures, his government had decided not to raise the Cyprus question in the hope that Britain would agree to bilateral talks. Otherwise, he concluded, the door to the UN 'always remain[ed] open'.[37]

The Papagos-Eden meeting and after

After spending three weeks resting in Crete, Eden went to Athens on his way back to Britain. Shortly before his departure, on 22 September, he met the Greek Prime Minister at the British Embassy. Given the prominence accorded to this particular event by many people, including Papagos, it is worth citing two subsequent accounts. First, that of the British Ambassador, who was present at the meeting:

Field-Marshal Papagos then raised the subject of Cyprus and said that he felt obliged to mention this question, but that anything that might pass between him and Mr Eden would be regarded as strictly secret, and he did not intend to tell his Ministers that he had spoken of it.

Mr Eden said that he feared that no discussion about Cyprus, whether private or no, could be fruitful. His position was that he could not consider, either now or in any predictable future, any change of sovereignty. In reply to a question from the Ambassador, Mr Eden agreed that the House of Commons would in no circumstances consent to any change in the status of Cyprus. In this matter we, like Greece, had to undergo the discipline of democracy. While in Greece there was a disposition to see Cyprus come to Greece, in the United Kingdom there was an opposite disposition, equally firmly held.

In reply to a question of the Ambassador, Field-Marshal Papagos agreed that the question was one based upon emotion.

Field-Marshal Papagos then briefly developed his arguments in favour of a change of sovereignty. Mr Eden said that Cyprus has never in fact belonged to Greece, and the only link between the two countries was a common language and the hierarchy of the Orthodox Church. After all there was a considerable Greek population in Alexandria and in New York, but he did not suppose that the Greek Government was demanding Enosis for them.

Field-Marshal Papagos seemed disappointed and said that, if this was to be our attitude, there hardly seemed any point in going on with the dis-

cussion. With this the Secretary of State and H.M. Ambassador agreed.[38]
Secondly, that of Field-Marshal Papagos himself:

> Then, coming to the subject, I developed to him how the Cyprus question
> stands, the difficult position in which the Greek government found itself
> following the Ethnarchy's appeal, why it did not sponsor it, and I insisted
> upon the need for finding a solution of the Cyprus problem to be found
> through bilateral friendly talks; these talks should particularly reinforce
> the good relations which we wish to have with Great Britain.
> Mr Eden listened to me attentively, yet he answered dryly: "I shall repeat
> what I have said on other occasions, that for the British government there
> exists no Cyprus question, either at present or in the future".
> Then I replied to him that, following that categorical statement, the Greek
> government will handle this matter in the way that it deems best and most
> expedient, and that it assumes full and absolute freedom of action.[39]

Certainly, these accounts fail to convey the atmosphere of mounting tension as two strong and vain personalities clashed.[40] The gist
of that meeting was leaked to the Greek press in Athens and Nicosia,
which reported the Field Marshal's pique.[41] On 15 October, the
Greek Ministry for Foreign Affairs addressed a formal note and an
aide-mémoire to the British Embassy in Athens, registering the
Papagos-Eden exchange and striking a note of warning – in view of
the negative British attitude, the Greek government assumed full
freedom of action in the future.[42] The British considered this a 'belated reservation' of the Greek position, which had not been made
during the Papagos-Eden meeting. To Peake it was 'no more than a
face saving gesture', designed to placate the champions of Enosis in
Greece and Cyprus.[43] The Foreign Office, for its part, decided not
to reply to the Greek note and relied on Peake to restate the British
position whenever necessary.[44]

On 10 November, Peake had his first meeting with the Greek
Prime Minister since Eden's visit. The subject was the latter's invitation to Papagos to visit London, but the talk naturally reverted to
the Cyprus question. Papagos felt unable to accept the invitation
without Cyprus on the agenda, since that would badly expose him
to domestic criticism. The conversation also touched upon the position of the United States. The Field Marshal appeared to believe that

the United States 'would not be averse to the Enosis'. Peake, for his part, had already contacted Cavendish Cannon, his new American colleague, who had assured him that there had been no change in the US position.[45]

From mid-November the Greek government began airing its intention to resort to the UN. On the 16th, Kyrou told Henry Cabot Lodge, the US Permanent Representative to the UN, that Greece would 'positively' raise the Cyprus question at the next General Assembly. He also handed Lodge a three-page memorandum intended for Dulles, in which Kyrou elaborated on the reasons for such a course: the island's ethnic character, British intransigence and the danger of the Communists exploiting national frustration in Greece and Cyprus. The Greek diplomat confidently dismissed the prospect of Turkish reactions and tried to reverse the British strategic argument, claiming that a friendly population would enhance the island's military value. Finally, he asked for Lodge's good offices in urging the British 'to show a little spirit of conciliation'.[46] Once again, the State Department refused mediation.[47]

The government made its intentions public in a Foreign Ministry press release issued on 25 November.[48] Stressing that the Cyprus question was 'being handled personally by the Field Marshal', it indicated a clear preference for bilateral talks, but, if the British were not forthcoming, a solution would be sought 'by any means which [the government] deems expedient'.[49] Stefanopoulos repeated this position in parliament five days later, while Kyrou, talking to journalists, asserted that 1954 would be 'the year of Cyprus'.[50] The Greek press was apt to interpret all this as evidence of secret Anglo-Greek negotiations.[51] Before the Greek Foreign Ministry issued a denial, these allegations had prompted a Turkish representation to the British.[52]

The prospects for Anglo-Greek relations further deteriorated as Peake delivered a message to Papagos from Eden, in which the Foreign Secretary stated that he 'should be sorry' if the Cyprus question prevented the Field Marshal from visiting London, but he could not change the British position on that account. He then expressed the hope that Papagos would 'find a way of avoiding the subject'.[53] This only served to add insult to the Premier's sense of injury.[54] The Ambassador continued his efforts to salvage the visit, hoping to bring the royal couple to London too. [55]

More friction in Anglo-Greek relations had been generated by the rejection of a request from the Greek Ministry of Education to be allowed to inspect Greek teachers in Cyprus. [56] This refusal provoked Greek *démarches* and threats that it might lead to the abrogation of the Anglo-Greek cultural convention – which, among other things, permitted the functioning of the British Council in Greece. [57]

To be sure, Peake, King Paul and even Papagos tried to maintain a level of communication between the two sides. Through the Ambassador and British visitors of some standing, such as Philip Noel-Baker, the King and the Prime Minister put forward a compromise formula, providing for a renewed constitutional offer and a promise to hold a plebiscite in a specific number of years. They both confirmed, however, that Greece would have to appeal to the UN as a last resort. [58] The British were unmoved. On 16 January 1954, Papagos embarked on a tour of France and the Low Countries. Britain was finally excluded from his itinerary. Instead, the Field Marshal accepted an invitation from General Francisco Franco to visit Spain, an act that the British interpreted as a snub. [59] While in Paris, Papagos reaffirmed that, in the absence of a bilateral settlement, Greece would 'spare no legitimate means in demanding her rights' over Cyprus. [60]

The change of guard in the colonial administration of Cyprus in February 1954 failed to have any appreciable impact on the course of the problem. Wright retired and was replaced by Sir Robert Armitage, who took office in February. Archbishop Makarios reaffirmed the line of non-cooperation and left for his regular early spring visit to Athens. There, for the first time, he was able to report progress in his cardinal aim – the internationalisation of the Cyprus question. [61] It was also clear that the initiative for the pursuit of Enosis had passed from Nicosia to Athens. According to Kyrou, Papagos had already made up his mind and the Archbishop's visit had little effect on the course of Greek policy. [62] From then on, every instance of British inflexibility would be matched with yet another affirmation of Greece's commitment to the UN course.

Makarios was still in Athens, when the British government broke its virtual moratorium on public pronouncements on Cyprus, which it had observed since the autumn. In February, Lord Winster, the former Governor, had introduced a motion on Cyprus in the House of Lords. Sensing trouble, both Peake and the Greek Ambassador in London, Vasilios Mostras, appealed for its withdrawal.[63] On the eve of the debate, he handed an informal note to John Selwyn Lloyd, Minister of State for Foreign Affairs, communicating the Greek decision to raise the Cyprus question at the next session of the General Assembly. At the same time, the British were assured that this move would be delayed 'until the last possible moment' in the hope that they would accept negotiations. Selwyn Lloyd, for his part, told Mostras that his government considered the political future of the island a matter of domestic jurisdiction and, therefore, outside UN competence.[64]

The debate in the House of Lords took place on 23 February 1954. Several alternative courses for British policy came in for scrutiny. Lord Munster made much of the recent efforts to promote the economic development of the island. In the political field, however, although it was generally acknowledged that the situation was unsatisfactory, no strong current was recorded in favour of change.[65]

On 1 March, Mostras called on Geoffrey Harrison, the Assistant Under-Secretary in charge of the Southern Department, and expressed satisfaction with 'the mild and unprovocative way' of the government spokesman in the Lords debate. The Ambassador repeated that his government would exhaust all time limits before placing the Cyprus question on the UN agenda.[66] Kyrou said as much in a radio interview.[67] Incidentally, these benign statements coincided with the shipment of the first load of arms to the island. It had been organised by the secret Struggle Committee, in which Makarios was involved.[68]

Whatever hopes the Greeks entertained for a relaxation of the British attitude, Eden dealt them a further blow. On 15 March, asked in the Commons by Labour MP Lena Jeger whether there had been any Greek approaches regarding bilateral talks on Cyprus, the Foreign Secretary acknowledged this and declared that his government could 'not agree to discuss the status of Cyprus'.[69] This statement, which said nothing new, provoked a fit of indignation in Greece and Papagos reportedly took it personally. On 18 March, he stated that his policy, which combined 'conciliation with decisiveness', would remain unaltered.[70] At the same time, he advised the King against accepting the invitation to visit England.[71]

Soon, reactions to Eden's statement assumed alarming proportions. The state radio began bitterly attacking British policy in Cyprus; the extreme right-wing *Ethnikos Kyrix* launched a campaign
of hatred against anything British; there were wholesale cancella-
tions of various events, such as lectures and football matches; demonstrations were organised, the most violent taking place in Rhodes,
where the windows of the British Consulate were broken and Greek
officials abused. In the end, Papagos had to come out and appeal for
restraint and public meetings were temporarily banned.[72] Eden summoned the Greek Ambassador to protest about the incidents. When
the latter complained that the Secretary's statement in the Commons 'had been too rigid', Eden confirmed that on this issue he
could be nothing but rigid. He also warned that, by pursuing the
UN course, the Greek government was 'staking their prestige as
well as their most important international friendships' – NATO and
the Turks, who could not be expected to remain silent.[73]

The trend of events prompted Queen Frederica to address a
highly emotional letter to Churchill, dated 24 March, in which she
begged for some modification of British policy. Peake was taken by
surprise. Two weeks later, the British Prime Minister informed Her
Majesty that he did not consider Cyprus a proper subject of correspondence.[74] The frosty climate in Anglo-Greek relations was confirmed by the eventual cancellation of the royal trip to London. On
announcing that, Mostras handed Eden a written communication –
the second since February – which included a message from Papagos.
After a lengthy historical exposition, the message concluded that, if
the British persisted 'in their inflexible policy', Greece would have
to resort to the UN in order to forestall a further deterioration in
Anglo-Greek relations.[75]

Turkish omens

During 1953, Greek-Turkish relations had remained as close as ever
– on the surface, at any rate. After signing the tripartite Treaty of
Friendship and Mutual Assistance with Yugoslavia in February, the
two countries were busy transforming it into a military alliance.[76]
In mid-June Papagos and Stefanopoulos paid a state visit to Turkey.

Talks were dominated by the Balkan Pact and the 'friendship offensive' of the new Soviet leadership to Ankara, following Stalin's death. Cyprus was not a topic, but some in Athens and Nicosia found cause for optimism in the passage of the joint communiqué, which stated that 'no question existed between the two countries that could not be solved in a friendly manner'.[77]

By autumn, however, this façade of harmony was somewhat tarnished. This time, the regular anti-Enosis campaign in Turkey was combined with a wave of protest against the alleged ill treatment of the Muslim minority in Greek Western Thrace. The lead was once more taken by the sensationalist and rabidly nationalistic *Hürriyet*, which used every occasion to cast doubt on the edifice of Greek-Turkish friendship.[78]

The second half of 1953 also witnessed an increased Turkish interest in Cyprus. This was manifested in matters such as the appointment of teachers, student exchanges, the election of a new *Mufti*, and the general welfare of the Turkish Cypriots. The traffic of visitors representing educational, business and religious interests, reached such proportions that, by early September, the Governor sought to have it curbed.[79] As a result, on 3 October, an official of the British Embassy discussed Wright's complaints with Orhan Eralp, the diplomat in charge of Cyprus affairs at the Turkish Foreign Ministry. The British pointed out that, at a time when the Greeks were making trouble, it was in Turkey's interest to avoid adding to the difficulties of the Cyprus administration. The point was taken by Eralp, who hastened to affirm the 'identity' of interests between the two powers on the Cyprus issue.[80]

Before the year was out, Turkish papers began criticising the government for its failure to react to the growing evidence that Greece intended to press her claim on Cyprus. The Menderes government issued a statement to the effect that while there was no Cyprus question at present, Britain could not possibly take any decision 'without first having the official opinion and consent of the Turkish Government'. The Secretary-General of the opposition RPP, Kasim Gulek, was even more outspoken: the Turks, he said, were satisfied with the current status of Cyprus. However, if there was to be a change, 'this change should be made in favour of Turkey'.[81] The effect of these statements on Greek attitude was negligible and

Ambassador Peake reported that both the King and Papagos seemed to discount the dangers for either the Balkan Pact or Greek-Turkish relations.[82]

The awareness of these perils had so far prevented the British from playing the Turkish card themselves.[83] The communication of the Greek decision to raise the Cyprus question at the UN helped the Foreign Office overcome earlier misgivings.[84] Eden, for one thing, was all for it.[85] On 24 February, the Embassy in Ankara asked the Turks to express their opposition to the raising of the Cyprus question to Washington and, perhaps, to Athens as well. The Turks agreed on the first score but were reluctant to approach the Greeks. Such a *démarche*, they pointed out, might involve them in a substantial discussion of the matter and thus undermine the common Anglo-Turkish position that the question was non-existent. They also made it clear that they expected the question, if it ever arose, to be settled on a tripartite basis. In the end, it was agreed that the British and Turkish embassies in Washington should co-ordinate their actions.[86]

Incidentally, the US Ambassador in Athens had already suggested a Turkish approach to Washington, while the State Department would have approved a similar approach to Athens.[87] On 26 February, the Director of the Turkish Foreign Ministry, Nuri Birgi, expounded the Turkish position to the US Ambassador, Avra Warren. Birgi stressed that a Greek recourse to the UN would provoke Turkish opinion and 'jeopardise [the] existing good relations' between the two countries.[88] A week later, Warren received a request for a US representation to Athens.[89] On 10 March, the State Department was handed an official memorandum containing Turkish views on Cyprus. Ankara came out in favour of the *status quo* and expressed concern with Greek intentions. This was probably the first time that a set of Turkish arguments against Enosis, emphasising geography and security, was officially advanced.[90] It should be noted that both Birgi and Ambassador Erkin targeted Kyrou, then Director-General of the Greek Foreign Ministry, as the prime mover of the Greek claim on Cyprus.

The Turkish *démarche* to Athens was eventually attempted on 15 March, on the heels of Eden's statement in the Commons. Yet it proved both ill-timed and out of place as Ambassador Kemal Tarray chose the evening reception in honour of German Chancellor Konrad Adenauer to speak to Stefanopoulos about the ill effects of the Cyprus venture on Greek-Turkish co-operation. Under the circumstances, he managed to convey his message in a 'diluted form'.[91] The British were further dismayed to find out that the Menderes government, which then faced a re-election campaign, was reluctant to undertake further and stronger *démarches*. The Turks made it clear that at that point they attached greater importance to the Balkan Pact and the Greek promises to improve the position of the Muslim minority in Western Thrace.[92] Until after the signing of the Bled military alliance on 9 August, the British would witness further signs of what they interpreted as Turkish equivocation.[93]

Still, in early April, replying to a question in parliament, Foreign Minister Köprülü reaffirmed the position that no Cyprus problem existed nor was a change in the status of the island desirable, but Turkey had every right to consider herself a primarily interested party.[94] This statement caused some uneasy comment in the Greek press and reports of an official Turkish representation on Cyprus saw the light. Their denial by the Greek Foreign Ministry complicated matters. Tarray protested to Kyrou that this created difficulties for his government 'in the midst of [its] election campaign'. He then asked that his approach to Stefanopoulos during Adenauer's reception be considered a formal representation. As a result, the Greek Foreign Ministry issued a 'correction', conceding that the Turkish government had conveyed 'in a friendly way, its doubts about unpleasant repercussions of a Greek recourse to the UN'.[95] If a solution was forthcoming, it was added, Greece was ready to accept any international guarantee safeguarding the position of the Turkish Cypriots.[96] Papagos also declared his personal commitment to improving the lot of the 'Turkish' minority in Western Thrace.[97] Yet the Greek government failed to explain its position on Cyprus to the Turks, in view of its recourse to the UN. Menderes' visit to Athens, on 7 June, was the most obvious opportunity and it was not taken.

A test for the 'special relationship'?

Faced with the prospect of a Greek recourse to the UN, the British sought to secure American support in earnest. To be sure, the US Ambassador in Athens was proving as helpful as could be expected. In October, he had expressed 'regret' to Stefanopoulos for the failure of the Greek government to restrain the 'more violent protagonists of Enosis';[98] two months later, he called again and tried to dispel any illusions the Greeks might have about their chances of getting US support on Cyprus.[99] Yet discreet prodding of this sort fell short of British requirements which were submitted to the State Department in an *aide-mémoire* dated 28 January 1954. First, it was made clear that there was no question of change and that Cyprus was a matter of Britain's domestic jurisdiction; thus, it supposedly lay outside the scope of 'legitimate discussion in the UN'. Then the British asked for assurances on three accounts: first, that the United States still adhered to the position that common strategic interests demanded that the status of Cyprus should remain unchanged; second, that it would continue to 'advise' the Greek government against pressing its claims; third, that the latter should be clearly told that the United States would oppose the raising of the Cyprus question at the UN.[100] Significantly, it would take the Americans five and a half months to deliver their reply.

The long delay notwithstanding, the British realised that, while being adverse to the airing of the Cyprus question at the UN, the State Department continued to take a liberal stand on the competence of the General Assembly to discuss any subject raised before it. What was more, it did not share the British view that discussion of this particular issue was debarred by Article 2(7) of the Charter as a matter of domestic jurisdiction.[101] To add to their dismay, the British were told that Cannon would be instructed to restrain the Greeks without disclosing what the US position would be in case the question was finally raised at the UN.[102]

Increasingly, however, the combined Anglo-Turkish influence was making an impact in Washington. The Greek Ambassador, Athanasios Politis, realised this when, on 5 April, he called on Henry Byroade, the Assistant Secretary for Near Eastern Affairs, to present Greek views on the Cyprus question. The Ambassador referred to Eden's rebuff of Papagos in September 1953 and his recent statement in the Commons as compelling factors in the Greek decision to refer the issue to the UN. Byroade seized the opportunity to express 'serious concern' about the effects of the Greek decision on allied unity and stability. Then he made it clear that no support should be expected if the Greek government persisted in its course. Politis replied that his government had always wanted to avoid that course, but it was unable to overlook domestic pressures and British intransigence.[103] On 10 April, Cannon made a similar representation to Stefanopoulos and Kyrou. Without commenting on the merits of the issue, he stated that the United States was 'firmly opposed' to a Greek recourse to the UN.[104]

The British also extended their diplomatic effort beyond Turkey and the United States and from early May they started approaching Latin American governments.[105] Commonwealth and NATO members were considered safe. The former, in particular, were expected to lend a helping hand in canvassing others.[106] Still, when Canada was sounded, it was revealed that, like the United States, it adhered to a liberal interpretation of UN competence to deal with issues such as Cyprus. Like Washington, Ottawa appeared sensitive to the popularity of self-determination among Canadian public opinion.[107] The Arab and Asiatic countries presented much more difficult ground. In this case, London sought the support of Turkey and Pakistan in projecting its position.[108]

Greek difficulties

In the beginning of April, the Papagos government experienced its first serious internal crisis when Markezinis, who was considered Papagos' heir apparent, resigned his post on 2 April. Although the reasons of his resignation, which cast doubt on the Rally government's omnipotence, remained shrouded for some time, it was common knowledge that the hyperactive Minister of Co-ordination had lately lost Papagos' ear. No doubt, Markezinis' high profile – his bombshell initiatives and his prolific activity abroad, including his much maligned deals with Dr Ludwig Erhard, his West German counterpart – had not endeared him to many of his colleagues in Cabinet and, at some point, annoyed the Field Marshal who also refused to satisfy his lieutenant's persistent bid for the Foreign Ministry.[109] Markezinis went on join the Rally's back benches before setting up his own party in November 1954.

This period was also one of mixed signals regarding Greek intentions on Cyprus. On 10 April Kyrou handed Cannon an unsigned
and undated memorandum, in which he attempted to meet the objections of the Americans, promised restraint and solicited their
'friendly services ... in adjusting this dispute'.[110] Stefanopoulos gave
an almost identical paper to the US delegation in Geneva, from
which, however, the request for American 'good services' was miss-
ing.[111] On 29 April the Greek Foreign Ministry announced that it
had addressed a memorandum to friendly governments, setting forth
the Greek position on Cyprus and asking for support.[112]

On 22 April, while in Paris for a NAC meeting, Stefanopoulos
stated that his government could accept a liberal constitutional regime for Cyprus under which the Cypriot people would determine
their fate 'within a certain time limit'.[113] This was nothing less than
the formula that all Greek governments had supported since 1951
and Papagos had unsuccessfully tried to put across to Eden the previous September. Makarios was also known to be in favour. During
his latest visit to Athens, Zinon Rossides, his adviser on international affairs, told US Embassy officials that the Ethnarchy was 'disposed to accept' a compromise of this sort, provided that a plebiscite took place within a short period of time.[114] Yet the Archbishop
recoiled. AKEL had seized Stefanopoulos' statement as an opportunity to denounce the Greek government and the Right for betraying the Cypriot cause.[115] Makarios promptly sent a message to
Papagos, in which he repudiated Stefanopoulos' statement as 'pro-
crastination' and called for immediate action at the UN.[116]

After this incident, Papagos' rhetoric became more uncompromising. On 3 May, stressing that this was his 'final word', he confirmed that, in view of British inflexibility, the Cyprus question would
be raised in the UN. The statement apparently aimed to reassure
Makarios, although, officially, it came as a reply to a remark by Henry
Hopkinson, the British Under-Secretary for the Colonies, who had
appeared to doubt Greece's determination to resort to the UN.[117]
A few weeks later, however, Papagos stated to an Italian journalist
that he would not have raised the question of 'annexation' if the
British had agreed to discuss the formula of a constitution cum plebiscite in two or three years' time 'at the latest'.[118]

In an effort to step up the pressure on Britain, the Greek gov-

ernment sought to raise the Cyprus question at the Consultative
Assembly of the Council of Europe. On 25 May the Greek deputies
asked for its inclusion in the general political debate which was due
to take place in September. The British delegation made its opposition clear and, when a Greek delegate took the floor, its members,
both Labour and Conservative, walked out. The Turkish delegates,
however, took part in the discussion, advancing in effect a counter
claim on Cyprus.[119] The matter was referred to the General Affairs
Committee where the dice was loaded against Greece – S. Bohy,
the Belgian rapporteur, worked closely with the British in producing a report against the Greek motion.[120] As a result, the Committee ruled that the question of Cyprus was not a proper subject for
the general political debate.[121]

The British constitutional offer

While delaying its reply to the British *aide-mémoire* of 28 January,
the State Department had made it clear that some positive and public gesture on the British part would help the Americans out of their
own dilemmas between principle and expediency. Some prospect
of constitutional development, it was repeatedly suggested, would
enable US diplomacy to resist more effectively the raising of the
Cyprus question at the UN.[122]

At that time, the 'special relationship' was going through a rough
period. Relations between Dulles and Eden, never exactly cordial,
had been seriously embroiled on account of the latter's opposition
to Western intervention in the French colonial war in Indochina.
Further irritants arose from the insistence of the United States to
block the entry of the People's Republic of China to the UN, and,
later on, the lack of British support for the US decision to veto the
appeal of the Guatemalan government against an American-inspired
invasion of dissidents.[123] In an effort to mend fences, Churchill and
Eden planned to travel to Washington on 25 June.

The visit was used by the Greek government to seek US mediation. Despite its public rhetoric, it still sought some conciliatory
British move which would enable Papagos to change course without losing face. The first sounding was not promising. Livingstone
Merchant, Assistant Secretary of State for European Affairs, pointed

out to Ambassador Politis the danger of 'relatively small areas ...
exacerbating international relations when relatively few people occupying these areas were influenced by nationalistic aspirations'.[124]
On the eve of the summit, the Greek Ambassador tried again, this
time with Byroade. His government, he said, only wanted the British to acknowledge the existence of a problem of 'mutual interest'
and agree to discuss it at a later date.[125] This time, Byroade presented a formula aimed at mutual appeasement. He proposed that
the British should recognise a Greek interest in the welfare of the
Cypriots and appear willing to 'receive the Greek views' on this
matter, while also introducing 'genuine' political reforms. Furthermore, the Greek government, for its part, should accept bilateral
talks excluding the question of sovereignty. Athens, in turn, should
induce the Greek Cypriots to co-operate with the plan 'as a step in
the direction of their ultimate objectives'. The Greek Ambassador
reacted favourably. The formula, however, was rejected by the British who replied that it was impossible to accord Greece 'a *locus
standi*' in Cypriot affairs.[126]

In the event, Cyprus did not receive much attention at the Anglo-
American summit. Significantly, the State Department would subsequently deny to Politis that the matter was ever discussed.[127] In
reality, however, Churchill referred to Cyprus as a good place for
the redeployment of British forces from Suez.[128] More important,
on 27 June Eden asked Dulles what the American attitude was towards the Greek claim. According to the British minutes, the US
Secretary of State, who had briefed the President on this issue a few
days earlier, professed a lack of detailed information. He conceded,
however, that American policy would be 'basically' with the British.[129] Still, another aspect of the Washington summit raised hopes
among optimists in Greece and Cyprus. At the conclusion of the
talks, a joint communiqué was issued committing the two powers
to uphold the principle of 'self-government' and to 'strive by every
peaceful means to secure the independence of all countries whose
peoples desire and are capable of sustaining an independent existence'.[130]

As Churchill had intimated to Eisenhower, the British Cabinet
had decided to transfer the Joint Middle East Headquarters to Cyprus, in view of the impending agreement with Egypt on the evacu-

ation of the Canal Zone.[131] The decision was announced by the British Ministry of Defence on 3 July. In reaction, Makarios sent a telegram of protest to the UN Secretary-General and to all NATO governments, warning that the British headquarters would be situated 'in a hostile environment so long as Cyprus remain(ed) under foreign domination'.[132]

At last, on 12 July the State Department delivered its reply to the British *aide-mémoire* of 28 January. The gist had been given to a member of the British Embassy on 25 June, so London knew what to expect – the US government could not confirm that common strategic interests required no change in the status of Cyprus. Still, it was conceded that important 'political considerations ... militat[ed] against such a change at this time'. The Americans also agreed to continue to discourage the Greeks. If the question was raised at the UN, however, no assurance was given that the United States would be voting with Britain. The dilemma of 'reconciling general political considerations' with respect for the principle of self-determination had yet to be resolved.[133] Significantly, upon delivering its reply, the State Department expressed the hope that the British would make 'a sincere effort ... to evolve an acceptable constitution for Cyprus'.[134]

The lack of political progress in Cyprus was already causing criticism in the British press and parliament. Woodrow Wyatt, Labour MP, described the government's policy as evasive and blind to the dangers ahead.[135] It was clear that the time had come for a fresh initiative. On 21 July the Cabinet rubber-stamped a new blueprint, which ruled out self-determination and sought to impose 'a more limited type of self-governing institutions'.[136]

The Americans were informed of British intentions on 26 July during the regular talks on colonial issues. The British tried to justify their less than liberal offer on the grounds of Communist strength in Cyprus. At the same time, they tested US reactions to their proposed tactics at the UN – the British delegation, the Americans were told, would withdraw from any debate on Cyprus, which would violate the Charter's clause on domestic jurisdiction; it would also threaten an 'agonising reappraisal' of British co-operation with UN organs on colonial matters. The Americans objected to both courses of action. Nor did the attempt to strike a bargain between Cyprus and other issues of interest to the two powers in the coming General Assembly bear fruit.[137] The British also tried to get the Americans to provide some comfort to the Greeks by saying things that they themselves were not prepared to say. For example, if the Greeks were patient and gave the constitutional offer a chance, then 'the time might well come' when Britain would 'listen sympathetically' to the national aspirations of the Cypriots, or even agree to talk to the Greeks.[138]

Armed with the constitutional offer the State Department went ahead with the *démarche* to Athens, as promised in its reply to the British *aide-mémoire*.[139] This came as a 'personal message' from Dulles to Stefanopoulos, delivered only hours before the British offer was announced in the Commons on 28 July. The Americans indirectly but clearly warned against the raising of the Cyprus question at the UN, stressing the 'serious and undesirable consequences' for allied cohesion in the region. What was more, they clearly recognised Turkey as a country 'primarily concerned with the future of Cyprus'. The solution to the problem, it was stated, should come from Britain and the Cypriots themselves 'in gradual stages', starting with a 'mutually acceptable constitution'. The Greek government was urged to help this process by using its influence with the Ethnarchy.[140] Upon reading the message, Stefanopoulos asked that its contents remain strictly secret.[141] As Politis explained to Byroade in Washington, no government could remain in power in Greece if it failed to 'respond to the will of the people by taking [the Cyprus question] to the UN'.[142]

In the early evening of 28 July the Parliamentary Under-Secretary for the Colonies proceeded to announce a new Cyprus policy in parliament. A day earlier, both the Greek and Turkish governments had been given notice.[143] In the case of Ankara, the Foreign Office took care to point out that the constitutional offer would take 'considerable time' to materialise and that it was designed to prevent 'extremists' from taking over.[144] As it happened, Hopkinson's statement came shortly after Eden had announced a preliminary accord with Egypt for the evacuation of the Suez Zone. This statement had provoked angry reactions from the so-called 'Suez Group' of Conservative hard liners.[145]

Hopkinson stated that the government intended to offer Cyprus a new constitution, which, he admitted, was less liberal than that offered in 1948. He ominously added that the Governor had been instructed to take all appropriate measures to ensure the early introduction of the constitution. Of course, there was no question of Britain abandoning her sovereignty. Subsequently, Hopkinson went at some length over the economic and other benefits of British rule in Cyprus. In conclusion, he acknowledged the 'close cultural links' of the Greek and Turkish-speaking parts of the population with Greece and Turkey, links that he did not see as incompatible with the objectives of British policy.[146]

From the stormy debate that followed[147] two points would have a particularly unfortunate effect on Anglo-Greek relations and the course of the Cypriot controversy. The first was Hopkinson's notorious 'never' in his reply to a question from Griffiths, the former Labour Secretary for the Colonies, regarding the ultimate status of Cyprus:

'It has always been understood and agreed that there are certain territories in the Commonwealth which, owing to their particular circumstances, can never expect to be fully independent. [...] I am not going as far as that this afternoon, but I have said that the question of the abrogation of British sovereignty cannot arise – that British sovereignty will remain'.[148]

There followed an assault by the left wing of the Labour party, whereupon Oliver Lyttelton, the outgoing Colonial Secretary, was summoned to save the situation. Having substituted 'at this stage' for Hopkinson's 'never', Lyttelton uttered a statement that could scarcely have been more provocative to the Greeks: 'I can imagine no more disastrous policy for Cyprus than to hand it over to an unstable though friendly power. It would have the effect of undermining the eastern bastion of NATO. It would have the effect of depressing the standard of life of everyone in Cyprus'.[149] No timely attempt was made to redress the impact of these statements on Greek and Cypriot opinion.

The constitutional offer was broadcast by Governor Armitage on 29 July. It provided for an appointed majority in the legislature and a limited representation of its members at the Executive Council.[150] The colonial administration also revealed its intention to use repression in order to pre-empt opposition. On 2 August, the Colony's Attorney-General, Criton Tornaritis, announced that the anti-sedition laws, which had been virtually ineffective since 1951, would henceforth be strictly enforced. The warning was particularly intended for the press – even the publication of material from British papers could result in prosecution for 'seditious intention', depending on 'the manner of publication and any comment thereon'.[151]

Reactions

The rejection of just any constitutional plan by the Greek Cypriot parties was a foregone conclusion [152] The Ethnarchy's Pancyprian National Assembly, which Makarios convened on 23 July, had done so in advance. Anticipating the British gesture, the Archbishop braced his flock for harder struggles. Although the campaign for Enosis, he said, had always been a peaceful one, events in Egypt 'demonstrated that violence is always necessary' against oppression.[153] Following Armitage's statement, the Archbishop warned that co-operation with the foreign ruler would be treated as treason. Not that there was much chance for such co-operation, since even moderate opinion in Cyprus was dismayed by what was on offer.[154] Only the Turks showed some satisfaction, considering the proposals 'safe'.[155]

Anti-sedition aggravated things further. On 4 August, the colonial authorities confiscated and destroyed all copies of the British *News Chronicle*, which contained an article 'highly critical' of British policy.[156] News vendors had to cancel orders for papers from Greece,[157] while the Greek Cypriot press suspended publication for a week.[158] Makarios, in an unprecedented move, received the Secretary-General and the mayors of AKEL, but publicly turned down their offer of support.[159] Still, both Right and Left contributed in the general strike of 12 August, brought all economic and social activity on the island to a standstill.[160] The adverse climate would also force the new Colonial Secretary, Alan Lennox-Boyd, to abandon his plan for a visit to Cyprus in August.[161]

In Greece, indignation was as expected universal. The press and radio rejected the constitutional offer as a mere sham for the perpetuation of colonial domination and widely predicted violence in Cyprus. Tornaritis was branded a traitor and threatened with death.

Enosis supporters organised a mass meeting in Athens, while Papagos called upon the people to 'express their sentiment and faith' in an orderly manner.[162] With regard to official reactions, Stefanopoulos expressed disappointment over the offer and declared that Greek policy remained unchanged.[163] The Ambassador in London protested against Lyttelton's disparaging remark. In response, Selwyn Lloyd had little difficulty in telling Mostras that, by using the word 'never', Hopkinson did not mean 'anything other than "never"'.[164]

Repression in Cyprus did not fail to provoke reactions in Britain where a growing section of the press began to give Enosis sympathetic comment.[165] As the colonial authorities admitted, the Cypriot press only had to select and translate material from British journals in order to keep Enosis on the front page without bringing charges of sedition upon itself.[166]

Faced with the 'sustained and general' criticism of the British press and, most important, the unfavourable reactions in the United States,[167] the British government fell back.[168] In a matter of days, Lennox-Boyd asked Armitage to try to soften the impact of Tornaritis' announcement. Thus, in a 'somewhat rambling radio address' delivered on 7 August, the Governor denied that the administration ever intended to suppress freedom of speech and the press.[169] There followed a 'corrective' statement by the Attorney-General to the effect that no prosecution could ever be instituted for anything said or written in Britain.[170]

On 3 August, amidst the furore sparked by Hopkinson's statement, Stefanopoulos gave Cannon his reply to the message from Dulles. It was a ten-page document that drew attention to 'the uncompromising, arrogant and discourteous' British rejection of all Greek overtures, fulminated against Turkish involvement in the dispute, blaming it on British machinations, and argued that the recourse to the UN actually served allied unity – if the Greek government abandoned Cyprus, friendship with Britain and Turkey would be destroyed, Moscow could claim a moral victory, and Greece's commitment to Western defence would diminish. For these and other reasons, the Greek government could not follow the course suggested in Dulles's message. Yet it expressed confidence that the United States would eventually 'stand by the side of Greece'.[171] A week later, Politis informed the State Department that the Greek appeal would be submitted to the UN Secretariat on 20 August.[172]

At about the same time, the British Embassy in Athens received two alternative suggestions emanating from Papagos: a mediation from the Council of Europe, where the Greek request for a discussion of the Cyprus question was still pending, or secret consultation on a new constitution, which Papagos would then try and sell to the Ethnarchy.[173] The British did not respond.

On the eve of the Greek recourse, Ambassador Cannon called on Papagos in a further attempt to make US opposition clear. According to the Embassy's report, the two men had a 'candid discussion', during which Cannon explained that, its long-standing advocacy of self-determination notwithstanding, US policy with regard to Cyprus was conditioned by global interests. There existed, he said, far more important issues on which the Americans and the British had to work together. Therefore, the Greek government should not expect 'a sympathetic attitude' if it raised that question at the UN. Papagos replied that he understood the US position and that he 'himself had favoured [a] more moderate and patient policy'.[174] Cannon also warned the Field Marshal to expect 'only disappointment' from the 'enlightenment committee', which the government intended to send to the United States in order to project the Greek case. Papagos admitted that he did not put much stoke in that committee, but he felt obliged to dispatch it in order to forestall domestic criticism.[175]

NOTES

1. 101799, 1017/22, Peake to Harrison, 1 July 1952; 101808, 1052/4, FO to Peake; 101807, 1051/5, FO minutes by Barnes and Cheetham, 4 Sept. 1952; 101800, 1017/42, 'The Record of the Plastiras Government', Lambert to Southern Department, 22 Oct. 1952.
2. 101808, 1052/6, memo of conversation between Melas and Eden, 10 Sept. 1952; 101808, 1052/7, memo of conversation between the Greek Chargé d'Affaires and Harrison, 15 Sept. 1952.
3. 101807, 1051/4, BBC Monitoring Service, 23 July 1952; 101808, 1052/5, Peake to Harrison, 26 Aug. 1952; referring to his relations with Venizelos, Peake commented that it was 'a mistake to get on terms of false intimacy with a man whom one profoundly distrusts and with whom it is often necessary to be stiff': 101807, 1051/4, Peake to Strang, 27 Aug. 1952; cf. 641.81/7-2252, Peurifoy to DS, tel. 271.

4. 101808, 1052/9, Peake to Eden, 25 Nov. 1952.
5. 101808, 1052/11, FO minute by Murray, 18 Nov. 1952; Linardatos II 1978, 27.
6. CAB 128, 25/CC (52) 101, 3 Dec. 1952.
7. Campbell 1960, 198-199; Eden *Memoirs* III, 244-245.
8. 107485, 10110/3, Cyprus Political Situation Report, Feb. 1953.
9. 107499, 1052/1, record of conversation between King Paul and Strang, 19 Feb. 1953.
10. 107485, 10110/3, Cyprus Political Situation Report, Feb. 1953; 10110/4, Cyprus Political Situation Report, March 1953.
11. 107501, 1081/9, Peake to FO, 7 March 1953; 1081/13, Peake to FO, 11 March 1953; 1081/17, letter from Peake to Stefanopoulos, 6 March 1953.
12. 107501, 1081/12, record of conversation between Mostras and Harrison, 9 March 1953; 1081/14, Peake to FO, 12 March 1953.
13. 107501, 1081/8, Athens Embassy to Western and Southern Departments, 4 March 1953; 781.00/3-2353, Anschuetz to State, desp. 1089; Linardatos II 1978, 72.
14. 107485, 10110/4, Cyprus Political Situation Report, March 1953.
15. United Nations General Assembly Resolution 637VII/16.12.1952 (Agenda Item 30.A/Res/40). On the adoption of this resolution and the opposition it encountered from the colonial powers and the US, see Xydis 1967, 592, n. 4.
16. 107501, 1081/25, Wright to CO, 27 April 1953; 1081/27, 29-31, drafts of Wright's reply to Makarios.
17. CO 926/66, Wright to CO, 18 May 1953; 747C.00/5-2953, Wagner to State, desp. 132; 747C.00/7-3153, Wagner to State, desp. 11.
18. 107485, 10110/4, Cyprus Political Situation Report, May 1953.
19. 107485, 10110/4, Cyprus Political Situation Reports, March-June; CO 926/10, Wright to Lyttelton, 8 June 1953; 747C.00/7-2153, Wagner to State, desp. 9; cf. Kelling 1990, 127.
20. Crawshaw 1978, 54; Kelling 1990, 127.
21. CO 926/10, Wright to CO, 8 June 1953; 107501, 1081/34, Wright to CO, 28 June 1953; 747C.00/7-153, Wagner to State, tel.1; Crawshaw 1978, 54; Kelling 1990, 122.
22. 747C.00/7-1353; Linardatos II 1978, 84-85; Servas I 1985, 162-164; Vlahos 1980, 62.
23. 107502, 1081/47, Cyprus government press communiqué, 4 July 1953; 747C.00/7-2153, Wagner to State, desp. 9.
24. 107485, 10110/5, Cyprus Political Situation Report, July 1953.
25. 107485, 10110/5, Cyprus Political Situation Report, July 1953.
26. 107485, 10110/, Cyprus Political Situation Reports, Aug.-Sept. 1953; Linardatos II 1978, 134.
27. 107484, 1019/5, Cyprus Political Situation Report, Sept. 1953.
28. 747C.00/9-953, Anschuetz to State, desp. 262; Crouzet I 1973, 380; Linardatos II 1978, 134-5.
29. The records relating to Dulles' plan to visit Cyprus are in file 107534, 1635/1-2.
30. *FRUS 1952-54*, IX, 156-157.

31. *FRUS 1952-54*,VIII, 676.
32. *FRUS 1952-54*,VIII, 678.
33. *FRUS 1952-54*,VIII, 676-7.
34. *FRUS 1952-54*,VIII, 677-8.
35. 107502, 1081/54, Seconde to Selby, 29 Oct. 1953; Linardatos II 1978, 135.
36. 107502, 1081/42, UKUN Delegation to FO, 31 Aug. 1953.
37. 747C.00/9-2353; 117622, 1081/66, Pierson Dixon to Eden, 19 Jan. 1955.
38. 107499, 1052/3, record of conversation between Papagos and Eden, 22 Sept. 1953.
39. *GPR*, meeting of 7 February 1955, 671.
40. As Crouzet remarks, Eden was recovering from jaundice, 'which could have aggravated a certain natural irascibility': Crouzet I 1973, 382, n. 108.
41. 107485, 10110/7, Cyprus Political Situation Report, Oct. 1953.
42. 107502, 1081/50, Peake to FO, 16 Oct. 1953; 1081/51. According to the Ambassador in London, the Greek Foreign Ministry failed to inform the London Embassy of the content of the Papagos-Eden conversation. When the Ambassador finally obtained the record some three months later, he found nothing in it indicating the 'sharp exchange' which later became common knowledge: Mostras, 44, n. 1.
43. 107502, 1081/50, Peake to FO, 16 Oct. 1953.
44. 107502, 1081/61, 'Cyprus', memo by Harrison, 18 Nov. 1953.
45. 107502, 1081/56, Peake to FO, 10 Nov. 1953.
46. 747C.00/11-1653, Lodge to Dulles; *ibid.*, Greek memorandum.
47. 747C.00/11-1653, Dulles to Lodge, Nov., 24, 1953. Lodge informed his British counterpart of Greek intentions, which Kyrou had also communicated to the Australian and New Zealand delegations. 107502, 1081/66, Jebb to FO, 1 Dec. 1953; 1081/70, Jebb to Kirkpatrick, 9 Dec. 1953.
48. The release was issued after Stefanopoulos' failure to mention Cyprus in his speech on foreign policy in parliament, a failure that had been widely criticised by the opposition and the press.
49. 107502, 1081/62, Peake to FO, 26 Nov. 1953; Linardatos II 1978, 136.
50. 112830, 10110/1, Cyprus Political Situation Report, Dec. 1953.
51. 107502, 1081/63, Eden to Peake, 26 Nov. 1953; 5 Dec. 1953.
52. 107558,WK1081/14, record of conversation between Berkol and Harrison, 18 Dec. 1953.
53. 107502, 1081/63, Eden to Peake, 23 Nov. 1953; 1081/69, Peake to Eden, 8 Dec. 1953.
54. 107502, 1081/69, Peake to Eden, 8 Dec. 1953.
55. 112843, 1081/3, 8 Jan. 1954; minutes by Cheetham and Harrison, 13 and 14 Jan. 1954.
56. Both Governor Wright and the Colonial Office had strongly objected such a concession, arguing that it was tantamount to 'permitting Greek infiltration in Cyprus' and that the mere presence of inspectors from Greece would incite sedition: 107502, 1081/71, Pearson, CO, to Selby, FO, 22 Dec. 1953.
57. 112843, 1081/5, Selby, FO, to Pearson, CO, 2 Feb. 1954; 1081/17, record of

conversation between Harrison and Mostras, 16 Feb. 1954; 1081/20.

58. 112843, 1081/3, Peake to Cheetham, 8 Jan. 1954; 1081/6, Peake to Cheetham, 23 Jan. 1954.
59. 112843, 1081/6, Peake to Cheetham, 23 Jan. 1954.
60. 112830, 10110/2, Cyprus Political Situation Report, Jan. 1954.
61. 112843, 1081/19, Peake to FO, 18 Feb. 1954.
62. 747C.00/3-1754, Cannon/Axelrod to State, desp. 860.
63. 112843, 1081/18, Peake to FO, 18 Feb. 1954; 1081/19, Peake to FO, 19 Feb. 1954; 112843, 1081/25, record of conversation between Harrison and Mostras, 20 Feb. 1954.
64. 112843, 1081/26, record of conversation between Selwyn Lloyd and Mostras, 23 Feb. 1954.
65. 112844, 1081/39, 'Cyprus', minute by Cheetham, 26 Feb. 1954.
66. 112844, 1081/32-33, oral communication by the Greek Ambassador to Harrison, 1 March 1954.
67. 112844, 1081/34, Athens Chancery to Western and Southern Departments, 2 March 1954.
68. Crawshaw 1978, 96; Linardatos II 1978, 166.
69. 112844, 1081/45, parliamentary question by Mrs Lena Jeger, 15 March 1954.
70. 112844, 1081/54, Athens Chancery to Western and Southern Departments, 20 March 1954.
71. 112920 1941/6, Peake to FO, 16 March 1954.
72. 112844, 1081/48, Peake to FO, 19 March 1954; 1081/54, Athens Chancery to Western and Southern Departments, 20 March 1954; 112845, 1081/71, Peake to Eden, 3 April 1954; 747C.00/3-2454, Holt to State, desp. 82; Linardatos II 1978, 167-168.
73. 112844, 1081/66, record of conversation between Eden and Mostras, 30 March 1954; Mostras ms, 65-66.
74. 112845, 1081/77, Lord Leceister to Churchill, letter from Queen Frederica, 24 March 1954; *ibid.*, Churchill to Queen Frederica, 7 April 1954; *ibid.*, Peake to Cheetham, 18 April 1954. See also Frederica 1971, 185-188, where the Queen's letter is incorrectly dated 4 March 1954.
75. 112845, 1081/72, record. of conversation between Eden and Mostras, 6 April 1954; 747C.00/4-1054, Cannon to State, tel. 2461. The message from Papagos, as Mostras noted, was riddled with grammatical errors, but the Foreign Ministry rejected any idea of correction: Mostras ms, 66, n. 2.
76. On the process that led to the conclusion of the two Balkan treaties of 1953 and 1954, see Iatrides 1968.
77. Hristidis 1967, 3-4; Iatrides 1968, 120; Linardatos II 1978, 83-84; Mihalopoulos 1989, 46-47.
78. 107494, WG10344/1, Izmir press notes, 29 April-14 May 1953; WG10344/2, Istanbul press review, 16 June 1953; 107558, WK1081/11, Ankara Embassy to Athens Chancery, 2 Nov. 1953.
79. 107589, WK1741/5, Ankara Embassy to Colonial Secretariat, Nicosia, 21 July 1953; WK1741/7, FO minute by Maby, 30 Sept. 1953; WK1741/8, Knox

Helm to Wright, 25 Sept. 1953.
80. 107558, WK1081/4, British Embassy, Ankara, to Colonial Secretariat, Nicosia, 3 Oct. 1953; WK1081/13, Knox Helm to Harrison, 3 Dec. 1953; *ibid.*, Cheetham, FO, to Pearson, CO, 6 Jan. 1954.
81. 107485, 10110/7, Cyprus Political Situation Report, Oct. 1953; Linardatos II 1978, 136.
82. 112843, 1081/3, Peake to Cheetham, 8 Jan. 1954; 1081/6, Peake to Cheetham, 23 Jan. 1954.
83. 112843, 1081/13, Ankara Embassy to FO, 13 Feb. 1954; *ibid.*, Eden to Ankara Embassy, 15 Feb. 1954.
84. 112843, 1081/23, minute by Cheetham, 17 Feb. 1954; 1081/28, Ankara Embassy to FO, 24 Feb. 1954.
85. 112843, 1081/11, Eden to Ankara Embassy, 11 Feb. 1954; 1081/12, Makins to FO, 12 Feb. 1954.
86. 112843, 1081/29, Ankara Embassy to FO, 25 Feb. 1954.
87. 112843, 1081/11, Peake to FO, 4 Feb. 1954; *FRUS 1952-54*, VIII, 680.
88. *FRUS 1952-54*, VIII, 680-681.
89. 747C.00/3-554, Warren to State, tel. 928.
90. *FRUS 1952-54*, VIII, 681-683.
91. 112844, 1081/51, Peake to FO, 22 March 1954; 1081/55, record of conversation between Cheetham and Berkol, 23 March 1954; 1081/62, Bowker to FO, 30 March 1954; 747C.00/3-1754, Cannon/Axelrod to State, desp. 860.
92. 112844, 1081/62, Bowker to FO, 30 March 1954; 112846, 1081/121, Scott Fox to Cheetham, 10 May 1954; 747C.00/3-3154, Warren to State, tel. 1024; 747C.00/6-2254, Warren to State, tel. 1366.
93. For example, on the occasion of a Turkish Cypriot visit in early July, a government spokesman in Ankara, while reaffirming that Turkey favoured the *status quo* in the island, denied press reports that there had been attempts to prevent Greece from bringing the issue before the UN: 112848, 1081/169, *Daily Telegraph*, 2 July 1954.
94. 112845, 1081/79, Ankara Embassy to FO, 7 April 1954; Pipinelis 1959, 35.
95. 112845, 1081/94, BBC Monitoring Service, April 1954; 112846, 1081/121, Scott Fox to Cheetham, 10 May 1954; 747C.00/4-3054, Cannon to State, tel. 2593; Mostras ms, 6. Regarding the Greek *démenti* and the subsequent 'correction', see *To Vima*, Athens daily, 25 and 28 April 1954.
96. 112846, 1081/102, *The Times*, 30 April 1954.
97. 747C.00/4-3054, Cannon to State, tel. 2593.
98. 747C.00/10-2353, Cannon to State, desp. 392.
99. 112843, 1081/11, Peake to FO, 4 Feb. 1954.
100. 112843, 1081/9, 'Cyprus', *aide-mémoire* from Washington Embassy to State Department, 28 Jan. 1954; 747C.00/1-2854, British *aide-mémoire*.
101. 112844, 1081/38, Salt to Cheetham, 4 March 1954.
102. 112844, 1081/47, Salt to Cheetham, 16 March 1954.
103. *FRUS 1952-54*, VIII, 685-687.
104. *FRUS 1952-54*, VIII, 684-685, 685, n. 3; 112845, 1081/80, Peake to FO, 12

April 1954.

105. 112845, 1081/88, minutes of meeting held in the CO, 14April 1954; 112846, 1081/147, FO circular dispatch, UP248128, 3 May 1954.
106. 112847, 1081/155, C.R.O. to High Commissioners in British Common-wealth countries, 22 July 1954.
107. 112847, 1081/150, minute of conversation betweenWilding and Robinson, 4 June 1954.
108. 112845, 1081/88, minutes of meeting held in the CO, 14 April 1954.
109. 747C.00/4-454, Salonika tel. 59; /4-2054, Athens desp. 994; Linardatos II, 154-161; Markezinis 1994, 44-56.
110. 747C.00/4-2154, letter from Cannon to Baxter.
111. 747C.00/5-1054, draft letter from Baxter to Cannon.
112. 112846, 1081/102, *The Times*, 30 April 1954
113. 112830, 10110/5, Cyprus Political Situation Report, April 1954; Vlahos 1980, 72; *Kathimerini*, 22 April 1954, and *To Vima*, 22 April 1954.
114. 747C.00/5-1354, Schnee to State, desp. 1054; Vlahos 1980, 72.
115. 112830, 10110/6, Cyprus Political Situation Report, May 1954.
116. 112846, 1081/110, record of conversation between Cheetham and Mostras, 3 May 1954; 747C.00/5-1354, Schnee to State, desp. 1054. According to the US Consul in Nicosia, Stefanopoulos' statement initially caused 'considerable dismay and confusion' to the Ethnarchy camp: 747C.00/6-354, Wagner to State, desp. 84.
117. 112846, 1081/112, Peake to FO, 5 May 1954; 747C.00/6-154, office memo from Howard to Wood; Crawshaw 1978, 74.
118. Linardatos II 1978, 200; Mayes 1981, 54.
119. 112847, 1081/136, Nutting to FO, 26 May 1954; 1081/137, Nutting to FO, 27 May 1954; Linardatos II 1978, 198.
120. 112847, 1081/140, minute by Nutting, 1 June 1954; 1081/148, letter from S. Bohy to Lord John, 26 May 1954; 1081/162, FO minute, June 1954.
121. 112851, 1081/271, FO minute, 18 Aug. 1954; 112855, 1081/398, Council of Europe Brief 94 (54), 2nd Meeting of the 5th Session, Sept. 13-25, 1954, 'Cyprus'.
122. 112846, 1081/128, Salt to Cheetham, 17 May 1954.
123. Calvocoressi 1987, 320, 478; *FRUS 1952-54*, IV, 1027 ff.
124. 747C.00/7-754, office memo from Howard to Baxter.
125. *FRUS 1952-54*, VIII, 691-692.
126. *FRUS 1952-54*, VIII, 691-692; 747C.00/6-2554, memo of conversation be-tween Beeley and Byroade; 112848, 1081/185, Salt to Young, 9 July 1954.
127. *FRUS 1952-54*, VIII, 692-693.
128. *FRUS 1952-54*, VIII, 690.
129. 112848, 1081/180, record of conversation between Eden and Dulles, 27 June 1954.
130. 112849, 1081/201, joint communiqué, Eisenhower-ChurchillTalks, Wash-ington, 29 June 1954.
131. 112848, 1081/174, *The Sunday Times*, 4 July 1954. The Headquarters would

be established at Episkopi, west of Limassol, in autumn 1955: Crouzet I 1973, 320-321.

132. 112830, 10110/7, Cyprus Political Situation Report, June 1954.

133. *FRUS 1952-54*, VIII, 695-6; 112851, 1081/274, US *aide-mémoire*, Scott to Eden, 10 Aug. 1954; Kelling 1990, 144-145.

134. *FRUS 1952-54*, VIII, 694.

135. 112848, 1081/197, parliamentary question by E.L. Mallalieu, 19 July 1954; 1081/200, parliamentary question by E.L. Mallalieu, 20 July 1954.

136. CAB 129, C (54) 245, memo by the Secretary of State for the Colonies and the Minister of State, 21 July 1954.

137. In exchange for US support on Cyprus, the British offered to 'do what (they) could' to help the United States on the Guatemalan issue or to defeat an Indian move intended to question the legality of US nuclear tests in the Trust Territory of the Marshall Islands in the Pacific: 112459, UP2416/8, Ramsbotham to Cope, 29 July 1954; *ibid.*, 'Colonial Talks in Washington. Cyprus', memo by UKUN Delegation; *FRUS 1952-54*, III, 1400-1402.

138. 747C.00/7-2854, memo of conversation between Wilson, US Embassy, and Martin, CO; *FRUS 1952-54*, VIII, 714 (Dixon to Lodge).

139. *FRUS 1952-54*, VIII, 696-697.

140. *Ibid.*, 697-699.

141. *Ibid.*, 699-700.

142. *Ibid.*, 700-701.

143. 112848, 1081/207, FO to Istanbul, 27 July 1954; 112849, 1081/214, FO to Athens Embassy, 27 July 1954; *FRUS 1952-54*, VIII, 696.

144. 112849, 1081/214, FO to Ankara Embassy, 27 July 1954.

145. On whether the statement on Cyprus deliberately followed Eden's announcement as a sop, see Crouzet, who tends to dismiss this inference: Crouzet I 1973, 402.

146. 112849, 1081/212, statement on Cyprus by the Minister of State for the Colonies in the Commons, 28 July 1954; Crawshaw 1978, 75-76.

147. An extensive account of the debate see in Crawshaw 1978, 75-80.

148. *Ibid.*, 76.

149. *Ibid.*, 79.

150. CAB 129 C (54) 245, memo by the Secretary of State for the Colonies and the Minister of State, 21 July 1954.

151. 112830, 10110/8, Cyprus Political Situation Report, 1 July-10 Aug. 1954; 112850, 1081/242, Armitage to FO, 6 Aug. 1954.

152. 747C.00/7-285, Wilson to State, enclosure: memo of conversation between Sir John Martin and Wilson. Martin had suggested that the Americans should try to provide some comfort to the disillusioned Greeks.

153. 112830, 10110/8, Cyprus Political Situation Report, 1 July-10 Aug. 1954; 747C.00/7-2954, Wagner to State, desp. 7; Linardatos II 1978, 202.

154. 112830, 10110/8, Cyprus Political Situation Report, 1 July-10 Aug. 1954; 747C.03/8-554, Wagner to State, desp. 10; cf. Durrell 1957, 147-148; Linardatos II 1978, 203-204; Vlahos 1980, 73-74.

155. 112830, 10110/8, Cyprus Political Situation Report, 1 July-10 Aug. 1954.
156. 112850, 1081/236, Armitage to CO, 4 Aug. 1954.
157. 112850, 1081/242, Armitage to FO, 6 Aug. 1954; CO 926/500, Armitage to Lennox-Boyd, 30 Aug. 1954.
158. 112830, 10110/8, Cyprus Political Situation Report, 1 July-10 Aug. 1954; Crawshaw 1978, 80; Linardatos II 1978, 204. Even the printing of the semi-official *Cyprus Mail* was suspended, as its press workers went on strike.
159. 112830, 10110/8, Cyprus Political Situation Report, 1 July-10 Aug. 1954; 747C.00/8-1154, Wagner to State, tel. 13; /8-1154, Rossidis to Wagner, memo; /8-2454, Wagner to State, desp. 17.
160. 112830, 10110/9, Cyprus Political Situation Report, 10-31 Aug., 1954; 747C.00/8-1954, Wagner to State, desp. 16.
161. 112853, 1081/314, FO minute by Young, 17 Aug. 1954; the visit was planned to take place between 17 and 21 August. The Greek Ambassador had already expressed 'great concern' regarding the effects of such a visit.
162. 112851, 1081/264, Lambert to Eden, 6 Aug. 1954; 747C.03/8-1154, Schnee to State, desp. 121; Linardatos II 1978, 204.
163. 112849, 1081/215, Lambert to FO, 29 July 1954; 747C.03/8-1154, Schnee to State, desp. 121; Linardatos II 1978, 203.
164. 112850, 1081/239, minute by Selwyn Lloyd, 4 Aug. 1954.
165. 112830, 10110/9, Cyprus Political Situation Report, 10-31 Aug. 1954.
166. 112830, 10110/10, Cyprus Political Situation Report, Sept. 1954; 10110/11, Cyprus Political Situation Report, Oct. 1954.
167. 112850, 1081/240, Washington Embassy to FO, 6 Aug. 1954; 112851, 1081/277, UKUN Delegation to FO, 13 Aug. 1954; 112856, 1081/415, extracts from US press reports, 19-25 Aug. 1954.
168. 112851, 1081/258, Lennox-Boyd to Armitage, 7 Aug. 1954.
169. 112851, 1081/258, Lennox-Boyd to Armitage, 7 Aug. 1954; 747C.00/8-754, Wagner to State, tel. 10; Crawshaw 1978, 80-81.
170. 112851, 1081/258, Lennox-Boyd to Armitage, 7 Aug. 1954; CO 926/311, Lennox-Boyd to Churchill, 10 Aug. 1954.
171. *FRUS 1952-54*, VIII, 702; 747C.00/8-454, memo, Jernegan to Dulles, Aug. 12, 1954.
172. 747C.00/8-1254, memo of conversation between Jernegan, Lincoln, Wood and Politis.
173. 112851, 1081/264, Lambert to Eden, 6 Aug. 1954.
174. 747C.00/8-1154, Cannon to State, tel. 344; 747C.03/8-1154, Schnee to State, desp. 121; 112852, 1081/287, Lambert to Harrison, 12 Aug. 1954.
175. 747C.00/8-1154, Cannon to State, tel. 344; 747C.03/8-1154, Schnee to State, desp. 121.

3

THE LIMITS OF DIPLOMACY

The Greek recourse to the UN

On 20 August the Greek government requested the UN Secretary-General to bring before the 9th session of the UN General Assembly the item 'Application under the auspices of the United Nations of the principle of equal rights and self-determination of peoples in the case of the population of Cyprus'. Three days earlier, Kyrou, the author of the appeal, had submitted a copy of the long explanatory memorandum to the US Ambassador in Athens.[1] The Greek recourse was based on the following provisions of the UN Charter: Article 10, which provided for the discussion of any question or matter within the scope of the Charter; Article 14, which permitted the General Assembly to recommend measures in situations 'likely to impair the general welfare or friendly relations among nations'; and Article 1(2), which recognised self-determination as a basis of such friendly relations. There followed a detailed exposition that stressed the Greek character of the island, the desire of its inhabitants for union with Greece, the negative and 'offending' British attitude and the state of opinion in Greece, which 'tended to jeopardise' Anglo-Greek relations and stability in the Eastern Mediterranean.[2]

The recourse was greeted in Greece with mass meetings and other manifestations organised by the PEEK across the country. At a gathering of some 150,000 in Athens, twenty reserve officers, who had marched all the way from Pyrgos in the Peloponnese, presented two bottles of their blood, one destined for Prime Minister Churchill, the other for Archbishop Makarios.[3] The meeting was followed by the usual clashes with the police, when some of the participants attempted to march on the British Embassy. In Salonika, anti-American sentiment was for the first time expressed by crowds which broke windows of the US Consulate-General.[4] Promptly, the Greek government offered its apologies.[5] In Cyprus, Makarios, defying the anti-seditious pronouncements of the authorities, delivered a passionate sermon at Faneromeni, where he swore with his congregation to remain faithful to Enosis unto death.[6]

The first reaction of the British government was to inform friendly governments that its delegation would not participate in a debate on the Cyprus question. Stressing its domestic jurisdiction argument, it also threatened to walk out and deny co-operation on colonial matters if the Greek item was inscribed.[7] These threats did not go down well with Commonwealth governments, which pressed London to reconsider its tactics.[8] Canadian Foreign Minister Lester Pearson, who questioned the validity of the British interpretation of Article 2(7) of the Charter, could only promise to abstain.[9] France and the Netherlands, on the other hand, which were facing similar motions on Tunisia, Morocco, and Western New Guinea respectively, pledged their support.[10]

On the day the Greek appeal was filed, Eisenhower wrote to Churchill and offered 'to do something'. In his letter, the US President expressed concern lest the British handling of the situation in Cyprus had a negative effect on American opinion and consequently put a strain on the 'durable and cordial' Anglo-American relationship.[11] The reply from the British Prime Minister did not arrive until 18 September. In the meantime, there were two American attempts at mediation through non-official channels. On 21 August Churchill was due to lunch with a Greek-American magnate, Spiros Skouras, President of 20th Century Fox. On Selwyn Lloyd's advice, Skouras left the Prime Minister a note with the following formula: the Greek government, by virtue of the difficult international situation, would have its appeal 'postponed', while the British would agree to discuss the Cyprus question when the time was ripe. The meeting with Churchill, however, did not go well. The Prime Minister appeared upset by Greek anti-British pronouncements – a 'campaign of calumny', as he put it – and did not particularly enjoy Skouras' company either. Thus, this first initiative was 'left to rest in peace'.[12]

About a week later, a second attempt was made, this time through Mrs Fleur Fenton Cowles, former wife of American publisher Gardner Cowles, editor of *Flair* magazine and socialite. Her main qualification, it seems, was her acquaintance with the Greek royal couple and the US President. With the approval of both Eisenhower and Dulles, Cowles proceeded to London and then to Athens in search of a formula which might enable the Greeks to withdraw their appeal.[13] On 2 September, she met Eden and Hopkinson in London, to whom she repeated Eisenhower's concern. In response to her request for 'some face-saving device', Hopkinson did jot something down, which provided for eventual talks with Greece and significantly Turkey on the future of Cyprus at the end of the period covered by the NATO treaty – although this was a point which the treaty itself left open to interpretation. In the event, the formula was not taken up. It was objected by Nutting and Sir Thomas Lloyd, the Permanent Under-Secretary for Colonial Affairs, while Eden himself did not hide his 'intense dislike for earnest and amateur diplomacy'.[14] The British Secretary of State sent a personal message to Dulles stating that his government could not make any statement, either in private or in public, which could be interpreted as yielding to Greek pressure.[15] In Athens Cowles met Papagos, who offered to tone down the Greek campaign once the Cyprus item was inscribed on the UN agenda. He also sent a personal letter to Eisenhower, expressing appreciation for Cowles' initiative.[16]

On 12 September, speaking to the British Ambassador, King Paul confirmed that Papagos 'would be only too thankful to find some pretext' for withdrawing from the UN. A few days later, it was Lodge's turn to sound Sir Pierson Dixon, his British counterpart, about a face-saving formula. Lodge suggested talks in three years' time.[17] On 20 September, however, Hopkinson told the US Permanent Representative that the British 'had racked their brains and had not been able to think of anything'.[18]

A further initiative to forestall the inter-Allied scuffle was taken by Belgian diplomacy. Foreign Minister Paul-Henri Spaak suggested to both London and Washington that the NAC rather than the General Assembly could serve as a place for the discussion of the Greek grievances. The Foreign Office, however, which had already examined this prospect, 'discreetly' discouraged Spaak's initiative.[19]

British diplomatic mobilisation

What British diplomacy was after was not American mediation but unqualified support. On 25 August, the British Chargé, Sir Robert Scott, called on Dulles and, playing up the themes of subversion and Communist exploitation of the Cyprus issue, pleaded for a US vote against the inscription of the Greek item on the agenda. Though 'not unsympathetic', Dulles reserved his position.[20] There followed a confidential memorandum seeking, among other things, assurances that the United States would not only vote against inscription but also try to persuade others to do likewise.[21]

This time British efforts were actively assisted by Turkish diplomacy. From 26 July onwards, Menderes abandoned his tactics of reserve and assured the British of full support in case Greece raised the Cyprus question at the UN.[22] On that day there were strong Turkish representations in Washington and New York. Ambassador Erkin complained that the United States had not done enough to discourage Greek intentions. Then, he handed in an informal memorandum, which, while concentrating on denying the Greek case, took care to stress the particular Turkish interest in the fate of the island. Moreover, the Turkish government fully subscribed to the argument that Cyprus was a matter of domestic jurisdiction, and declared its intention to 'co-ordinate very closely' with Britain at the UN.[23] The Anglo-Turkish concert was publicly confirmed by Menderes in Istanbul on 28 August.[24] A few days later, acting upon a British request, the Prime Minister sent a message to Dulles, in which, after deploring Greek policy and reaffirming Turkey's 'vital' interests in Cyprus, he asked that the United States oppose the Greek item at every stage.[25]

It took American diplomacy a fortnight to formulate its position on the Greek item, as Dulles was absent on a trip to Manilla for the signing of the South East Asian Defence Treaty (SEATO) Pact. Meanwhile, its representatives tried to use Cyprus as a bargaining counter on the question of Chinese representation. This attempt remained inconclusive.[26] The US position was finally communicated to the parties concerned on 15-6 September. It distinguished between the procedural aspect – the competence of the General Assembly to discuss any item, which it could not oppose – and the substantial –

the passage of a resolution on Cyprus, to which it objected. Thus, it chose to abstain from the vote on inscription. To the British and Turks, the Americans pledged to discourage a debate on substance and to 'actively oppose any resolution'. They also argued that by abstaining they would be better placed to 'exert a moderating influence on Greece'.[27] To the Greeks, they repeated their objection to a debate and asked them not to press for the passage of a resolution.[28] Significantly, the Greek government had since 25 August been asking the State Department what a desirable type of resolution would be.[29] Finally, all parties were urged to display moderation and to avoid criticisms of one another.

While expressing disappointment,[30] the British persevered. On 17 September, the State Department and the Supreme Allied Commander in Europe received a three-page 'top secret' note from the British Chiefs of Staff, which elaborated on the strategic importance of Cyprus and concluded that the retention of British sovereignty was a *sine qua non* for the fulfilment of their military obligations in the Middle East and beyond.[31] There followed the reply from Churchill to Eisenhower's letter of 20 August. Among other things, it referred to Greece's poor record of administration of the Dodecanese, the British intention not to be present at a discussion of Cyprus at the UN, and the adverse impact on British opinion if the United States failed to vote against inscription.[32] These arguments were recapitulated in a factual note, delivered on 20 September. With regard to self-determination, the Foreign Office contended that 'to allow the United Nations to discuss Cyprus on the pretext of self-determination would open the flood gates for the pursuit of territorial claims elsewhere'. Enosis was portrayed as an expansionist pursuit, not dissimilar to Hitler's *Anschluss* of Austria in 1938. In characteristic understatement, it was claimed that the British attitude was 'not entirely negative' – democratic processes were to be introduced and, once they had time to work, the Cypriots would realise 'where their true interests' lay.[33]

Three days before the General Committee was due to consider the Greek item, Dixon and Hopkinson made a last-minute effort to extract a reversal of the US decision. Lodge gave them no hope and argued that, in view of the coming congressional elections, the administration could not risk alienating the Greek-American vote.[34]

The British Ambassador in Washington ingeniously suggested that the US delegation might wish to abstain from the preliminary vote at the General Committee but could then cast a negative one in plenary.[35] There followed a rather disappointing meeting with Secretary Dulles, on 21 September. When Hopkinson and Dixon evoked allied solidarity in order to justify their plea for American assistance in persuading certain Latin Americans to abstain, Dulles chillingly remarked that the United States might decide to be as helpful as the British had been on the issue of Guatemala![36]

In the event, however, the Americans gave some ground. Dulles promised some canvassing of General Committee members by disclosing US opposition to the discussion of the Cyprus question – something that the American delegation had been doing already.[37] If the Committee's recommendation was against inscription, then it would vote to uphold it in plenary; if the item was put on the agenda – and this was the important thing – Dulles pledged that the United States would 'actively oppose the passage of any resolution'.[38]

At the same time, the British stepped up their diplomatic effort both in foreign capitals and in New York. The Western European and 'white' Commonwealth countries eventually closed the ranks. The 'northern tier' countries – Iran, Iraq and Pakistan – could also be counted upon not to support Greece. The British successfully lobbied India as well. Its Permanent Representative, Krishna Menon, appeared convinced that Enosis was a mere territorial dispute between two European powers, not a colonial problem that deserved Indian support.[39] On the other hand, the Arab countries, with the exception of Iraq,[40] related more closely to the Greek case.[41] The Political Committee of the Arab League, meeting in Cairo in early September, urged its members to use their influence with both parties to settle their differences through direct talks. If either party insisted on the inscription of the item, they should vote in favour and, after the debate, they should try to promote a resolution urging both parties to settle the dispute outside the UN.[42]

London also benefited from Turkish good offices, which were used with various member states, including the Scandinavian and Muslim countries and Yugoslavia.[43] While delivering strongly-worded memoranda against the Greek case to foreign governments,[44] the Turkish government sought to project an image of equanimity and moderation. Mass meetings and demonstrations on Cyprus were prohibited. On 9 September Menderes issued a statement explaining that it would be a mistake for his government to commit the same 'fallacious' actions as the Greeks, and expressed the hope that the latter would eventually see the light.[45] At the same time, he assured that his government was resolved to protect Turkey's national interests and rights.[46]

The battle of inscription

On the eve of the General Committee session, both the British and the American delegations to the UN proposed to have a third party table a motion to postpone any decision on the Greek item.[47] According to the American plan, the Greek and British delegations would present their cases and support direct talks between Britain and Cypriot representatives. Then, the General Committee could take a vote on postponement.[48] The Foreign Office opposed the idea, while the State Department vacillated[49] until the Greeks got air of the scheme. In Athens, deputy Premier Kanellopoulos 'urgently' called for a member of the American Embassy and asked that the United States oppose such a move.[50] This *démarche* perhaps caused the State Department to put a freeze on the scheme later that day.[51]

The composition of the General Committee appeared favourable to the Greeks. Of the fifteen members, only Australia, France[52] and the Netherlands were considered safe for the British. The United States and the two Latin American members, Colombia and Ecuador, were expected to abstain. The results of the voting on 23 September bitterly surprised the British: the Dutch representative, as President of the Assembly, chose to show impartiality by abstaining, while Ecuador came out as a strong supporter of the Greek case. In all, nine members voted in favour of inscription, while three voted against and three abstained.

With regard to the arguments advanced by the contending sides, Kyrou concentrated on British intransigence. By refusing to contemplate talks with Greece and to recognise the Cypriots' right to self-determination, he claimed, the British themselves had forced Greece's hand in filing the item. The head of the British delegation,

Selwyn Lloyd, focused on legal arguments, projecting the issue as one of domestic jurisdiction. He further warned that, by condoning the discussion of a territorial question settled by a valid treaty, the General Assembly was setting a very dangerous precedent for international relations.[53]

On the following day, the British missed a good opportunity to get the Greek item out of the way. As the report of the General Committee came in the plenary for consideration, the Iraqi representative tabled a motion to postpone decision for a few days in order to allow further study of the Greek and British statements. The real aim was, of course, to buy time for the British effort to muster more votes. Yet, having inspired the Iraqi initiative, the British delegation chose to abstain and let other friendly members, such as Turkey or South Africa, do likewise. Despite American support, the result was a tie (24-24) and the motion failed.[54]

There followed a second round of speeches. Greek Foreign Minister Stefanopoulos warned that, but for UN intervention, things for Cyprus, Anglo-Greek relations and regional peace and stability would take a turn for the worse. His reference to the Treaty of Lausanne as barring Turkish involvement proved unfortunate. Selwyn Lloyd used it to turn the tables against the Greeks – if their item was inscribed, he claimed, this would invite others to dispute legitimate frontiers anywhere. The British Minister of State also referred to Turkish Cypriot reactions, British commitments and the prospect of constitutional development. Finally, he warned that, if the item was inscribed, his delegation would not participate in further discussion. In a mild speech, Turkish Permanent Representative Selim Sarper argued against inscription on the grounds that it was a matter of domestic jurisdiction. Sarper reserved the right to speak on the merits of the case, if and when there was a debate on the substance. Krishna Menon's speech revealed the effectiveness of British tactics of using the *Anschluss* analogy. If it was for the freedom and self-determination of the 'Cypriot nation', Menon said, India would have supported the Greek appeal;[55] by seeking, however, to annex the island, Greece was merely posing a territorial claim and was overlooking the 'nationhood' of the islanders.[56]

In the event, the item was inscribed on the agenda by 30 votes in favour, 19 against and 11 abstentions. Significantly, with the exception of Iceland, which voted in favour, and the United States, which abstained, all Western European and NATO states voted against. All five Soviet bloc members,[57] half the Latin Americans and five out of six Arab states voted in favour. It was clear that Greece was still a long way behind the two-thirds majority required for the passing of a General Assembly resolution.[58]

Closing the ranks

On 2 October, during the London talks on the future of Western European defence and the question of German rearmament, Eden raised the Cyprus question with Dulles and the US Ambassador, Winthrop Aldrich. Referring to a suggestion of tripartite talks between Greece, Turkey and Britain, Eden declared that he 'could not sit down with [the] Greeks'. He also objected to a resolution postponing discussion until the next General Assembly. He agreed, however, with the proposal of Ambassador Aldrich to have Cyprus placed at the bottom of the agenda. The aim was to avoid a discussion before the Congressional elections of 2 November, which already accounted for much of American reserve. The latter's hope was that the item might not come up for discussion at all.[59] When Cyprus was indeed placed last, Kyrou, who knew that the Americans were behind this, declared that his delegation would insist on discussion at all levels, before the closing of the Ninth session of the General Assembly.[60]

The British appeared to play it tough until the last possible moment. Thus, they informed friendly governments that they did not wish them to promote a 'mild' resolution; rather, the Greeks should be allowed to table their own draft, and the more substantive it was, the better; the aim was to have it beaten and to prevent the passage of *any* resolution; finally, the British delegation would not participate in any discussion on substance.[61] They also tried to get a friendly state to canvass those UN members which had voted for inscription or abstained. Norway was approached first but refused. Canada was more forthcoming.[62] The Cyprus administration, for its part, let it be known to the Americans that there was no question of going ahead with the constitutional proposals until after the Greek appeal had been disposed of by the General Assembly.[63]

When the British parliament reconvened in October, the Cyprus issue was due for debate. The government sought to redress the unfavourable climate of opinion persisting since the summer. Hopkinson's 'never' was still a thorn on its side, having proved of considerable propaganda value to its adversaries. The issue was deemed important enough to warrant the intervention of the aged Prime Minister. During a Commons debate on 19 October, Churchill claimed that it had not been the intention of the Colonial Under-Secretary to use that word, which, he explained, 'is one which in politics can only be used in its general relativity to the subject'. Yet, in order to prevent improper interpretations, Churchill added that 'wiping out the word "never" does not mean that you substitute any other date'.[64] The other source of discomfort, the anti-seditious legislation and the lack of political progress in Cyprus, was addressed by the Colonial Secretary, who assured the Commons that press controls in the island had been relaxed. He had, however, nothing positive to say on the constitutional issue, nor did he, like Churchill before him, hold out any prospect of change even in a distant future.[65]

On the Greek part, the delegation to the UN, led by Kyrou, actively lobbied its case. Ambassador Politis was sent on a tour of Latin American capitals and his colleague in Australia attempted to enlighten the Indian government. More important, in its effort to win Arab-Asian and Latin American support, the Greek delegation changed its voting patterns on many issues in favour of anti-colonial positions. This change was manifested during the discussion of the Morocco, Tunisia and West New Guinea items at the Political Committee as well as in the Committees on social issues and non-self-governing territories.[66]

Kyrou also sent for Archbishop Makarios who, before coming to New York, visited Athens. There, he openly advocated a more assertive foreign policy and once more alluded to the prospect of violence in response to British intransigence.[67] In London he scored a public relations success, as the BBC invited him on its domestic programme. This led the Foreign Office to protest and ask a similar treatment of the Cyprus administration.[68] Makarios also had several contacts not only with opposition but also with certain 'philhellene' conservative politicians, who appeared sympathetic with

the Greek Cypriot cause. While in the British capital, he was reported to have stated that a constitutional offer could be accepted if
it was accompanied by a provision for a plebiscite within a given
number of years – the very formula which he had repudiated the
previous spring. The statement baffled the Ethnarchy camp back in
Cyprus, though it failed to attract any response from the British
government. Thus, before leaving for New York, the Archbishop
publicly reverted to his uncompromising position: no constitution
whatsoever was acceptable, but only the immediate recognition of
the Cypriot people's right to self-determination.[69]

Shortly before Makarios' arrival in London, the Labour party
had adopted a position on Cyprus during its annual conference at
Scarborough, which partly accounted for the ebullience of his public statements. As has been noted, Cyprus policy was proving quite
unpopular with the press and presented a good opportunity to criticise the Conservative government. The Liberal Party was all out for
the Cypriots' right to self-determination, but its political influence
was negligible. Things were different with Labour. Its Scarborough
resolution, taken on 29 September, deplored Tory policy and urged
the parliamentary Labour party 'to oppose it on all occasions'. This
rather vague text was greeted with enthusiasm by the Greek press,
which chose to interpret it as a serious blow on the colonial consensus in Britain. The fact was that the resolution did not mention a
transfer of sovereignty; rather, self-government, albeit of a more
liberal form than what had been offered in July, equally appealled to
many in the Labour Party as it did to many a diplomat or colonial
official.[70] Seeing the influence of Makarios' apparent optimism on
Greek policy makers, Ambassador Mostras inquired Labour leaders
as to their actual intentions if returned to power. Philip Noel-Baker
undertook to explain that, 'in his view', the Cyprus policy of his
party would be to grant a liberal constitution with the prospect of
self-determination in ten or fifteen years.[71]

Makarios' presence in New York upset the British. Although
Dulles refused to meet him,[72] his lobbying was attracting consider-
able attention. While doing their utmost to curb his activities at the
UN seat, the British also tried to create a diversion – a three-mem-
ber Turkish Cypriot delegation left for New York in September.
Modelled on the Ethnarchy missions, the team passed through An-

kara and London.[73] Under 'discreet' British patronage, its members did some lobbying with the American and other delegations, held a press conference and circulated a text setting forth arguments against Enosis and in favour of British rule.[74] Yet, as the British admitted, the Turkish Cypriot activity 'passed almost unperceived'.[75] So did the visit of the *Mufti* of Cyprus in December, shortly before the Cyprus item came up for discussion.[76]

Papagos only briefly joined the Greek diplomatic effort in person. On 23 October, he met Dulles in Paris, during an interval of his long tour of the Iberian peninsula.[77] While he was absent, Ambassador Cannon had made it clear to acting Prime Minister Kanellopoulos that the United States would oppose any substantive resolution.[78] Perturbed by this statement, Papagos pleaded for strict US neutrality. He also handed Dulles a long memorandum, complaining of the pro-British bias of US policy on the Cyprus question. Attached to this there was a personal message to Eisenhower, which contained a clear warning about the future of Greek-American relations: if the current trend of US policy continued, 'the sympathies of the Greek people' would be estranged, with dangerous repercussions for Greek foreign policy.[79] Papagos and Dulles left Paris with conflicting impressions. The Greek Premier believed that the United States would stick to neutrality,[80] whereas, according to the American record of the conversation, the Secretary of State had 'made no commitment', although he had not clearly expressed US opposition to *any* type of resolution. Significantly, during the conversation, Papagos had suggested that the United States, if it could not remain neutral, might help to have the item postponed for that year.[81]

As it turned out, far from clarifying the US position, the Papagos-Dulles meeting caused a further misunderstanding: subsequent Greek communications reflected the belief that Dulles had promised complete neutrality and no canvassing of other countries.[82] Indeed, as much was stated by Kyrou to Lodge on 26 October. When he was told not to expect 'much encouragement', if his government decided to submit a resolution, the head of the Greek delegation wondered whether this meant a change in US policy. If the Greek recourse to the UN failed, Kyrou retorted, then violence would be the only alternative in Cyprus.[83] At the same time, the Americans came in for bitter attacks in the Greek press for violat-

ing their alleged promise of neutrality. As if to give credibility to
Papagos' warning to Eisenhower, editorials increasingly appeared
calling for a more independent policy *vis-à-vis* the United States
and the West.[84]

With considerable delay, Dulles undertook to reply to Papagos'
message to Eisenhower and try to clear matters up. After expressing regret for the 'misunderstanding' of the US position, he essentially repeated what had been stated in his message of 28 July to
Stefanopoulos: the United States would have 'to oppose the passage
of any substantive resolution' in order to protect allied unity; the
problem could only be solved by the 'parties most directly concerned', the Cypriots and the British, and 'by gradual steps'; the
Greek government ought to support such a course; finally, the future attitude of the United States would depend on 'the degree of
willingness' that the Cypriots and the British displayed in solving
'their common problems'.[85] The letter was delivered on 16 November, shortly before the municipal elections, which were to be a
grave test for the Greek government's popularity. For this reason,
Stefanopoulos again pleaded for 'strict secrecy'.[86] In his reply, sent
on 1 December, Papagos would refuse to support a purely Anglo-
Cypriot dialogue.[87]

Yet Greek diplomacy continued as if the Americans could still
be relied upon to remain neutral. On 16 November, as the message
from Dulles to Papagos was being delivered, Kyrou furnished Lodge
with the first Greek draft resolution. It contained two operative
paragraphs, and, of course, was as substantial as anything the Americans wished to avoid.[88] A fortnight later, Kyrou came up with a
revised text with only one operative paragraph, which expressed a
wish that self-determination be applied in the case of the people of
Cyprus. A further paragraph, calling for the inclusion of the item in
the next General Assembly, had been dropped.[89] On 1 December,
Stefanopoulos handed Cannon a similar draft and requested 'ideas
and guidance' in formulating a text compatible with American criteria. Of course, he got no encouragement.[90]

Towards the end of November, the Greek government appeared
somewhat demoralised. Papagos' party had suffered a minor split,
as Markezinis and his supporters walked out and formed their own
party. More serious was the setback of the municipal election re-

sults, particularly the loss of the city of Athens to the Centre-Left front candidate. Under the circumstances, and anticipating a poor result at the UN, Stefanopoulos decided not to travel to New York, leaving Kyrou to lead the 'battle'.[91]

Side-tracking the Greek item

Right after the Congressional elections, US diplomacy made a new effort to persuade the contending parties to accept postponement. The American plan envisaged moderate Greek and, hopefully, British statements at the General Assembly to be followed by a motion to 'postpone further discussion'.[92] Dulles also discussed it with the outgoing Greek Ambassador on 16 November. Politis appeared interested, although he predicted domestic difficulties.[93] Eden, however, and the Foreign Office found the American 'manoeuvre' unacceptable, since it did not exclude the reappearance of the issue at the next General Assembly. The British reply, delivered on 23 November, professed determination to deal with any Greek resolution, come what may.[94] Eventually, the Greek government was not forthcoming either.[95] The Turks, for their part, having received assurances of US opposition to any substantial discussion of the Greek item,[96] solidly supported the British.[97] The only type of resolution that Turkey would accept, it was declared, was one rejecting the Greek claim on Cyprus.[98]

The rejection of postponement irritated the Americans. Lodge told Nutting and Dixon that all he could promise, and half-heartedly so, was to vote against a Greek resolution. No 'button-holing' of delegates or active lobbying on British behalf should be expected, if they insisted on having the Greek item 'dealt with' and 'killed'.[99] The Americans, however, did not know that the British no longer sought a straight fight. On 3 December, Dixon sounded James Wadsworth, deputy head of the US delegation, about a procedural motion 'not to discuss' the issue.[100] Five days later, the idea was discussed with Lodge. The climate in Anglo-American relations had improved due to the British contribution in the release of US airmen held by communist China. Thus, a plan of action was swiftly drawn: the motion should be made at the outset of the debate; no prior sign should be given to any but a handful of confidants; until

the last moment, the British would continue to declare their resolve to defeat any Greek resolution and, significantly, could claim
American opposition to it.[101]

Next, the British appraised the old Commonwealth delegations
and Turkey. The proposed motion was laconic: 'The Assembly decides not to consider further the Cyprus item'.[102] Although the
Anglo-American plan was based on the element of surprise, Dulles
chose to give the Greek government a foretaste. On 11 December,
Stefanopoulos was told that the United States would vote against
the latest Greek draft resolution.[103] On the following day, Cannon
delivered an 'urgent' message from Dulles to Papagos. After reaffirming US opposition to the Greek draft, the Secretary of State
urged the acceptance of the 'not to discuss' formula as best serving
'Western unity as well as Greek prestige'. Sweetening the pill, Dulles
added that such a decision would not bind future Assemblies.[104]

Before receiving the message from Dulles, Papagos had approved
a draft resolution inviting Great Britain and Greece to seek a solution through various peaceful means (negotiation, enquiry, mediation, etc.), as provided by Article 33(1) of the Charter.[105] Dulles'
letter and subsequent American actions led Athens to withdraw this
draft, and the Greek delegation to the UN was left with the text
that had first appeared on 30 November.[106]

On the morning of 13 December, the *New York Times* carried a
front page report, inspired by Lodge himself, to the effect that the
US delegation would vote against any Greek draft and that Athens
had been notified accordingly.[107] Stefanopoulos confirmed this, but
still appeared hopeful that the United States might find another draft
more acceptable.[108] In Washington, the new Greek Ambassador,
Georgios Melas, waved at the State Department the prospect of a
'desperate situation' arising in his country, if the Assembly ignored
the substance of the Greek item. The Americans were unmoved.[109]
Kyrou also called on Lodge, who disclaimed any connection with
the *New York Times* story and expressed regret for having 'to pull
the chestnuts out of the fire'.[110] Then he let Kyrou know that, on
the following morning, a 'friendly delegation' would make the anticipated procedural motion.[111]

Indeed, on 13 December, Leslie Munro, Permanent Representative of New Zealand, introduced the motion. There followed active

Anglo-American lobbying of various representatives. Reservations regarding the procedural propriety of the motion had to be overcome.[112] On the following day, two draft resolutions were placed before the Political Committee by Greece and New Zealand respectively. Munro asked to intervene on a point of order and spoke first. There followed a long wrangle on questions of procedure: which draft resolution should take precedence in discussion and voting? Did the New Zealand draft amount to a reversal of the Assembly decision to inscribe the item? If that was the case, a two-thirds majority would be required for either its discussion or its adoption. Urrutia, the Colombian Chairman of the Committee, came under relentless pressure to drop his reservations and to accept a simple majority vote on the matter of priority. This the New Zealand draft secured by 28 votes to 15, with 16 abstentions.[113]

There followed brief statements by Munro, Lodge and Nutting, focusing on the dangers arising from a discussion of the item for Greek-Turkish relations and regional stability. The substance of the issue was dealt with in the long speeches of the Greek and Turkish representatives, at the afternoon session of the Committee. Kyrou concentrated on countering the British arguments as expressed by Selwyn Lloyd during the debate on inscription – the Greek request neither aimed at a transfer of sovereignty nor did it represent a threat to valid treaties and existing frontiers; it was a 'perfectly disinterested' initiative aimed at recognising the right to self-determination for the people of Cyprus. This was the desire of their overwhelming majority, whose Greek identity was beyond doubt. He also dismissed the risk of communal strife, if self-determination was applied.[114]

Unlike his performance during the inscription debate, Sarper launched a ferocious attack, which took Kyrou by surprise. First, he tried to discredit the Greek case and to deny the authenticity of the Enosis movement: its aim, he claimed, was not self-determination but annexation, reminiscent of *Anschluss*; no racial connection existed between the populations of Greece and Cyprus; Enosis had been artificially created and sustained by Greece; the Greek claim amounted to unilateral abrogation of the Treaty of Lausanne. His second aim was to assert Turkey's interest. Cyprus was a continuation of Anatolia and there could be no lasting settlement, if the question ever arose, without the consent of his country.[115] The British were gratified 'to have at least one delegation hitting the Greeks hard'. In their view, Sarper's speech had served to vindicate Nutting's claim that 'it was playing with fire for the United Nations to have a full-dress discussion of the Cyprus issue'.[116]

Seeing the Greek chances waning, Kyrou concentrated on qualifying rejection. He agreed with five Latin American representatives to introduce two preambular amendments to the New Zealand draft.[117] The first, sponsored by Colombia and El Salvador, which had proved a staunch supporter of the Greek case, was based on the resolution adopted on the Morocco item two days earlier and read: '*Considering* that, for the time being, it does not appear appropriate to adopt a resolution on the question of Cyprus'. The second, introduced by the representative of the Philippines, was the following: '*Having in mind* the principles and purposes of the Charter'.

Uncertainty about the outcome led the Anglo-Americans to be more flexible. When the Committee resumed its work on 15 December, their delegations estimated that, despite two days of intense canvassing, most Asians appeared inclined to abstain, while the Latin Americans could not be relied upon either. Failing to get Colombia and El Salvador to withdraw their amendment, the British indicated that they would acquiesce in it, provided there was no further change. Thereupon, Kyrou announced that he accepted the amended resolution and the Filipino representative introduced the second amendment. This caused the sharp reaction of Munro, Sarper and Nutting, who, seconded by their Brazilian and Iraqi colleagues, insisted that 'such phraseology was out of place in a purely procedural motion'. In the end, the Phillippino amendment was withdrawn. The preamble was approved by 44 votes to none, with 16 abstentions, and then the amended New Zealand draft passed by 49 votes to none, with 11 abstentions.[118] The Greek draft resolution was never put to the vote.

On 17 December, the General Assembly gave its final approval in plenary by 50 votes to none, with 8 abstentions to what became Resolution 814 (IX).[119] Predictably, the contending parties indulged in conflicting interpretations of the outcome. The British and Turkish delegates had explained their vote as not implying recognition of UN competence to discuss the item 'on any future occasion'. In contrast, Kyrou argued that, by the inscription of the item on the agenda, the General Assembly 'had recognised the international character of the issue', and that the resolution merely amounted to a moratorium, which left the door 'wide open' to future discussion.[120] Both sides appeared to ignore the fact that resolutions were in no way binding for future Assemblies.

Shortly after his return to Athens, Kyrou, the architect of the first Greek recourse, was placed *en disponsibilité* at his own request. He was never to resume a post with any bearing on the Cyprus question.[121] Yet the government continued to interpret the outcome as the best possible and to declare that the policy of internationalisation would remain unchanged until the complete fulfilment of (Greek) Cypriot national aspirations.[122]

The bitter aftermath

While the Greek item was being disposed of at the UN, a side show that revealed much about the limits of Greek foreign policy was taking place in Paris. On 15 December, Stefanopoulos, who was in the French capital for the NAC, was instructed by Papagos to proceed to the UN seat 'at once' and take charge of the Greek effort. The Foreign Minister, however, only had to wait a little longer until the die was cast in the Political Committee. In the meantime, he called on Dulles, with whom he pleaded for some alteration of the New Zealand resolution or a statement indicating that the door to future discussion at the UN was always possible.[123] Stefanopoulos appeared primarily concerned with easing the 'tremendous public opinion problem' that his government was certain to face once the decision of the General Assembly was announced. The Foreign Minister, whose absence from the UN had been criticised in parliament,[124] wanted to show that he had done something, despite his staying in Paris.

Dulles preferred to reserve his position until the following day. Then, he consented to make 'some helpful comment' to the press, although he thought that the Greeks should be satisfied with the resolution as amended.[125] As the news of anti-American riots in Greece were reaching Paris, the US and Greek delegations to NATO arranged what would be presented as Dulles' spontaneous state-

ment.[126] The British were also given advance notice.[127] On 18 December, a text was passed to selected Greek correspondents. In
this, after heaping praise on Stefanopoulos, Dulles sought to take
credit for the amendment to the New Zealand resolution, which he
linked with his meeting with Stefanopoulos and an alleged intervention of his with the US delegation to the UN. Of course, this was
inaccurate and provoked a British denial.[128] The Secretary of State
further contented that the US attitude had been misunderstood in
Greece, but reiterated his confidence in the strength of Greek-American friendship. As a token of appreciation – or a sop – he proposed
the holding of the next NAC in Athens.[129]

   Dulles' gesture had been necessitated by the scale of reactions
not only in Greece and Cyprus but also from among the Greek-
American community, whose representatives swamped the State Department with letters of protest. It was all the more disquieting that
popular reactions in Greece targeted the United States, the insidi-
ous patron, rather than Britain, the apparent rival. After the *New
York Times* had revealed US opposition to the Greek effort at the
UN, the press in Greece and Cyprus freely interpreted the American attitude as a 'stab in the back'.[130] On 14 December, anti-American feeling was manifested during a student demonstration in Athens, where the quarters of the US and British Missions were stoned
and cars were damaged. Papagos sent Cannon official regrets but
no formal statement was issued.[131] Rather, the Prime Minister saw
it fit to let steam off and combined the announcement of a cabinet
reshuffle with some criticism of 'the friends and allies' who had
failed to honour the principles of the United Nations. His government, he affirmed, would continue the struggle for the self-determination of the Cypriot people. That evening, all sections of the
Greek parliament expressed their bitterness. The Left interpreted
the outcome at the UN as the result of the government's unconditional attachment to the West.[132] The most violent outbreak of anti-
American feeling took place in Salonika on 16 December. There,
another student demonstration resulted in the storming of the US
Information Service premises, leaving the library smashed and other
property damaged. More than fifty people were injured in clashes
with the police. This incident provoked strong American representations and an official ban on all demonstrations.[133]

The riot coincided with Ambassador Melas' visit to the Acting Secretary of State, Herbert Hoover Jr. Just as he had expressed regret for previous incidents, he was presented with the news from Salonika. Hoover asked for concrete steps not only in the field of security but also in terms of publicity. The Greek government, he urged, ought to correct the impressions of the Greek public about the US attitude at the UN, get things back to normal and safeguard the Greek-American relationship. Cannon spoke in the same vein to Papagos, on 17 December.[134] As a result, the Greek Prime Minister expressed 'deep regret' and 'strongly' condemned the anti-American riots.[135] Three days later, King Paul broadcast a message urging the Greek people to 'remain faithful to [their] friends, despite recent disappointments'.[136]

The impact of popular reactions on Anglo-Greek relations, while no less painful, was predictable. Since the summer, Greek broadcasts to Cyprus had been virulently anti-British.[137] At first the British chose to ignore them, but, from October onwards, they repeatedly protested to Mostras and Stefanopoulos.[138] The Americans, of course, were given due notice of this campaign. Apart from his occasional representations, Ambassador Peake saw it fit to 'lie low' and to avoid public appearances. His personal contacts with Greek leaders were kept to a minimum, with only two meetings – with King Paul and Papagos – registered during that five-month period.[139]

Predictably, the UN 'battle' did not leave Greek-Turkish relations unscathed. Commencing in the summer, a war of words through the columns of the press raged until after the General Assembly's decision. The whole edifice of friendship and alliance between the two countries was cast in doubt and old animosities rekindled. Sarper's speech in the Political Committee had largely reflected this climate of opinion. Its venom, however, had even astonished the British and did not fail to provoke a Greek representation to the Turkish Ambassador in Athens.[140] In order to mitigate the impact, Menderes issued a statement on 20 December, couched in friendly terms. The Cyprus problem had been 'definitely settled', the Turkish Prime Minister stated, and it was time 'to pay great care and attention in order that the slightest shadow should not dim the friendship' between Greece and Turkey.[141] Stefanopoulos would reciprocate a few weeks later, during the parliamentary debate on Cyprus.[142]

The government's handling of the Cyprus question came in for debate in the Greek parliament on 7 February 1955. Papagos concentrated on the Greek efforts towards a bilateral settlement and their rejection by the British. He clearly indicated that his personal rebuff by Eden in September 1953 had been a decisive moment in the process towards internationalisation.[143] This was not missed by the British Embassy, which otherwise appeared content with the Prime Minister's 'moderate language' and matter-of-fact approach.[144] Stefanopoulos, for his part, concentrated on the diplomatic aspect and tried to defend his own part in it. Weeks before the debate, he had consulted the US Embassy on certain points of his speech. Although he had been urged to keep discussion of the American role to a minimum,[145] the Foreign Minister devoted more than two-thirds of his speech to this particular subject, quoting long extracts from Dulles' messages to Papagos. Although the prevailing tone was one of bitterness, Stefanopoulos 'warmly' thanked the Americans for their alleged support of the Salvador-Colombian amendment. Towards the end of his speech, however, he attempted to take credit for the government's 'courage' in defying the American warnings.[146] Significantly, the Foreign Minister chose to downplay Turkey's role at the UN, as did every other speaker with the exception of Markezinis, who criticised Papagos for his failure to have a frank talk with Menderes, in June 1954.[147]

In Cyprus, the lull that had prevailed since the Greek recourse in August was brought to an end. The General Assembly resolution sparked an outburst of violent protest: press comment was as indignant as could be expected; a general strike was observed on 18 December, a day marked by mass demonstrations; in the cities, army units were called in to deal with the situation; in Limassol, where the crowd assaulted a police station taking down the British flag and hoisting a Greek one, the troops opened fire wounding several demonstrators.[148] Nationalist passions also affected communal relations, as Greek demonstrators smashed the windows of Turkish shops and, on 19 December, a group of Turks retaliated, leading the US Consul to observe that, at least momentarily, 'the thin veneer of Greek-Turkish harmony' rubbed off badly.[149] Amid this hardly conducive atmosphere, Governor Armitage chose to make a statement in favour of constitutional development. In Britain, the disturbances came

in for debate at the Commons on 20 December. Warning that the
constitutional offer was doomed to failure, James Griffiths, the
former Labour Colonial Secretary, suggested a meeting of communal representatives with the Colonial Secretary to discuss the future
of the island.[150]

The eve of violence

After the failure of its UN policy, the Greek government appeared
to lose the initiative to Archbishop Makarios and his supporters.
According to the British Embassy, Papagos attempted to dissuade
Makarios from visiting Athens on his way back from New York, fearing that this might provoke further anti-Western incidents.[151] The
Archbishop did come and immediately made his intentions clear.
Until the Cyprus question was solved, he declared, it ought to remain 'the main factor … of Greece's foreign policy' and the yard-
stick in her relations with the 'so-called friends and allies'.[152] His
visit prompted the Archbishop of Athens and PEEK to declare a
week of nation-wide manifestations for the fifth anniversary of the
Ethnarchy plebiscite. This provoked an American *démarche* and the
government had to extend the ban on demonstrations.[153] Back in
Cyprus, Makarios commemorated the anniversary with an impassioned sermon at Faneromeni, fulminating against 'the sordid bargaining' at the UN, which had deprived the Greek Cypriot people
of a victory certain 'until the last moment'. Any constitutional offer
was a 'trap', he warned, unless it recognised the right to self-determination, while anyone who might be inclined to co-operate with
the oppressor would be branded as a traitor and incur the wrath of
the people.[154]

   This uncompromising attitude was apparently a reaction to the
feelers that the Governor of Cyprus had been extending to Makarios
through various intermediaries for some time. While the Archbishop
was still in Athens, Armitage had requested the British Embassy to
sound him out regarding a meeting to discuss 'public order'. Without waiting for instructions from the Foreign Office, Peake had the
message conveyed. Makarios appeared to agree on two conditions:
that he should meet the Governor 'as an equal' and that self-determination should also be discussed. Yet Nikos Kranidiotis, the Arch-

bishop's secretary, leaked the contact to the press and the scheme foundered. The Foreign Office did not like it either and criticised Peake for not awaiting instructions.[155] Nonetheless, Armitage continued his efforts after Makarios' return to Cyprus.[156]

During the first four months after the General Assembly resolution, a deceptive calm returned to Cyprus. To be sure, for some time the British had been receiving various signals that more dynamic methods might be employed in the pursuit of Enosis. Information regarding the infiltration of 'extremists' and arms trafficking from Greece into the island had been reaching the colonial authorities at least since October 1954.[157] On 25 January 1955, a Greek caique, the 'Agios Georgios', was seized with a cargo of explosives off the Paphos coast. This and the arrest of Sokratis Loizidis, former secretary of PEK, was a clear indication of what was in store. The Americans were also aware that trouble was brewing.[158]

During the same period, official Anglo-Greek contacts remained limited to points of friction, such as the Greek request for the inspection of teachers in Cyprus or the British complaints about Greek broadcasts to the island.[159] Other channels of communication, however, were kept open, transmitting various views, even if on an informal and tentative basis. The Greek palace and the British Embassy had remained in touch throughout. The visit of Patrick Maitland, Conservative MP, to Athens and Nicosia in January also helped convey moderate Greek views to Whitehall. Moreover, according to US records, in early February, and for the first time since 1946, a Foreign Office official acknowledged to the Greek Ambassador the prospect of an eventual change in the status of Cyprus. Stressing that he had no authority to make a statement, Sir Ivone Kirkpatrick, Parliamentary Under-Secretary for Foreign Affairs, explained to Mostras that changes in the nature of warfare were leading to a revision of strategic requirements in places such as Cyprus. In his view, this sort of evolution could lead to a 'mutually satisfactory' solution 'in five or ten or fifteen years' – a period, he mused, which was 'but [a] brief moment in [the] life of [a] nation with history as ancient as Greece'.[160]

Meanwhile, the Greek Ambassador in Washington was engaged in his fruitless efforts to solicit a more sympathetic US attitude. His first approach, as has been noted, had coincided with the riots in

Salonika. Still, Melas found the nerve to elaborate on Greek disappointment with the American attitude and to ask for assistance in bringing about a settlement.[161] When, early in 1955, the Ambassador called on George Allen, Assistant Secretary for Near Eastern Affairs, it was clear that the Americans were tiring of Melas' lengthy and emotional rhetoric: just as the Ambassador had risen to leave, Allen wryly remarked that 'he had enjoyed the talk and he hoped to continue another time so that they could discuss the strong feelings which Turkey had about Cyprus'.[162]

By the end of March 1955, there were hints that, despite official reticence, British thinking was slowly evolving towards a more relaxed position. The State Department, which was also moving towards a reassessment of its Cyprus policy, was inclined to encourage this trend, which envisaged a renewed constitutional offer and an indirect recognition of eventual self-determination for the Cypriots.[163] With this in mind, the Americans urged the Greeks not to incite spirits in Cyprus,[164] and to be prepared 'to take advantage of any changed circumstances' in the near future. Athens, for its part, appeared disappointed by the absence of any visible change in British attitude and, as before, asked for American good offices.[165]

This was the rather dim diplomatic background against which the National Organisation Cypriot Fighters (EOKA) planted its bombs in the early morning hours of All Fool's Day, 1955. Five days later, Eden succeeded Churchill as Prime Minister — the same day that Britain joined Turkey and Iraq in forming the so-called Baghdad Pact, a new defence arrangement for the Middle East. Within a few months, in late August 1955, the Greek government would virtually recognise Turkey's role in the future of Cyprus by taking part in the British-sponsored Tripartite Conference in London. Gradually but surely, self-determination for the Cypriot majority was being driven beyond the realm of practical politics.

NOTES

1. 747C.00/8-1754, Cannon to State, tel. 394.
2. The Greek text of the appeal is given in: Kyrou 1955, 443-450; its official French translation can be found in 112852, 1081/308, UKUN Delegation to FO, 20 Aug. 1954; an English translation is in 747C.00/8-1754, Schnee to

State, Embassy desp. 135; an extensive summary see in Xydis 1967, 4-6.
3. It appears that the Pyrgos reservists were not the first to bottle their blood for
   nationalistic purposes. Back in 1933, like-minded Turkish Cypriots had sent a
   bottle to Mustafa Kemal Atatürk as a tribute to the founder of modern Turkey:
   87716, 1081/45, Charles to McNeil, 30 Jan. 1950.
4. 112853, 1081/327, Peake to Churchill, 21 Aug. 1954; 747C.00/8-2154, Cannon to State, tel. 428; 781.00/8-2154, Williams to State, desp. 8; Crawshaw
   1978, 82-83; Linardatos II 1978, 206.
5. 747C.00/8-2454, memo of conversation between Jernegan, Baxter and Politis.
6. Linardatos II 1978, 206, 208; Vlahos 1980, 77.
7. 112852, 1081/308, UKUN Delegation to FO, 24 Aug. 1954.
8. 112459, UP2416/7, minute by Cope, 30 July 1954; 112853, 1081/335, FO
   minute of meeting in the CRO, by Buxton, 24 Aug. 1954; 112854, 1081/
   351A, Jockel, Australian External Affairs Office, to Cleary, CRO, 2 Sept. 1954;
   112855, 1081/376, Williams to Cleary, 13 Sept. 1954.
9. 112858, 1081/454, UK High Commissioner in Canada to CRO, 3 Sept. 1954.
   Pearson suggested that the British government seek the opinion of 'some im-
   partial body such as the International Court of Justice' – an idea already considered and rejected by the Foreign Office.
10. 112853, 1081/318, minute by Young, 25 Aug. 1954; 747C.00/9-954, memo
    of conversation between Baxter and Carraud, Second Secretary of the French
    Embassy.
11. *FRUS 1952-54*, VIII, 709-710, n. 3.
12. 112852, 1081/298, minute for the Prime Minister about Spiros Skouras, 18
    Aug. 1954; *ibid.*, minute by Roberts, 24 Aug. 1954; 747C.00/9-954,
    Butterworth to State, tel. 1244.
13. 747C.00/8-2454, memo of meeting between Dulles and Fleur Cowles; /8-
    3054, memo from Baxter to Dulles.
14. 112860, 1081/534, minute by Nutting, 2 Sept. 1954; minute by Hopkinson,
    2 Sept. 1954; 112861, 1081/559, minute by Nutting.
15. *FRUS 1952-54*, VIII, 714, n. 2.
16. 747C.00/10-754, memo from Byroade to Dulles. Mostras writes that he felt
    obliged to put an end to Cowles' activities, because it threatened to raise
    doubts about the firmness of Greek policy: Mostras ms, 47, n. 2.
17. 112862, 1081/582, Dixon to FO, 18 Sept. 1954.
18. *FRUS 1952-54*, VIII, 714.
19. 112859, 1081/477, Broothby to FO, 8 Sept. 1954; FO to Brussels Embassy,
    17 Sept. 1954; see also 112862, 1081/586.
20. 112853, 1081/320, Washington Embassy to FO, 25 Aug. 1954.
21. 747C.00/8-2554, memo of conversation between Jernegan, Foster and Scott;
    /8-2654; British Embassy memorandum.
22. 112849, 1081/224, Scott Fox to Young, 26 July 1954; 112852, 1081/286,
    Bowker to Eden, 13 Aug. 1954.
23. 747C.00/8-2054, memo of conversation between Richards, Wood and Baydur;
    /9-1354, office memo from Howard to Baxter.

24. 747C.00/9-1354, office memo from Howard to Baxter.
25. 112852, 1081/301, FO to Ankara Embassy, 23 Aug. 1954; 112854, 1081/
    353, Istanbul Consulate General to FO, 27 Aug. 1954; *FRUS 1952-54*, VIII,
    703, n. 2. The message, labelled 'personal and confidential', remains classified
    in file 747C.00/8-3154. Its content is given in 747C.00/9-1354, office memo
    from Howard to Baxter. Since Dulles was absent in Manilla, an interim reply
    to Menderes' letter was sent by Acting Secretary of State Smith on 6 Septem-
    ber. In this, the Turkish Prime Minister was assured that the US government
    would 'weigh with [the] fullest sympathy' the views of his government in de-
    termining its policy: *FRUS 1952-54*, VIII, 703. The reply from Dulles came on
    21 September, almost verbatim repeating the arguments for the US decision
    to abstain, which had already been communicated to Ankara on 15 Septem-
    ber: *FRUS 1952-54*, VIII, 716-717.
26. *FRUS 1952-54*, III, 779-785. The question of having the nationalist Republic
    of China replaced by the People's Republic of China as permanent member of
    the Security Council was a recurring one in UN General Assemblies, until
    1970. In 1954, the United States was seeking a resolution 'not to consider'
    any proposal to remove its protégé, nationalist China, from the UN seat. The
    British, who had extended recognition to the People's Republic since 1950,
    acquiesced in the resolution adopted by the previous session of the General
    Assembly 'to postpone' consideration of the issue for its duration.
27. 112861, 1081/543, Makins to FO, 15 Sept. 1954; *FRUS 1952-54*, VIII, 708-
    709; 747C.00/9-1654, Wadsworth to State, tel. 165.
28. No record of the communication of the US decision to the Greeks, conveyed
    by William Baxter, Deputy Director of the Bureau for Greece, Turkey and
    Iran, to Greek Chargé Phaidon Cavalierato on 16 September, has been found
    in the records of the Department of State. Its substance is given in the State
    Department telegram to Athens of 15 September: *FRUS 1952-54*, VIII, 709.
    Greek sources give two rather conflicting versions. Kyrou, in his story of the
    first Greek recourse to the UN (Kyrou 1955, 278), sums up the US commu-
    nication as follows: (a) the US delegation would not take part in the debate on
    inscription and would abstain from the voting in both the General Committee
    and the Plenary; (b) the US government would not give advance notice of its
    decision to abstain to third parties and, generally, would avoid influencing
    anyone; (c) if the item was inscribed, the final attitude of the US delegation
    would depend on the *mildness* of the draft resolution. Kyrou evoked these
    three points in a conversation with Lodge on 26 October, claiming that they
    were made by Cannon on 16 August and then 'practically *verbatim*' repeated
    in Baxter's communication – although with regard to (c) Kyrou mentioned
    the *nature* – not *mildness* – of the draft resolution: 747C.00/10-2654, New
    York tel. 143. Yet points (b) and (c) explicitly run counter to the actual deci-
    sions of the State Department. Drawing upon Cavalierato to Athens tel. 3813/
    16.9.1954, Mostras, Greek Ambassador in London at the time, gives a sub-
    stantially different version of Baxter's communication: (a) the US govern-
    ment considered a debate on Cyprus inopportune and for this reason it would

abstain from the voting; (b) if the item was inscribed, its attitude on the substance would depend on the *content* of the draft resolution; (c) if asked by other governments, the US government would limit itself to informing them of its own decision. Mostras adds that Cavalierato's remark to Baxter that the communication would deeply disappoint the Greek government and people could hardly be justified if Kyrou's version is accepted: Mostras ms, 36. Mostras' version is both better documented and more in keeping with American records than the one advanced by Kyrou.

29. 747C.00/8-2554, memo of conversation between Key *et al.*, Beeley and Salt.
30. 112861, 1081/543, Makins to FO, 15 Sept. 1954.
31. 112859, 1081/490, COS (54) 303, 'Strategic Importance of Cyprus', Chiefs of Staff Committee, 13 Sept. 1954; 747C.00/9-1354, British Embassy note to State; /9-2054, memo W/ATT, from British Ambassador to General Smith; *FRUS 1952-54*, VIII, 710, n. 5.
32. 112863, 1081/607, Churchill to Eisenhower, 18 Sept. 1954; *FRUS 1952-54*, VIII, 709-710.
33. 112863, 1081/620, Factual Note, FO to Washington Embassy, 20 Sept. 1954; *FRUS 1952-54*, VIII, 711-712.
34. *FRUS 1952-54*, VIII, 713-715.
35. 747C.00/9-205, memo of conversation between Merchant and Makins.
36. 747C.00/9-2154, memo of conversation between Dulles, Cook, Dixon and Hopkinson. On Guatemala, see 112848, 1081/185, Salt to Young, 9 July 1954; *FRUS 1952-54*, VIII, 726; *FRUS 1952-54*, IV, 1027 ff.
37. For example, 747C.00/9-1554, memo of conversation between Monsen, Mangano and Soutello-Alves, Brazilian Embassy. This canvassing did not go unnoticed by the Greek delegation: Kyrou 1955, 290-291.
38. *FRUS 1952-54*, VIII, 715-716.
39. 112850, 1081/228, Young, FO, to Morris, CO, 4 Aug. 1954; 112854, 1081/371A, CRO to UK High Commissioner in India, 10 Sept. 1954; 112858, 1081/468, Hopkinson to Nutting, 6 Sept. 1954. The aversion of Indian leaders to the sort of 'ethnic' rather than 'territorial' nationalism preached by the Greek and Greek Cypriot spokesmen was well known and can be easily understood in the light of India's ethnic problems in areas like Kashmir.
40. 112862, 1081/588, Baghdad Embassy to FO, Sept. 1954.
41. 112856, 1081/386, Stevenson to FO, Cairo, 1 Sept. 1954; 112859, 1081/481, Scott to FO, Beirut, 9 Sept. 1954; Gardener to FO, Damascus, 13 Sept. 1954; 112861, 1081/562, Stevenson to FO, 19 Sept. 1954; 112863, 1081/609, Beirut Embassy to FO, 21 Sept. 1954.
42. 112859, 1081/481, Gardener to FO, 13 Sept. 1954; 112860, 1081/512, Stevenson to FO, 10 Sept. 1954.
43. 112852, 1081/301, Wright to FO, Oslo, 19 Aug. 1954; 112854, 1081/353, Istanbul Consulate General to FO, 27 Aug. 1954; 747C.00/8-3054, Strong to State, Damascus; 112860, 1081/519, Istanbul Consulate General to FO, 13 Sept. 1954.
44. 112857, 1081/418, Bowker to Young, 1 Sept. 1954.

45. 112856, 1081/407, Ankara Embassy to FO, 31 Aug. 1954; 112860, 1081/514, Bowker to FO, 10 Sept. 1954; 747C.00/8-254, Kohler to State, desp. 63; /9-954,Warren to State, tel. 268; /9-1354, office memo from Howard to Baxter.
46. 112856, 1081/407, Ankara Embassy to FO, 31 Aug. 1954; 112865, 1081/657, Ankara Chancery toWestern and Southern Departments, 22 Aug. 1954.
47. 112860, 1081/501, 506, Dixon to FO, 10 Sept. 1954; *ibid.*, FO to UKUN Delegation, 15 Sept. 1954; 747C.00/9-1554, Lodge to Dulles, tel. 235; *ibid.*, Dulles to Lodge, tel. 157, Sept. 18, 1954; *FRUS 1952-54*, VIII, 713, n. 1; *ibid.*, 714-715; 747C.00/9-2054, Smith to USUN Delegation, tel. 161.
48. 747C.00/9-1554, Lodge to Dulles, tel. 235; *ibid.*, Dulles to Lodge, tel. 157, Sept. 18, 1954.
49. Kyrou 1955, 291.
50. 747C.00/9-2254, Birgfeld to State, tel. 661; 112864, 1081/631, Selwyn Lloyd to FO, 22 Sept. 1954.
51. 112864, 1081/631, Selwyn Lloyd to FO, 22 Sept. 1954.
52. The French had in fact joined the British and the Turks in urging the Americans to vote against inscription: 747C.00/9-954, memo of conversation between Baxter and Carraud.
53. 117622, 1081/66, Dixon to Eden, 19 Jan. 1955; Crawshaw 1978, 83; Kyrou 1955, 291-292.
54. 112865, 1081/665, UKUN Delegation to FO, 24 Sept. 1954; 117622, 1081/66, Dixon to Eden, 19 Jan. 1955; 747C.00/9-2554, Lodge to Dulles, tel. 20.
55. Menon's contention, while defective on other accounts too, overlooked Resolution 742 (VIII), which provided that non-self-governing territories could attain 'self-government' through independence but also by 'association with another state if done freely and on the basis of absolute equality'. Xydis 1967, 9.
56. 112866, 1081/687A, Hopkinson to Lennox-Boyd, 25 Sept. 1954; cf. Crawshaw 1978, 83-85; Hristidis 1967, 87; Kyrou 1955, 293.
57. In order not to lend itself to criticism from its NATO partners, the Greek delegation had avoided canvassing the Eastern bloc delegations. Kyrou, however, met their representatives at various social occasions and ascertained their intention to give support. Significantly, Kyrou requested the head of the Soviet delegation, Andrej Vyshinsky, not to intervene in support of the Greek item in the debates.The latter complied: Kyrou 1955, 283.
58. 117622, 1081/66, Dixon to Eden, 19 Jan. 1955. In the aftermath of the inscription vote, the head of the Egyptian delegation attempted to promote the Arab League proposal for a direct Anglo-Greek settlement outside the UN.This envisaged a compromise resolution inviting the two parties 'to meet in order to clarify their position', while leaving the Assembly to consider the question at its next session. Kyrou was in favour. Predictably, since anything smacking of bilateral talks was an anathema to the British, Dixon 'threw cold water' on this proposal. 112867, 1081/745, Crosthwaite to Young, 29 Sept. 1954; Kyrou 1955, 294-5.
59. 112867, 1081/741, minute of conversation between Eden and Dulles, 2 Oct.

1954; 117622, 1081/66, Dixon to Eden, 19 Jan. 1955; *FRUS 1952-54*, VIII, 717-718.

60. 117622, 1081/66, Dixon to Eden, 19 Jan. 1955; Kyrou 1955, 298.

61. 112867, 1081/735, FO to various Missions, 2 October 1954; 117622, 1081/66, Dixon to Eden, 19 Jan. 1955.

62. 112869, 1081/821, CRO to UK High Commissioner in Canada, 12 Oct. 1954.

63. 747C.00/10-2954, Courtney to State, desp. 34.

64. 112871, 1081/913, extract from House of Commons debates, 19 Oct. 1954.

65. 112872, 1081/920, statement by the Secretary of State for the Colonies on Cyprus, 28 Oct. 1954; 747C.00/11-154, Rutter to State, desp. 1243.

66. 117622, 1081/66, Dixon to Eden, 19 Jan. 1955; 747C.00/11-1754, Schnee to State, desp. 446; Kyrou 1955, 296-297.

67. Linardatos II 1978, 220.

68. 112870, 1081/867, minute by Young, 15 Oct. 1954.

69. 112873, 1081/948, weekly summary of the Cypriot press, 17-23 Oct. 1954; 747C.00/11-154, Rutter to State, desp. 1243; Crawshaw 1978, 86.

70. 112867, 1081/720, Peake to FO, 1 Oct. 1954; 747C.00/10-2054, Wilson to State, desp. 1092; see also the comment of Labour *Daily Herald* in 747C.00/11-154, Rutter to State, desp. 1243.

71. 112871, 1081/910, minute of conversation between Harrison and Mostras, 18 Oct. 1954.

72. 747C.00/11-2254, letter from Dulles to Scopas; /11-2954, letter from Senator Irving M. Ives to Dulles.

73. 112859, 1081/487, Istanbul Consulate General, 8 Sept. 1954; FO to Istanbul Consulate General, 10 Sept. 1954.

74. 112866, 1081/701, Hopkinson to Lennox-Boyd, 23 Sept. 1954; 112868, 1081/772, UKUN Delegation to FO, 5 Oct. 1954; 112873, 1081/964, UKUN Delegation to FO, 5 Nov. 1954. The letters were in response to the letters from Archbishop Makarios and the mayor of Nicosia, which the Greek delegation had managed to circulate as official documents.117622, 1081/66, Dixon to Eden, 19 Jan. 1955. The Greek Cypriot letters were dated 25 September and 12 October respectively. See YUN 1954, 96.

75. 112868, 1081/772, UKUN Delegation to FO, 5 Oct. 1954; 117622, 1081/66, Dixon to Eden, 19 Jan. 1955.

76. 112876, 1081/1057, Ankara Embassy to FO, 2 Dec. 1954; 112882, 1081/1215, FO to Ankara Embassy, 11 Dec. 1954.

77. Papagos' leisure trip lasted from 7 October to 2 November. His choice of Spain did not fail to annoy the British, who drew a parallel between the Spanish claim to Gibraltar and the Greek one on Cyprus.

78. *FRUS 1952-54*, VIII, 721, no. 390, n. 4.

79. *FRUS 1952-54*, VIII, 720, no. 390, n. 3; 747C.00/10-2354, Papagos message to President Eisenhower, Paris, 23 October 1954; *ibid.*, Greek memo to the US Secretary of State. Papagos' message to Eisenhower was delivered twice, the second time by Ambassador Politis, on 26 October.

80. 747C.00/10-2654, Lodge to Dulles, tel. 143; *FRUS 1952-54*,VIII, 723.
81. *FRUS 1952-54*,VIII, 719-720; *ibid.*, 720, n. 3, 745; that Papagos had spoken of postponement was confirmed by Markezinis in parliament: *GPR*, 7 February 1955, 686. A similar suggestion emanated from Kyrou. His purpose, however, was to prod the Greek government into a more determined posture *vis-à-vis* the Americans: Kyrou 1955, 298; cf. Xydis 1967, 599, n. 72.
82. *FRUS 1952-54*,VIII, 723.
83. Kyrou also promised Lodge an advance copy of the Greek draft resolution: 747C.00/10-2654, Lodge to Dulles, tel. 143; cf. Kyrou 1955, 299.
84. 747C.00/10-1954, Schnee to State, desp. 336; /11-1754, Schnee to State, desp. 446.
85. *FRUS 1952-54*,VIII, 727-728.
86. *FRUS 1952-54*,VIII, 730.The American record belies Stefanopoulos' contention in parliament that the Greek government had 'demanded' that the US keep 'secret [its] decision and not disclose it until the time of the voting': *GPR*, meeting of 7 February 1955, 675. Kyrou had also asked for secrecy but for different reasons: *ibid.* [Stefanopoulos], 690.
87. *FRUS 1952-54*,VIII, 733. Although the text of the reply remains classified, in conveying its substance the US Ambassador in Athens remarked that it was 'on [a] somewhat higher plane and in more moderate language' than previous messages. Perhaps this had something to do with Kyrou's absence in New York since late October.
88. 747C.00/11-1854, Lodge to Dulles, tel. 255.
89. 747C.00/11-3054, Lodge to Dulles, 311; /12-154, Cannon to State, tel. 1167.
90. *FRUS 1952-54*,VIII, 730-731.
91. The decision was communicated to New York in 25-27 November: *GPR*, meeting of 7 February 1955 [Markezinis], 687; the US Embassy was duly informed: *FRUS 1952-54*,VIII, 732.
92. 112873, 1081/970, Washington Embassy to FO, 5 Nov. 1954; *FRUS 1952-54*,VIII, 722-3.
93. *FRUS 1952-54*,VIII, 728-9.
94. 112873, 1081/972, Dixon to FO, 8 Nov. 1954; 112875, 1081/1028, FO to Washington Embassy, 23 Nov. 1954; 747C.00/11-2454, State to Athens Embassy, tel. 1238.
95. *FRUS 1952-54*,VIII, 730-732.
96. *FRUS 1952-54*,VIII, 952.
97. 747C.00/11-154,Warren to State, tel. 478; /12-554,Warren to State, tel. 590.
98. 747C.00/12-754,Turkish memorandum.
99. 112875, 1081/1032-1033, Nutting to FO, 25 Nov. 1954; 747C.00/11-2554, Lodge to Dulles, tel. 286.
100. 117622, 1081/66, Dixon to Eden, 19 Jan. 1955; *FRUS 1952-54*,VIII, 737, n. 3.
101. 112878, 1081/1094-1095, UKUN Delegation to FO, 8 Dec. 1954; 117622, 1081/66, Dixon to Eden, 19 Jan. 1955; *FRUS 1952-54*,VIII, 735-6.
102. 117622, 1081/66, Dixon to Eden, 19 Jan. 1955.

103. *GPR*, meeting of 7 February 1955 [Stefanopoulos], 675.
104. *FRUS 1952-54*,VIII, 738.
105. 747C.00/12-1354, Schnee to State, desp. 1263.
106. 117622, 1081/66, Dixon to Eden, 19 Jan. 1955, annex II; Kyrou 1955, 306, n. 1.
107. 117622, 1081/66, Dixon to Eden, 19 Jan. 1955; Kyrou 1955, 300-301. On 11 December, the *New York Times* editor, Cyrus Sulzberger, published an article strongly critical of the Greek recourse to the UN, in which US objections were clearly stated: 747C.00/12-2054, Schnee to State, desp. 576.
108. 747C.00/12-2054, Schnee to State, desp. 576.
109. Melas suggested a preambular clause to the 'not to discuss' formula, adding that 'the matter will be discussed between the parties': 747C.00/12-1354, memo of conversation between Key, Jernegan, Baxter, Popper, and Melas.
110. Kyrou 1955, 301-302; cf. 747C.00/11-854, letter from Lodge to Dulles.
111. The British had been informed of this meeting in advance: 112880, 1081/1165, UKUN Delegation to FO, 13 Dec. 1954.
112. To those who expressed misgivings, it was pointed out that the proposed arrangement 'would permit of a fair hearing for the Greeks' and enable the British not to realise their threat to boycott the Committee proceedings: 112880, 1081/1165, UKUN Delegation to FO, 13 Dec. 1954; 117622, 1081/66, Dixon to Eden, 19 Jan. 1955.
113. 117622, 1081/66, Dixon to Eden, 19 Jan. 1955; Kyrou 1955, 302-307.
114. Kyrou 1955, 349-433 *passim*. The head of the British delegation, Nutting, appraised Kyrou's speech as 'studiously moderate' and 'rather dull': 112883, 1081/1232, UKUN Delegation to FO, 14 Dec. 1954; 117622, 1081/66, Dixon to Eden, 19 Jan. 1955.
115. 112881, 1081/1181, UKUN Delegation to FO, 14 Dec. 1954; 1081/1195, UKUN Delegation to FO, 15 Dec. 1954; *YUN 1954*, 94-96.
116. 112881, 1081/1195, minute by Wilding, 16 Dec. 1954; 117622, 1081/66, Dixon to Eden, 19 Jan. 1955; cf. Kelling 1990, 147.
117. Kyrou 1955, 307-308.
118. 112881, 1081/1193, UKUN Delegation to FO, 15 Dec. 1954; 117622, 1081/66, Dixon to Eden, 19 Jan. 1955; 747C.00/12-1754, Butterworth, tel. 2803; Kyrou 1955, 310-312.
119. Its text read as follows: '*The General Assembly, Considering* that for the time being, it does not appear appropriate to adopt a resolution on the question of Cyprus, *decides* not to consider further the item entitled 'Application, etc.', *YUN* 1954, 96.
120. 112883, 1081/1222, UKUN Delegation to FO, 18 Dec. 1954; Kyrou 1955, 314-315, 450-454; cf. Crawshaw 1978, 88; Xydis 1968, 143.
121. 117620, 1081/2, Peake to FO, 31 Dec. 1954; Kyrou 1955, foreword, 7. During the first semester of 1955, Kyrou would primarily occupy himself with the writing of a treatise on Greek foreign policy, the second part of which constitutes a lengthy apology of the first Greek recourse to the UN: *ibid.*, 269-454.

122. 117620, 1081/15, Peake to FO, 27 Dec. 1954.
123. *FRUS 1952-54*,VIII, 740.
124. 747C.00/12-2054, Schnee to State, desp. 576; Linardatos II 1978, 255.
125. *FRUS 1952-54*,VIII, 741-742.
126. Stefanopoulos saw the text in advance and concurred: 747C.00/12-1754, memo from Brewster to Merchant.
127. 747C.00/12-2154, memo from Merchant to Dulles.
128. 112883, 1081/1250,Washington Embassy to FO, 20 Dec. 1954.
129. *FRUS 1952-54*,VIII, 749-750.
130. Regarding the anti-American tone of the entire Greek Cypriot press, see CO 926/209, Cyprus Political Situation Report, Dec. 1954; 747C.00/12-1754, Sprecher to State, desp. 47. As the US Consul in Nicosia put it, commentary on the US position on Cyprus in the nationalist papers was indistinguishable from that of *Neos Dimokratis*, the AKEL organ.
131. 112882, 1081/1211, Peake to FO, 15 Dec. 1954; 747C.00/12-2054, Schnee to State, desp. 576.
132. 112882, 1081/1225, Peake to FO, 17 Dec. 1954; 747C.00/12-2054, Schnee to State, desp. 576; Linardatos II 1978, 255-256.
133. *FRUS 1952-54*,VIII, 743-745; Linardatos II 1978, 255-256.
134. *FRUS 1952-54*,VIII, 746.
135. 747C.00/12-2054, Schnee to State, desp. 576; *FRUS 1952-54*,VIII, 746.
136. 112884, 1081/1273, BBC Monitoring Service, 20 Dec. 1954; 747C.00/12-2354, Schnee to State, desp. 587. According to unspecified US Embassy sources, the message, which was drafted by the government, was the result of the King's own initiative. King Paul, however, before delivering his message, had told the British Ambassador that 'he did not want to make a broadcast, but had been strongly advised by (Papagos) to do so': 117620, 1081/1, Peake to Young, 29 Dec. 1954.
137. 112848, 1081/175, FO to Athens Embassy, 21 July 1954; 112852, 1081/303, Peake to FO, 19 Aug. 1954; Crouzet, 428-432.
138. 112873, 1081/954, minute of conversation betweenYoung and Mostras, 2 Nov. 1954; 1081/959, Peake to FO, 3 Nov. 1954; 1081/969, minute by Nutting, 3 Nov. 1954; 112876, 1081/1043, Peake to FO, 26 Nov. 1954.
139. These meetings took place shortly before and after the inscription of the Greek item: 112860, 1081/520, Peake to FO, 12 Sept. 1954; 112868, 1081/789, Peake to Harrison, 30 Sept. 1954.
140. 117621, 1081/26, Bowker toYoung, 31 Dec. 1954.
141. 112883, 1081/1240, Ankara Embassy to FO, 20 Dec. 1954; 747C.00/12-2154,Wendelin to State, desp. 276.
142. *GPR*, meeting of 7 February 1955, 679; cf. Hristidis 1967, 91.
143. *GPR*, meeting of 7 February 1955, 670-673.
144. 117624, 1081/100, Lambert to Eden, 9 Feb. 1955.
145. Thus, Stefanopoulos was prevented from saying that the Americans had actively supported the El Salvador and Colombian amendment — the face-saving device that had permitted Greece to vote for the New Zealand resolution:

747C.00/1-1255, Cannon to Dulles, tel. 1456; State to Athens tel. 1701.
146. *GPR*, meeting of 7 Feb. 1955, 673-680; 117624, 1081/100, Lambert to Eden, 9 Feb. 1955; cf. Linardatos II 1978, 138-9, 263-4;Terlexis 1971, 154-156.
147. *GPR*, meeting of 7 February 1955, 687.
148. 112884, 1081/1257, situation report, Nicosia, 18 Dec. 1954; 747C.00/12-2154, Courtney to State, desp. 48; Crawshaw 1978, 89.
149. CO 926/209, Cyprus Political Situation Report, Dec. 1954; 747C.00/12-2354, Courtney to State, desp. 49.
150. 112884, 1081/1271, extracts from House of Commons debates, 20 Dec. 1954.
151. Kelling 1990, 149.
152. 117220, 1081/13, *Daily News Bulletin*, Prime Minister's Office, Department of Information, Athens, 3 Jan. 1955; Linardatos II 1978, 260, 262.
153. 747C.00/1-555, memo of conversation between Cavalierato and Baxter.
154. CO 926/209, Cyprus Political Situation Report, Jan. 1955; 747C.00/1-2055, Sprecher to State, desp. 62; Linardatos II 1978, 262.
155. 117620, 1081/6, Armitage to Athens Embassy; 117621, 1081/23, FO to Athens; see also 1081/28, 30; 117623, 1081/68; 747C.00/1-1155, memo of conversation between Mackenzie, FO adviser on UN matters to the Cyprus Governor, and Wood.
156. Kelling 1990, 150.
157. 112830, 10110/11, Cyprus Political Situation Report, October 1954.
158. 747C.00/2-1155, Sprecher to State, desp. 68.
159. Under discreet American pressure, the government would take steps to tone down these broadcasts. Although Enosis remained the central theme, the vocabulary became less inflammatory. According to the US Embassy, 'Greek Cypriots collaborating with [the] British formerly labelled outrightly traitors [are] now termed Anglophiles. Allegations of oppression and persecution [are] still prominent ... but barbarism, terrorism, and Hitlerism [are] in less frequent use'. Incitement to violent resistance also tended to be replaced by references to manifestations of support from British and American opinion: 747C.00/3-1555, Cannon to Secretary of State, tel. 1931.
160. 747C.00/2-955, Aldrich to State, tel. 3537. Like previous 'unauthorised' statements (Peake's to Venizelos, in June 1952, and Harrison's to Mostras, in March 1954), this one too is not to be found in Foreign Office records declassified under the thirty-year rule. Mostras, without mentioning the meeting, makes a reference to the views expressed by Kirkpatrick: Mostras ms, 48, n. 2. Yet that statement is indicative of an existing and significant trend of thought within the Foreign Office, and as such it was passed on to the Americans.
161. *FRUS 1952-54*, VIII, 743-745.
162. 747C.00/1-2555, memo of conversation between Allen, Wood and Melas.
163. 117628, 1081/205, Young to Salt, 1 April 1955; 747C.00/3-1755, Nicosia tel. 68; /3-2855, Sprecher to State, desp. 80.
164. 747C.00/-5, Cannon to Dulles, tel. 1931.
165. 747C.00/3-1555, Dulles to Athens, tel. 2275; *FRUS 1955-57*, XXIV, 533-534.

PART TWO

4

RESISTING CHANGE:
THE FORMULATION OF BRITISH POLICY

Labour and British rule in Cyprus

For decades, British primacy in the Mediterranean and predominance in Greece had ensured that Cyprus did not become a contentious issue in Anglo-Greek relations, even during the 1931 uprising. As World War II drew to its close, however, the portents were clear and it was a matter of time before British rule in the island would be challenged by the Greek Cypriots themselves or a Greek government less dependent on British support. The question only seemingly constituted an area of colonial responsibility. The fact that it cut across relations with Greece and, increasingly, Turkey effectively made it the joint responsibility of the Foreign and the Colonial Offices. Since early 1945, the former had repeatedly examined the cession of Cyprus to Greece as an option likely to serve longer-term British interests and objectives. A timely cession, it was reasoned, could bolster the popularity as well as the pro-British orientation of the post-war Greek regime, which faced formidable challenges from both the extreme Right and the Communist Left. This assessment was shared by the powerful British Ambassador in Athens, Reginald Leeper, and, for some time, Foreign Secretary Bevin seemed attracted to it too.[1]

As was to happen repeatedly in this story, short-term considerations militated against longer-term objectives. From the point of view of the Colonial Office bureaucracy, the cession of a Crown Colony, apparently on grounds of national self-determination, would set a dangerous precedent affecting British possessions elsewhere. Economic and constitutional antidotes might offset nationalist pres-

sures, provided they were combined with an unequivocal affirmation of Britain's resolve to keep the island within the Empire.[2] This
line of thought eventually prevailed, aided by the mighty strategic
argument that was to dominate bureaucratic discourse on Cyprus
for more than a decade. In September 1945, the COS called attention to the fact that Cyprus was the only territory in the entire
Eastern Mediterranean and the Middle East where the British exercised full possession rights 'unfettered by treaties'. This fact allowed
them to develop and exploit the island's strategic potential to the
full whenever they wished in peace or war. These interests, the COS
concluded, rendered the retention of British sovereignty essential,
'even at the risk of increased agitation in the island and of unfavourable reaction in Greece'.[3]

Arguments against the cession of Cyprus did not emanate simply from the colonial bureaucracy, the COS or even the upper echelons of the Foreign Office. The Fabian Colonial Bureau, Labour's
think tank on colonial matters, had elaborated the 'strategic colony'
concept, which was to influence British thinking well into the next
decade. Imperial military and political arguments were fused in order to make a case for the retention of strongholds along the imperial lines of communication. This concept, of course, might have
trodden on the principle of self-determination, which the British
Socialists were expected to uphold in the aftermath of World War
II. The problem was acknowledged but, clearly, imperial interests
came first. According to the brochure issued by the Fabian Colonial
Bureau in October 1945, 'The constitutional history of Malta, Gibraltar and Cyprus illustrates, for example, the difficulty of deciding what limits must be imposed on the people attaining responsible self-government when imperial strategic needs have to be
served'.[4] With regard to Cyprus, it was claimed that the island would
find a better future in its 'association with Britain'. Acknowledging
the strength of the Enosis movement and the question of the Turkish minority, the study urged the early introduction of economic
and constitutional incentives against the tide of nationalism.

It took Bevin and his advisers more than a year to adopt a definite position against the cession of Cyprus. The Foreign Secretary
was aware of the damaging impact an inflexible attitude might have
on both Anglo-Greek relations and Britain's image abroad. By late

September 1946, however, he was persuaded to sanction the formula that no change in the status of the island was contemplated.[5]
During 1947 the government's about-face became complete. That
was the time when responsibility for Greece and Turkey was relin-
quished to the Americans, Palestine had to be abandoned and even
the future of the Suez Zone base looked uncertain. Thus, the cession of Cyprus in return for base rights in bitterly divided Greece
did not appear to be sound policy.[6] Once convinced of the vital
importance of the Middle East for imperial strategy, Clement Attlee
himself advocated the retention of Cyprus as a sure 'foothold' in the
region.[7] Last but not least, having given independence to the Indian
subcontinent, the Labour government was then careful not to lend
itself to Conservative accusations that it was about to 'scuttle' the
Empire.[8]

At the same time, it was realised that something had to be done
in order to redress the glaring inconsistency between Labour colonial pronouncements and the situation in Cyprus. As was the case
elsewhere, a combination of economic and political advance was
opted for.[9] In Attlee's view, constitutional politics and a taste of
responsible government would encourage the formation of political parties 'based on internal policies economic and social and thus
wean (the Cypriots) from the delusion of Greek nationalism'.[10] This
was not to be as nineteen months lapsed between the announcement of the intention to grant a constitution in October 1946, and
the publication of Lord Winster's draft, in May 1948. This delay
allowed nationalist opposition to mount and contributed to the loss
of interest on the Left. The restricted character of the proposed
regime was a further disincentive. As Nancy Crawshaw rightly observes, 'the Labour Government had set itself the impossible task of
trying to introduce a more liberal regime and at the same time
preclude any risk of either Enosis or Communist control of the Legislature'.[11]

The acute polarisation of Cypriot politics and the absence of a
middle-of-the-road party – which was, at least in part, the result of
repression since 1931 – proved a serious obstacle to the constitutional initiative. To be sure, the line of 'self-government leading to
union', which AKEL adopted in 1947,[12] might have raised this party
to responsible opposition status, had the British been prepared to

concede a more liberal regime. Unlike the Ethnarchy, which stuck
to its tactics of non-cooperation, the Left had proved capable of
working with the administration in municipal and labour affairs.
Some British officials had come to regard it as the only constructive
factor in Cypriot politics.[13] On the whole, however, the colonial
authorities tended to treat AKEL, with its considerable record of
militancy, as a subversive force and a menace to public order. Scores
of its members were sentenced to various terms in jail or fined and
its press organs were occasionally suppressed.[14] Until very late in
the day, it was not clear whether the British, both at local level and
in Whitehall, recognised the nationalist Right, rather than the Left,
as the main threat to their rule in Cyprus.

Apart from the Left-Right divide within the Greek majority, British policy had to take the island's ethnic configuration into account.
The exacerbation of ethnic politics in Cyprus after World War II
owed a great deal to the fact that colonial rule, in line with standard
practice elsewhere, had largely preserved the pre-existing pattern
of political representation. This pattern, inherited from the Ottoman *millet* system, not only guaranteed a good measure of autonomy
in religious, educational and social matters; more importantly, it
accorded an essentially political role to the spiritual leadership –
the Archbishop and the *Mufti* – of the Greek-Orthodox and the
Muslim communities respectively. Ethnic-religious segmentation was
further institutionalised in local politics: the Greek and the Turkish
Cypriots voted for separate councils in municipal elections, and a
similar provision was made for the election of the legislature in the
abortive Winster constitution. This context was scarcely conducive
to communal co-operation. Despite notable exceptions, such as
AKEL's sincere effort to gain a foothold among the Muslim working class, the ethnic cleavage was never bridged.[15]

The effect of political segmentation on the island's political future would prove devastating. It would be misleading, however, to
attribute the upholding – or even the consolidation – of the communal pattern to some sinister 'divide-and-rule' design. At least until
they were faced with the rigours of internationalisation and armed
struggle,[16] the British were satisfied with exercising hegemonic control over the island's population and considered it unwise to med-
dle with long-standing religious or other divisions. Besides, until

after the drive for Enosis began in 1950,[17] incidents of communal friction were practically unknown.[18] This attitude was best reflected in the field of education: it was never the British policy to foster a collective 'Cypriot' identity, above and beyond the existing ones, nor was there any serious effort to prevent the island's communities from being 'contaminated' by Greek or Turkish nationalism. As Governor Wright put it in 1953, it was always the 'hope and intention' of the colonial administration that the Greek and Turkish Cypriots 'should develop from their past history' as 'good Greeks' and 'good Turks' respectively.[19] The implications of such nonchalance would be tremendous for both rulers and ruled.

The colonial authorities occasionally sought to take some control of education by what proved to be half-measures. Primary schools were taken over in 1929, but many teachers and textbooks, including readers, continued to come from Greece and Turkey.[20] Secondary education remained in the hands of the Greek and Turkish communities, its content being largely modelled on the respective national systems. It was only in July 1952 that the administration would attempt to break this monopoly by offering state funding in return for control over teacher appointments and school curricula. The measure was optional and proved ineffective as it was resisted by the Greek and Turkish communities alike.[21] A second attempt would follow with the education law amendment of July 1953, when the authorities sought to enforce stricter discipline over the Greek *gymnasia*, already the hotbeds of militant nationalism.[22] The promotion of some sense of 'Cypriotism' would be given serious attention by the Foreign Office only after the first Greek recourse to the UN.[23] By that time, however, whatever steps were taken proved spasmodic and ineffectual.[24]

Though a less slippery ground, economic development also proved a formidable task. Living standards in Cyprus, while superior to those in Civil War Greece, were still unacceptably low. As late as 1953, the *per capita* income stood at only one-third of the British average. Infrastructure was inadequate, the processing sector rudimentary, and the Colony ran a trade deficit.[25] In spite of its geographical position, trade was oriented towards the West. Its main economic role in the Middle East, according to a Foreign Office official, was 'as a centre for goods smuggling between Israel and the

Arab states'.[26] In response, from 1946 onwards, the colonial administration embarked on a ten-year development plan costing a rather modest £18 million. While some improvement would be achieved, particularly in roads, land improvement and public health, the administration would find it difficult to finance the entire scheme. Thus, at the end of the period, the Cypriot economy would preserve its underdeveloped, agricultural, import-dependent character. Only after 1954, with the dramatic increase in transfers for military purposes, the island's gross domestic product would score a substantial growth, which, however, was little related to internal factors.[27]

Interpreting Enosis

After Winster, the Governors of Cyprus were always inclined to see the Enosis movement as primarily the result of external influence and machinations. Wright's preoccupation with the alleged role of Greece in fomenting anti-British agitation in Cyprus neared obsession. Thus, he regularly pleaded for official and public display of British firmness and diplomatic pressure on Athens,[28] starting with his demand for the removal of the Greek Consul-General in December 1949.[29] With regard to Turkey, though appreciating her potential role in countering Enosis, the Governor proved equally keen to guard British sovereignty against excessive manifestations of Turkish interest in Cypriot affairs.

It appears that the colonial bureaucracy in London was capable of a more subtle analysis of the Enosis drive. A discussion between Mary Fisher, the imaginative Desk Officer for Cyprus, and Margaret Tibbetts, attaché of the US Embassy in London, is quite illuminating. Fisher interpreted the escalation of the Enosis campaign as the result of the antagonism between the Ethnarchy and AKEL. The former, she acknowledged, adhered to Enosis for a variety of reasons – emotional, sentimental, resentment against British rule – but its 'desire not to let the Communists steal the credit' for championing Enosis had put it on a course, which neither side could abandon without losing face.[30] Although Fisher's emphasis on the role of AKEL must be taken with a pinch of salt, since it was the British practice to play up this factor when talking to Americans, this analysis is all the more remarkable in that it did not attempt to explain Enosis agitation as being primarily the result of outside influence.

From Athens, Ambassador Norton also disputed Wright's line of argument: there was not much that any Greek government, short of a military dictatorship, could do to help the Governor, since Enosis was already an immensely popular issue both in Greece and Cyprus.[31] Wider political considerations made the diplomats reluctant to press matters as far as Wright wished. The preservation of British influence in Greece was one consideration. By late 1949, the last British troops were being withdrawn and London had joined Washington in pressing Athens for leniency at home and conciliation abroad.[32] Ambassador Norton steadily warned of the risks of high-handedness for Anglo-Greek relations: it was Greek 'affection and gratitude' for Britain, he wrote, that 'had prevented the [Cyprus] thing from getting out of hand hitherto'. British *démarches*, he further pointed out, could undermine the position of the Greek government and dissatisfy the Americans, who wanted political stability.[33]

For a time, the attitude of the Greek government satisfied British demands without further ado. Norton had also been able to enlist the US Ambassador's active support.[34] It should be noted that Bevin was in favour of using American influence in order to discourage Greek agitation about Cyprus and authorised an approach to Washington.[35] In this effort, the British made full use of the fact that the Communist AKEL and Eastern bloc media were championing Enosis. The advantages of this argument were not missed by Norton.[36] British officials, in their representations to the American and Greek governments, would steadily warn that Enosis agitation directly played into the hands of the Communists and threatened allied unity in the region.

An abortive revision

Despite the official position that no Cyprus question existed, the mounting Enosis agitation both in Cyprus and Greece and its implications for Anglo-Greek relations generated a number of interesting suggestions from various levels of the British establishment. Leo

Amery, the 'long time imperial statesman', proposed the dual citizenship formula, whereby Greek Cypriots who so wished could establish a kind of 'personal Enosis' with Greece. This, Amery argued, might satisfy national sentiment, while allowing for the 'island's real estate' to remain British.[37] This proposal, while rejected by the Colonial Office, later inspired Mary Fisher to venture a sort of 'appropriation of Enosis'. Foreseeing 'storms ahead' in the absence of any tangible political or economic progress, she suggested that the authorities recognise the Hellenic identity of the Greek Cypriots and tolerate its manifestations on the cultural level. This, in her view, might encourage the local population to co-operate with a constitutional regime, while leaving British sovereignty intact.[38]

Apart from these ideas, which aimed at perpetuating British rule, there were more far-reaching propositions. Even before the Ethnarchy plebiscite and the first stirrings towards internationalisation, Ambassador Norton had repeatedly expressed misgivings about the attitude of his government. He was stating the obvious when he remarked that, as Greece gained in strength and self-confidence, Britain would find it increasingly difficult to influence her policy on Cyprus. In a letter to Charles Bateman, on 29 November 1949, he clearly read the signs:

I cannot conceal from myself that the dice are heavily loaded against us. The march of even very backward peoples in the Middle East to independence, the cases of India, Burma, etc., the heroship accorded all over the world to Pandit Nehru, our own somewhat 'diminished state', Great Britain's necessity being Ireland's opportunity, etc.. And the very high intellectual level of the Greeks, compared e.g. with the Senussi.[39]

What Norton proposed was a sort of mild 'Balfour declaration', possibly in answer to a parliamentary question, which, while condemning agitation, would not exclude a future reconsideration of British policy.[40] In subsequent letters to Bateman, the Ambassador further complained that he had never received any guidance on Cyprus, 'the one topic', he wrote, 'of daily burning interest' in Anglo-Greek relations.[41] He also criticised the fragmented way in which the Cyprus question was being treated, claiming that not a single

department was 'in a position to consider the whole problem ...
objectively'. In order to meet this deficiency, he urged the setting
up of an interdepartmental committee 'to establish a policy and an
information policy in regard to Cyprus'.[42]

Norton's views sounded all the more 'heretical' as they closely
echoed proposals put forward by Greek officials from time to time.
They were also in line with American thinking, but well ahead of
conventional wisdom in Whitehall. Yet the Southern Department
duly took them into account. Its head, Sir Anthony Rumbold, shared
the Ambassador's opinion that, no matter how many Greek disclaim-
ers were obtained, the British would find it increasingly hard to
maintain their position in Cyprus in the face of mounting local reaction. His prediction was that violence would break out just as it
had done in 1931. In response to Governor Wright's request for the
removal of the Greek Consul-General, Rumbold prepared a memorandum for Bevin, in which he forcefully questioned the entire basis of Cyprus policy. He observed that the only valid argument for
maintaining colonial rule over a 'civilised and educated population'
was the strategic one, as had been defined by the COS in 1945 and
1947. In his view, this argument was not 'watertight' as the Greek
offer of bases and military rights in return for Cyprus could be
framed in such a way 'as to make it impossible for either side to
break it'. Rumbold concluded that there was a case for the re-examination of British policy and seconded Norton's proposal for an
interdepartmental approach to the problem. This, he ventured, might
reveal that 'the early cession of Cyprus to Greece would be not only
the most just but also the most expedient solution'.[43]

In the same memorandum, dated 16 December 1949, Rumbold
conscientiously listed the options available, were his government to
reject change. Strong measures, perhaps of the type advocated by
the Governor, should be necessary in order to keep the island under
control, even at the risk of 'antagonising the Greek government'.[44]
This was closer to mainstream thinking at the time. Bateman stressed
that Britain was in Cyprus for strategic reasons and no one could
predict when, 'if indeed ever', these reasons would cease to be
valid.[45] Wright, for his part, was opposed even to a preliminary
study on the future of Cyprus. Rumbold retorted that Wright 'would
himself prefer to see the island go to Turkey than to Greece'.[46]

The isolation of revisionist trends was reflected in the instructions which, following his complaints, Norton received in the early days of 1950. Minister of State Younger advised him that the retention of full British sovereignty on Cyprus should be considered 'axiomatic', a point that the Ambassador ought to make clear to the Greek government without raising undue expectations about the future. As Norton wondered what more a British diplomat could say whenever the subject was brought up, Younger suggested 'a shew of impatience. .. You know the sort of thing: a little foot-tapping, lip biting and a changing of the subject in, what P.G.Woodhouse would call, a marked manner'.[47] Finally, with regard to the plebiscite, the British government chose to ignore it, apparently underestimating its value as a propaganda weapon and a rallying point for the supporters of Enosis.[48]

The prevailing trend in British policy was confirmed by the joint study that the Foreign and the Colonial Offices duly prepared in April 1950. Its authors admitted that a redefinition of Cyprus policy was needed in view of the international publicity which the Ethnarchy plebiscite was already attracting. Then they examined the pros and cons of a change of sovereignty. Such a move, it was argued, would relieve Britain of a considerable administrative and financial burden, which was certain to increase if unrest ever broke out; relations with Greece would benefit and a cause of 'a good deal of unwelcome criticism' would be removed. On the negative side, attention was given to the opposition of the Turkish Cypriot community and the likely reaction of Turkey. The emphasis, however, was placed on the perceived ill effect on Britain's credibility as a great power in the Middle East: the cession of the only British sovereign territory in an area which Bevin had declared to be 'of cardinal importance, second only to the UK itself',[49] would be interpreted by local opinion 'as another manifestation of (Britain's) growing weakness, even if accompanied by the retention of all necessary strategic facilities'. The bitter experience in Egypt, where the British were embroiled in fruitless negotiations over the future of their military base rights, loomed large in the official mind; nor could the possibility of a Communist or extreme nationalist regime taking over in Greece and endangering British rights be discounted. Quite obviously, the report was carefully weighted against any fun-

118 *Isle of Discord*

damental change in British policy.[50]

A further, largely unspoken, consideration concerned the government's anxiety not to expose itself to Conservative criticism on an imperial matter. This consideration weighed more heavily after the general elections held in February 1950, as the Labour Party emerged with a slender majority of 2 seats.[51]

Subsequently, the Colonial Office asked the COS for their imprimatur. Their report, delivered in early June 1950, came as the final blow against any revisionist tendency. As Rumbold put it, that document was a not a report on the actual strategic value of the island, but rather 'a fervent essay ... for keeping Cyprus'.[52] Indeed, the strategic requirements of Britain in Cyprus were couched in vague terms and often appeared as a matter of the future: 'a free hand to station ..., in peace, that part of British Middle East Forces which may be considered necessary, at any time, to meet the strategic situation'; 'the right to develop the airfields necessary to support allied strategy'. Rather, what counted most was the British position in the Middle East which, the COS asserted, could only be safeguarded if Cyprus remained in British hands. Even a promise to review the situation in the future, they argued, would merely invite further subversive activities in the island and discourage Britain's allies in the Middle East. It would also 'seriously affect relations with Turkey', and might also have an effect on the United States.[53] Upon receiving the report, Mary Fisher noted: 'We must resign ourselves to being primarily an occupying power (in Cyprus)'.[54]

The subject was briefly reopened in spring 1951, as the British faced a novel element in the situation – the demand for the cession of Cyprus, which Greek Prime Minister Venizelos was obliged to express in reaction to Kenneth Younger's ineptitude in the Commons, on 14 February. From Athens, Norton despondently reported that, although it was still possible a year earlier to extract official statements to the effect that it was inopportune to press national aspirations on Cyprus, the best that could be obtained was 'the comment that the problem must be solved "in the framework of Anglo-Greek friendship"'.[55]

Once again, the Ambassador tried to impress on his department the need for a 'more realistic approach'. In a letter to Strang, dated 13 March, he repeated that no Greek government short of 'a non-parliamentary military regime' should be expected to be helpful on the question of Cyprus.[56] Norton then put forward a 'stick and carrot' formula, which he had discussed with the Americans a few weeks earlier.[57] According to this, the US and British military chiefs should declare that, owing to the tense international situation and Western defence requirements, no change in the status of the island was feasible. At the same time, however, the British government should indicate that the time would come when it 'would agree to take steps to ascertain the real wishes of the inhabitants'.[58] It should be noted that as Norton's views reached London, the US Vice-Consul in Nicosia reported high-ranking members of the colonial administration in Cyprus admitting in private that their government might consider ceding the island to Greece, after international tensions had abated.[59]

Apparently, such ideas were designed to keep the matter in manageable proportions and prevent an Anglo-Greek falling out; they also seemed to meet the minimum expectations of both the Greek government and Archbishop Makarios and could count on wholehearted American support.[60] On the other hand, the prospect of compromise was strongly resisted by both Cypriot nationalists and Governor Wright.[61] The Labour government, for its part, proved unwilling or unable to modify its course. Approaching the end of its parliamentary tether, it dug itself into convenient immobilism.

These abortive attempts at revising British policy confirmed the difference of perspective between the agents charged with policy-making on Cyprus — the diplomats were inclined to probe into alternative courses, the colonial bureaucracy never doubted the need of retaining full sovereignty, and the military was always ready to underwrite this view. The result was the sort of inertia referred to above. A degree of confusion of authority was also inevitable, and this, according to Robert Holland, 'allowed the Cyprus government over a long period to evade effective accountability'.[62]

Wright's way

Unlike his predecessor, Sir Andrew Wright was a career colonial administrator with a long record of service in Cyprus. Under Governor Storrs, he had seen the Government House burned down

during the 1931 rebellion, and in 1937 he became Governor Rich-
mond Palmer's Colonial Secretary. Thus, he had played his part in
the repressive regime of that period, an experience that probably
accounted for his predilection for strong-arm methods. Sympathetic
contemporaries invariably described Wright as a man 'of the old
order',[63] too much attached to the memories and methods of the
past to be a sound judge of the situation after two momentous decades.[64] Coming from Gambia to Cyprus, the new Governor was
given a mandate to seek means to break the deadlock left by the
failure of Winster's effort. Soon he concluded that political evolution should be preceded by the 'development and consolidation' of
British rule. Frustrated by the incessant Enosis agitation and the
refusal of Greek Cypriot nationalists to co-operate, he consistently
advocated repression as a prerequisite to constitutional advance.
Mary Fisher ventured a milder interpretation, stating that repressive measures were designed not necessarily to be implemented but
'to make an impression': 'if you wave sticks at Cypriots', she quipped,
'you don't have to call out the garrison'.[65] Thus, on the eve of the
1950 plebiscite, Wright addressed a letter to the Colonial Secretary
asking authorisation to reinforce the colony's anti-seditious legislation.[66]

In advocating a wide range of repressive measures over the following three years,[67] Wright could count on some support from
within the Colonial Office, particularly from Permanent Under-
Secretary Sir Thomas Lloyd, but little more. There were strong reservations, owing to the more recent bitter experience in Palestine
and Egypt, where high-handedness had proved counter-productive.
This was not far from the views of Creech Jones's successor, Griffiths,
who, as Robert Holland observed, would distinguish himself 're-
sisting the pressures emanating from Nicosia'.[68]

By September 1950, the US Consul in Nicosia found Wright
'frustrated in his desire to "put the Cypriots in their place"'.[69] Shortly
afterwards, he went to London to plead his case with Griffiths. He
stressed that the proposed measures were designed to pre-empt subversion, which he believed to be inevitable. In case his request was
not granted, Wright indirectly wondered what other policy might
'relate' to his own reading of the situation, 'the general accuracy' of
which he considered beyond doubt. His style seemed to exasperate

some in the colonial bureaucracy. A 'highly placed' official told the Americans that there could be little progress in Cyprus as long as Wright remained at his post.[70] In the event, Griffiths was able to postpone a decision for the second time that year, promising to re-examine the Governor's request after six months.[71] Yet, by January 1951, Wright was given the green light to strengthen the anti-seditious legislation of the colony.

Obviously, the mere announcement of tough measures could not possibly scare the Cypriots into compliance; there had to be some enforcement. This did not happen. The Labour government soon saw the whole thing as a tactical mistake which had attracted unfavourable attention at home and abroad, at a time when a Greek recourse to the UN was a possibility. By April, even the military admitted that they had failed to improve matters in Cyprus 'in any noticeable way'.[72]

Unable to apply anti-sedition at will, Wright singled out AKEL as a more promising target. When he visited London in the summer of 1951, he sought authorisation to proscribe Communist activity. His request was based on political rather than security grounds. The aim, he argued, was to drive a wedge between the Ethnarchy and the Left, and, by removing the pressure of the latter, to make it easier for moderate nationalists to come forward and co-operate with the authorities. To Griffiths all this was wishful thinking. He reminded Wright that it was the Ethnarchy, not AKEL, which now championed Enosis, and that action against the latter would fail 'to touch the real issue in Cyprus'. Besides, repression under any guise would not make a popular issue at the next UN General Assembly. Once more Wright returned empty-handed.[73]

The Turkish card

When the cession of Cyprus to Greece had been discussed as an option in 1945-6, the Foreign Office had assumed that 'Turkey would not object to having Greece on her southern flank as long as it was her policy to be friendly with Greece'.[74] Turkey's attitude during World War II was a further factor working to her disadvantage. As Christopher Woodhouse put it, 'the Turks had neither the legal right nor the moral standing nor even the inclination to object' to a British decision to cede Cyprus.[75]

By 1949 of course, things were different. Turkish opposition to
Enosis was manifest and the British were suspected, not only by the
Greek press, for fomenting it. For one thing, the British government did nothing to discourage the expression of Turkish interest in
the fate of Cyprus, whenever the question gained prominence. The
Foreign Office preferred to 'leave the initiative [of discouraging Turkish claims] with the Americans'.[76] The reason, of course, was that
the British themselves increasingly felt inclined to use the Turkish
counter-claims as one of their main arguments against Enosis. The
goodwill of the Turkish Cypriot community was a further important consideration. According to the US Consul in Nicosia, after
Winster's resignation, Acting Governor Turnbull had 'taken particular pains to woo [the Turkish Cypriots] with assurances that the British
will not allow union to take place and will continue to protect the
out-numbered Turkish citizens from the Greek majority'.[77] At the
same time, the Foreign Office was fully aware of the danger of Greek-
Turkish animosity being revived as a result of Cyprus, and still felt
that it was in the British interest to prevent such development.[78]

The 'special relationship'

From 1950 onwards, British policy makers had to seriously take
into account the possibility of the Cyprus question becoming an
international one. The Ethnarchy mission of 1950 was in a way the
forerunner of internationalisation. The British reacted by putting
pressure on Athens. Having 'stiffened up' the Plastiras government
as instructed, Norton advised London that Greek leaders should be
left to deal with the situation as best they could.[79] Yet, after pronouncements in support of Enosis in the Greek parliament, the Ambassador himself suggested a strong statement – in common with
the Americans, if possible – in order to dispel any undue expectations of change.[80] There followed Dugdale's reply to a parliamentary question, the first in a long row of official statements that not
only reiterated the standard British position but succeeded in offending Greek susceptibilities.[81]

By early summer, the possibility of a country other than Greece
bringing the matter before the UN General Assembly caused con-

cern on either side of the Atlantic. AKEL's own mission to various
Eastern European capitals seemed to give substance to this appre-
hension.[82] Self-confidence, it appears, was in short supply: as Mary
Fisher admitted, the British case could not be easily defended: 'No
attempt to explain away, qualify, or discredit the plebiscite of last
January could disguise the fact that a clear majority of the people in
Cyprus want union with Greece'.[83]

In view of Britain's declining capability to influence the course
of Greek foreign policy, American co-operation was fast becoming
indispensable. As Ambassador Norton put it to Bevin, 'no other single factor is likely to have so much influence [in Greece] as the
knowledge that the US Government are opposed to the raising of
the question in present circumstances'.[84] Indeed, the assistance of
successive US Ambassadors and senior personnel in seconding British *démarches* on Cyprus was proving a valuable asset. To secure
public American support for the British position, however, proved
an impossible task.

For one thing, the British had to contend with the anti-colonial
reflexes of American opinion as expressed in Congress, the press
and, to some extent, official circles. In order to bring their position
home to the Americans, they relied primarily on the strategic importance of Cyprus, the Communist involvement in the Enosis campaign and the opposition of the Turkish factor. Yet all these arguments were riddled with deficiencies: the strategic argument was
not borne out by the existing, under-developed, defence facilities
on the island; the strength of AKEL in Cyprus was a double-edged
argument, since it could lend the British to criticism of being 'soft'
to communism; finally, until at least early 1950, the State Department strongly deprecated the involvement of Turkey in Cyprus and
warned the British against using this card.

From the outset, the British became aware of significant divisions of opinion within American diplomacy on the point that concerned them most – a public statement against the raising of the
Cyprus question at the UN. The regional offices of the State Department were expected to be helpful, but UN Affairs and the delegation to the UN were known to be unsympathetic on colonial
issues.[85] They also realised the effect of Greek-American lobbying
and pressure in Congress. In search of a potent ally, they turned to

the US military leaders. According to the Washington Embassy, American lukewarmness was in large part due to insufficient appreciation of the British strategic argument.[86] Thus, the COS were called upon to help convince their American counterparts that the interests of the Western alliance would be better served if British rule over Cyprus continued indefinitely.[87]

As has been seen, the British effort went some way towards gaining tacit American support, though no public statement was forthcoming. The issue was bound to recur in the Sixth session of the General Assembly, in 1951. In view of the regular Anglo-American talks on colonial matters, the Foreign Office sought a reaffirmation of the strategic grounds of Cyprus policy. The COS obliged: a 'stable and firmly held British stronghold is of the greatest strategic importance', they opined, while any sign of diminishing British presence in the Middle East could only provoke further instability. As an antidote, the military recommended 'a firm and unequivocal statement' of Britain's determination to stay on the island.[88] On this basis, the diplomats resumed their effort to persuade the Americans to come out against the raising of the Cyprus question at the UN.[89] They also tried to link Cyprus with the impending admission of Greece and Turkey into NATO.[90] These efforts not only failed but also generated American pressures for some positive steps in Cyprus. In the view of the Colonial Office, this was quite impossible. The latter's recommendation was to keep the issue 'out of the news' as much as possible. Thus, by the summer of 1951, British diplomacy could only take relief in the fact that the prospect of a Greek recourse to the UN had receded, at least for that year.[91]

The Conservative comeback

The Conservatives, who came to power in October 1951, were traditionally regarded as the 'Party of the Empire'. Yet, in spite of Churchill's imperial attachment, the point at issue was not whether the peoples under British tutelage would be led to self-rule, preferably within the Commonwealth, but the scope and pace of that change.[92] The new government, of course, was against any premature moves, in accordance with the prevailing mood at Westminster.[93] The adherence of the Labour leadership to the ideal of the

Commonwealth and to Britain's role as a world power made the government's task much easier.[94] In the case of Cyprus the record of the Labour government further contributed to a virtual consensus beyond party lines.[95]

Sympathy for the national aspirations of the Greek Cypriots in Britain was largely confined to the traditional philhellene circles of classical scholars and Byronic romantics, well-intentioned but politically ineffective, and the left wing of the parliamentary Labour Party: MPs like Lena Jeger and Kenneth Robinson, who were elected in north London constituencies with strong Cypriot communities, 'Bevanites' like Richard Crossman, Thomas (Tom) Driberg, E.L. Mallalieu and Woodrow Wyatt, or the more moderate Francis Noel-Baker, whose family had special ties with Greece.[96] Conversely, the Conservative government faced strong reactions from within its own ranks against any idea of relinquishing British rights in the region: the so-called 'Suez Group', mustering some thirty to forty backbenchers, was basically opposed to a deal with Egypt for the evacuation of the Canal Zone and was certain to make an issue out of a change in Cyprus policy.[97] With a majority of only seventeen in the Commons, the government was to an extent hostage to this vocal group of imperial incorrigibles.

The Conservative come-back also gave Governor Wright's plans a new impetus. While in London, in February-March 1952, he once more requested authority to suppress newspapers by executive action or else to proscribe AKEL, as a prerequisite to any attempt to constitutional advance. It immediately became clear that the new government did not wish to desist from the immobilism of its predecessor and the new Secretary of State for the Colonies, Lyttelton, rejected both repression and reform. As second best, Wright pleaded for a 'very firm statement' of Britain's intention to retain sovereignty and to grant a constitution only if the political atmosphere improved'.[98] On the recommendation of the Foreign Office, Eden opposed such action as bound to provoke 'trouble' both in Cyprus and in Greece, where Enosis agitation was reportedly ebbing.[99]

With respect to the constitutional question, Wright and Lyttelton agreed to have a draft prepared for use whenever 'a political opportunity offered itself'. The task was delegated to Chief Justice Sir Edward Jackson, the Chairman of the 1947 Consultative Assembly.

Yet Jackson left Cyprus to serve on the Allied High Commission in
Germany without having dealt with his task.[100] Indicative of the
government's actual intentions was the fact that Cyprus was not
included in the Colonial Office priority list of constitutional work
for 1953. Significantly, Malta was top of that list.[101] The rejection of
Wright's requests and the postponement of reform virtually extended the period of inaction initiated by the previous government.
The colonial administration went on with what the US Consul described as 'the practice of the art of government in a vacuum, …
every day becoming more removed from, and more foreign to, the
ruled'.[102] This went in parallel with a virtual eclipse of interest in
Cyprus in the British parliament, which lasted until February 1954.

While public statements were avoided, Eden was in no way prepared to entertain Greek approaches on the question. His rebuff of
Averof in Rome, in November 1951, was a typical example of the
'stiff doses of acid diplomacy'[103] which he and his aides prescribed
for similar occasions. Yet there were a few remarkable deviations.
One was the unofficial views expressed by Lord Halifax to King
Paul in May 1952, that the Cypriot people after achieving self-government 'could no doubt choose for themselves'.[104] This was far
from pleasing to Eden, who deplored the former Foreign Secretary's lack of firmness.[105] Yet a month later, according to an American report, much the same was stated in Ambassador Peake's reply
to an approach from Venizelos.[106] Surely, intimations to the effect
that the Cypriots would eventually 'be free to work out their own
destiny' were out of keeping with the official line and never surfaced above the level of speculation.

Cyprus and Britain's contraction in the Middle East

During the early 1950s, the British position in the Middle East un-
derwent a fairly rapid transformation as a result of the country's
declining capabilities and the dynamics of Arab nationalism. The definition of a new role that would permit Britain to retain her influence was urgently required. As the Americans secured the admission of Greece and Turkey into NATO, the British concentrated on
promoting a new regional defence arrangement, initially termed
'Middle East Command', in which Turkey – though not Greece –

was expected to play a crucial part. The objective was to salvage British military presence in the Suez Zone by involving Egypt and as many Arab states as possible in the planned defence organisation. Yet the plan got off to a bad start, as Cairo refused to participate. On 8 October 1951, the Egyptians denounced the 1936 treaty of alliance with Britain and demanded the withdrawal of the British garrison from Suez. An attempt to relaunch the plan as a 'Middle East Defence Organisation' failed to break the deadlock. The overthrow of King Farouk and the military take-over did not ease things for Britain.[107] By late 1952, Foreign Secretary Eden would recommend the gradual shedding of Britain's 'informal empire' in the Middle East and South Asia as a necessary evil. This process, however, enhanced the value of strategic strong points like Cyprus in British planning for the region.

Indeed, in October 1952, the COS considered the transfer of their Middle East headquarters from Egypt to Cyprus. Their lack of enthusiasm was understandable as the island was no real substitute for Suez, since it lacked in infrastructure and natural facilities, harbours in particular, and could not play host to substantial ground or naval forces.[108] The transfer was sanctioned by the Cabinet on 3 December 1952, as part of a major reassessment of Middle East policy. Eden was quick to point to the perceived political advantages of such a move which would be 'very acceptable' to Turkey, while it 'should help to convince the Greeks' that the British were in Cyprus to stay.[109] Left-wing scepticism was expressed by Charles Richards in the *Statesman and Nation*, who remarked that little had been done to foster social and cultural bonds between the colony and Britain, and that this, coupled with the lack of political progress, had produced 'an isolated, dissatisfied people'.[110]

Anglo-Greek relations: From courtship to estrangement

The end of political instability in Greece and the coming of Field Marshal Papagos to power in November 1952 seemed to open new prospects. Ambassador Peake in particular appeared to entertain high hopes for the future of Anglo-Greek relations. From the point of view of regional stability, Peake argued that the staunchly pro-Western and anti-Communist orientation of the new government

served British interests, even if some of its policies were not always
approved. Hence, he did his best to stimulate interest in Greece,
proposing high-level visits, an invitation to Greece to join MEDO,
and, more important, increased levels of trade and investment. With
regard to Cyprus, the Ambassador found Papagos' early caution
encouraging: the question, he ventured, could be kept 'in reasonable proportion', if only British companies purchased the entire
tobacco crop for the following two years![111]

Moreover, Peake hoped to shore up British influence, which had
been on the wane since 1947. His assessment was that the high-
handed American methods of intervention and patronage were already causing disaffection and the time might well come when Greek
élites once more turned to the British 'as the absent friend'. Such
wishful thinking was in fact encouraged by Greek leaders themselves, from King Paul to Papagos.[112] The British Ambassador was
also worried by the rise of rival foreign influences. His reports regularly warned of West German and Russian advance, as a result of
increased volumes of trade and generous credit policies. He seemed
to fear that, economically at least, Greece was slipping from American to German tutelage, and thought that Britain ought to remain a
respectable third by extending at least modest financial support.[113]

Yet London failed to meet Peake's expectations. Greek participation in MEDO was out of the question. In the economic field, the
Treasury, judging from past experience, estimated that 'whatever
money is put into Greece is lost'.[114] Eden confirmed this view when
he minuted that Britain had 'no money for Greece'.[115] Thus, when
Minister of Co-ordination Markezinis visited London in July 1953,
instead of being able to attract capital investment, he was confronted
with British demands for the settlement of the pre-war Greek
debt.[116] Not much stock was put in the country's political reliability either.[117]

Thus, Peake concentrated on improving the façade of Anglo-
Greek relations. He tried less costly means, such as cultural events
and visits of British dignitaries, including R.A. Butler, Chancellor
of the Exchequer, his Labour predecessor Hugh Gaitskell, and
Anthony Eden himself. By August, the Embassy was able to profess
some optimism for the future.[118] However, its public relations campaign had succeeded in arousing American mistrust. Peurifoy, the

outgoing Ambassador, saw in it an 'obvious intention of reasserting the traditional British primacy in Greece, if the opportunity is offered.'[119]

Eden was due to visit Athens in April. The Embassy and the Foreign Office saw in it not only an opportunity to upgrade Anglo-Greek relations, but also a lever to induce the Greek government to meet British requirements on points of friction.[120] On the question of Cyprus the Southern Department concluded that the Greek government could not be expected to be more 'realistic' than its predecessors.[121] Papagos, it was lamented, had failed to live up to his promise to discourage public emotion about Cyprus and treat the issue 'discreetly as between friends' — not that the British, of course, were prepared to enter into discussions at any time. This was made abundantly clear in Eden's brief, where it was reaffirmed that 'on strategic grounds alone' the British government could 'contemplate no change of sovereignty in the foreseeable future'.[122] Peake himself was now in favour of a 'sharp reminder'.[123] In the event, the postponement of Eden's visit and the adherence of the Foreign Office to a moratorium on public statements helped keep Anglo-Greek relations calm for another six months.[124]

In the event, Eden's visit in September 1953 and his rebuff of Papagos ushered in a new period of confrontation. This prospect led to a brief review of the British position on the Cyprus question. A Foreign Office study, dated 18 November 1953, revealed that its authors were inclined to treat the claims of Greece and Turkey on the island as equally 'arguable'. This position, which, a few years later, would inspire plans of partition, presently served to justify British rule. 'Expediency', it was argued, demanded that Cyprus 'should go to neither' of its claimants. Instead, three options were put forward: (a) a public reaffirmation of British resolve to keep the island; (b) the introduction of 'a measure of self-government, leading possibly to independence within the Commonwealth'; and (c) an effort to get public American support. The Foreign Office still considered the first option counter-productive. Eden minuted the second with a plain 'No'.[125] The remaining option could be pursued by the Foreign Secretary during the forthcoming three-power conference in Bermuda. Harrison, head of the Southern Department, suggested that Dulles and Georges Bidault might be induced to ex-

press a 'vital interest' in the continuing British control of 'strong
points' such as Hong Kong, Gibraltar and Cyprus.[126] Eden was reserved.[127] In Bermuda, he would be too busy seeking American
support over British difficulties with Egypt to be able to interject
Cyprus effectively.

For a few more months, British diplomacy chose to adhere to
what Peake described as 'masterly inaction',[128] or, alternatively, 'con-
spiracy of silence'.[129] As the Foreign Office explained to the Ambassador in Ankara, it was its policy to keep the Cyprus question in
the background, at least as long as the Greek government did likewise.[130] These views were shared by Ambassador Peake too, who,
like his predecessor, had come to regard the usual representations
about Cyprus a 'highly disagreeable task'.[131] Moreover, he still hoped
to bring Papagos to London.[132]

The question of Papagos' visit dragged on for some time and
further poisoned Anglo-Greek relations. Upon receiving Peake's report of his talk with Papagos on 10 November, Eden approved a
reply to the effect that, however much he would like to see the
Greek Premier in London, he could not concede to discuss Cyprus;
thus, if Papagos could not find a way of avoiding the subject, then,
'with the greatest regret, he had better not come'.[133] Peake realised
that such an answer, if delivered, would ruin Anglo-Greek relations,
to the benefit of the West Germans and the Russians. Thus, he pleaded
for the omission of the final passage and proposed to delay delivery
of the message until after the Greek government had dealt with a
flare-up of public discussion on Cyprus.[134] In the Southern Department, Harrison was against making things 'too easy' for Papagos to
which Eden concurred.[135]

Peake did not give up and suggested a formula similar to that
used during Archbishop Damaskinos' trip to London eight years
earlier – either party could say that the Cyprus question had been
raised by Papagos, but that, 'in Her Majesty's government's view,
the time was not opportune to discuss it'. This, he claimed, would
enable the Greek Premier to withstand his domestic pressures, while
not committing the British in any way.[136] A hard line, however, prevailed in the Southern Department and Peake's plan fell through.[137]

Continuity

GovernorWright's retirement in early 1954 offered an opportunity for a fresh look at Cyprus policy. Yet the selection of his successor indicated that the Colonial Office did not consider the situation to require innovative or outstanding skills. Sir Robert Armitage was of the 'standard, off the shelf' type of colonial administrator.[138] He had served most of his career in Kenya and then in the Gold Coast, a model colony in West Africa already enjoying self-government.[139] His African background, however, would be of little value in the intricate political climate of Cyprus. Like his predecessors, Armitage was given wide discretion to determine whether to 'impose' a constitution or to 'continue as at present', although his briefing conveyed no sense of urgency.[140] Furthermore, the new Governor would perform his task in isolation from local realities: upon his arrival, in February, his staff took care not to include in his contact list persons who might have declined the invitation. Thus, they happily reported that, wherever Armitage went on his first tour, he was received 'with courtesy and friendliness'.[141]

The Foreign Office, while definitely less complacent, appeared at that time to be resigned to the assumption that in Cyprus Britain 'had to hold (her) position and make the best out of it'. The initiative for proposing some means to that end was taken by the Under-Secretary for Commonwealth Relations, Douglas Dodds-Parker. His suggestions included the following: the co-ordination of military, colonial and international policies by the head of the British Middle East Office (BMEO), which was in charge of development policy for British-controlled territories in the region; the use of a combination of warnings and promises in dealing with the Greek government, including an assurance that an elected assembly would be introduced in Cyprus; 'vigorous action' to turn the island into 'one of the commercial centres of the Levant'. The Foreign Office objected that the extension of BMEO authority over Cyprus might antagonise the colonial administration; secondly, it was not clear whether the new Governor was in favour of an elected assembly; thirdly, in the commercial and economic field, some progress could already be observed, but opportunities for expansion were small and political dividends slow to come.[142] This was probably the last time that economic development and trade expansion were given some thought as possible antidotes to Enosis. Harrison, reflecting the views of his political superiors, commented that the point was not to project the strategic importance of the island nor its political and economic development, but to make plain Britain's resolve not to discuss its future with Greece. Agreeing to discuss at some future date, he warned, 'would simply be the thin edge of the wedge'.[143]

These views were reflected in Eden's reply to Lena Jeger's parliamentary question on 15 March, which broke the moratorium on public statements observed since 1952. The repeated refusal to discuss Cyprus with Greece came on a day that Eden had mostly spent arguing in Cabinet in favour of a compromise with Egypt over the evacuation of the Suez Zone. Although Churchill was still opposed to the idea, there was agreement on the redeployment of British forces from the Zone to places like Cyprus, Libya and Jordan, from where Britain hoped to 'exert effective power' in the region.[144] What was more, Eden's reply in the Commons was given with little regard for Greek reactions[145] and without prior consultation with Ambassador Peake. The latter, having learnt of the statement from the Greek press, complained bitterly.[146]

Peake was still trying to avert a complete wreck of Anglo-Greek relations. Even before Eden's statement of 15 March, the Ambassador had proposed a renewed constitutional offer, partly as a means to 'stimulate American sympathy'. In his communications, he took care to stress that he was not preaching 'for the sake of improving Anglo-Greek relations', knowing that this particular cause did not appeal to Eden.[147] Peake's proposal was conveyed to Governor Armitage, whose thinking was evolving to a different direction. While admitting that the 1948 offer was no longer applicable, Armitage argued that the announcement of a new constitution had to wait until after the Greeks had their turn at the UN General Assembly. No constitutional proposal, he claimed, could stand a chance of success, unless the prospect of internationalisation was out of the way.[148] Peake's proposal was turned down[149] only to be taken up a few months later in order to win over American support.

Although the official position on Cyprus remained as rigid as ever, British visitors to Greece tended to hold out hopes for some relaxation in the future. In early April, Charles Mott-Radclyffe, Conservative MP, met leading Greek figures in Athens, including the royal couple, to whom he intimated that, 'in the long run', Britain's aim was to give Cyprus independence 'within or outside the Commonwealth'. This provoked the reaction of the Colonial Office, which reminded that official policy did not go beyond 'self-government within the Commonwealth'. Harrison, on the part of the Foreign Office, wondered whether it was not still the case that 'Cyprus, together with Malta, Gibraltar and Aden, is never to be given the right of complete secession'.[150] That was, of course, a rhetorical question, which proves that Hopkinson's notorious 'never' some three months later merely reflected a fairly common – though largely unspoken – assumption.

For some time, against Ambassador Peake's advice, British ministers went on replying to parliamentary questions undeterred. Between 26 January and 23 July 1954, the Cyprus question would be debated in parliament at least eight times.[151] In May, Parliamentary Under-Secretary Nutting assured Mostras that not only the Conservative Party but also the majority of the opposition were behind the government's position that neither Cyprus nor any other colonial issue could be a matter of discussion with a foreign power.[152]

The bid for external support

The main objective of British policy was to forestall a Greek recourse to the UN. Yet the time when it was possible to restrain the Greeks single-handed had long passed. As had been the case since 1950, the Americans were expected to help.[153] As much was requested in the *aide-mémoire* which the British Embassy delivered to the State Department on 28 January 1954. As the Americans took their time to reply, the Foreign Office soon abandoned its initial reserve and appealed to Ankara for support in pleading the British case with Washington.[154]

As has been noted, the British had always been tempted to play the Turkish card in their dealings with Greek officials as well as in their approaches to the Americans.[155] This is not to say that Turkish reactions were 'invented'[156] or even that they did not count for real. Turkey played a central role in British plans for the Middle East and London was always careful not to alienate Turkish opinion. Eden, in

particular, was quite disturbed by reports which arrived from both
Ankara and Nicosia during the second half of 1953, to the effect
that the Turks had 'little confidence' in the 'gentle' British methods
and felt 'discouraged' by signs of 'weakness' in the face of Enosis
agitation.[157] For this reason, the Foreign Office had resisted Governor Wright's demand for a representation to Ankara against the interference of various agencies in Turkish Cypriot community affairs.[158] When the matter was eventually raised, it was done in an
atmosphere of mutual understanding which ensured that the traffic
between Turkey and Cyprus would continue unhindered. There was
also some British funding of counter-Enosis activities in Turkey. According to American sources, this was done on an unofficial level,
on the initiative of Turkish organisations which solicited funds from
'British business'.[159]

Tolerating and making good use of Turkish interest in Cyprus
was one thing; soliciting the active support of Ankara against the
Greek recourse was quite another. One of the proponents of such a
course was Ambassador Knox Helm, who saw advantages in encouraging a counter-Enosis movement among the Turkish Cypriots. He also recommended the preferential treatment of Turkish
interests in Cyprus for the simple reason that, unlike Greece, Turkey did not advance a territorial claim on the island. Even if such a
claim developed in the future, Helm argued, it would pay the British well, if they 'quietly worked in with the Turks' and carry them
with British policy in the matter.[160] The Foreign Office, for its part,
admitted that it had 'no very concrete ideas' about how this could
be achieved and was wary of its effects on Anglo-Greek relations.[161]
Shortly before retiring, Wright expressed opposition to Anglo-Turkish co-operation.[162] Peake added his own qualms, warning that the
Greek-Turkish friendship was 'still a very tender plant'.[163] Even the
Embassy in Ankara was aware of the risk, lest, in the pursuit of
support against Enosis, the British led the Turks to expect 'something of the status of partnership in the Cyprus question'.[164] Reservations, however, would tend to recede as it became obvious that
Greece intended to raise the question at the UN General Assembly.

As it turned out, the attitude of both Washington and Ankara
would keep the British seething with anxiety for several months.
The Americans delayed their reply to the British request until July.

This 'flabbiness' – a term often used by British diplomats – was only in part explained by the current difficulties in relations between Dulles and Eden. Above all it was due to the delicate dilemmas facing US decision-makers. Thus, they increasingly pressed for some conciliatory gesture on the British part, preferably in the form of a new constitutional offer, which would enable them to support the continuation of colonial rule in Cyprus. On the other hand, US attitudes helped to reinforce British suspicions 'that the Americans are out to take our place in the Middle East'.[165]

The Menderes government, after its initial commitment to assist, also seemed to vacillate and refused to undertake further representations to Athens. It was not before August that Turkish support would be fully available. All this led the Foreign Office to consider strong *démarches* to both Ankara and Washington. It kept its temper, however, preferring less forceful methods of 'hotting up' the two powers.[166]

Much of the British government's ability to muster international support would, of course, depend on its line of defence on the UN floor. For some time, its contingency planning hinged on the question of competence. According to the British interpretation of Article 2(7) of the Charter, colonial issues – unlike those of trusteeship – fell within the domestic jurisdiction of the administering power and as such were exempted from discussion by UN bodies. The underlying objective was for Britain 'to be left alone to continue its work [in the colonies] without irresponsible criticism from the UN'.[167] On these grounds, the Colonial Office had always insisted that the British delegation should walk out of any debate dealing with Cyprus – as the French had done in the case of Morocco and Tunisia.[168] Yet the Foreign Office was well aware that this line of argument ran contrary to the prevailing trend of opinion in the UN,[169] and its prediction was that, in all probability, Greece should be able to muster a majority in favour of the inscription of a Cyprus item.[170]

With regard to self-determination – the probable basis of a Greek recourse – the British view, as expressed during the discussion of the issue by UN organs, could be summed up as follows: difficulties of definition apart, this was essentially 'a political principle that might have to be subordinated, in its application, to other principles, in particular the maintenance of peace'. In this spirit, the British delegation had voted against Resolution 637A (VII), which recommended that UN members 'recognise and promote' the 'right' of self-determination in the case of non-self-governing and trust territories.[171]

In mid-April, the Colonial Office took the initiative for an interdepartmental formulation of the response to the Greek recourse.[172] It was decided to start diplomatic preparations with the aim to prevent both the inclusion of the Cyprus question on the agenda and its discussion at committee level. Legal arguments should be combined with threats of a walk-out. Anxiety about the American delay in replying to British pleas was reflected in the suggestion of a new *démarche* which should emphasise the strategic argument and the exploitation of the controversy by the Communists. With respect to the Commonwealth and NATO states, Britain should stress the strategic value of Cyprus to NATO and the Middle East defence, the British record of 'good government' and Turkish reactions.[173] The Asian-Arab group should be approached through Pakistan and Iraq. To that end, Turkish services were required, a factor which was considered essential for the entire diplomatic effort.[174] Yet, despite the definition of aims, differences of opinion arose, particularly over tactics at the UN. As a result, the British diplomatic effort did not get off the ground until well into the summer.

Too late and too little: The 'constitutional offer'

The government's rigid line not only complicated its diplomatic effort abroad but was also coming in for criticism at home. To be sure, the Cyprus question had received little attention until Eden's statement of 15 March. From then on, reactions from the leading national papers multiplied: the *Observer* came out in support of self-government in Cyprus to be coupled with a pledge for a plebiscite in, say, ten years' time, even if it was all but certain that it would go in favour of Enosis. The *Manchester Guardian* wondered whether the British government could not agree to 'disentangle' long-term military interests from its present denial of 'an obstinately affirmed Hellenic character' of the island. The *Times* spoke of self-determination as a 'reasonable' prospect at the end of a pe-

riod of self-government and also argued that it was possible to safeguard British military interests 'even if the Cypriots eventually and
peacefully opted for union with Greece'.[175] On 1 May, the same
paper could see no harm in 'private and informal' Anglo-Greek
talks.[176] By July, even the *Economist* lamented Eden's 'frank but
over-brusque declaration' of 15 March, and criticised the government's 'inability' to recognise the 'sincerity and intensity' of Greek
Cypriot national sentiment.[177]

Things in Cyprus, as reflected in the political reports of the colonial authorities, also provided little comfort. The island, the Commissioner of Limassol reported in May, was 'passing through one of
these cycles, when nearly everyone ... has come to believe that Enosis
is on the way'. Civil servants could be seen taking part in 'Greek
nationalist occasions'. A novel feature of the situation, it was claimed,
was a serious crisis of confidence in Britain's resolve to retain her
grip on the island – not only the prospect of a Greek recourse to
the UN raised hopes of imminent liberation among the Greek Cypriots,[178] but even the colonial civil servants were doubtful about the
future and were inclined to adopt a 'wait and see' attitude.[179]

Under the circumstances it was only natural that Whitehall should
realise the shortcomings of a purely negative policy and start seeking an alternative. Peake's earlier proposal for a renewed constitutional offer was taken off the shelf. The Ambassador in Ankara saw
some merit and argued that the Turks might be 'well disposed' to it
if self-determination was excluded.[180] The deputy head of the British delegation to the UN also commented in favour, explaining that
the official line, which focused on the interpretation of Article 2(7),
could hardly win votes. Pierson Dixon suggested to Eden that, if
there was to be a constitutional offer, then it should be announced
shortly before the opening of the General Assembly.[181] From Washington Barbara Salt warned that if the current policy persisted, the
most that could be expected from the United States was an abstention from the vote on a Cyprus item, while a vote in favour could
not be excluded; a positive gesture, however, should enable the
Americans either to abstain or to support the British position, depending 'on how substantial and how public the gesture was'.[182]
Inside the Foreign Office, C.L.S. Cope of the Department for UN
Political Affairs added his own argument in favour stating that a

timely relaxation of British attitude might enable the Greeks to withdraw their appeal without losing face. Addressing the main objection to this argument, Cope hit the nail on the head: 'might not a
gesture made in 1955 seem more like weakness than one made in
1954? Might it not, in particular, seem like some recognition of
UN's right to prod us into acting in our Colonies?' The British themselves, he reminded his colleagues, had prodded the French in previous sessions, when the latter had boycotted debates on Morocco
and Tunisia.[183]

On 3 May, Harrison summed up the case for a thorough revision
of British policy. The Greek appeal could easily be exploited by 'un-
friendly powers', all the more since the British position seemed
devoid of 'constructive' elements; something should be done to al-
leviate the Greek government's feeling of 'being unnecessarily
snubbed by an old friend and ally'. Therefore, it should be informed
of British intentions and assured that the Cypriots would eventually
be given the right to self-determination. The remaining difficulty,
he pointed out, was the question of timing.[184] In conveying these
views to Hopkinson, the Parliamentary Under-Secretary for Colonial Affairs, Anthony Nutting did submit the idea of a statement
expressing Britain's 'eventual intention' to concede self-determination. The motive, he explained, was pure anxiety for 'the possible repercussions' of the Cyprus question on Britain's foreign relations.[185]

Eden, who was known to oppose 'appeasing' the Greeks, was
then in Geneva, devoting his energies to the settlement of the
Indochina problem. His Minister of State continued to state in reply
to parliamentary questions that the government was not prepared
to discuss Cyprus with Greece. Selwyn Lloyd himself, an experienced General Assembly 'player', had no illusions about Britain's
chances to defeat a Greek motion at the UN, if the latter was based
on self-determination. He himself wanted the British delegation to
take part in the debate, despite the claim that the question was one
of domestic jurisdiction.[186]

British ministers also found out that the current line on Cyprus
did not go down well with their partners in the Commonwealth.
The Canadians, on whom the British relied for canvassing the other
members, did not share their interpretation of Article 2(7) of the
UN Charter regarding the question of competence. They also com-

plained that the strategic value of Cyprus had never been adequately explained.[187]

Soon, the 'revisionist' trend was joined by the Governor of Cyprus himself. Armitage was now favour of a constitutional offer made in advance of the General Assembly. He further suggested a 'firm statement', though not of the type advocated by his predecessor: it should mention self-government, or, as Armitage put it, 'self-determination in internal affairs'; it might also go as far as to include a promise of eventual complete self-determination. Regarding Turkish Cypriot reactions, he thought that they could be met with adequate safeguards.[188]

Dissenting voices were initially few. The Ambassador in Ankara, Sir James Bowker, retorted that it was concern for political reactions at home and the effects on possessions such as Gibraltar and Malta that lay behind the British refusal to discuss Cyprus. These considerations, he implied, were still valid.[189] When the formulation of Cyprus policy entered its final phase, the Embassy would insist on safeguards, the exclusion of self-determination in particular, which would satisfy Turkey and secure the co-operation of the Turkish Cypriot community with the colonial authorities.[190]

Meanwhile, all three embassies involved in the question, Athens, Ankara and Washington, had been asking for clear guidance.[191] This only served to reinforce the sense that the time was 'overripe' for a statement of British policy.[192] By mid-June, the Colonial Office had prepared a draft policy paper which contained two alternative premises: one recognising ultimate self-determination for the Cypriots, and a second postulating the indefinite retention of British sovereignty, primarily for strategic reasons.[193]

When the draft was submitted to the Foreign Office for comment, Harrison's successor in the Southern Department, W. Hilary Young, did not hesitate to challenge the strategic imperative. To say that this dictated the indefinite retention of sovereignty over Cyprus, he pointed out, was tantamount to saying that the strategic situation would never change. He further wondered whether the rejection of the Greek offer of strategic facilities in return for Cyprus did not imply that the Greeks were considered no more reliable than the Egyptians.[194] Young should have known that, at least as far as Eden was concerned, this question was a rhetorical one.

What was more, the diplomats had come to resent the fact that
the Colonial Office had the upper hand in what was fast becoming
an essentially international problem.[195] Eventually, in an effort to
achieve interdepartmental consensus, a meeting was held at the
Foreign Office on 29 June in which the Foreign, Colonial and Commonwealth Offices were represented at ministerial level – Selwyn
Lloyd, Lord Reading and Dodds-Parker respectively. At the meeting, dissenting voices were few, notably that of Sir Frank Roberts,
Deputy Under-Secretary for Foreign Affairs. Those present reaffirmed the strategic imperative with all its concomitants: the indefinite retention of British sovereignty, the offer of self-government rather than self-determination, the deterioration of Anglo-
Greek relations, unpopularity in the UN. With regard to the Americans, Selwyn Lloyd argued that it was too much to expect full support, though an offer of self-government should have a positive impact. The meeting ended by urging the diplomats to 'concert' with
the Colonial Office in preparing a Cabinet paper.[196]

There followed a lower-level meeting on 1 July, in which Armitage was present. A few weeks after he had expressed himself in
favour of eventual self-determination, the Governor now argued
that there could be no chance for constitutional progress and stability, unless the Cypriots were convinced of Britain's resolve to retain
sovereignty.[197] A few arrests, he claimed, would suffice to keep things
under control. The only reservation was expressed by Harrison, the
outgoing head of the Southern Department, who questioned the
expediency of arresting Greek Cypriot leaders on the eve of the
UN General Assembly. It was further agreed that the situation called
for a constitution 'less liberal' than that of 1948, and that it would
'take a long time to prepare' it.[198] This made it clear that the whole
thing was little more than a tactical manoeuvre, dictated by the need
to defeat the Greeks at the UN.[199]

Now Armitage had fairly clear terms of reference in preparing
his constitutional offer. Attempting to draw lessons from Winster's
bitter experience, he suggested that any new constitution 'should
be imposed without any prior consultation'. The Governor favoured
a corporatist model providing for a semi-appointed legislature, with
the minority drawn from organised interest groups rather than constituencies; suffrage should be limited to men, and communal rep-

resentation was to be upheld. Armitage proposed a legislature of thirty three seats: fifteen elected (twelve Greek and three Turkish Cypriots), six *ex-officio* and twelve members nominated by the government.[200] Realising the essentially unattractive character of his plan, the Governor started talking of it as a 'first step along the road of constitutional advancement'.[201] He also insisted on creating 'an appropriate atmosphere' by enforcing the anti-seditious legislation of his predecessor.[202]

The draft Cabinet paper on Cyprus policy was ready on 20 July. It was primarily the work of the Colonial Office and incorporated the Governor's proposals. It addressed both the political status of the island and the question of British tactics at the UN. On the first score, it concluded the following: 1) strategic reasons (i.e. those defined by the COS in 1950) dictated the retention of full sovereignty for the foreseeable future; 2) the prospect of ultimate self-determination should not be raised, since it might be interpreted as a sign of weakness; 3) a constitution less liberal than the one of 1948 should be 'imposed at the earliest practicable date'; and 4) the Governor could take all necessary steps 'to ensure the enforcement of existing laws'.

Regarding tactics at the UN, the draft paper went back to the standard line of defence: the inscription of the Greek item should be opposed mainly on the grounds of domestic jurisdiction and, if it was inscribed or came in for debate, the British delegation could threaten to withdraw. With respect to the anticipated deterioration of Anglo-Greek relations, the paper only called for a combination of 'firmness with courtesy', against Papagos' 'firm but conciliatory policy'; nor was much reliance placed on the United States: the aim should be to prevent it from supporting the Greek case.[203] The draft paper reached the Cabinet on 24 July. As Churchill would admit a few weeks later, it 'slipped through at the end of Business without detailed consideration'.[204] As it happened, a blueprint of policy had been approved which entirely failed to take into account the changing climate of opinion about the course of British policy. Its patent inadequacy would be revealed a few days later.

Voices in the wilderness

Hopkinson's statement in the Commons on 28 July provoked the
first major debate on Cyprus policy and helped reveal some of the
assumptions behind it. The notorious 'never', for one thing, was
compatible with the concept of strategic colonies, elaborated by
the Labour Fabian Bureau nine years earlier. There was nothing extraordinary in the position, expressed by Hopkinson, that 'the exact
degree of independence which a colony could achieve would depend on its circumstances'. The opposition of Turkey to Enosis was
more than a tactical excuse, given her importance for British strategy in the Middle East. In comparison, Greece was reduced to an
unreliable, second-rate ally. Last but not least, the British withdrawal
from the Suez Zone could only reinforce the strategic imperative
for keeping Cyprus. The debate also revealed various other perceptions and prejudices entertained by members of parliament: that
the Cypriots were neither Greek nor European; that only a minority really wanted Enosis; that there would be enough of them to
come forward and co-operate in putting the constitutional offer to
effect; that Greece not only was a bad administrator but could always turn Communist; that Cyprus was second best to the Suez Zone.
    The debate gave the Labour opposition the opportunity to re-
mind the government of the bitter fruits of British obstinacy elsewhere in the Middle East and issue warnings about the future: a
strategic stronghold first and foremost required the consent and
co-operation of the local population; the Greek Cypriots' desire for
Enosis was widespread and genuine; the government's intransigence
over Cyprus was a sop to the 'Suez Group', which had bitterly opposed the Anglo-Egyptian accord only hours earlier.[205]
    The government's performance in parliament drew criticism
from official circles, too. The Cyprus officer at the Colonial Office,
talking to a member of the US Embassy, admitted that there had
been only limited preparations for a debate following Hopkinson's
opening statement. 'In this', he complained, the Under-Secretary
'had gone completely off his prepared brief and taken an unfortunately rigid stand against eventual independence'.[206] It seemed reasonable, therefore, to attribute his 'never' to a lapse. Regarding Lyttelton's reference to Greece as a friendly but unstable power, the

same official also attributed it to 'a slip of the tongue' before 'an aroused and angry Opposition'.[207] Foreign Office minutes reveal that, though 'wounding and tactless', Lyttelton's remark reflected a common assumption, which for the sake of diplomatic propriety ought to have remained unspoken.[208] As Young minuted, there was 'nothing to be gained from seeking to convince the Greeks that they are unstable'.[209]

The debate in parliament had brought forward a point on which even bitter critics of the government policy were in agreement: Britain needed a 'firm base' on Cyprus.[210] On this basis, Labour MP Woodrow Wyatt had advanced a plausible alternative to sovereignty over the entire island: Britain, he argued, could retain 'a kind of Hong Kong', namely a 'permanent cession' of territory sufficient to provide for her military requirements. This solution, he pointed out, would be 'consistent with the rights of the inhabitants of the country concerned'.[211]

Wyatt's suggestion, which in fact presaged what Britain actually got after Cyprus became independent,[212] was taken up in the Foreign Office, where revisionist tendencies once more surfaced following the fiasco of the 'new' Cyprus policy. Kirkpatrick, the Permanent Under-Secretary for Foreign Affairs,[213] wondered whether a 'free lease' of territory, in the pattern of Hong Kong or of the US base in British West Indies, might not provide the best answer to longer-term British military needs; if that was found to be the case, Greece could be told that, 'in a calmer time',[214] a solution could be discussed. In a memorandum to Selwyn Lloyd and Eden, dated 10 August, Kirkpatrick proceeded to question the entire premise of Cyprus policy. Drawing on his personal experience[215] and the fast changing strategic environment,[216] he disputed both the validity of the strategic imperative and the expediency of keeping a colony against rising political and financial costs; such a policy, he argued, found no strong public support in England, whereas international opinion was on the Greek side. The situation, he concluded, called for 'bold and imaginative efforts', whatever the final choice.[217]

Before submitting the memorandum, Kirkpatrick had shown it to Hopkinson, who, surprisingly, concurred 'generally'.[218] His bid for a revision of policy was supported by Young and Under-Secretary Roberts. The former, while seeing only disadvantages in either keeping or ceding Cyprus, admitted that the COS dictum of 1950 was out of keeping with current realities.[219] Roberts elaborated on this further, pointing at the recent U-turn in government policy on the Suez Zone and Churchill's assessment of the 'revolutionary' impact of the hydrogen bomb on strategy. If a deal was struck over Cyprus, Roberts argued, the British should be able to safeguard their bases, even if Greece turned Communist. With regard to the prospect of a Greek-Turkish crisis, which seemed to worry Young, he was confident that the Turks could get a good deal for their minority, given the existence of a 'much richer' Greek community in Istanbul. Roberts was in favour of talking to the Greeks and predicted severe strains on Britain's international relations, if the current policy continued.[220] The Commonwealth Relations Office added its own misgivings: the line taken on Cyprus threatened to undermine its efforts to cultivate Commonwealth opinion in favour of British colonial policy.[221]

Once again, the political leadership of the Foreign Office proved impermeable to change. Only corrective action was deemed necessary, which would evolve in three directions: the dampening of anti-sedition in Cyprus; a fresh assessment of the island's strategic importance by the COS; and a 'publicity' campaign designed to win support for the government's Cyprus policy at home and, primarily, abroad.

As it happened, the brand for the apparent fiasco of the constitutional offer and its concomitants was borne by the Governor of Cyprus. Instead of pre-empting criticism, anti-sedition had resulted in a public relations disaster. When the British press lashed out against the confiscation of newspapers and other related incidents, Churchill took a personal interest in the matter. This one-time Liberal found it intolerable that local papers were being persecuted for reproducing 'in a seditious context' material from the British press. He blamed Armitage for choosing a most slippery ground on which to make a stand, disregarding the fact that the Governor had obtained advance approval for his actions. Churchill also decided to have the matter reopened in Cabinet and asked the new Secretary of State for the Colonies, Lennox Boyd, to 'summon the Governor home in the near future'.[222] When this visit took place in October, Armitage would have to fight hard to keep his anti-seditious arsenal intact, conceding only an amendment of the press law.[223]

The strategic imperative revisited

As requested, the COS dutifully prepared a re-evaluation of the strategic imperative. The context was quite different from that of four years earlier. After successive failures to build a regional arrangement around Egypt and the Suez Zone, the British had turned to the 'Outer Ring' of states in order to preserve a role in Middle East security. In this new effort, Ankara proved an eager partner. The Turkish-Pakistani agreement in April 1954 was the first step, followed by earnest Turkish approaches to Iraq and Iran.[224] Therefore, it is hardly surprising that Eden came to rate the alliance with Turkey 'as the first consideration' in British policy in the Near East.[225] This factor only added to the British determination to retain Cyprus.

The military Chiefs' study began with a general outline of British security objectives: to prevent war by maintaining the economic strength of the 'Free World' and aiding 'backward' countries against Communist infiltration; to create stability and contain communism by building alliances and rearming; and, above all, to strengthen Britain's position as a major power and maintain her influence worldwide. The COS reaffirmed the vital importance of the Middle East and Britain's special role there because of her 'long-established economic interests', treaty obligations and the need to safeguard Commonwealth sea and air communications. The fulfilment of that role, they argued, militated against the cession of Cyprus to Greece. Although both powers belonged to NATO and their interests would coincide in global war, this might not be the case in regional emergencies. Thus, they tried to counter the American view, to the effect that it did not really matter which power controlled Cyprus, provided it was an allied one.[226]

With regard to the strategic role of Cyprus, the COS envisaged it not so much in the framework of global or even allied strategy, but rather in the context of Britain's own status and contingency planning for an increasingly unstable, nationalistic and anti-British Middle East. Although the island could never really take the place of the Canal Zone, it offered the only sure base from where to 'exert British influence and to meet sudden emergencies of any kind'. Citing the haunting analogy of Egypt, the COS once again objected to a deal whereby the United Kingdom would only retain military rights by treaty.[227]

As a matter of fact, three quarters of a century after its acquisition, Cyprus was about to assume the role of a 'place of arms' that
Benjamin Disraeli had envisaged in 1878.[228] Following the Anglo-
Egyptian agreement of 19 October 1954, it was decided that a 'permanent garrison' of no more than 9-10,000 troops be set up in
Cyprus. Construction work for installations at Episkopi and Dhekelia
and an airfield at Akrotiri had already begun during 1954.[229]

Compared to the 80,000 strong Suez garrison, the projected
British force on Cyprus should look a token one. Yet, at that junc-
ture, the British position in the Middle East rested upon symbols
rather than substance. Cyprus was the 'only remaining British territory' in the region and to cede it on the heels of the decision to
evacuate Suez, the COS sternly warned, would be a further blow to
Britain's prestige and credibility in the entire region.[230] These two
latter factors were all-important elements in Eden's proposal for a
gradual and calculated reduction of British commitments in the
Middle East, which the country's financial predicament urgently
required.[231] The official obsession with projecting an unflinching
image against mounting nationalistic pressures found a convenient
outlet in Cyprus.

The 'publicity' campaign

On the 'publicity' front, a steering ministerial committee[232] undertook to sell Britain's case at home and abroad. It met twice in early
September, and decided to lay stress on the strategic value of the
island, the risk of Communist subversion and Turkish reactions. The
main target areas would be the United States, where the British
case was getting a bad press, and the countries of the Commonwealth, Western and Northern Europe, and the Eastern Mediterranean.[233]

The strategic imperative was projected, as has been seen, by
making extensive use of the latest COS study. The 'red peril', on the
other hand, was an argument that the British had always felt inclined to use in order to discredit Enosis.[234] In September 1954, it
was considered the best excuse for the unpopular anti-sedition campaign. The British Information Service (BIS) saw to it that US opinion makers were furnished with Communist radio and press com-

ment supporting the national cause of the Greek Cypriots.[235] Enosis was portrayed as an issue 'gradually exploited and blown up by the Communists, both in Cyprus and Greece, as a Cold War gambit, until the Greek Government felt obliged to come forward themselves as its public champion'.[236] Yet, after a three-month effort, John Russell of the BIS office in New York cautioned that Cyprus was not a subject on which the British could expect to swing American opinion.[237]

The third objective of British propaganda was to 'get Turkish views reported as extensively as possible'.[238] This ran parallel with the close Anglo-Turkish co-operation on the diplomatic front. Turkish arguments against Enosis were channelled to the foreign press, while British services arranged all possible publicity for Turkish Cypriot parties visiting London and New York during the session of the General Assembly.[239]

The propaganda campaign was also extended to Cyprus, too, where a Public Information Office was set up,[240] benefitting from the 'energy and imagination' of its director, Lawrence Durrell, the famous author who had been staying in the island since 1953.[241] Apart from cultivating foreign journalists, the Office sought to project the disparity beween Greece and the colony in such matters as living standards, legal rights and obligations – conscription in particular – in an effort to convince the Cypriots that they were better off under British rule. It also tried to cultivate Turkish Cypriot opinion.[242] At one point, Durrell proposed the appointment of a Turkish cultural attaché to Cyprus, but the Foreign Office objected.[243]

The home front was a further task. To be sure, with the exception of the 'Bevanite' left-wing of the Labour Party and the severly reduced Liberals, there was no great support for an immediate transfer of sovereignty in Cyprus. Labour pronouncements on Cyprus, like the Scarborough Resolution, were more 'anti-Tory' than a pledge to concrete action. Yet they inspired fears in official circles lest the government's case went by default. At Selwyn Lloyd's suggestion, a White Paper was prepared.[244] Under pressure from Nicosia, the Foreign Office also undertook to 'engineer' one or two statements from 'known Enosis sympathisers' in Britain which could have a sobering effect on optimistic nationalists.[245]

Regarding the 'war of words' launched by the Greek press and radio since the summer of 1954, the British government at first adopted a benign attitude, refusing to respond in kind.[246] It was only a month after the inscription of the Greek item that Eden urged the steering committee under Hopkinson to retaliate. British 'publicity' should expose the alleged role of the Greek government in fomenting sedition in Cyprus, its intolerance of internal criticism, the 'religious pressure' of the Ethnarchy on the faithful, and, of course, the Communist connection.[247] Inspired questions should also help bring the 'hostile tone of Greek broadcasts' to the attention of the parliament.[248] This counter-offensive, however, was conducted in a rather dilatory manner. Young admitted that the only outcome was 'four rather unexciting pamphlets about communism and the Greek Orthodox Church' and one article in the *Times*.[249] Eden was exasperated. Those in charge of 'publicity', he minuted, should stop bothering about 'avoid[ing] to annoy the Greek government'.[250] By the time the battle at the UN General Assembly was over, there would be more guidelines and little action. Hopkinson's committee had already reached the conclusion that publicity, unless it was 'of a very startling nature', such as gun-running, was unlikely to influence voting at the UN. Hence, it was decided to focus on opinion in Cyprus and Britain, with the aim to discredit Enosis leaders, Makarios in particular.[251]

In a related effort, the British sponsored the activities of Turkish Cypriot delegations abroad. They also attempted to fish in the troubled waters of Balkan ethnic politics. In October, their delegation to the UN was approached by Rev Luben Dimitroff, a leading member of a Bulgarian-Macedonian immigrant organisation, who offered to co-operate in harassing the Greeks at the UN. Dimitroff asked the British to sponsor a petition to the UN Secretary-General denouncing repression in Greek Macedonia. The delegation liked the idea, while the Foreign Office, in true Machiavellian fashion, let it be known that, although it could not be openly associated with the petition, it would 'not be sorry to see it circulated'.[252] Eventually, a text was submitted, provoking the Greek delegation to speak of an unholy collusion between 'British gentlemen and criminal *comitadjis*'.[253]

UN tactics

Until the eve of the General Assembly, tactics at the UN continued to be a matter of debate. The Colonial Office was the hardliner, asking that member states be warned in advance of British determination not only to walk out from any discussion of the Cyprus question but also to refuse co-operation on all colonial matters. To sanction a discussion by being present, it argued, would be against the best traditions of British colonial policy in the UN.[254] The Foreign Office was more concerned with preserving Britain's image 'as the leader of moderate Western opinion'.[255] Under the impact of US and Commonwealth objections,[256] the Foreign Office decided to reserve its position on a walk-out and to drop the non-cooperation threat altogether. Realising that the British interpretation of the domestic jurisdiction clause alone could not attract many votes, it focused on arguments of expediency including the risk of setting a 'dangerous precedent' for border stability, strategic considerations and Turkish reactions.[257]

On the eve of the opening session, the picture at the General Assembly was hardly encouraging. The only concrete achievements had been the promise of the Scandinavian countries to vote against inscription, and of India, Pakistan, Iraq and Iran to abstain. Although the US decision to abstain had been expected, its announcement was received as a 'body blow' to the hopes of mustering a majority against inscription.[258] Anticipating the outcome, Dixon had already suggested a moratorium, whereby the General Committee, leaving the question of competence aside, would suggest that the Greek item should not be discussed during the current session of the General Assembly. This suggestion, first submitted on 10 September, actually presaged the eventual resolution, three months later. It was also taken up by the US delegation and won State Department approval. Yet, at that point, it was rejected by the Foreign Office, which still preferred a straight fight.[259]

The first results were disappointing and the adverse vote at the General Committee was followed by the unsuccessful attempt to have the matter deferred. The British delegation justified its fateful decision to abstain on the Iraqi motion as 'a nice calculation of the advantage of impartiality'.[260] For Cabot Lodge, however, the US

permanent representative, it was sheer lack of organisation and forward planning.[261] The final result of the vote in plenary did give
some cause of satisfaction, since the British had achieved the best
vote ever recorded on a colonial issue, while the Greeks were a
long way from the two-thirds majority required for a decision.[262]

Anticipating the inscription of the Greek item, the Foreign Office had been preparing its second line of defence. The original objective was to prevent the passage of any resolution, and, if possible,
to do it in such a way that would discourage the Greeks from raising
the issue year after year. This, of course, was too ambitious a task.
What worried the British most was the prospect of a Greek draft
moderate enough to muster a majority in the General Assembly.
Therefore, they consistently urged friendly delegations not to take
interest in a mild text, but, rather, to let the Greeks table a resolution calling for concrete action, which would be easier to assail for
violating Britain's domestic jurisdiction.[263] Again, things did not look
safe. Having declared their intention to walk out,[264] the British be-
latedly realised that such a move would deprive them of any control
over subsequent proceedings. What was more, there were still grave
doubts about US attitude, despite Dulles' assurances to Churchill.
In this climate, Young reiterated Dixon's earlier proposal for a procedural motion 'not to discuss' the item, which would bar further
action at the UN.[265]

Owing to reactions from the Colonial Office[266] and tactical reasons, the official line continued to be for a straight fight.[267] Thus,
the American proposal for a postponement motion was rejected
not only because it left the door open to future discussion, but also
because the Foreign Office did not wish to 'release' Dulles from his
promise to oppose any resolution.[268] The apparent half-heartedness
of the Americans, Lodge's refusal to canvass against the Greeks in
particular,[269] and the risk of the item being postponed for the next
session[270] rendered the procedural formula increasingly attractive.[271]
After a further disappointing meeting with Lodge, Nutting, who
had taken charge of the delegation in New York, asked Eden for 'a
wide measure of discretion' in determining tactics in the UN.[272]
This was granted,[273] and the 'not to discuss' formula was put to the
Americans. From that point onwards, the two delegations would
act in concert. With regard to the phrasing of the motion,[274] the

Foreign Office preferred to remain flexible, its main aim being 'a good majority'. Thus, it was prepared to acquiesce in the preambular amendment later proposed by Colombia and El Salvador.[275] The onus, it was maintained, would be on the Greek side to prove that any future time was right to consider the issue.[276]

The offer that was not to be

Pending the outcome of the Greek recourse, the internal aspect of the Cyprus question was given its due of interdepartmental attention. Both Armitage and the Colonial Office insisted that there could be no prospect of constitutional advance until the Cyprus item had been disposed of at the UN.[277] Within the Foreign Office, however, the Southern Department remained the hotbed of bureaucratic initiative. In early October, Young, Wilding and their colleagues laid out two alternative approaches that were to dominate the discourse on Cyprus policy until the outbreak of violence half a year later. The first provided for the transformation of Cyprus into a 'British' island and its people into 'willing members of the Commonwealth' by a 'judicious mixture of severity and liberal constitutionalism' – a process envisaged by the Governor and the Colonial Office. The second reflected ideas advanced on several past occasions,[278] which aimed at a partial recognition of the national and cultural ties between Greece and Cyprus – dual nationality, an extended cultural convention[279] and closer trade links. These concessions, it was further proposed, should be extended to Turkey as well. In fact, the Southern Department had taken up an idea first advanced by the *Economist* in July,[280] whereby both countries would be given a say in Cypriot affairs through the appointment of two Ministers Resident, one Greek and one Turk, in Nicosia. In October 1954, the Southern Department had cautiously recommended it as 'the most practicable policy',[281] and, viewed in retrospect, it was an obvious precursor to the 1958 MacMillan plan for a tripartite condominium.

Other sections of the Foreign Office were much more attracted to the idea of developing 'Cypriotism'.[282] Yet, even there, the futility of the current Cyprus policy was clearly recognised. As W. Selby, who acted as a liaison with the Colonial Office, predicted:

If we go on stressing our determination to stay on Cyprus *ad infinitum* and that the Cypriots will never be free to determine their own future, I am quite sure that public opinion abroad and at home will, and before very long, drive us out of the Island.[283]

By early December, the division of opinion between the Governor and the Colonial Office, on the one hand, and the Southern Department on the other, had come to the fore. The former's reluctance to proceed with constitutional development and his advocacy of repression,[284] was denounced by Young as 'despondent and negative'. The head of the Southern Department was exasperated with the tendency of the colonial apparatus to attribute 'the ills of Cyprus' to Greek interference 'and not to any failings in (their) own policy or administration'.[285] Wilding was equally critical.[286]

In this constant interplay between realism and inhibition, the Southern Department proved admirably capable of proposing ways for putting into effect a policy in which it apparently did not believe. Young's minutes contain a number of proposals designed to strengthen Britain's grip on Cyprus: firstly, the reform of the educational system by establishing closer links with the colonial metropolis; towards this end, Young suggested the setting up of a university or a university college in the island; secondly, a generous investment programme, which *inter alia* would provide for a new harbour, tourist facilities and a new broadcasting station; thirdly, the stiffening of anti-sedition laws.[287] It should be noted that Eden would later find this set of ideas particularly to his taste.[288]

Right after the conclusion of the General Assembly, Churchill called all sections involved in the Cyprus question to join in producing 'a firm and realistic policy for the future'.[289] The Colonial Office faithfully recapitulated the familiar set of 'conceivably possible' alternatives. Among these, it listed Greek and Turkish co-operation on specific issues, provided that British sovereignty was recognised.[290] In its subsequent recommendation to the Prime Minister, it concluded that all courses other than the current one presented 'insuperable difficulties'. Formal talks with Greece were also rejected on the grounds that they would be interpreted as a sign of weakness – hence a blow to British prestige.[291] Eden, Armitage and Peake subscribed to this conclusion.[292] What remained was unilat-

eral British action, probably in the form of a new statement.
Early in the new year, the Colonial Office was briefed on the
state of Cypriot affairs by Fletcher Cooke, the Colony's Secretary.
His assessment was that the constitutional offer had no chance of
being accepted by Greek and Turkish Cypriots alike and that no
progress could be made in this respect unless the Greek government stopped supporting Enosis. He assured, however, that the situation was 'not explosive' and could remain under control 'until
Doomsday', if only the Governor was allowed to proceed with his
long-advocated combination of repression and financial incentive.
With regard to the latter, Armitage had contended that nothing was
more likely to convince the Cypriots of Britain's intention to stay
than large-scale projects such as port development.[293] Similar ideas
were current in Colonial Office circles, as can be surmised from
Dodds-Parker's memoranda.[294] Yet political uncertainty and financial stringency militated against development schemes. As Fletcher-
Cooke's interview revealed, owing to 'the scare of Enosis', the five-
year plan of the colonial administration could raise no money on
the London market. Whitehall, for its part, not only refused to underwrite this bid openly but had curtailed its own 'Colonial Development and Welfare' allocation for the same period.[295]

Having been overshadowed by New York for some time, the Athens Embassy re-entered the debate. Peake estimated that, under
pressure from Makarios and the Church, the Greek government
would redouble its efforts. He also warned that nationalist circles in
Greece would try to undermine 'by fair means or foul' any constitutional initiative in Cyprus.[296] With respect to future policy, Peake
also faced the stifling dilemma of how to make a breakthrough without appearing to be yielding to pressure. As a possible way out, he
proposed a discussion at the NATO Council, in an effort to redress
the impact of Hopkinson's 'never', and reiterated his old recipe of
increased imports or some investment as a means of building goodwill in Greece.[297] The Embassy Counsellor, Anthony Lambert, who
visited London, suggested a combination of ultimate self-determination with immediate 'strong measures' as the only conceivable
way out of the stalemate.[298]

Slowly, the 'stick and carrot' combination gained ground. The
Foreign Office was certain to support it.[299] Nutting, who had greatly

benefited from his recent experience at the General Assembly, summed up the merits of the recognition of self-determination, even at an unspecified, distant future: it would win the wholehearted support of the United States and others at the UN; it could give the Greek government a good excuse not to proceed with a second recourse; and it might secure enough support for a new constitution in Cyprus. The Minister of State warned of grave dangers ahead, if the current 'policy of drift' continued.[300] The attractions of a liberal constitution cum ultimate self-determination were further expounded by Patrick Maitland in a personal letter to Eden, following his visits to Athens and Nicosia.[301] In another volte-face, Armitage came out in favour too, while anxiously seeking to make contact with Makarios.[302]

Once again, the task of formulating a blueprint was relegated to the Colonial Office. This time, it proposed an indirect and qualified recognition of the principle of self-determination, which could be phrased in a double negative: although a change in the status of Cyprus could not be foreseen 'at present', the government could declare that it saw 'no reason why, when the international situation permits and when a system of internal self-government has been fully developed and successfully worked, we should not reach agreement with the Cypriots on this question'.[303] With regard to the new constitution, provision was made for a legislature with a narrow majority of elected members.[304] When Eden saw the text, he asked for a further safeguard requiring a two-thirds majority for any motion affecting the question of sovereignty. As was the case with previous schemes, the underlying assumption was that constitutional life might foster 'a vested interest in remaining separate from Greece'.[305]

When these proposals came for discussion between the Foreign and Colonial Secretaries, on 23 March, Eden made it clear that he accepted the recognition of ultimate self-determination only as a tactical manoeuvre, designed to rally support at the UN and gain time for British rule in Cyprus. He also insisted on two preconditions: the first stemmed from his mistrust for the Greeks, to whom no foretaste of British intentions should be given, lest it was construed as a sign of weakness. Secondly, the Turkish government had to be taken into full confidence and be assured that the British had no intention to hand Cyprus to Greece.[306] Considering Turkey the principal prop of British policy in the Middle East, Eden would do nothing to prejudice her continuing support and goodwill.[307] By way of logical extension, this meant the recognition of a virtual Turkish veto on Cyprus policy – 'should [the Turks'] reaction be violently hostile', Nutting told Lennox Boyd, 'we might even have to think again about our proposals'.[308]

By late March, the situation looked ripe for positive action and Armitage was ready to proceed.[309] Peake was eager to give King Paul some advance notice of British intentions: the King, he reported, awaited the signal to step in and 'induce his Ministers to be sensible'.[310] Interest in the British Parliament had revived.[311] The Americans had been urging an accommodation all along and had recently despatched a State Department official to London, Athens and Nicosia.[312] In the event the government took its time. Eden always insisted on giving the Turks advance notice and thus ruled out any chance of a statement before the Easter parliamentary recess.[313] By 1 April, the new policy had not yet reached the Cabinet.

That morning, Young had just signed a despatch to Ms Salt in Washington, briefing her on the state of Cyprus policy, when the news of EOKA bombing attacks broke in. Young noted down a first-hand reaction in postscript: the timing of the new constitutional offer would 'almost certainly be affected by this outbreak of violence'.[314] As it happened, it would soon be counted among its fatalities: the new Prime Minister, Eden, would have the plan shelved as his estrangement from the Greeks and his attachment to the Turkish alliance became complete.

A 'gutless' people?

With rare exceptions, the use of force in the pursuit of Enosis was never considered a serious contingency by British officials. Despite occasional outbreaks of violence, such as the Paphos riots in June 1953, the colonial authorities continued to speak of a 'mass of moderate, law-abiding people, who privately deplored extremism'.[315] There was a widespread conviction that not only the terrain but the Cypriot character were not conducive to armed struggle.[316] This trend of thought persisted right up to the end. After a four-day visit

to the island, S.H. Evans, of the Colonial Office Information Department, wrote of the Cypriots' 'tribal temperament' that was translated as 'niceness, lethargy or plain lack of guts'.[317] During the parliamentary debate on Cyprus on 22 October 1954, a Conservative
MP, Dick Brooman-White, exclaimed: 'It seems inconceivable that
the Cypriots should become vicious like the Egyptians.'[318] Durrell,
who had a much longer experience of the island and its people, was
no less optimistic.[319] Interestingly enough, Colonel Grivas also considered the Cypriot character, moulded by centuries of foreign domination, a 'disadvantage' to his insurrectionary plans.[320] All these
views, however, disregarded the Greek community's considerable
record of violence in local politics, trade unionism and social life.[321]
Equally overlooked was the risk of 'imported' violence.[322]

Official complacency was not due to lack of warning. In early
September 1954, Georgios Hryssafinis, a former member of the
Executive Council, warned that 'irresponsible' elements from Greece
might come to Cyprus and commit acts of violence.[323] By December, the colonial authorities were aware of 'rumours' regarding the
arrival of 'Greek extremists' and arms smuggling. Although the prospect of violence was held up in order to justify the pleas for a get
tough policy, the administration continued to regard the Communists – not the nationalists – as the main threat to peace.[324] Perhaps,
the more far-sighted judge of the situation was Ambassador Peake
who alone took the prospect of violence seriously in the aftermath
of Greek failure at the UN. On 10 December, he warned:

What I have in mind is the possibility that the next stage in the Enosis
campaign may be smuggling of arms and explosives into Cyprus; the oc-
currence of outrages resulting in bloodshed which may force the Government there to take repressive measures. If blood should flow in Cyprus, I
do not for a moment think that the Greeks would pause to consider who
was at fault... The impulse to moral fervour and moral indignation, which
is so far lacking, would at once have been supplied, and Anglo-Greek friendship would vanish overnight.[325]

Even the seizure of the 'Agios Georgios' and the arrest of several
men on the spot failed to put the authorities on the alert. As
Crawshaw observed, 'the relative ease with which the plot was dis-

covered and its perpetrators brought to trial may well have induced a sense of false security in British official circles'.[326] Indeed, on the day that the 'Aghios Georghios' was being seized, a Colonial official in London noted that the island authorities were 'sufficient' to deal with any kind of emergency 'that can at present be considered even remotely possible' despite the fact that the colony possessed an understaffed and underpaid police force in a state of neglect – as London was by then well aware.[327]

Equally misplaced was the marked tendency among British colonial and diplomatic circles to dispute the national identity of the Greek Cypriots on grounds of racial origin. Selwyn Lloyd did likewise before the General Assembly during the debate on the inscription of the Greek item. This contention was criticised in the columns of the British press and in parliament as pointless and self-defeating. Before long, colonial and diplomatic officials came to realise that to dispute the national self-identification of the Cypriots by the use of terms, such as 'Greek-speaking Cypriots', only stimulated anti-British feeling. The disadvantages were clear to those who understood that they could 'get nowhere' in Cyprus without the loyalty, or at least, the acquiescence of the Greek majority.[328]

More deep-rooted was the tendency to underestimate pro-Enosis feeling both in Greece and Cyprus. The Embassy in Athens repeatedly questioned the 'strength and momentum' of the Enosis movement[329] or the depth of public emotion.[330] British officials found it hard to understand how the Greek Cypriots could ever prefer the material hardships, which a transfer to Greek rule was bound to entail. Some in the Foreign Office seemed to hope that, for economic reasons, a majority of the Greek Cypriots 'would probably prefer independence to Enosis', a view shared by British residents in Cyprus.[331] The colonial administrators had traditionally attributed Enosis to a minority made up of the Orthodox hierarchy, the Communists and the literate, and generally disputed its authenticity. Instead, they often referred to a 'silent majority' that supported British rule.[332] As late as July 1954, Armitage assured the Cabinet that 'only a minority in Greece and Cyprus' really demanded Enosis.[333] Even in the thick of the UN confrontation, there were several repetitions of what was essentially wishful thinking.[334] British communications to foreign governments still targeted the Greek government as the prime mover of irredentist agitation, implying that a change of policy in Athens would deflate the Enosis movement.[335]

The alleged traits of the Cypriot character were often used to draw a rather deceptive picture. The British 'publicity' campaign made much of the 'calm, apathy and friendliness' as well as the 'natural' compliance of the Cypriot in an effort to explain away Enosis as the result of either foreign interference or the, primarily moral, pressure of the Church.[336] There were also attempts to explain the Enosis campaign as motivated by ecclesiastical self-interest. The Church, it was argued, only wished to safeguard its rights, both spiritual and material, from the encroachments of a tactless civil administration. This was the view of Lord Quickswood, best man and life-long friend of Winston Churchill, who thought that the Archbishop of Canterbury and his advisers were better suited to deal with Makarios than an 'ordinary diplomatist or official'.[337] Curiously, this view was, at least in part, shared by Armitage. In seeking to establish contact with the Archbishop in the early part of 1955, he claimed that he could strike some common ground by appraising Makarios as to the risks of union with Greece for 'the position of the Church and its properties'.[338]

Yet private assessments were quite different: despite his crucial role in official propaganda, Durrell the writer would later give a vivid description of the 'suffocating inertia' and bitter frustration prevailing in the island in the months before violence.[339] Visitors with less local experience were no less perceptive. In late October 1954, the First Secretary on Information of the British Embassy in Ankara, K.S. Butler, reported: 'Travelling through the island … the sullen and resentful attitude of the Greek population was noticeable in all Greek areas; Enosis slogans and the Greek flag were much in evidence'.[340] The following year Patrick Maitland despondently observed that 'Both a sense of economic frustration and a whole range of affronts at the Greek character of most of the people, have built up an escapist mood for which Enosis is the name'.[341] Graffiti next to the coffee shop of the village of Alona captured that mood: 'We want Greece and may we eat stones'.[342]

NOTES

1. Louis 1984, 207-208; cf. Kelling 1990, 68-69, 72.
2. Louis 1984, 205-207.
3. *Ibid.*, 210-212; cf. Kelling 1990, 69. For a critique of the COS' attachment to the traditional tenets of conventional warfare in the atomic era, see Louis 1984, 28-29.
4. Crawshaw 1978, 35.
5. Louis 1984, 215-216; cf. Kelling 1990, 70-71. For an outline of the colonial policy of the Labour government in 1945-1948, see Darwin 1988, 69-79.
6. Louis 1984, 222-224; cf. Kelling 1990, 73, 79-80.
7. Louis 1984, 223-224; cf. Darwin 1988, 76-77; Devereux 1990a, 191; Kelling 1990, 68, 73, 77-78. Not that there was any lack of Cassandras: Sir Oliver Harvey, Deputy Under-Secretary at the Foreign Office, prophesied in November 1947: 'When the Greeks in despair turn to the methods of the Irish, the Jews, the Hindus and the Egyptians, then, I suspect, the British people will rise and compel the Government to evacuate (Cyprus)': quoted in Louis 1984, 225.
8. Darwin 1988, 73.
9. Cf. the conclusions on the basis of the Malayan experience in Darwin 1988, 158-159.
10. Louis 1984, 221-222.
11. Crawshaw 1978, 39. Regarding Attlee's suspicion of AKEL's support for self-government, see Louis 1984, 221; cf. Kelling 1990, 77-78.
12. For the origins of this line in the policy of Eleftherios Venizelos, in 1928-1932, and the left-wing Greek Cypriot 'Committee for Cyprus Autonomy', in wartime London, see Attalides 1986, 144-145. According to Servas, Ezekias Papaioannou, future Secretary-General of AKEL, had been a member of this committee.
13. 849C.00/4-1849, Porter to State, A-35; Crawshaw 1978, 34.
14. 849C.00/3-2349, Rankin to State, desp. 224; /4-1849, Porter to State, A-35; Crawshaw 1978, 39-41.
15. On British perceptions of colonial societies and the impact of their rule on Cypriot politics, see Pollis 1973, 575-593. See also Attalides 1981, 419-421; Kitromilides 1981, 452; Kyriakides 1968, 163-164.
16. Pollis 1973, 578.
17. CO 67/368, Wright to Griffiths, 23 May 1950; cf. Mihalopoulos 1989, 24.
18. As late as June 1953, the Cyprus administration observed that 'inter-racial conflict [had been] unknown in Cyprus for forty years': 107501, 1081/38, Colonial Secretary's Office, Nicosia, to Chancery, Ankara, 16 June 1953. On the relations between the Greek and Turkish Cypriot communities under British rule, see Attalides 1981; Hill 1952; Kyrris 1977; Pollis 1973, 587-593.
19. 107558, WK1081/13, Helm to Harrison, 3 Dec. 1953; cf. Grivas *Memoirs*,

3, where the General, recalling his happy childhood in early twentieth century Cyprus, speaks of the days 'when I marched behind the blue and white banners on some national day and felt the Hellenic passion for liberty burning in us all'.

20. Kyriakides 1968, 19.
21. Crawshaw 1978, 52; Kelling 1990, 126; Mayes 1981, 45.
22. 107502, 1081/47, Cyprus government press communiqué, 4 July 1953; 747C.00/7-2153, Wagner to State, desp. 9; cf. Durrell's experience as teacher at the Greek Gymnasium of Nicosia, which he described as 'the perfect laboratory in which to study national sentiment in its embryonic state': Durrell 1957, 127ff..
23. See, for instance, 112869, 1081/801, FO minute by Wilding, 8 Oct. 1954; cf. Crouzet I 1973, 113-115; Durrell 1957, 136, who noted the cultural impoverishment of Cyprus in the early 1950s, including the lack of a university. Later, Eden, as Prime Minister, would realise the importance of such an institution as an antidote to the 'cultural attraction of Athens': Eden 1960, 398.
24. The US Consul in Nicosia referred to 'petty obstruction' against the more obvious expressions of national sentiment, such as the removal of the word 'Hellas' from school badges: 747C.00/12-954, Courtney to State, desp. 46.
25. In 1952 exports amounted to £17.6 million and imports to £21.2 million: *The Economist*, 6 March 1954, cited in Terlexis 1971, 89.
26. 112844, 1081/39, minute by Beckett, 2 March 1954.
27. Crouzet I 1973, 70-93, notes the artificial character of the post-1954 boom, as it was largely based on the 'massive injection of capital from Great Britain for financing military expenditure'. Indeed, military spending in Cyprus increased from £1,45 million in 1950 to £6,73 million in 1954 and £10,10 million the following year, accounting for more than 10 per cent of GNP. For an account of the practical benefits of British colonial administration, see Reddaway 1986, 9-39. John Reddaway had served as senior official of the Cyprus government.
28. 78425, R11375, Wright to Creech Jones, 1 Dec. 1949; 95115, 1081/16, Bennett, CO, to Cheetham, FO, 27 July 1951.
29. 78425, R11375, Wright to Creech Jones, 1 Dec. 1949; R11540, Wright to Creech Jones, 10 Dec. 1949; cf. Kelling 1990, 99.
30. 747C.00/5-1850, Tibbetts to State, tel. 2434.
31. 87719, 1081/104, Norton to Rumbold, 19 May 1950.
32. 78424, R10544, Rumbold to Norton, 14 Nov. 1949.
33. 78425, R11111, Norton to FO, 26 Nov. 1949; 78426, R11683, Norton to Bateman, 29 Nov. 1949.
34. 78425, R11617, Norton to FO, 13 Dec. 1949.
35. Bevin had also suggested inducing the US JCS to stress to the Greeks 'the importance of keeping things quiet in Cyprus': 87715, 1081/10, minutes of meeting at the FO, 23 Dec. 1949.
36. 87715, 1081/32, Norton to FO, 18 Jan. 1950.
37. *The Sunday Times*, 6 April 1947; Kelling 1990, 97-98.

38. 78422, R4853, Fisher, CO, to Peck, FO, 10 May 1949; Kelling 1990, 98.

39. 78426, R11683, Norton to Bateman, 29 Nov. 1949.

40. *Ibid.*

41. 78427, R11866, Norton to Bateman, 29 Dec. 1949.

42. 78425, R11615, Norton to Bateman, 8 Dec. 1949.

43. 87715, 1081/10, 'Cyprus', FO minute from Rumbold to Bevin, 16 Dec. 1949.That British sovereignty over Cyprus was in the long run untenable was a view apparently shared by Permanent Under-Secretary Sir William Strang: 87715, 1081/10, minute by Strang, 17 Dec. 1949. Strang, however, was not the type of official who would undertake 'to promote new initiatives'; rather, he was described as 'reserved, tactful, cautious to a fault': Adamthwaite 1988, 20.

44. 87715, 1081/10, 'Cyprus', FO minute from Rumbold to Bevin, 16 Dec. 1949.

45. 87716, 1081/41, minute by Bateman, 7 Jan. 1950.

46. 87716, 1081/45, minute by Rumbold, 6 Feb. 1950.

47. 78427, R11866, Norton to Bateman, 29 Dec. 1949; Younger to Norton, 6 Jan. 1950.

48. 87719, 1081/91, paper on Cyprus by the Colonial Office and the Foreign Office, April 1950; cf. Crouzet I 1973, 271-272.

49. CAB 129, CP (49) 183, 'Middle East Policy', note by the Secretary of State for Foreign Affairs, 25 Aug. 1949.

50. 87719, 1081/91, paper on Cyprus by the Colonial Office and the Foreign Office, April 1950.

51. This view was elaborated in an article published in the leading Liberal daily *To Vima*, on 19 May, which the British Embassy appreciated as 'the only recent attempt … in a Greek newspaper to state the anti-Enosis point of view': 87719, 1081/108, Chancery to Southern Department, 20 May 1950.

52. 87719, 1081/104, Rumbold to Norton, 13 June 1950.

53. 95132, 1081/32, 'Cyprus', FO minute from Barnes to Morrison, 30 March 1951; CAB 129, C(54) 245, Annex 2.

54. Holland 1993, 153.

55. 95133, 1081/47, Norton to Morrison, 18 April 1951.

56. 95132, 1081/32, Norton to Strang, 13 March 1951.

57. *FRUS 1951*, V, 529; 747C.00/3-1950, Peurifoy to Acheson, tel. 3074.

58. 95132, 1081/32, Norton to Strang, 13 March 1951.

59. 747C.00/3-1451, Bartch to State, desp. 155.

60. 747C.00/3-1951, Peurifoy to Acheson, tel. 3074.

61. See the memorandum from Wright to Griffiths, drafted by the newly appointed Colonial Secretary John Fletcher Cooke on 16 April 1951, in Holland 1993, 156-157.

62. Holland 1993, 152.

63. A high official of the Colonial Office, whose name is not disclosed by the reporting US diplomat, described Wright as 'a fine Victorian type now almost extinct in the British Colonial Service', who 'looked on the Cypriots somewhat as children who needed a firm hand, an occasional spanking and definite limits to their political activities': 747C.00/11-2850, Tibbetts to State, desp.

2549. For further assessments of Wright's personality see Crouzet I 1973, 244; Holland 1993, 150; Kelling 1990, 96-97; 78422, R4853, Fisher, CO, to Peck, FO, 10 May 1949; 747C.00/9-1950, Porter to State, desp. 39.

64. As Crouzet puts it, 'Wright knew Cyprus in detail, but, perhaps, too well for the trees not to hide the forest from him': Crouzet I 1973, 244.

65. Holland 1993, 149-150, 155; cf. Kelling 1990, 101.

66. Holland 1993, 149.

67. Indicative of Wright's anxiety to clamp down on Enosis 'agitators' was his handling of the so-called street signs incident: taking exception of the renaming of the Limassol main sea front walkway from 'Palmer' (after the repressive pre-war Governor) to '28 October boulevard' (after the anniversary of the Greek entry into World War II), the Governor had the entire Greek City Council detained: Crawshaw 1978, 50; Holland 1993, 153-154; Kelling 1990, 101.

68. Holland 1993, 151-152.

69. 747C.00/9-1950, Porter to State, desp. 39.

70. 747C.00/11-2850, Tibbetts to State, desp. 2549; cf. Kelling 1990, 100.

71. Holland 1993, 154.

72. DEFE 5, COS (51) 245, 'Sovereignty of Cyprus. Background', memo by COS Committee, 24 April 1951; 95133, 1081/61, note by the War Office, 24 April 1951; cf. Holland 1993, 156.

73. 95115, 10113/16, Bennett, CO, to Cheetham, FO, 27 July 1951; Holland 1993, 158-159.

74. This position, stated on 15 January 1946, is quoted in 78427, R11889, Charles to FO, Ankara, 21 Dec. 1949.

75. Quoted in Louis 1984, 212, n. 23; cf. Stephens 1966, 206.

76. 78427, R12052, Rumbold, FO, to Bennett, CO, 2 Jan. 1950.

77. 849C.00/3-2349, Rankin to Acheson, desp. 224.

78. 78420, R200, FO to H.M. Representatives, 26 Jan. 1949.

79. 87719, 1081/100, Norton to FO, 18 May 1950; *ibid.*, FO to Athens, 23 May 1950.

80. 87791, 1081/104, Rumbold to Norton, 30 May 1950.

81. 87720, 1081/139, Norton to FO, 23 May 1950; 87721, 1081/152, Norton to Younger, 29 June 1950.

82. 87720, 1081/128, Stephens to Rumbold, 2 June 1950; 87719, 1081/104, Rumbold to Norton, 13 June 1950; 747C.00/9-1450, Tibbetts to State, desp. 1269.

83. 747C.00/9-1450, Tibbetts to State, desp. 1269.

84. 95132, 1081/3, Norton to Bevin, 2 Jan. 1951.

85. 87720, 1081/128, Stephens to Rumbold, 2 June 1950.

86. 87722, 1081/158, Hoyer Millar to Rumbold, Washington, 14 July 1950; 87723, 1081/193, Franks to FO, Washington, 20 Sept. 1950.

87. 87723, 1081/171, FO to Washington, 19 Aug. 1950; 1081/193, FO to Washington, 25 Sept. 1950; 1081/195, Franks to FO, Washington, 4 Oct. 1950; 1081/199, letter from Lord Tedder to General Bradley.

88. DEFE 5/31, COS (51) 245, COS Committee, 'Sovereignty of Cyprus', 24 April 1951; 95133, 1081/61, note by the War Office, 24 April 1951.

89. 95132, 1081/32, 'Cyprus', FO minute from Barnes to Morrison, 30 March 1951.

90. 95133, 1081/68, Norton to Morrison, 16 May 1951; 95134, 1081/80, Burrows to Cheetham, 6 July 1951; 1081/85, Norton to Cheetham, 1 Aug. 1951.

91. 95134, 1081/80, Martin, CO, to Mason, FO, 10 July 1951.

92. As early as 1949, a Conservative brochure declared that 'self-government within the British Empire and Commonwealth is an aim to be achieved as soon as Colonial peoples are ready for it': quoted in Ansprenger 1989, 180-181.

93. Adamthwaite 1988, 1, 8-11, who notes that, after the traumas of 1950-1, further 'withdrawals became much harder to stomach'.

94. Darwin 1988, 126-130; 168-169; Kelling 1990, 119-120; Smith 1978, 78-79.

95. This was repeatedly pointed out by Mostras, the Greek Ambassador to London in 1953-6: Mostras ms, 16ff.

96. Crawshaw 1978, 58-59; Crouzet I 1973, 412-419.

97. Adamthwaite 1988, 10; Darwin 1988, 216; Ovendale 1988, 141, 146; Sked 1984, 116. One of the leaders of the 'Suez Group' was Julian Amery, sponsor of dual nationality for the Cypriots.

98. 101810, 1081/16, Lyttelton to Eden, 10 April 1952; cf. Holland 1993, 160; and Kelling 1990, 125.

99. 101810, 1081/16, Eden to Lyttelton, 29 April 1952; cf. Holland 1993, 161.

100. CO 926/91, Wright to Martin, 12 Dec. 1952; cf. Holland 1993, 159-160.

101. CO 926/91.

102. 747C.03/4-1852, Wagner to State, desp. 268.

103. Holland 1993, 161.

104. 101807, 1051/2, notes by Lord Halifax, 9 May 1952.

105. 101807, 1051/2, minute by Eden.

106. 101811, 1081/33, Peake to Harrison, 17 June 1952; 747C.00/6-2852, Peurifoy to Acheson, tel. 5512.

107. Devereux 1990b, 241-248; Louis 1984, 731-732; Ovendale 1988, 136-139.

108. CAB 128/25, C.C. (52) 91, agreed conclusions of Cabinet Committee meeting, 29 Oct. 1952; cf. 95133, 1081/, article by S. Delmer in *Daily Express*, June 1951; Crouzet I 1973, 318-319; Eden III, 1960, 244-245; Kelling 1990, 97. Earlier in the year, Cyprus had been seen as a likely location for the headquarters of the projected Middle East Command: Devereux 1990b, 245.

109. CAB 128/25, C.C. (52) 101, agreed conclusions of Cabinet Committee meeting, 3 Dec. 1952.

110. 107501, 1081/7, article by Richards, *Statesman and Nation*, 28 Feb. 1953.

111. 101808, 1052/9, Peake to Eden, 25 Nov. 1952; 101800, 1017/54, Peake to Harrison, 17 Dec. 1952.

112. 101807, 1051/1, minutes by Murray, 14 Feb. 1952.

113. 107483, 1017/20, summary note on the situation in Greece, 17 July 1953; 107502, 1081/64, Peake to FO, 30 Nov. 1953. In an other report, Peake spoke of 'such formidable Russian and German competition' that he could not

'neglect a single chance of keeping (the British) well in the news': 112843, 1081/3, Peake to Cheetham, 8 Jan. 1954.

114. 87732, 1113/5, Stevenson,Treasury, to Legh, Bank of England, 5 June 1950.

115. 101808, 1052/9, minute by Eden, undated.

116. Linardatos II 1978, 90.

117. According to a Greek member of the British Embassy staff, by 1953, the Foreign Office still treated Greece as a country 'economically and politically finished', which could not be relied 'as a strong *point d'appui* in Southeastern Europe': 641.81/4-1753,Yost to State, desp. 1185.

118. 107483, 1017/23, Galsworthy to May, 13 Aug. 1953; 1017/24, Galsworthy to May, 21 Aug. 1953.

119. 611.81/8-453, Peurifoy to State, desp. 123.

120. 107501, 1081/13, Peake to FO, 11 March 1953; 1081/14, Peake to FO, 12 March 1953.

121. 107501, 1081/21, brief on Cyprus for the Secretary of State, 19 March 1953.

122. 107501, 1081/21, brief on Cyprus for the Secretary of State, 19 March 1953; cf. Kelling 1990, 129.

123. 107501, 1081/26, Peake to FO, 28 April 1953.

124. 107501, 1081/24, minutes by Murray, 29 April 1953; 107501, 1081/27, 29-31, FO and CO drafts of GovernorWright's reply toArchbishop Makarios, delivered on 11 May 1953.

125. 107502, 1081/61, 'Cyprus', memo by Ward, 18 Nov. 1953.

126. 107502, 1081/61, 'Cyprus', brief by Harrison, 19 Nov. 1953.

127. Eden would have preferred the Americans to 'volunteer' a statement 'at some time agreed': 107502, 1081/61, 'Cyprus', memo, marginal minutes by Eden, 21 Nov. 1953.

128. 112843, 1081/6, Peake to Cheetham, 23 Jan. 1954.

129. 112830, 10110/3, Cyprus Political Situation Report, Feb. 1954.

130. 107502, 1081/62, minute by Selby, 29 Nov. 1953; 107502, 1081/63, Selby, FO, to Pearson, CO, 5 Dec. 1953; 107558, WK1081/13, Cheetham, FO, to Pearson, CO, 6 Jan. 1954; 112843, 1081/8, Selby, FO, to Pearson, CO, 4 Feb. 1954.

131. 107501, 1081/14, Peake to FO, 12 March 1953.

132. 107502, 1081/64, Peake to FO, 30 Nov. 1953; 112843, 1081/1, Peake to Harrison, 18 Dec. 1953.

133. 107502, 1081/61, 'Cyprus' memo, 18 Nov. 1953; 1081/63, Eden to Peake, 23 Nov. 1953.

134. 107502, 1081/64, Peake to FO, 30 Nov. 1953.

135. 107502, 1081/64, minute by Harrison, 1 Dec. 1953; *ibid.*, minute by Eden, 8 Dec. 1953.

136. 112843, 1081/3, Peake to Cheetham, 8 Jan. 1954.

137. 112843, 1081/3, minute by Cheetham, 13 Jan. 1954; *ibid.*, minute by Harrison, 14 Jan. 1954. Instead, the Foreign Office concentrated on the proposal for a state visit by King Paul and Queen Frederica to England. It was hoped that this 'might help ease the strain' of Cyprus on Anglo-Greek rela-

tions, and, also, match the success of the royal couple's recent visit to the
United States: 112843, 1081/3, minute by Cheetham, 13 Jan. 1954.
138. Kelling 1990, 140; cf. Holland 1993, 162-163. For a kinder view, see Durrell
1957, 144-146.
139. A brief account of the devolution of colonial power in the Gold Coast (present-
day Ghana), see in Darwin 1988, 174-179.
140. The directive for Armitage on the constitutional issue read as follows: 'The
new Governor would therefore make his own assessment, when he has had
time, and communicate to the Secretary of State his views on whether any
form of initiative by the Government towards a constitution on the 1948
pattern is practical politics, whether advance along any other road would be
preferable or whether the time is ripe for any form of constitutional experi-
ment': CO 926/91, Directive for Armitage, Oct./Nov. 1953; cf. CO 926/
91, 'Cyprus: Political and Constitutional Considerations', memo by Mediterranean Department, Oct. 1953; 112844, 1081/39, 'Cyprus', minute by
Cheetham, 26 Feb. 1954.
141. 112830, 10110/3, Cyprus Political Situation Report, Feb. 1954; cf. Durrell
1957, 119-123; 145-146; Holland 1993, 163.
142. 112844, 1081/39, 'Cyprus', minute by Cheetham, 26 Feb. 1954; minutes
by Harrison and Beckett, 2 March 1954. By December 1954, the US Consul
would report that, despite some real progress, there was 'room for a great
deal more to be done ... in the fields of soil and water conservation, improvement of ports and communications, easing of restrictions upon trade, social
insurance': 747C.00/12-954, Courtney to State, desp. 46.
143. 112844, 1081/39, minute by Harrison, 27 Feb. 1954.
144. Ovendale 1988, 148.
145. There was a further sign of hardening attitude. Eden discouraged the visit to
Greece of Conservative MP Julian Amery, who had been invited by Kyrou and
intended to discuss with him his father's proposal of a dual citizenship for
Greek Cypriots. The proposal was given study by the Colonial Office and was
dismissed on the grounds that it left out the Turkish Cypriots: 112844,.1081/
37, Amery to Eden, 4 March 1954; 1081/56, CO note, 24 March 1954.
146. 112845, 1081/71, Peake to Eden, 3 April 1954.
147. 112844, 1081/69, 112845, 1081/71, Peake to Eden, 3 March 1954.
148. 112845, 1081/84; 1081/85, brief for the Secretary of State, (received on)
22 April 1954; 112830, 10110/5, Cyprus Political Situation Report, April 1954.
112845, 1081/88, minutes of meeting held in the Colonial Office, 14 April
1954.
149. 112845, 1081/83, FO to Athens, 15 April 1954.
150. 112845, 1081/89, minute on Charles Mott-Radclyffe's memoranda by
Cheetham, 26 April 1954; *ibid.*, minute by Cheetham, 7 May 1954.
151. 112848, 1081/206, FO minute, 23 July 1954. On 12 May, for example,
Selwyn Lloyd repeated the 'not discuss' position of his government: 112846,
1081/123, reply to Parliamentary Question by E.L. Mallalieu, 12 May 1954.
152. 112846, 1081/125, record of conversation between Nutting and Mostras,

14 May 1954.
153. 107502, 1081/70, Jebb to Kirkpatrick, 9 Dec. 1953.
154. 112843, 1081/11, Eden to Helm, 11 Feb. 1954; 1081/23, minute by
    Cheetham, 17 Feb. 1954; 1081/28, British Embassy, Ankara, to FO, 24 Feb.
    1954.
155. 87719, 1081/104, Norton to Rumbold, 19 May 1950.
156. As Kelling rightly observed, 'while the British made good use of [Turkish
    anti-Enosis] feeling, they did not invent it': Kelling 1990, 128; cf. Crouzet,
    445-446; Mostras, 8, 13.
157. 107589, WK1741/5, British Embassy, Ankara, to Colonial Secretariat, Nicosia,
    21 July 1953; 107558, WK1081/11, British Embassy, Ankara, to Chancery,
    Athens, 2 Nov. 1953; 107502, 1081/61, 'Cyprus' memo by Ward, 18 Nov. 1953.
158. 107589, WK1741/8, Helm to Wright, 25 Sept. 1953; 107589, WK1741/7,
    minute by Maby, 30 Sept. 1953; 112830, 10110/3, Cyprus Political Situation
    Report, Feb. 1954. Wright appeared particularly anxious to avoid Turkish in-
    terference in the field of education, fearing that this would establish a prec-
    edent for similar Greek demands: 107558, WK1081/13, Helm to Harrison,
    3 Dec. 1953.
159. 747C.00/8-254, Kohler to State, desp. 63.
160. 107558, WK1081/13, Helm to Harrison, 3 Dec. 1953.
161. 107558, WK1081/13, Cheetham, FO, to Pearson, CO, 6 Jan. 1954; 107494,
    10344/4, Chancery, Ankara, to FO, 13 Aug. 1953; 107558, WK1081/11, British
    Embassy, Ankara, to Chancery, Athens, 2 Nov. 1953; 112843, 1081/14, Peake
    to FO, 15 Feb. 1954; 112848, 1081/177, Scott-Fox to Young, 30 June 1954.
162. CO 926/183, Wright to Martin, 2 Feb. 1954
163. 112843, 1081/14, Peake to FO, 15 Feb. 1954; 107502, 1081/64, Peake to
    FO, 30 Nov. 1953; 112843, 1081/1, Peake to Harrison, 18 Dec. 1953.
164. 112843, 1081/13, Ankara to FO, 13 Feb. 1954.
165. As much was admitted by the Ambassador in Washington, Sir Roger Makins,
    in a memorandum dated 25 January 1954, i.e. only three days before the
    British officially requested US support on Cyprus: quoted in Louis 1985, 396.
166. 112844, 1081/62, 64, minutes, April 1954.
167. Mathieson, UKUN Delegation, at the Anglo-American colonial policy talks,
    Washington, 25 Sept. 1952: *FRUS 1952-54*, III, 1261.
168. 101811, 1081/30, minute by Dunnett, 20 June 1952; 112846, 1081/105,
    FO to H.M. Representatives, 25 Oct. 1952.
169. As a Foreign Office circular put it at the time of the Seventh General Assem-
    bly, 'the majority of UN members have shown little inclination to grasp the
    formidable nature of the task of advancing backward people through the stages
    of social and political evolution which in Europe took many centuries. Instead
    they tend to propose solutions which are superficial and facile, are therefore
    impossible of achievement, and play into the hands of Communists': 112846,
    1081/105, FO to H.M. Representatives, 25 Oct. 1952.
170. 101812, 1081/43, minute by Royce, 14 July 1952. When the prospect of a
    Greek recourse to the Ninth General Assembly arose, the Foreign Office con-

sidered the advisability of requesting the Assembly to seek an advisory opinion from the International Court of Justice on whether colonial affairs constituted a matter of domestic jurisdiction or not. The Colonial Office was not in
favour. The Department of UN Political Affairs also advised against involving
the International Court, on the grounds that its interpretation of treaties relied extensively on the principle of 'subsequent practice'. It also doubted Britain's ability to influence the terms of discussion in that body. Thus, the only
way left was for the British Delegation to the UN to 'voice its dissent' whenever the internal affairs of member states came in for discussion: 112460,
UP2417/1, FO to CO, 17 Feb. 1954; *ibid.*, CO to FO, 18 March 1954; *ibid.*,
Cope, FO, to Wilson, CO, 12 May 1954. On the same grounds, the Foreign
Office would reject a similar proposal from the Canadian Foreign Minister, on
the eve of the General Assembly: 112858, 1081/454, High Commissioner,
Ottawa, to Commonwealth Relations Office, 7 Sept. 1954.
171. Xydis 1967, 592 n. 4; *YUN 1954*, 209.
172. 112844, 1081/49, Pearson, CO, to Selby, FO, 18 March 1954.
173; cf. 112847, 1081/155, Commonwealth Relations Office to UK High Commissioners in British Commonwealth countries, 22 July 1954.
174. 112845, 1081/88, minutes of meeting held in the Colonial Office, 14 April
1954. This reliance tended to overlook Arab suspicion towards Turkey on account of her strongly pro-Western policy and alleged ambitions in the Middle East.
175. 112830, 10110/4, Cyprus Political Situation Report, March 1954.
176. 112846, 1081/103, *The Times*, 1 May 1954.
177. 112849, 1081/202, *The Economist*, 24 July 1954.
178. 112830, 10110/5, Cyprus Political Situation Report, April 1954.
179. 112830, 10110/6, Cyprus Political Situation Report, May 1954; 112830,
10110/7, Cyprus Political Situation Report, June 1954.
180. 112845, 1081/92, Bowker to Harrison, 21 April 1954; cf. Kelling 1990, 143.
181. 112846, 1081/108, Dixon to Eden, 30 April 1954.
182. 112846, 1081/128, Salt to Cheetham, 17 May 1954.
183. 112846, 1081/108, minute by Cope, 20 May 1954.
184. 112846, 1081/107, minute by Harrison, 3 May 1954.
185. 112846, 1081/107, Nutting to Hopkinson, 11 May 1954.
186. 112847, 1081/132, minute by Selwyn Lloyd, 24 May 1954.
187. 112847, 1081/150, record of conversation between Wilding and Robinson,
Canadian High Commissioner's Office, 14 June 1954.
188. 112847, 1081/156, Armitage to Lloyd, 3 June 1954.
189. 112846, 1081/129, Bowker to Harrison, 18 May 1954.
190. 112848, 1081/178, Scott-Fox to Young, 30 June 1954; 1081/188, Bowker
to FO, 8 July 1954.
191. 112848, 1081/179, minute by Young, 7 July 1954.
192. CO 926/209, minute by Smith, June 1954.
193. 112847, 1081/145, draft Cabinet paper, CO, 16 June 1954.
194. 112847, 1081/145, minute by Young, 16 June 1954.

195. 112848, 1081/164, minute by Harrison, 18 June 1954.
196. 112848, 1081/166, record of meeting held by the Minister of State, 29 June 1954.
197. 112848, 1081/174, *The Sunday Times*, 4 July 1954; cf. Holland 1993, 166.
198. 112848, 1081/183, record of conversation between Harrison, Morris, CO, and Armitage 5 July 1954.
199. Armitage would admit as much later: Holland 1993, 166.
200. 112848, 1081/193, Armitage to Lyttelton, 13 July 1954.
201. 112848, 1081/193, Armitage to Lyttelton, 19 July 1954.
202. 112849, 1081/204, Armitage to CO, 25 July 1954; cf. Crouzet I 1973, 406.
203. 112849, 1081/208, draft Cabinet paper by the Colonial Office, 20 July 1954; CAB 129, C(54) 245, memo by the Secretary of State for the Colonies and the Minister of State, 21 July 1954.
204. CO 926, 499, Churchill to Lennox-Boyd, 11 Aug. 1954. On the shortcomings of the Churchill Cabinet, see Adamthwaite 1988, 2-3, 21.
205. This latter contention is disputed: Crouzet I 1973, 402.
206. 747C.00/8-2554, London desp. 593; cf. Crouzet I 1973, 403; Holland 1993, 167-169.
207. 747C.00/8-2554, London desp. 593.
208. 112850, 1081/233, minutes by Young and Harrison, 4 Aug. 1954; cf. above, n. 99.
209. 112850, 1081/233, minutes by Harrison and Young, 4 Aug. 1954.
210. Crawshaw 1978, 75-80.
211. Crawshaw 1978, 80; 747C.00/11-354, office memo from Howard to Wood. The former Greek Under-Secretary for Foreign Affairs, Averof, had also suggested a similar idea to the Americans in 1952: he had spoken of a lease of territory for 99 years: *FRUS 1952-54*, 675.
212. In November, Wyatt's idea struck Harry Howard, UN adviser of the NEA Bureau in the State Department, as a possible solution, but it was not pursued further: 747C.00/11-354, office memo, Howard to Wood.
213. Kirkpatrick had succeeded Sir William Strang in November 1953. Unlike his over-cautious predecessor, he was described as 'brisk, combative and outgoing': Adamthwaite 1988, 20.
214. Initially, Kirkpatrick had noted 'five or seven years', as indicative of the time after which the British should be prepared to discuss: 112851, 1081/260, 'Cyprus', FO minute by Kirkpatrick, 10 Aug. 1954.
215. In his memorandum, Kirkpatrick related an episode which highlighted the doubtful rationality of strategic options: 'At the beginning of 1951 the Air Ministry declared that it was vital to retain Heligoland as a bombing target. When German squatters made bombing impossible, I undertook to remove them and to keep the island clear, provided I could obtain an R.A.F. launch. The Air Ministry replied that they would sooner give up this target than incur the trouble and expense of providing a launch. So we made arrangements for an alternative target in the North Sea': 112851, 1081/260, 'Cyprus', FO minute by Kirkpatrick, 10 Aug. 1954. Incidentally, as early as 1921, a report

on the strategic value of Cyprus had styled it 'the Heligoland of the Eastern Mediterranean': Svolopoulos 1985, 240.

216. Like many others, Kirkpatrick was particularly impressed by the devastating impact of the recently developed hydrogen bomb on the concept of large military bases, which could be wiped out at one thermonuclear stroke. This argument had been taken up by Churchill in sanctioning the decision to withdraw the British garrison from the Suez Zone: Adamthwaite 1988, 4-5; Ovendale 1988, 150. Yet this was only one of certain factors influencing that decision, and definitely not as crucial as Britain's recurring balance of payments crises: Kent 1994, 62.

217. 112851, 1081/260, 'Cyprus', FO minute by Kirkpatrick, 10 Aug. 1954.

218. *Ibid.* As seen in Chapter 3, at the time of Fleur Cowles' abortive mediation in September, Hopkinson would suggest tripartite talks on the status of Cyprus at the end of the period covered by the NATO treaty.

219. 112851, 1081/260, minute by Young, 18 Aug. 1954.

220. 112851, 1081/260, minute by Roberts, 20 Aug. 1954.

221. 112856, 1081/410, Osmerod, CRO, to Wilson, CO, 1 Sept. 1954.

222. CO 926/499, Prime Minister's personal minute, 6 Aug. 1954; *ibid.*, Churchill to Lennox-Boyd, 11 Aug. 1954; *ibid.*, Churchill to Lennox-Boyd, 13 Aug. 1954; *ibid.*, Lennox-Boyd to Armitage, 16 Aug. 1954; C (54) 245, para. 18, subsection 6; cf. Holland 1993, 1170-1171.

223. CO 926/500, Churchill to Lennox-Boyd, 30 Sept.; *ibid.*, record of meeting between the Prime Minister, the Colonial Secretary and the Governor of Cyprus, 18 Oct. 1954. On 28 October, it was stated in parliament that the press law in Cyprus was to be brought into line with that in Britain: CO 926/500, Lennox-Boyd to Armitage, 22 Oct. 1954.

224. Devereux 1990a, -184; Holden Reid 1988, 159-179.

225. Eden *Memoirs* III, 462.

226. This point was made by the Foreign Office in a telegram to the Washington Embassy, in view of the Pentagon's apparent difficulty in coming out in favour of indefinite British sovereignty over Cyprus. What the Pentagon experts overlooked, it was claimed, was the contingency of operating 'from Greek bases against an enemy with which Greece was not herself at war': FO to Washington, 25 June 1954, referred to in 112848, 1081/185, Salt to Young, 9 July 1954.

227. 112859, 1081/490, COS (54) 303, 'Strategic Importance of Cyprus', Chiefs of Staff Committee, 13 Sept. 1954.

228. Stephens 1966, 18.

229. Crouzet I 1973, 319, n. 24, 320-321; Devereux 1990a, 174-175.

230. 112859, 1081/490, COS (54) 303, 'Strategic Importance of Cyprus', Chiefs of Staff Committee, 13 Sept. 1954.

231. Adamthwaite 1988, 9. For an analysis of British defence policy in the Middle East at the time, see Devereux 1990a. According to this author, after the Anglo-Egyptian agreement of October 1954, Britain's role in the Middle East was effectively limited to 'showing the flag': *idem.*, 191-2; cf. Kent 1994, 55-63.

232. The committee was made up of Foreign, Colonial, and Commonwealth Relations ministers, plus a representative of the COS. It was subsequently placed under Hopkinson's supervision.

233. 112855, 1081/379, minute by Caccia, undated (Sept. 1954); 112856, 1081/413, Nutting to Hopkinson, 4 Sept. 1954; 112859, 1081/500, interim report to the Secretary of State, 9 Sept. 1954.

234. J.S. Benett of the Colonial Office Mediterranean Department was among the few to question the expediency of making communism a 'publicity' issue. 'The Enosis problem', he reminded, 'existed before Communism and would continue without it': CO 926/180, minute by Benett, 18 Aug. 1954.

235. 112851, 1081/278, UKUN Delegation to FO, 14 Aug. 1954; 112853, 1081/309, 'International Communism and the Cyprus question' FO minute, 19 Aug. 1954; 747C.00/9-154, 'International Communism ...', note from the British Embassy to the State Department; 112856, 1081/409, 'Publicity on Cyprus', FO minute by Young, 1 Sept. 1954. This material almost exclusively emanated from the outlawed KKE: as British diplomats admitted, Soviet and satellite propaganda in favour of Enosis had decreased in recent months, in line with Moscow's attempt to improve relations with London.

236. 112851, 1081/278, UKUN delegation to FO, 14 Aug. 1954.

237. 112874, 1081/998, Russell, B.I.S., New York, to Makins, Washington, 12 Nov. 1954.

238. 112857, 1081/422, Oslo to FO, 4 Sept. 1954.

239. 112859, 1081/487, FO to Istanbul, 10 Sept. 1954; 112866, 1081/701, Hopkinson to Lennox-Boyd, 23 Sept. 1954; 112868, 1081/772, UKUN Delegation to FO, 5 Oct. 1954; 112874, 1081/995, Mackenzie to UKUN Delegation, 30 Oct. 1954.

240. 112855, 1081/379, minute by Caccia, undated (Sept. 1954); 112856, 1081/413, Nutting to Hopkinson, 4 Sept. 1954; 112859, 1081/500, interim report to the Secretary of State, 9 Sept. 1954.

241. 112875, 1081/1014, Butler to FO, 8 Nov. 1954; cf. Durrell 1957, 143ff.

242. 112860, 1081/530, FO to Athens, 30 Sept. 1954; 112875, 1081/1014, Butler to FO, 8 Nov. 1954.

243. 112875, 1081/1014, Butler to FO, 8 Nov. 1954.

244. 112867, 1081/759, Selwyn Lloyd to Eden, 2 Oct. 1954; *ibid.*, Wilding, FO, to Wilson, CO, 8 Oct. 1954; 112872, 1081/920, statement by Lennox-Boyd on Cyprus, 28 Oct. 1954.

245. 112875, 1081/1019, Mackenzie, Nicosia, to Young, 16 Nov. 1954.

246. 112848, 1081/175, FO to Athens Embassy, 21 July 1954. Although the deterioration in Anglo-Greek relations had been accepted as the inevitable cost of standing pat on Cyprus, Greek polemics and other manifestations of ill feeling did not fail to irritate British leaders. Churchill, in particular, minuted on the cancellation of British Fleet visits to Greek ports on 25 August as follows: 'It should be a mistake to go there at the present time, when they are insulting us so grossly and showing every form of ingratitude. There are plenty of pleasant places to go to in the Mediterranean': 112853, 1081/330, Prime

Minister's personal minute, 25 Aug. 1954.
247. 112870, 1081/880, 'Cabinet Committee on Cyprus', minute, 21 Oct. 1954.
248. 112871, 1081/886, minutes by Young and Eden, 19 Oct. 1954; 112872, 1081/921, Rae, FO, to Mott-Radclyffe, Member of Parliament, 28 Oct. 1954; 112873, 1081/952, Parliamentary Question, 1 Nov. 1954. This particular effort failed to attract much publicity, since it was accorded low order and was answered in writing. Yet the 'offending extracts' to which it referred were subsequently channelled to the *Times* and the *Economist*: 112876, 1081/1044, 'Publicity on Cyprus', minute by Young, 24 Nov. 1954. Upon Eden's request, a further question was inspired in December: 112878, 1081/1109, Parliamentary Question by Gilbert Longden, 8 Dec. 1954.
249. 112876, 1081/1044, minute by Young, 24 Nov. 1954.
250. 112877, 1081/1073, minute by Eden.
251. 112877, 1081/1081, 'Compendium of Publicity Material on Cyprus', FO minute, 9 Dec. 1954; 1081/1086, 'Cyprus'. Hopkinson Committee', minute by Young, 6 Dec. 1954.
252. 112871, 1081/893, UKUN Delegation to FO, 20 Oct. 1954; *ibid.*, FO to UKUN Delegation, 29 Oct. 1954.
253. 112880, 1081/1164, BBC Monitoring Service, 27-28 Nov. 1954; Linardatos II 1978, 215.
254. 112459, UP2416/4, Wilson, CO, to Cope, FO, 14 July 1954; *ibid.*, minute by Buxton, 20 July 1954; UP2416/7, Wilson, CO, to Buxton, 29 July 1954; 112852, 1081/296, 'Cyprus and the United Nations', CO minute by Mathieson, 5 Aug. 1954.
255. 112459, UP2416/7, minute by Cope, 30 July 1954. 112852, 1081/308, FO to British Embassies, 24 Aug. 1954; 112853, 1081/318, minute by Young, 25 Aug., 1954.
256. 112459, UP2416/8, Ramsbotham to Cope, 29 July 1954; 112853, 1081/335, FO minute of meeting in the Commonwealth Relations Office, 24 Aug. 1954; 112854, 1081/351A, Jockel, Australian External Affairs Office, to Cleary, CRO, 2 Sept. 1954.
257. 117622, 1081/66, Dixon to Eden, 19 Jan. 1955.
258. 112861, 1081/543, Makins, Washington, to FO, 15 Sept. 1954.
259. 112860, 1081/501, 506, UKUN Delegation to FO, 10 Sept. 1954; *ibid.*, FO to UKUN Delegation; 112861, 1081/562, UKUN Delegation to FO, 16 Sept. 1954.
260. 112865, 1081/665, UKUN Delegation to FO, 1954; 117622, 1081/66, Dixon to Eden, 19 Jan. 1955.
261. 747C.00/9-2554, Lodge to Dulles, tel. 20.
262. The British were particularly gratified by the Indian abstention, which had been explained as opposition to Enosis, but were furious with the Arabs, except Iraq, whose conduct they blamed on Egypt: 112866, 1081/687A, Hopkinson to Lennox-Boyd, 25 Sept. 1954; 1081/692, UKUN Delegation to FO, 28 Sept. 1954.
263. 112854, 1081/343, minute by Williams, 25 Aug. 1954; 112855, 1081/376, Williams to Cleary, CRO, 13 Sept. 1954; 112867, 1081/735, FO to various

Missions, 2 Oct. 1954; 112869, 1081/810, memo on the Cyprus item, UKUN Delegation, 9 Oct. 1954.

264. 112867, 1081/735, FO to various Missions, 2 Oct. 1954.

265. 112867, 1081/740, Young to Crosthwaite, UKUN Delegation, 8 Oct. 1954.

266. 112872, 1081/931, Mathieson, CO, to Young, 29 Oct. 1954.

267. 747C.00/11-154, Warren to State, tel. 478.

268. 112867, 1081/741, minute of conversation between Eden and Dulles, 2 Oct. 1954.

269. 112867, 1081/740, Young to Crosthwaite, UKUN Delegation, 8 Oct. 1954; 112873, 1081/972, Dixon to FO, 8 Nov. 1954.

270. This seemed possible in early November due to the backlog in the Political Committee. As the Greek item had been placed at the bottom of the agenda, even a short extension of the agreed closing date of 10 December might not permit the General Assembly to deal with it. In that case, the item would automatically be referred to the next session, an outcome practically identical with a postponement decision.

271. 112873, 1081/972, Dixon to FO, 8 Nov. 1954.

272. 112875, 1081/1033, Nutting to Eden, 25 Nov. 1954.

273. 112875, 1081/1033, FO to UKUN Delegation, 30 Nov. 1954.

274. Although a 'not to discuss' formula had initially seemed preferable, the British delegation eventually opted the 'not to consider' one as being more 'far-reaching': *FRUS 1952-54*, VIII, 736; 112878, 1081/1095, FO to UKUN Delegation, 10 Dec. 1954; 117622, 1081/66, Dixon to Eden, 19 Jan. 1955.

275. 112878, 1081/1095, FO to UKUN Delegation, 10 Dec. 1954; 747C.00/12-1754, Butterworth to Dulles, tel. 2803.

276. 112883, 1081/1224, UKUN Delegation to FO, 18 Dec. 1054.

277. 112830, 10110/11, Cyprus Political Situation Report, Oct. 1954; 112879, 1081/1120, Smith, CO, to Wilding, FO, 10 Dec. 1954; 747C.00/10-1254, Courtney to State, desp. 25; /10-2954, Courtney to State, desp. 34; /12-954, Courtney to State, desp. 46.

278. For example, by Leo Amery in 1947 and Mary Fisher in 1949.

279. The Foreign Office had been considering the granting of inspection rights on education in Cyprus to both Greece and Turkey since late 1953, when the Greek Ministry of Education had advanced a request to this effect. At that time, the Greek request had been turned down on Governor Wright's insistence: 112843, 1081/5, Selby to Pearson, 2 Feb. 1954.

280. 112849, 1081/202, *The Economist*, 24 July 1954.

281. While in favour of the second course R. W. Wilding, the Southern Department official who drafted these proposals, admitted that the government should not appear as 'contemplating another retreat in the Imperial field': 112869, 1081/801, 'Cyprus and the future of Anglo-Greek relations', FO minute by Wilding, 8 Oct. 1954.

282. 112869, 1081/801, minute by Muirhead, 19 Nov. 1954; *ibid.*, minute by Selby, 22 Nov. 1954.

283. 112869, 1081/801, minute by Selby, 22 Nov. 1954.

284. As the 'battle' at the UN drew to its close, the Governor proposed to take

measures against both AKEL activity and Enosis propaganda: 112878, 1081/
1096, B.M.E.O. to FO, 8 Dec. 1954; 112879, 1081/1120, Smith, CO, to
Wilding, FO, 10 Dec. 1954; 112880, 1081/1150, Armitage to Lennox-Boyd,
(?) Dec. 1954; 747C.00/12-954, Courtney to State, desp. 46.
285. 112881, 1081/1198, minute by Young, 9 Dec. 1954.
286. 112879, 1081/1120, minute by Wilding, 13 Dec. 1954.
287. 112881, 1081/1198, minute by Young, 9 Dec. 1954.
288. Eden *Memoirs* III, 398.
289. 112883, 1081/1247, Prime Minister's personal minute, 15 Dec. 1954.
290. 112885, 1081/1276, Eastwood, CO, to Young, FO, 20 Dec. 1954; 117621,
1081/50, Lennox-Boyd to Churchill, 12 Jan. 1955; cf. Crouzet I 1973, 409.
291. CO 926/311, CO minute to the Prime Minister, 7 Jan. 1955.
292. 117621, 1081/32, minute by Young, 10 Jan. 1955.
293. 117622, 1081/56, 'Cyprus', record of talks at CO and FO, 11-12 Jan. 1955.
294. CO 926/91, memoranda by Dodds-Parker, Sept.-30 Dec. 1954.
295. 117622, 1081/56, 'Cyprus', record of talks at CO and FO, 11-12 Jan. 1955;
CO 926/223, minute by Smith, 28 Jan. 1955.
296. 117620, 1081/18, Peake to Eden, 5 Jan. 1955.
297. 117620, 1081/21, Peake to Young, 7 Jan. 1955.
298. 117622, 1081/56, 'Cyprus', record of talks at CO and FO on 11-12 Jan., by
Wilding, 18 Jan. 1955.
299. 117622, 1081/56, minute by Wilding, 14 Jan. 1955; 117624, 1081/96,
minute by Young, 27 Jan. 1955.
300. 117624, 1081/97, 'Cyprus', minute by Nutting, 8 Feb. 1955.
301. 117624, 1081/89, Maitland to Eden, 3 Feb. 1955.
302. 117624, 1081/104, Armitage to Lloyd, 1 Feb. 1955; cf. Crouzet I 1973,
409; Kelling 1990, 150.
303. 117628, 1081/205, Young to Salt, Washington, 1 April 1955; cf. CO 926/
264, draft paper on constitutional proposals by Smith, March 1955.
304. CO 926/264, draft paper on constitutional proposals by Smith, March 1955.
305. 117628, 1081/199, record of meeting between Eden and Lennox-Boyd, 23
March 1955; 117628, 1081/205, Young to Salt, Washington, 1 April 1955.
306. 117628, 1081/199, record of meeting between Eden and Lennox-Boyd, 23
March 1955.
307. It was a time when the British government felt indebted to Menderes for his
effective promotion of the Turkish-Iraqi Pact, which purported to safeguard
British military rights in Iraq: Holden Reid 1988, 176.
308. 117627, 1081/196, minutes of meeting between Lennox-Boyd and Nutting, 15 March 1955; cf. Kelling 1990, 150.
309. 747C.00/3-1755, Courtney to State, tel. 68.
310. 117628, 1081/200, Peake to Ward, 23 and 31 March 1955.
311. CO 926/253, reply from Lennox-Boyd to parliamentary question supple-
mentary, 2 March 1955.
312. 117628, 1081/205, Young to Salt, 1 April 1955.
313. 117627, 1081/199, minute by Eden, 24 March 1955; cf. Kelling 1990, 150.
314. 117628, 1081/205, Young to Salt, Washington, 1 April 1955.

315. 107485, 10110/5, Cyprus Political Situation Report, July 1953.
316. 112848, 1081/183, record of conversation between Harrison, C.O. Morris, CO, and Armitage, 5 July 1954.
317. CO 926/179, report by Evans, Information Dept., CO, pt 1954
318. Quoted in Holland 1993, 148.
319. 112884, 1081/1269, Durrell to CO, 7 Dec. 1954; cf. Durrell 1957, 119, 125-126, 148-149.
320. Grivas *Memoirs*, 16-17.
321. Crawshaw 1978, 99.
322. Evans had mentioned this in his report of 29 September: CO 926/179; cf. Kelling 1990, 153.
323. 112859, 1081/486, Morris, CO, to Armitage, 8 Sept. 1954; cf. Kelling 1990, 151.
324. CO 926/209, Cyprus Political Situation Report, Dec. 1954; 112878, 1081/1096, B.M.E.O. to FO, 8 Dec. 1954; cf. Anderson 1994, 177-179; Crawshaw 1978, 102.
325. 112880, 1081/1172, Peake to FO, 10 Dec. 1954. As a means of preventing this, Peake suggested a recourse to the NATO Council or even to the UN Security Council, if there was proof of Greek complicity in stirring up armed rebellion in Cyprus: 112881, 1081/1174, Peake to Ward, 10 Dec. 1954. Young agreed that such proof would greatly help to 'inhibit Greek agitation': 112885, 1081/1276, minute by Young, 21 Dec. 1954.
326. Crawshaw 1978, 112.
327. Anderson 1994, 182-183.
328. 112868, 1081/781, Morris, CO, to Young, FO, 6 Oct. 1954; cf. Durrell 1957, 120-121; Kyrou 1955, 368-371, n. 1.
329. 107502, 1081/49, Galsworthy to May, 1 Oct. 1953.
330. 112843, 1081/6, Peake to Cheetham, 23 Jan. 1954.
331. 107502, 1081/61, 'Cyprus', memo by Ward, 18 Nov. 1953; Durrell 1957, 134-135.
332. Instances of such claims by Winster, Turnbull and Fletcher-Cooke, see in Louis 1984, 218-219 and n. 39; Kelling 1990, 86, 109.
333. 112848, 1081/193, Armitage to Lyttelton, 19 July 1954.
334. 112853, 1081/327, minute by Young, 21 Aug. 1954; 1081/330, Peake to FO, 23 Aug. 1954. 112859, 1081/470, FO to San Jose, 9 Sept. 1954; 112863, 1081/620, Factual Note, FO to British Embassy, Washington, 20 Sept. 1954; *FRUS 1952-54*, VIII, 710-712.
335. CO 926/500, Armitage to Lloyd, 13 Sept. 1954; cf. Durrell 1957, 146.
336. 112884, 1081/1269, Durrell to CO, 7 Dec. 1954.
337. 117623, 1081/72, Churchill to Lennox-Boyd, 5 Jan. 1955.
338. CO 926/174, minute by Armitage, 16 March 1955.
339. Durrell 1957, 134-136.
340. CO 926/183, 'Report on a Visit to Cyprus, 23-27 Oct. 1954' by Butler, Ankara.
341. 117624, 1081/89, Maitland to Eden, 3 Feb. 1955.
342. Photograph reproduced in Seferis, *Meres* VI, 140.

5

PRINCIPLES AND EXPEDIENCY: THE
FORMULATION OF U.S. POLICY

Anti-Communism versus anti-Colonialism

Cyprus, like other colonial issues involving allied powers, presented
the US administration with a grave dilemma between principle and
expediency. Anti-colonialism, as a genuine and widely shared set of
principles, was an integral part of the American self-image, particularly as it had emerged from the glories of World War II. Ideology, however, could hardly be expected to get in the way of a world
power's self-interest. In setting the priorities of US foreign policy,
as Professor W. Roger Louis observed, principles were 'easily rec-
onciled with defence requirements and economic opportunities'
and increasingly became 'subordinate to the more urgent problem
of anti-communism'.[1] In the case of Cyprus, this reconciliation
proved no easy matter, as the United States had to take the conflicting interests of its allies into account.

Towards the end of World War II, the State Department's post-
war planning appeared to favour the cession of Cyprus to Greece as
part of the peace settlement.[2] Yet, as inter-allied relations deteriorated, this position never became official policy. Being aware of both
Greek national aspirations and British imperial interests, American
planners were primarily concerned with containing Soviet expansion in an increasingly important region.[3] However, that early position reappeared at the time of the Truman Doctrine. During the
Congressional hearings on the Greek and Turkish Aid bill, in March
1947, a 'working paper' on Cyprus slipped in the background material provided by the State Department. This text recognised the
Cyprus question as 'the one unresolved issue of Anglo-Greek rela-

tions of importance to the United States', which was 'likely to grow
more acute' as Greece became less dependent upon Britain. The
State Department, for its part, 'would welcome a direct settlement
of this issue between Greece and Britain, which would adequately
safeguard legitimate security interests and trade routes in the Mediterranean and the welfare of non-Greek Cypriot minorities'.[4]

When this document was leaked to the press, the State Department felt compelled to withdraw it, explaining that it expressed
only a tentative position 'not approved on [the] highest level as official US policy'.[5] Still, it was a trend of thought which the British
found extremely disquieting. Since a strong British presence in the
Middle East was considered to be in the American interest, Washington became more circumspect.

Reviewing the US position on the future of the British Empire in
June 1948, the State Department attempted to tackle its fundamental dilemma which was bound to recur in its Cyprus policy. It
was recognised that 'the general policy of favoring eventual self-
determination of peoples' ought to be balanced against current strategic considerations, particularly the continuing British role in safeguarding Western interests in various parts of the world.[6] This approach was promptly undersigned by the military.[7] It also came in
good time, as the Cyprus question resurfaced in early August, following King Paul's interview in the *New York Times*. Though careful not to come out openly in support of either side, the Americans
endorsed the strategic argument in favour of British sovereignty
and quietly exercised their influence in order to restrain the Greeks
from pressing their national claims.[8] This attitude continued into
the next year. Ambassador Grady's prodding considerably helped
the British to extract the Greek statements discouraging Enosis agitation in December 1949.[9]

American diplomats clearly perceived the destabilising potential of the Cyprus question for Greek relations with Britain and
Turkey. The heads of the US missions in the Middle East, meeting in
Istanbul in late November 1949, urged the US government to 'do
everything possible to promote stability on the island'. This entailed
not only discouraging Greek nationalist aspirations but also making
it clear to the Turks that they should expect no support for any
claims they might have on Cyprus. While acknowledging the is-

land's importance to the defence of Turkey, the 'men on the spot' were obviously alarmed by the 'irresponsible and inflammatory' pronouncements of Turkish newspapers and patriotic groups.[10] The British were also given a warning against using the Turkish card.[11] Within months, however, the State Department would itself be using the Turkish interest in Cyprus in order to discourage Greek lobbying.

What also worried American diplomats and policy-makers was the attempt of the Communists within and without Cyprus to exploit the problem for their own ends. They resented the rise of AKEL and its attempt to dominate the drive for Enosis.[12] The vigorous sponsoring of the Greek national cause by Eastern bloc media was further proof of Communist complicity. According to the US Consul in Nicosia, by early 1950, the 'loud and distorted comment' of satellite broadcasts to Cyprus could 'be heard in most Cypriot coffee shops or *tavernas* between the hours of five and nine p.m.'.[13] All this convinced the Americans that Moscow realised the disruptive potential of the Cyprus question and meant to make full use of it.

As has been noted, US diplomats tended to regard the British as partly responsible for this unsatisfactory state of affairs. According to the Consul in Nicosia, the official Greek reticence towards Enosis, being the result of British pressures, allowed AKEL to pose as the true champion of patriotism. Above all, the Americans were displeased by the 'inadequacy' of British methods in dealing with the 'red menace' in the island. This led the State Department, on the eve of the 1949 municipal elections, to propose the involvement of Greece and Turkey in checking AKEL's influence. The rejection of this proposal only helped to arouse American suspicions. The heads of US missions in the Middle East suggested that the colonial administration of Cyprus be urged to tackle the problem and to 'increase their efforts to promote security'. One representative argued that the British 'tended to let the Communists have too free a run so as to play them off against the Nationalists'.[14]

American concern with AKEL did not merely reflect the prevailing anti-communism of US foreign policy; it also stemmed from the party's proven capacity to disrupt American business interests by industrial action, which had occasionally taken violent forms in the troubled 1940s.[15] In view of the continuing failure of the colonial authorities to take drastic action against Communist activity,[16]

the US Consulate undertook its systematic surveillance itself. By
1952, it kept 120 informants on its payroll, many of them within
AKEL ranks.[17] Such inside information permitted the Consulate to
keep the State Department abreast of developments in the Cypriot
Left on a regular basis.[18]

Enosis crosses the Atlantic

Despite its early awareness of the problem, by early 1950 the State
Department conveniently claimed that there was no specific policy
on the Cyprus question, simply because 'it was not a matter of direct concern to the US'.[19] Yet the American position was fast becoming the concern of others. Following the Ethnarchy plebiscite,
it was clear that the Enosis campaign would, sooner rather than
later, cross the Atlantic. The possibility of the Cyprus question being raised at the UN provoked an in depth discussion at the State
Department on 2 May. From this meeting, where eleven officials,
including Consul Porter, were present, it transpired that the official
position was that the United States was not and did not wish to
become party to the dispute. The officials directly involved in the
affairs of the region were in favour of urging the British to relax
their attitude. Leonard Cromie, the officer in charge of Greek affairs at the State Department, wondered whether it was 'wise to
continue our hands-off policy ... trying to sit with our British allies
on a boiling pot and asking the Greeks not to add fuel to the flames'.
Britain, however, was a major ally in the Middle East, and the administration did not wish to add to her difficulties on account of a
minor spot like Cyprus. Thus, the meeting concluded in favour of
Anglo-American talks with a view to producing, if possible, a co-
ordinated position.[20]

A further question, which the British often raised and the State
Department meeting addressed, concerned the Greek ability to assume the financial and administrative burden of a transfer of sovereignty in Cyprus.[21] It seems that the Americans, who actually ran
the Greek economy until 1952, had no confidence in its ability to
cope with this task. In Ambassador Grady's view, Enosis, if effected,
would pose an administrative burden which war-torn Greece simply could not shoulder.[22] Cromie remarked half-jokingly that 'a

moderate dose of actual Greek administration would quickly discourage further Enosis agitation'.[23] The economic argument was
subsequently used in State Department communications to Congressmen sympathetic to the Greek case.[24]

The matter acquired some urgency as Cypriot delegations were
out in search of a sponsor for their bid to raise their cause at the
UN. While the British requested support against such a prospect,
the State Department feared that a Soviet satellite might take the
initiative and embarrass the West on yet another colonial issue.[25]
Further pressure was generated by the lobbying activities of the
Greek-American community. This campaign could capitalise on the
community's electoral strength in certain important states, such as
New York or Massachusetts, and, of course, on anti-colonial sentiment. To the persistent correspondence of Congressmen and other
dignitaries in support of Cypriot emancipation, the State Department undertook to explain that, although the United States generally supported the principle of self-determination of peoples, broader
'legal and political considerations' dictated its non-involvement in
this particular case, in which no significant American interests were
at stake; Enosis was opposed by Britain, Turkey and the 'not incon-
siderable non-Greek minorities' of the island; it was also sponsored
by Moscow and international communism, which stood to benefit
from the airing of inter-allied differences at the UN.[26] If the Greek-
Americans succeeded in attracting more Congressional support, the
State Department was prepared to explain, 'orally and confiden-
tially', that the government based its opinion on wider considerations and not on the 'merits of the arguments for and against'
Enosis.[27]

All this amounted to a clear position against the raising of the
question at the UN, which would remain unaltered over the following four years. The State Department continued to give to the recurrent approaches of pro-Enosis lobbyists the standard reply that
it would not be 'appropriate' for the United States to involve itself
in the problem, because it was 'essentially' one for the British and
the Cypriots to settle, whereas 'the principal parties' concerned –
Britain, Greece and Turkey – had deep and conflicting interests,
and the international situation made the whole thing 'inopportune'.[28]

Indeed, the outbreak of the Korean War and the heightening of

international tensions had provided a convenient argument in favour of the *status quo* in Cyprus. Enosis agitation coupled with the
slow progress in Greek-Yugoslav relations proved an irritant to US
policy-makers, as shown by Acheson's strong-worded despatch to
Athens of 27 June.[29] The State Department asked US missions abroad
to guard against any indication that some state might sponsor Enosis
before the coming General Assembly. If that happened, the Americans would be confronted with a further dilemma, since it was their
general policy to support the discussion of any item raised before
the UN.[30] After the Korean invasion, this line was modified: the US
delegation to the UN was instructed 'to work actively to discourage
[the] placing of [the] question' on the agenda, while reserving its
position on inscription.[31]

   The matter was re-examined in the light of rumours, originat-
ing with AKEL, that a Soviet bloc delegation might raise the question. Only a few days before the deadline for putting items on the
agenda and opinion within the State Department remained divided:
the Offices of European and Near Eastern Affairs came out against
inscription, despite previous practice. The UN delegation, however,
seconded by the Office of United Nations Political and Security
Affairs, insisted on being allowed to determine its position according to the circumstances: unless there was an Eastern bloc initiative,
abstention should be the furthest it could go. As it put it, it would
be against the best American traditions, if the delegation were to
'vote negatively when the issue is tinged with "colonialism"'.[32] Eventually, the dilemma did not arise in practice, but it was not resolved either.

Sitting on the fence

From the first UN scare of summer 1950, the Americans would be
confronted with periodic requests to come out in support of the
British position. As it turned out, the US military was at first more
susceptible to British strategic arguments than the diplomats. Following Lord Tedder's letter to Bradley in October 1950, the JCS
agreed that British sovereignty over Cyprus served Western military planning in the region. They also concurred that Greece should
be pressed 'to cease agitation'.[33]

   The responsiveness of the JCS largely reflected the importance that it still attached to the role of Britain in Middle Eastern defence rather than any particular strategic interest in Cyprus. This is not to say that the latter was non-existent: British air fields were available to the US Air Force for medium-range operations in case of emergency, while the Americans assisted in the installation of early warning radar stations on the island.[34] The State Department also enjoyed operating rights for two 'Voice of America' radio stations, whereas, in the private sector, the American-owned Cyprus Mines Corporation, which exploited the island's rich copper deposits, was regarded as the 'backbone of the island's economy'. Yet it was far from self-evident that these interests were best served by the retention of British sovereignty.

A hint to this effect was included in the State Department's statement of policy with respect to Greece, Turkey and Iran. This statement, issued in late December 1950, for the first time contained a special reference to Cyprus. In the short run, it favoured the continuation of British rule due to 'strategic considerations'. The Greek government should be urged at least to stick to its position that the matter be settled within the framework of Anglo-Greek friendship when the time was propitious. Any idea of a recourse to international bodies or the 'conspicuous discussion' of the question in Greece and Cyprus should be discouraged. On the other hand, the State Department recognised the need for some positive steps on the British part too: economic improvement, progress towards self-government, and, without prejudice to the question of sovereignty, the development of 'closer ties between Cyprus and Greece'. From all this it became clear that the Americans far from shared the British axiom that the matter was closed. Their long-term perspective did not exclude a revision of the status of the island. As much as was admitted in the same study, which stated that the 'continued examination of this question is essential in order to provide a long-range solution'.[35] From all this it was clear that, for as long they valued the British military contribution to the security of the region, the Americans were in favour of the *status quo* in Cyprus. Yet, in order to be able exercise their influence on both sides of the dispute, they refused to commit themselves openly. Thus, they steadily rejected all British requests for a joint or a unilateral public statement against Enosis.

The prospect of difficulties at the UN once more arose in early 1951, following Governor Wright's anti-sedition measures and the official Greek pronouncements in support of Enosis.[36] From Nicosia, Vice-Consul Carl Bartch suggested a thorough re-examination of policy. He did not believe that the innocuous measures suggested by the Department in its December study would suffice to placate the Ethnarchy. Nor did he conceal his disapproval of the colonial administration's policy, arguing that the anti-sedition laws were 'more severe than the laws enacted against the American colonists prior to our own war of independence'. Seeing grave dangers ahead, he could only envisage a way out in a British undertaking to let the people of Cyprus decide their own future, once international tension abated.[37]

This formula was embraced by Ambassador Peurifoy,[38] whereas, according to reports from Athens and Nicosia, Ambassador Norton, Venizelos, Makarios and officials of the colonial administration had also expressed themselves in favour at some point. What then seemed a basis for a settlement, combined with pressures in Congress and a Greek request for mediation, led the State Department to pursue the idea. Among the set of ideas which Anschuetz informally put to the British Embassy in Washington in early April, the emphasis was clearly on a promise of eventual self-determination.[39] Yet nothing came out as Makarios publicly repudiated the formula and the British remained unmoved.

Following this abortive mediation, the State Department reaffirmed its position in favour of the *status quo*. At that point, it did not wish to add to the 'many current areas [of] friction' between the United States and Britain on account of a relatively minor issue such as Cyprus.[40] By the time Enosis resurfaced in the spring of 1952 the official position of the United States was that it did not wish to become party to a dispute which was between friends, although it did not think that the time was opportune for the Greeks to press their case at the UN.[41] The qualification about timing was an important feature in that it could serve as a soothing formula each time the Greeks were rebuffed, while permitting the Americans to retain some flexibility as to the future.

Yet Washington refrained from stating this position in public, although it was invited to do so by both the British and Greek governments. The latter's prodding was interpreted as an attempt to attribute to the Americans the unpopular decision not to resort to the UN. Venizelos' play of US objections in the past tended to confirm this. What was more, Peurifoy had warned that the developing hostility towards Britain might also affect the Americans if they appeared to oppose Greek aspirations.[42] The Department, for its part, realised the unpopularity of its pro-British positions with Middle Eastern opinion and preferred to continue to work discreetly. This time, it asked Peurifoy to point out the risks for Greek-Turkish relations. In the Department's view, a 'sharp Turk[ish] reaction' was to be expected if the Greeks chose to raise the matter at the UN.[43]

Throughout this early period, the US Embassy in Athens had assisted the British in discouraging Enosis agitation, albeit, as it was observed, 'with varying degrees of discomfiture'. The British Embassy also commented that the Americans took more seriously than themselves the 'strength and momentum' of the Enosis movement both in Cyprus and Greece, and were much more concerned with its disruptive potential.[44] Indeed, US reports repeatedly spoke of the 'potentially explosive frustration and negativism' prevailing in Cyprus as a result of British policy.[45] Furthermore, even after the advent of the strong Papagos government, the Athens Embassy did not tend to dismiss lightly the domestic pressures facing any Greek government on account of Cyprus.[46]

In the aftermath of the Anglo-American colonial talks of July-September 1952, the State Department, in concert with the Pentagon, approved its first articulate position paper on the matter. In short, the document recognised 'impelling strategic reasons' for the retention of Cyprus 'as a military British base' – an important qualification regarding the question of sovereignty. The views of the JCS in favour of the retention of 'full (British) sovereignty over the island' featured prominently. Due notice was also given to the Turkish opposition to Enosis. The document urged 'every effort' to keep the question out of the limelight and to prevent it from reaching the UN. Finally, the paper listed a number of suggestions for 'checking the campaign for Enosis': constitutional government; suspension of the anti-sedition laws; curtailment of AKEL influence; dual nationality or other measures designed to placate Greek Cypriot national sentiment; encouragement of moderate opinion; and development of non-Communist trade unions.[47]

The 'New Look' and Cyprus

Until 1952, and despite the momentous changes enunciated by the
Truman Doctrine, US strategy in the Middle East had largely rested
on the assumption that the security of the area was primarily a British responsibility. This view was no longer valid by July 1953. Following his tour of the region, the new Secretary of State, Dulles,
fully realised that British influence had waned, possibly beyond re-
pair, and that identification with the policies of Britain and France
in the region was damaging to US interests. From the military point
of view, two years of efforts for a regional defence structure hinged
on a strong British presence in Egypt had come to nought. From
then on, while maintaining Anglo-American co-operation 'to the
greatest extent practicable', the United States should be prepared
to act either with local powers, Turkey in particular, or on its own.
The 'Northern Tier' – comprising Turkey, Iran, Iraq and Pakistan –
had grasped Dulles' imagination as the best defence arrangement
against Soviet expansionism. It also had the advantage of covering
the unstable inner core of the Arab states and Israel without postulating their participation.[48] In this context, Turkey emerged as the
linchpin between the European and the Middle East systems of defence – a factor with considerable bearing on America's Cyprus
policy.

With regard to Cyprus, the Americans had long realised that, as
the British were likely to withdraw from the Suez Zone, they were
bound 'to look upon Cyprus as the last bit of territory standing
between them and their total eclipse in the Middle East'.[49] Yet US
planners did not see eye to eye with their British counterparts. The
concept of a Mediterranean defence line stretching from Gibraltar
to Malta and Cyprus was considered out-dated. By 1954, the strategic role of the island was primarily seen in providing air support
to operations along the 'Northern Tier'.[50] The fact that the British
had done very little to develop that potential also tended to reduce
its immediate strategic value in American eyes.

When, in November 1953, the State Department became aware
of the Greek intention to raise the Cyprus question at the coming
General Assembly, its reaction was low-key. The US permanent representative to the UN, Lodge, was told that the United States 'ought

not to interfere' in a matter that was between two friendly powers 'over a small island' and had to be settled by them alone.[51]

This initial nonchalance was broken by the British request for support, officially submitted in the *aide-mémoire* of 28 January 1954. To a great extent, US policy on Cyprus would be formulated in response to the three points raised in that document. Thus, the Americans had to decide whether the strategic interests of both powers in the Eastern Mediterranean demanded 'that there should be no change in the status of Cyprus'. Further, they should consider a commitment to continue to discourage the Greeks from pressing their claim. Finally, if the Greeks went undeterred, could they pledge to 'oppose the placing of the Cyprus question on the General Assembly agenda or any other attempt' to have it discussed at the UN?[52]

The formulation of the American reply to the British *aide-mémoire* proved a slow, almost agonising process, affected as it was by departmental heart-searching and the ups and downs of Anglo-American relations. The British *aide-mémoire* forced upon US decision-makers the dilemma they had been evading since 1950, namely that of reconciling general principles with concrete political and strategic interests. At first sight, the Cyprus question put the American anti-colonial tradition to the test. Yet a careful reading of the US record at the UN would reveal that this tradition could be bent whenever this suited relations with allied colonial powers – the US delegation had opposed discussion of the Morocco and Tunisia questions and had abstained from the vote on Resolution 637A (VII) supporting self-determination. As a study by the Policy Planning Staff admitted in May 1954, the United States was often 'forced into supporting' the colonial powers against not only the rising tide of nationalism in areas like the Middle and the Far East but also 'its own instincts and traditions'. By doing so, it not only sacrificed part of its 'moral influence' and exposed itself to Communist 'charges of imperialism',[53] but also forfeited its ability to exploit Soviet 'colonialism', i.e. the domination of the peoples of Eastern Europe and Central Asia by Moscow.[54]

Imaginative officials ventured various formulations for overcoming this dilemma. According to the US Consul in Nicosia, principles should be judged by the outcome. In the case of Cyprus, it was clear that self-determination threatened 'to weaken the free world for no reason except an emotional one'.[55] For the official in charge of the Greek affairs at the State Department, Chalmers Wood, the question was really one of timing as the United States did not favour a change in sovereignty *at that time*, but did favour the eventual self-determination of colonial peoples.[56]

A second dilemma arose in connection with the British request for a clear commitment against having the issue on the General Assembly agenda. However much the Americans disliked the washing of allied dirty linen at the UN, a commitment of this sort would be against standard practice.[57] What was more, it would mean that the United States abandoned the line adhered to since at least 1951, and took sides in a dispute between friends. Some, like the Ambassador in London, believed that this was better than appearing to be 'sitting on the fence'.[58] Others, like Wood, advised against openly supporting either side, so that the Americans could retain, if need be, their ability to mediate.[59]

As a possible way out from a UN discussion and its tantalising dilemmas, the State Department examined the possibility of containing the dispute within the Western family by having it referred to the NAC. The suggestion emanated from the Office of UN Affairs, but it was not followed up, as it was realised that NATO simply lacked the mechanism 'for the collective handling of disputes' between its members. It was further feared that the airing of such a controversial issue would only add to the strains of the Alliance, at a time when the question of German rearmament and the fate of the European Defence Community remained unsettled.[60]

At a preliminary meeting of the Offices involved on 8 February, it was decided to obtain the assessments of the 'people on the spot' and the views of the military on the strategic importance of Cyprus. The tentative conclusion of that meeting was that, since the United States opposed the airing of inter-allied differences at the UN, it should be able to satisfy the first two British requests – supporting the *status quo* in Cyprus and discouraging Greek intentions. Yet no commitment could be made as to its subsequent course of action if the Greeks did raise the Cyprus question at the UN.[61] Interestingly enough, the meeting contemplated asking the Turks to exercise a restraining influence on the Greeks, in view of the 'close ties' existing between the two neighbouring countries.[62]

The replies from the diplomatic missions did not delay. For some time, reports from Athens had been critical of British inflexibility: far from achieving its task – to convince the Greeks that Enosis was unattainable and agitation futile – that attitude only helped to stiffen them in their resolve to step up their campaign; at the same time, it pre-empted any attempt to 'mitigate the issue' when necessary. Ambassador Cannon, who privately blamed Peake, Eden and Papagos for 'the Cyprus mess',[63] estimated that the problem was bound to grow more acute. In order to avoid this, he suggested that the British be clearly warned not to expect the US position to remain the same indefinitely. Instead, they should be advised to consider a 'gradual evolution' for Cyprus, and, in the short run, to accept to talk to the Greeks on current issues affecting the island. From the Embassy's 'vantage point', a constitution including a provision for self-determination after a specified period offered the 'best possibilities' for a solution.[64]

Cannon also questioned the ability of the United States to influence Greek policy effectively, particularly since the Papagos government was 'substantially less dependent on US aid' than its predecessors.[65] By mid-March, the Embassy estimated that Athens had already made up its mind and, in doing so, had taken into account likely reactions. A more forceful presentation of the American views, it warned, could jeopardise bilateral co-operation 'in other important sectors'. On the question of the *status quo*, the Embassy submitted that the security of Cyprus could be dissociated from the retention of British sovereignty. Instead, it perceived merits in some form of condominium, which would adequately protect British military interests. Despite the shortcomings of 'divided authority', it was argued, this would be preferable to an unresolved Cyprus question 'rankling within the Western alliance'.[66] From Nicosia, Joseph Wagner also saw no point in a policy of pressing the Greeks against pursuing their own interests at the UN 'year after year'. After three years at that post, he had come to doubt whether 'the trend of events' towards some sort of climax could be reversed.[67]

By way of contrast, both London and Ankara came out in favour of all three British requests, as a matter of consistency. Ambassadors Aldrich and Warren argued that a discussion of the Cyprus question at the UN should be opposed on the strategic and political grounds

that were mentioned in recent British and Turkish representations –
the dangers to allied relations, regional stability and the British position, and the corresponding Soviet gains.[68]

The reply from the Pentagon did not arrive before 19 May. The
British Embassy in Washington partly attributed this delay to the
'conspicuously weak' co-ordination between the State Department
and the Pentagon.[69] At any rate, it was a significant departure from
previous endorsements of the British strategic imperative – while
reaffirming the importance of Cyprus to US strategic interests, the
JCS were no longer prepared to underwrite the continuation of
British sovereignty; rather, they 'would prefer those arrangements
which are most likely to permit [the] continued use [of base facili-
ties] by the armed forces of the United States'. In communicating
this opinion to the State Department, the Pentagon made it clear
that this was its final word: it was unwilling to take sides 'in a dispute between two of our allies in which the U.S. interest is not
clearly affected'.[70]

The fact that the American reply to the British *aide-mémoire*
delayed another two months was not unrelated to the strains and
stresses of the 'special relationship'. As has been noted, Indochina
had caused a springtime chill between Dulles and Eden. Despite
mending efforts in June, the climate was once more aggravated owing
to the British abstention from the vote on the Guatemalan appeal to
the Security Council, which the United States wished to suppress.
When, in early July, State Department officials were about to take
their draft reply to Dulles for clearance, his Assistant Secretary, General Bedell Smith, warned them that, if they did so, 'they would be
thrown out of the room'.[71] At the same time, however, the personal
involvement of the Secretary of State in Cyprus policy should not
be exaggerated. Until after the issue had been placed on the UN
agenda, Dulles often went on record as being 'not informed in detail',[72] 'perplexed'[73] knowing 'nothing about it',[74] while instructions bearing his signature were sometimes issued with 'no high
level clearance'.[75]

Eventually, in its reply of 12 July to the British *aide-mémoire*,
the State Department distinguished between strategic and political
considerations. While the former did not necessarily preclude a
change in sovereignty in Cyprus, political expediency 'militated'

against such a development, but only 'at this time'. On the point
most burning to the British, that of the US attitude towards a Greek
recourse to the UN, the Department reserved its position and merely
restated its fundamental dilemma of reconciling 'general political
considerations with the importance which it attaches to the principle of the self-determination of peoples'.[76]

Pressures and mediation

Meanwhile, American diplomacy had engaged in a relatively discreet effort to discourage the Greek recourse to the UN. Since the
beginning of April, US officials had been telling the Greeks not to
expect support if they went ahead with their plan, but they never
threatened to oppose it.[77] The risks for Greek-Turkish relations and
the projected military alliance between Greece, Turkey and Yugoslavia featured prominently in State Department thinking about
Cyprus.[78] Yet reports from the field were rather sanguine. Its stern
warnings to the Greek government notwithstanding, the US Embassy in Athens optimistically reported that, if the discussion at the
UN could 'be kept within bounds', Greek-Turkish co-operation and
the Balkan Pact could well survive the rigours of the Greek appeal.[79] Equally reassuring was the assessment from Ankara. Impressed by Turkish moderation, Warren estimated that, at that point,
the Turks did not want 'to undermine [the] Gr[ee]k position *vis-à-
vis* [the] British'.[80]

It seems, therefore, that, not unlike the British, US diplomacy
tended to play up Turkish reactions in its effort to discourage Greek
intentions. This is not to say that Washington did not pay due attention to these reactions. Turkey was the most powerful and stable ally
of the United States in the region and, in comparison to Greece,
had always been considered of greater strategic importance. With
hindsight, the first five years of the Menderes government have been
described as the 'honeymoon' period of US-Turkish relations.[81]
Besides, the State Department had been referring to Turkey as one
of the 'principal parties' to the Cyprus dispute since 1950. All this
was reflected in the message which Dulles sent to Stefanopoulos on
28 July. The original draft went much further than recognising Turkey's interest in the future of Cyprus: it spoke of 'deep popular

feelings' which the Turkish government could not ignore, and stressed that the US government was 'cognizant of the interests of Greece *and Turkey*'.[82] These points were strongly objected by Ambassador Cannon[83] and were subsequently deleted.

Owing to the revision process, Dulles' message was delivered to Athens a fortnight later than intended, thus preceding Hopkinson's ill-fated announcement in the Commons only by a few hours. Yet, even in its final form, it was a forceful enough expression of American disapproval. In line with the Department's position since 1950, it came out in favour of Anglo-Cypriot talks with a view to resolving the problem 'in gradual stages' without third-party interference.[84] This became the standard recipe which the Americans would repeatedly but unsuccessfully try to impress upon the Papagos government.

Pending the Greek reply, the Embassy in Athens estimated it was too late for Papagos to reverse his policy 'without risking [the] disintegration [of] his government'.[85] Cannon also began to sound apprehensive about the future of Greek-American relations and suggested additional aid to Greece and an invitation to Papagos to visit the United States before the opening of the General Assembly.[86] The proposal was not followed up. The State Department was inclined to be more confident than either Greek officials or the Embassy in Athens regarding the ability of the Greek government to survive a failure at the UN.[87]

The administration had also to contend with the repeated Greek requests for mediation. The aim was to secure a relaxation of British attitude and, in return, the Greek government would abandon its recourse to the UN. At first, the State Department refused to be involved, save its lower-level approach to the British during the Churchill-Eden visit to Washington, in late June.[88] While drafting the US reply to the British *aide-mémoire*, the Department had also contemplated a verbal appeal to the British regarding the need for a constitutional offer 'acceptable' to all sides in Cyprus.[89] It was only after the debacle of Hopkinson's statement and the Greek recourse to the UN, that President Eisenhower himself sanctioned informal attempts at mediation, such as those of cinema magnate Skouras and Ms Cowles.[90]

By that time, British moves had undermined Washington's effort to restrain Athens.[91] What was more, the way the British had chosen to introduce their constitutional offer in Cyprus had created a public opinion problem within the United States. Until then, what little comment the Cyprus question attracted in the American press was largely sympathetic to the Greek case. The news, however, of the 'anti-seditious' repression in Cyprus was bound to test the anti-colonial reflexes of American public opinion. The media began to refer to the British policy as an instance of out-dated, if not 'immoral', colonialism. Ernie Hill, the London correspondent of the *Chicago Daily News* and the *Washington Post*, commented that the British intended to maintain their stronghold in Cyprus 'even if they have to put half the population in jail'.[92] There were reactions in Congress too. During the debate on the Foreign Aid bill, Senator Wayne Morse referred to Cyprus warning that, despite repression, the 'spirit of freedom will rise again to plague Great Britain and to plague the United States, if we aid and abet the policy of colonialism'.[93] All this, of course, was grist to the mill of the Greek-American lobby.

Neutrality of sorts

The tactics of the US delegation to the UN *vis-à-vis* the Greek recourse became a matter of intense debate between the various branches of the State Department involved. For one thing, Cyprus could not be isolated from the wider colonial problem, which was expected to be 'the single most controversial issue' at the Ninth General Assembly.[94] As had been the case in 1950, when the problem was only hypothetical, the Office for European Affairs supported either a negative vote on inscription or a motion to postpone the consideration of the Greek item; the Offices for UN and Near Eastern Affairs favoured a positive vote or abstention, whereas the former opposed postponement.[95] The matter came to a head after 25 August, when the British, seconded by the Turks, asked for an explicit US commitment to oppose inscription and to canvass other member states to do likewise.

By the end of August, the US position swayed between abstention and a negative vote. On the 31st, the State Department informed various US missions, including the delegation to the UN,

that it was moving in favour of a negative vote.[96] On the following
day, however, things changed and the missions were informed that
no firm position would be taken for at least another ten days, pending Dulles' return from Manila. What caused this change overnight
is not clear, though a cable from Cabot Lodge, head of the US delegation to the UN, may hold the clue.[97] London, Athens, Ankara
and Nicosia were duly sounded as to local reactions.[98] Ankara anticipated no serious or long-lasting effect on Turkish opinion, if abstention was opted.[99] According to the London Embassy, the British government was resigned to losing the fight on inscription; therefore, a US abstention would not have a 'seriously unfavourable impact'.[100] Things with Athens were more complex. Ambassador Cannon reiterated his concern about the future of US influence in
Greece, if the inscription of the Cyprus item was opposed. As a
result, he warned, Greek co-operation in military matters would
be restricted, the pro-American Papagos government would be discredited, political instability would return, rival foreign influences,
primarily the Soviet but possibly the German too, would benefit,
while the Greeks might even be tempted to try French-style neu-
tralism.[101]

Such concern was duly reflected in the position paper, which
was prepared by the Office of UN Political and Security Affairs on
14 September. The overriding objective was to safeguard allied cohesion, the Greek-Turkish partnership, in particular. The ability of
the United States to act as an 'honest broker' was a further consideration. This, of course, precluded outright opposition to either side.
Abstention was thus recommended as the most expedient course. If
the Greek item was inscribed, it should not be allowed to mature:
the United States should try to keep discussion at a minimum and
to 'avoid Assembly action' of the kind requested in the Greek appeal. This meant that the Americans were prepared to oppose a substantial resolution on Cyprus, and, by doing so, they went some
way towards meeting British wishes. US diplomacy should also continue pressing the point home with the Greeks that 'direct discussions' between the British and the Cypriots offered the best prospect for a settlement.[102]

It should be noted that, in discussing the Cyprus question, the
State Department paid only cursory attention to the 'red peril' in

Cyprus. The prospect of the Soviets exploiting inter-allied differences caused much more concern. Assistant Secretary Smith had told the British that, if a plebiscite were to be held, he did not believe that Cyprus would become Communist.[103] Clearly, the Americans had grown less receptive to the portrayal of Enosis as a Communist plot. If the British were really concerned with Communist influence in Cyprus, they argued, they could easily take steps to curb it.[104]

Eventually, in conveying their decision to abstain to London and Ankara, the Americans pledged to 'discourage debate' on substance and to 'actively oppose any resolution'.[105] This sweeping commitment was repeated in letters from Dulles to Churchill and Menderes, sent on 21 September.[106] At the same time, the Greeks were urged not to press 'for [the] passage of any resolution'.[107] For some reason, no personal message was sent to the Greek Prime Minister. Yet the American opposition to the discussion of the Cyprus question 'at this time' was made abundantly clear in the standard replies of the State Department to its numerous correspondents.[108]

Indeed, during the thirty-odd days between the placing of the Greek appeal and the opening of the Ninth session of the General Assembly, Greek-American lobbying intensified. Congressmen, Governors and other public figures were writing to the government in support of Cypriot self-determination.[109] The matter acquired additional importance in view of the mid-term Congressional elections, which were due for November. Anti-colonial opinion and, more precisely, the strategically concentrated Greek-American vote were factors that could not be lightly ignored. All this apparently accounted for the President's personal interest in the matter and his offer, in his letter to Prime Minister Churchill, 'to do something'.[110] Not that Dulles was immune to domestic considerations either. Thus, in his letter to Churchill on 21 September, he did drop a hint at the effect on US opinion.[111] What was more, he still bore the British some grudge for their abstention from the vote on the Guatemalan appeal, the previous June.[112]

Perhaps the main force behind the less than committed US attitude towards the British was Cabot Lodge, the permanent representative to the UN. For one thing, he loathed the public identification of the United States with the colonial policies of its allies. This

was a fact well known to Department officials, who, when wishing
to assist the British, hoped that Lodge 'would be absent on a fishing
expedition'.[113] Thus, when the State Department seemed to verge
upon British policy, he would forcefully come out in opposition.
Having the President's ear,[114] Lodge enjoyed enough status to be
able not to execute instructions he found distasteful. He could also
call Dulles and talk him into changing a position. Moreover, as a
politician and former Republican Senator,[115] he was particularly
sensitive to questions affecting the electoral chances of the Grand
Old Party. Cyprus was such an issue because of the Greek-American vote, which was of crucial importance in Lodge's native Massachusetts. Thus, he strongly resisted the communication of US opposition to the Greek item prior to the Congressional elections.

No wonder, then, that the British tended to see Lodge as the
'nigger in the woodpile'.[116] His objections were to put to the test
Dulles' pledge to oppose the passage of any resolution. Lodge did
not hide his disapproval of the commitments made in the Secretary's letter to Churchill of 21 September. The promise to uphold a
– however unlikely – negative vote on the Greek item in the General Committee, he argued, 'would make [the Americans] look like
a friend to backward colonialism to the outside world and would
create enormous difficulties for candidates for Congress in this country'. As a result, Dulles promised to 'take a fresh look', but the
'unexpected' did not happen.[117] Following the inscription of the
Greek item, his intervention forestalled the communication to the
Greeks of the US decision to oppose any resolution on Cyprus and
to canvass others against it. Lodge thought it 'highly unwise' to say
anything so upsetting to Greek-American opinion, all the more since
the Greek item had been placed at the bottom of the agenda and
would not turn up well after the mid-term elections.[118] As a result,
Dulles would say nothing of this decision to Papagos, when the two
men met in Paris on 23 October, nor to the Greek Ambassador,
who called on him three days later. At the same time, the British
delegation to the UN was asked not to 'breathe a word' of Dulles'
promise until after the elections.[119]

Like the majority of US officials, Lodge basically wished to avoid
the choice of evils posed by the Greek appeal. Thus, his recommendation was for the US delegation to work 'behind the scenes and

procedurally to prevent the issue from coming to a head' at the General Assembly.[120] President Eisenhower, ever anxious about the effect of the controversy on Western unity, warmly consented.[121] Dulles, who already felt uncomfortable with the unconditional promise he had given to oppose *any* resolution, instructed the State Department to 'explore ways and means' for side-tracking the Greek item.[122] To this end, the idea of a procedural resolution to postpone discussion was resurrected,[123] but when it was tried out with the British and the Greeks, the results were disappointing.

Matters came to a head, as the Greeks, who were unaware of Dulles' pledge to Churchill, sought assurances of US neutrality; Papagos' letter to Eisenhower of 23 October also awaited a reply. Dulles suggested that the President should not be personally involved; rather, he would inform the Greek Prime Minister that the Americans had never committed themselves to neutrality and that, for a number of reasons, they felt 'obliged to oppose the passage of any resolution'.[124] Eisenhower saw the draft reply and found it 'cold and abrupt'.[125]

The matter was discussed at a State Department meeting, on 12 November, at which Dulles was present. The Secretary of State claimed that in promising Churchill to oppose *any* resolution he had actually meant any 'substantive' one, that is one 'smacking of action or intervention in the affairs of Cyprus'; thus, a resolution 'adjourning or cutting off' discussion for the present was all right. Department officials, however, retorted that the British insisted on a literal interpretation of the US commitment. Of course, they did not know that British thinking was also evolving towards a procedural formula. In reality, the meeting of the minds between the Americans and the absent British was almost complete: after discussing the pros and cons of a postponement motion, Dulles admitted that it would be better if the General Assembly decided 'not to consider the matter further at this time'.[126]

At the same meeting, it was agreed to clarify the US position to the Greek government without further delay. Two points should be stressed: first, that US 'neutrality' did not extend over a discussion or a resolution on the 'substance' of the Cyprus issue by the General Assembly; second, that, for the sake of allied unity, the United States would 'oppose the passage of any substantive resolution'.[127]

The letter to Papagos was finally delivered on 16 November. The effect was that, until the eve of the debate, the Greeks would seek in vain to come up with a less than a 'substantive' resolution.[128]

Further complications arose as Dulles was caught between his conflicting pledges to Papagos and Churchill. As the time for the discussion of the Greek item approached, the British were asking the Americans to fulfil their promise of *active* opposition to any resolution by canvassing other member states. Cannon warned that Papagos was firmly convinced of the Secretary's undertaking to avoid such action.[129] Lodge did not mince his words: lobbying against the Greeks would amount to 'pulling the [British] chestnuts out of the fire with a vengeance'.[130] Eventually, it was decided to inform both sides that the United States would abstain from any canvassing whatsoever.[131]

This decision was also a sign of American exasperation with British inflexibility. Thus, it came as a great relief when the British, at last, assented to a procedural motion. This, together with their contribution to the release of US airmen held in China, helped to restore Anglo-American co-operation on the eve of the discussion of the Greek item. Even Lodge proposed to do some lobbying after the motion had been tabled, although he did not want the Americans to sponsor it themselves.[132] The niceties of phrasing the motion also attracted some attention: Lodge and the Department thought that a 'not to discuss' formula would be 'less painful to the Greeks' than a 'not to consider' one, and more likely to muster a good majority.[133] This was the initial position of the British delegation, which later changed its mind.

There remained the problem of selling the formula to the Greeks. Although the State Department would have preferred Lodge to handle the matter in New York,[134] Dulles decided to apprise Papagos. In his message of 12 December, he saw it fit to insert a few tricks. Thus, he deliberately confused the proposed 'not to discuss' formula with the suggestion the Greek Prime Minister had made in Paris. Yet, according to the American record of that meeting, Papagos had referred to having the issue postponed *for that year*. Indeed, in order to sweeten the pill, the Secretary of State did not hesitate to add in his message that 'future Assemblies would be unbound' by the proposed decision.[135] This remark, however, was contrary to what Lodge and the British had agreed in NewYork; what was more, it contradicted the delegation's instructions to 'ward off' any amendments opening the door to future reconsideration of the issue.[136] In the end, of course, in order to secure the Greek assent, the Americans would accept the amendment of their original, straight formula.

'Tactics of forbearance'

Although tactics at the UN had paid off, the outbursts of anti-American feeling in Greece were undoubtedly a disturbing development. As the First Secretary of the Embassy in Athens noted, the experience of the last few months had created 'a more favorable atmosphere for Communist objectives …, foreign policy reorientation, anti-Americanism, enhanced standing of the USSR, identification of Greece with anti-colonialism, overthrow of the Rally Government, and violence in Cyprus'.[137] Thus, after Cannon's early representations, the State Department decided to try 'tactics of forbearance'.[138] Subsequent American communications to Greek officials stressed the need to get things back to normal.[139] In this context, and despite his initial reluctance,[140] Dulles conceded Stefanopoulos' request for a reassuring statement to the Greek press.

There were also reactions from within the United States, too. A typical letter of protest to the White House or the State Department would criticise the administration's attitude for overlooking the principles and traditions of US foreign policy and offering an advantage to Soviet propaganda, and would ask for its reversal. The standard reply of the State Department would attempt to explain the US position as primarily dictated by concern for allied unity, reminding, as appropriate, that it had not opposed the inscription of the Greek item on the agenda.[141]

Yet the State Department eschewed a full-scale public relations campaign, as suggested by its people in the field.[142] Instead, it chose to adopt a policy of 'no comment', which was reflected in the conspicuous absence of the Cyprus question from 'Voice of America' commentaries.[143] Ambassador Cannon, for his part, continued to urge a more positive approach, reiterating his proposal for an invitation to Papagos to visit Washington. This, he argued, might bolster

the government's standing at home, help to mend Greece's relations with her allies, and counter the friendship offensive of the
Soviet Union and its satellites.[144]

Although the rise in anti-American sentiment and the phasing
out of aid were expected to make the Greek government less com-
pliant than earlier, US agencies were not unduly preoccupied about
the future: American influence in Greece, they predicted, would
remain predominant; the Cyprus question was 'likely' to remain an
irritant in Greece's relations with Britain, Turkey and the United
States, but it was not expected to 'strain' the country's alliances; if
anything, it was unlikely that the orientation of Greek foreign policy
would change. The prospects for internal stability, however, looked
increasingly uncertain: Papagos' illness was apparent, his early withdrawal from the scene and the demise of his party were considered
possible, as was a return to unstable coalition governments. If that
was the case, military intervention could not be excluded.[145] In
fact, the CIA was aware that IDEA, the clandestine society of low-
to-middle-ranking officers, had prepared for a *coup d'état* in case
that Papagos stepped down. The head of the organisation, Major-
General Solon Gikas, claimed to have the approval of the palace.[146]
This prospect did not seem to worry US agencies either: any attempt at imposing a dictatorship, they assumed, 'would depend to a
large degree on IDEA's estimate of the US reaction'.[147]

Back on the sidelines

Even before the General Assembly had dealt with the Greek item,
US diplomats recognised the need for a more positive British attitude if the problem of Cyprus was not to drift on to the next General Assembly. As they emphasised an Anglo-Cypriot understanding, they realised that the appropriate atmosphere did not exist and
had to be created.[148] Yet US diplomacy shied away from taking a
major initiative.

After the General Assembly was over, the State Department intended to urge upon the British a more liberal constitution combined with steps to curb Communist activity; the contention that
the latter move would facilitate a *rapprochement* with non-Communist leaders was strongly reminiscent of Governor Wright's ar-

guments which had failed to convince successive British ministers.[149]
On 27 January, the US Ambassador in London was instructed to
raise these points with the Foreign Office and ask for Anglo-American consultation at working level. In the absence of any progress,
the State Department thought it 'unrealistic' to expect that the
General Assembly could be indefinitely prevented from discussing
a substantive resolution. Yet the Ambassador discouraged US involvement at that stage, arguing that the British were aware of the need
to modify their attitude and were working on that.[150]

US interest in the course of the Cyprus question was finally expressed in March. Wood, the desk officer for Greek affairs, was sent
on a *tour d'horizon* to London, Athens and Cyprus. Although most
of the relevant correspondence remains classified,[151] it appears that
Wood returned rather unimpressed by the pace and the substance
of the revised constitutional proposals, which the Colonial Office
had been working out for some time. He also found out that Governor Armitage was prepared to work for a constitutional settlement
that would mention eventual self-determination for the Cypriots.[152]
Anticipating a British move, Cannon was instructed to remind the
Greek government of the need to encourage the Cypriots to 'adopt
a reasonable attitude' towards their British rulers.[153]

The prospect of violence was present in American considerations during the early months of 1955. Apart from the hints of Greek
and Cypriot leaders or the rhetoric of Greek wireless propaganda,
the State Department had begun receiving disquieting reports about
repeated attempts at smuggling arms and explosives into the island.
Following the seizure of the 'Agios Georgios' with its cargo of explosives, the manager of the Cyprus Mines Corporation, Robert
Hendricks, confirmed that there had been at least four previous
attempts, some of them successful. Hendricks candidly predicted
that the Greek Cypriots were approaching 'a point where they would
sacrifice their lives for their cause'. By then, it had also become
obvious that it was not the Communists who threatened to disturb
the peace of the colony.[154]

NOTES

1. Louis 1985, 409; see also *idem.*, 395-399.
2. Louis 1984, 205, n. 1.
3. As Creech Jones put it in 1948, 'the United States ... is at present too much preoccupied with communism to spare much time for "British imperialism"': quoted in Darwin 1988, 145.
4. 849C.00/9-3049, Acheson to Nicosia, tel. 55.
5. The State Department's version of this episode was the following: the paper on Cyprus was 'included accidentally' in the material on Greek policy given by the Department to the press. It was intended for use 'without attribution' to its source and not as 'fixed and final US policy'. This injunction was disregarded, and certain papers reported that the United States favoured the cession of Cyprus to Greece. As a result, the State Department withdrew the paper in question and omitted any reference to Cyprus in its final statement of policy: 849C.00/9-3049, Acheson to Nicosia, tel. 55; cf. Kelling 1990, 80.
6. *FRUS 1948*, III, 1091-1099; cf. Kelling 1990, 81.
7. RG 218 (Joint Chiefs of Staff records), Geographic File 1948-1950, 381, Eastern Mediterranean and the Middle East Area, Section 1, memo by Joint Strategic Plans Committee, 883/1, 12 July 1948; cf. Mihalopoulos 1989, 32.
8. 849C.00/3-2349, Rankin to Acheson, desp. 224; cf. Mihalopoulos 1989, 29-30.
9. 78427, R11914, Norton to F.O., 24 Dec. 1949; 747C.00/1-350, Grady to Acheson, tel. 9.
10. 78427, R12052, Rumbold, F.O., to Bennett, C.O., 2 Jan. 1950; *FRUS 1949*, VI, 171.
11. 747C.00/1-1250, memo of conversation between Cromie and Jellicoe.
12. 747C.00/1-2550, Porter to State, desp. 10.
13. *Ibid.*
14. 849C.00/4-1849, Porter to State, A-35; *FRUS 1949*, VI, 171; 78427, R12052, Rumbold, F.O., to Bennett, C.O., 2 Jan. 1950.
15. 849C.00/3-2349, Rankin to Acheson, desp. 224.
16. 747C.001/10-351, Wagner to State, desp. 91.
17. 747C.00/8-2352, letter from Wagner to Porter.
18. An interesting account of 'the historical development of AKEL', which is also a good example of the Consulate's methodical monitoring of leftist activity in Cyprus, is given in 747C.001/1-3153, Anschuetz to State, desp. 879.
19. 747C.00/2-150, Jernegan to Mr Spiros Minotos, Feb. 10, 1950.
20. 781.022/5-250, policy meeting on affairs concerning Cyprus and the problem of Enosis. At the same meeting, F.G. Ranney of the Office for Britain and North Atlantic drew an interesting parallel between the Enosis problem and Irish partition, warning that, if the United States changed its position in favour of Enosis, it could find itself at odds 'with everyone else concerned', implying Turkey of course.

21. The question was also raised on a somewhat broader level by diplomat and poet Seferiadis (Seferis) in the privacy of his notes: 'Are we worthy of ruling Cyprus, without harming this people, making them better, without turning them into a Greek province, like Corfu, like Salonika?': Seferis, *Meres*VI, 98.

22. 747C.00/1-350, Grady to Acheson, tel. 9.

23. 781.022/5-250, policy meeting on affairs concerning Cyprus.

24. 747C.00/6-250, office memo from Hare to McFall.

25. 87720, 1081/128, Stephens to Rumbold, 2 June 1950.

26. 747C.00/6-250, memo from Hare to McFall.

27. *Ibid.*

28. 747C.00/6-2650, Hare to Paul Ralli; /10-350, Brown to Senator George Malone, Oct. 13, 1950; /10-1250, Ruckh to M.E. Mavromatis, Dec. 5, 1950; /10-950, McGhee to H.G. Michael, Archbishop of North and SouthAmerica, Oct. 31, 1950; /8-152, Cook to Anthony Miller, Sept. 11, 1952; Cook to the Hellenic American Community, May 5, 1954.

29. *FRUS 1950*,V, 378-379.

30. 747C.00/7-2650, Acheson to American diplomatic officers.

31. 747C.00/10-250, memo from Wainhouse to Hickerson; 87723, 1081/193, Franks to F.O., 20 Sept. 1950.

32. 747C.00/10-250, memo from Wainhouse to Hickerson; 87723, 1081/195, Franks to F.O., 4 Oct. 1950.

33. 747C.00/10-1650, letter from Lovett to Acheson.

34. DEFE 5/31, COS (51) 245, COS Committee, 24April 1951; RG 218, Geographic File 1951-53, 381, Eastern Mediterranean and the Middle East Area, Section 4, JCS 1887/20, 175-185, memo by Chief Naval Operations on the Malta talks, January 22-24, 1951, appendix D; 747C.00/2-254, Wagner to State, desp. 56.

35. *FRUS 1950*,V, 256, 260; 95132, 1081/8, Jellicoe to LordTalbot, 5 Feb. 1951.

36. 95132, 1081/33, British Embassy to Morrison,Washington, 15 March 1951.

37. 747C.00/3-1451, Bartch to State, desp. 155.

38. 747C.00/3-1951, Peurifoy to Acheson, tel. 3074.

39. 95133, 1081/45, Jellicoe toTalbot, 3 April 1951.

40 *FRUS 1951*,V, 533-534.

41. 107501, 1081/21, brief on Cyprus for the Secretary of State, 19 March 1953. This position was repeated in Department toAthens, tel. 5076, May 14, 1952: 747C.00/7-1852, Acheson to Athens, tel. 236.

42. 747C.00/7-852, Peurifoy to Acheson, tel. 83.

43. 747C.00/7-1852, Acheson to Athens, tel. 236.

44. 107502, 1081/49, Galsworthy to May, 1 Oct. 1953.

45. 747C.03/4-1852, Wagner to State, desp. 268; 747C.00/7-1553, office memo from Porter to NEA; /7-2153, Wagner to State, desp. 9.

46. This was, for example, the assessment of the US Chargé inAthens, Yost: *FRUS 1952-54*,VIII, 677.

47. 747C.00/9-3052, Baxter, GTI, to Popper, UNP; finalised text in Lot File 61 D214, dated October 13, 1952.

48. 153rd meeting of NSC, July 9, 1953, in: *FRUS 1952-54*, IX, 394-395; NSC 155/1, 'US Objectives and Policies with Respect to the Near East', July 14, 1953: *ibid.*, 399-400; NSC 5428, July 23, 1954: *ibid.*, 525-527; RG 218, Geographic File 1951-53, 381, Eastern Mediterranean and the Middle East Area, Section 6, JCS 1887/33, 28 Dec. 1953; cf. Devereux 1990b, 247-250; Holden Reid 1988, 163; Lucas 1990, 258-260; Ovendale 1988, 145, 152.

49. 747C.00/7-1752, Wagner to State, desp. 8. According to Joseph Wagner, US Consul in Nicosia, 'a Britain strongly entrenched on Cyprus would still be a force to be reckoned with and as such an agent for stability in the area'. At the same time, however, he wondered whether this provided a solid basis for US area planning, in view of the 'complications' of the Cyprus question.

50. 747C.00/8-1854, 'British Thinking on the Cyprus Question', memo by Park Armstrong, Jr., Special Assistant to the Secretary of State.

51. 747C.00/11-1653, letter from Dulles to Lodge, Nov. 24, 1953.

52. 112843, 1081/9, 'Cyprus', *aide-mémoire* from British Embassy to State Department, 28 January 1954; 747C.00/1-2854, British *aide-mémoire*.

53. NND 927313, E 1568, Box 86, Policy Planning Staff Records, 1954, Lot File 65 D101, memo from PPS to the Secretary of State, May 16, 1954.

54. This sort of tactic was considered by the Office of Dependent Area Affairs of the State Department, but it was ruled out as bound to put the sincerity of the United States to the test before friend and foe alike: *FRUS 1952-54*, III, 1407.

55. 747C.00/2-254, Wagner to State, desp. 56.

56. 747C.00/8-1054, office memo from Wood to Richards.

57. Regarding the US practice at the UN, the British Ambassador in Washington remarked that it tended to distinguish between inscription of items on the agenda of the Security Council, which had powers of action, and inscription on the agenda of the General Assembly, which was largely a talk shop. In the latter case, the Americans took a much more liberal view: 112853, 1081/320, Makins to F.O., 25 Aug. 1954.

58. 747C.00/3-1954, Aldrich to Dulles, tel. 4026.

59. 747C.00/8-1054, office memo from Wood to Richards.

60. *FRUS 1952-54*, VIII, 688-689. The Ambassador in Athens also objected: 747C.00/7-654, Cannon to Dulles, tel. 28.

61. This was the suggestion of the Office for UN Political and Security Affairs: 747C.00/2-554, office memo from Popper to Key.

62. *FRUS 1952-54*, VIII, 679-680.

63. Sulzberger 1969, 1011.

64. 747C.00/3-1754, Cannon and Axelrod to State, desp. 860.

65. 747C.00/2-2554, letter from Cannon to Baxter.

66. 747C.00/3-1754, Cannon and Axelrod to State, desp. 860.

67. 747C.00/3-254, Wagner to State, desp. 62.

68. 747C.00/3-1854, Rutter to State, desp. 3157; /3-1954, Aldrich to Dulles, tel. 4026; *FRUS 1952-54*, VIII, 683-684.

69. 112843, 1081/25, Chancery, Washington, to Western and Southern Departments, 19 Feb. 1954.

70. RG 218, Geographic File 1954-56, 381, Eastern Mediterranean and the Middle East Area, Section 18, Admiral Radford, JCS Chairman, to Anderson, Secretary of State for Defense, May 5, 1954; Anderson to Dulles, 19 May, 1954, in: *FRUS 1952-54*, VIII, 687.

71. 112848, 1081/185, Salt to Young, 9 July 1954.

72. 112848, 1081/180, record of conversation between Eden and Dulles, 27 June 1954.

73. 112853, 1081/320, Makins to F.O., 25 Aug. 1954.

74. *FRUS 1952-54*, VIII, 718, n. 1.

75. *Ibid.*, VIII, 718.

76. *Ibid.*, 695-696.

77. See, for example, the Department's instructions to Athens in *FRUS 1952-54*, VIII, 684-685; also, Byroade's remarks to Ambassador Politis, *ibid.*, 686.

78. 747C.00/6-1454, State to Athens, tel. 3518; repeated to Ankara, tel. 1374.

79. 747C.00/6-1954, Cannon to Dulles, tel. 3021.

80. 747C.00/6-2254, Warren to Dulles, tel. 1366.

81. Quoted in Vàli 1971, 38.

82. Emphasis added: 747C.00/7-1254, personal message from Dulles to Stefanopoulos, draft; also in *FRUS 1952-54*, VIII, 698, notes 2-3.

83. Cannon warned that the Greek government, in accordance with its tendency to interpret Turkish reactions as British-inspired, would 'find it hard to understand' the prominence accorded to Turkey and would consider the Americans party to British manoeuvring: 747C.00/7-2454, Cannon to Dulles, tel. 196.

84. 747C.00/7-1254, personal message from Dulles to Stefanopoulos, draft; *FRUS 1952-54*, VIII, 696-699; 747C.00/8-1054, office memo from Wood to Richards.

85. 747C.00/7-2454, Cannon to Dulles, tel. 196; /8-1154, Schnee to State, desp. 121.

86. In fact, Papagos had been pressing for such a visit since September 1953: 781.5MSP/8-1154, letter from Cannon to Byroade, Aug. 4, 1954; E 1294, Lot File 59 D36, box 1, office memo from Lincoln to Wood, Aug. 31, 1954.

87. 781.00/9-2854, Department memo from Armstrong to Smith.

88. Even then, State Department officials anxiously denied that they intended 'to get into the position of intermediaries': 747C.00/6-2554, memo of conversation between Byroade, Baxter and Beeley; 112848, 1081/185, Salt to Young, 9 July 1954.

89. *FRUS 1952-54*, VIII, 694.

90. In the case of the latter, Eisenhower was all for it, while Dulles saw no harm in Cowles's talking 'informally and socially' to Eden: 747C.00/8-2454, memo of meeting between Dulles and Ms Cowles.

91. 747C.00/8-1654, office memo from Wood to Baxter; /8-2554, Rutter to State, desp. 593.

92. 112850, 1081/240, Embassy in Washington to F.O., 6 Aug. 1954; 112851, 1081/277, UKUN Delegation to F.O., 13 Aug. 1954; 112856, 1081/415, extracts from consular reports, 19-25 Aug. 1954.

93. 112850, 1081/240, Embassy in Washington to F.O., 6 Aug. 1954.
94. *FRUS 1952-54*, III, 1407.
95. 747C.00/8-2354, memo of conversation between Taylor, UNP, and representatives of UNA, EUR and NEA.
96. 747C.00/8-3154, State to Athens, tel. 525; repeated to Ankara, London, Nicosia.
97. 747C.00/8-3154, USUN Delegation to State, tel. 182 (classified).
98. 747C.00/9-154, State to Athens, tel. 538; repeated to Ankara, London, Nicosia.
99. 747C.00/9-154, Warren to State, tels. 239, 244.
100. 747C.00/9-954, Butterworth to Dulles, tel. 1238.
101. 747C.00/9-754, Cannon to Dulles, tel. 541.
102. *FRUS 1952-54*, VIII, 704-708.
103. 747C.00/9-2154, Smith to USUN Delegation, tel. 2.
104. 747C.00/10-2254, letter from Courtney to Wood; *FRUS 1952-54*, VIII, 734.
105. *FRUS 1952-54*, VIII, 708-709.
106. *Ibid.*, 715-717.
107. *Ibid.*, 709.
108. A good example of a reply of this sort is contained in: 747C.00/9-2254, Ben H. Brown, Acting Assistant Secretary, to Representative Earl Chudoff, Sept. 28, 1954.
109. Among those writing to the State Department on the Cyprus question were Senator Alex Wiley, Chairman of the Foreign Relations Committee (747C.00/9-254), Senator Everett M. Dirksen (747C.00/9-854), Representatives Thomas B. Curtis (747C.00/9-2054), Earl Chudoff (747C.00/9-2254), Thomas P. O'Neill, Jr. (11-2354), and Governor Theodore R. McKeldin (747C.00/12-1054).
110. *FRUS 1952-54*, VIII, 709-710, n. 3.
111. *Ibid.*, VIII, 715.
112. 747C.00/9-2154, memo of conversation between Dulles, Cook and Hopkinson, Dixon; *FRUS 1952-54*, VIII, 726.
113. A 'personal comment' from Byroade to Beeley, in 112848, 1081/185, Salt, Washington, to Young, 9 July 1954.
114. Lodge had been appointed presidential adviser in December 1953 and would serve as Permanent Representative to the UN throughout Eisenhower's term of office.
115. Lodge had lost his seat in the Senate in the 1952 elections.
116. Foreign Office officials had reached the conclusion that 'what Dulles says and what Lodge does are two quite separate things': 112867, 1081/740, Young to Crosthwaite, 8 Oct. 1954.
117. 747C.00/9-2254, memo of conversation between Dulles and Lodge; *FRUS 1952-54*, VIII, 716, n. 6.
118. *FRUS 1952-54*, VIII, 718-719; 747C.00/10-2654, memo from Byroade to Dulles.
119. 112872, 1081/927, Crosthwaite to Young, 27 Oct. 1954.
120. *FRUS 1952-54*, VIII, 719; 747C.00/10-2654, Lodge to Dulles, tel. 143.

121. 747C.00/10-2554, office memo from Popper to Key.
122. *FRUS 1952-54*, VIII, 724.
123. 747C.00/10-2754, Cannon to Dulles, tel. 928.
124. *FRUS 1952-54*, VIII, 721-722.
125. *Ibid.*, 721, n. 4.
126. With this remark, Dulles unwittingly prescribed the eventual outcome: *FRUS 1952-54*, VIII, 726.
127. *FRUS 1952-54*, VIII, 724-726.
128. *Ibid.*, 730-732.
129. *Ibid.*, 723.
130. 747C.00/11-854, letter from Lodge to Dulles; /11-2554, Lodge to Dulles, tel. 286.
131. *FRUS 1952-54*, VIII, 728, 734.
132. *Ibid.*, 735-736.
133. *Ibid.*, 736-737.
134. 747C.00/12-1154, office memo from Murphy to Dulles.
135. *FRUS 1952-54*, VIII, 738.
136. *Ibid.*, 737.
137. 747C.00/12-2054, Schnee to State, desp. 576.
138. *FRUS 1952-54*, VIII, 746.
139. *Ibid.*, 745, 746.
140. *Ibid.*, 740, 742.
141. 747C.00/12-2054, C.F. Kiernan, Representative of the Commonwealth of Massachusetts, to President Eisenhower; 747C.00/12-1054, Morton to Governor Theodore McKeldin, Annapolis, Dec. 31, 1954; /12-2054, Baxter to Rev. Spiros Zodhiates, Dec. 31, 1954.
142. The Embassy in Athens proposed such an effort which, among other things, should try to explain to the Greek public that the US attitude at the UN concerned the 'timing and methods' of the Greek appeal rather than its substance: 747C.00/12-1354, Cannon to Dulles, tel. 1269; *ibid.*, State to Athens, tel. 1466, Dec. 17, 1954.
143. 747C.00/12-1354, State to Athens, tel. 1466, Dec. 17, 1954.
144. Lot File 59 D36, box 1, office memo from Allen to Dulles, 29 March 1955.
145. These views were expressed in the National Intelligence Estimate, published by the CIA on 18 Jan. 1955, and in a draft memo from Allen to Nolting, dated Feb. 14, 1955: *FRUS 1955-57*, XXIV, 528-531.
146. Lot File 59 D36, box 1, memo of conversation between Richardson, CIA, and Wood, GTI, Feb. 4, 1955.
147. *FRUS 1955-57*, XXIV, 528.
148. For example, the US Consul in Nicosia particularly lamented the absence of a moderate Centre, which could become a partner in a programme of political advance: 747C.00/12-954, Courtney to State, desp. 46.
149. *FRUS 1952-54*, VIII, 734-735; 747C.00/12-954, Courtney to State, desp. 46.
150. 747C.00/1-2755, Dulles to London, tel. 3865; /1-3155, Aldrich to Dulles, tel. 3355.

151. As of August 1995. The correspondence is contained in the 747C.00 partial folder for March 1955.

152. 117628, 1081/205, Young to Salt, 1 April 1955; 747C.00/3-1755, Nicosia tel. 68; /3-2855, Nicosia, desp. 80.

153. 747C.00/3-1555, Dulles to Athens, tel. 2275.

154. 747C.00/2-1155, Sprecher to State, desp. 68.

6

THE COUNTER-CLAIMANT:
TURKISH REACTIONS TO ENOSIS

Turkish values

Turkish reactions to the Greek claim on Cyprus in the period under discussion were influenced by two, largely incompatible, considerations: distrust of Greek motives and intentions in seeking territorial aggrandisement along the coastline of Anatolia; and the need to preserve Greek-Turkish friendship for security reasons of a more immediate character.[1] The first consideration, largely based on geopolitical assumptions, was reflected in the record of Turkish opposition to the acquisition of the Eastern Aegean Islands and the Dodecanese by Greece. Indeed, once Cyprus became an issue, the Turkish grudge for the 'loss' of those 'coastal islands' resurfaced. 'Feeling hemmed in by the Greek islands in the Aegean', Tozun Bahcheli notes, the Turks could not allow Greece to control access to her southern ports too.[2] With regard to the second consideration, the *rapprochement* with Greece was largely based on a community of interests in the face of the external threat represented by the Soviet bloc. Since 1947, the Truman Doctrine, participation in West European organisations and membership of NATO and the Balkan Pact had led to an era of Greek-Turkish co-operation without precedent. It was expected to endure at least as long as the commonly perceived threat remained an overriding factor.[3]

The presence of a sizeable Turkish minority in the contested island was a further important element. For decades, both the mother country and the minority itself had acquiesced in British domination. Although the colonial regime had not been an unmixed blessing, minority leaders consistently supported the continuation of

British rule as long as annexation to Greece seemed the only likely
alternative.[4] Besides, intercourse between the Turkish state and the
minority had been limited until after World War II. The latter's traditional, religious outlook kept it out of pace with Mustafa Kemal's
secular reforms, whereas the authoritarian practices of the colonial
administration after 1931 acted as a check on the stirrings of Turkish and Greek nationalism alike. Turkey's neutrality in the war further circumscribed her ability to influence minority affairs. It was
only after 1945 that a nationalist Turkish Cypriot movement manifested itself primarily in reaction to Enosis. Even then, it would
retain a strong Islamic trait.[5] However rudimentary and fragmented,
at least until 1950,[6] this movement would be fully exploited by
Britain and Turkey as a counter to Greek irredentism.[7] Yet its influence on Turkish policy should not be overestimated. Turkish Cypriot activists could attract the attention of nationalistic circles and
the press in Turkish cities but they never assumed the independent
role of the Ethnarchy and its energetic supporters in Athens.

It remains to establish whether Turkish reactions to Enosis were
merely defensive or, since the return of Cyprus to Turkey was increasingly propagated, they signified a further departure from the
Kemalist renunciation of claims on former Ottoman possessions.
This renunciation, enshrined in the so-called National Pact of 1920
and article 16 of the Lausanne Peace Treaty (1923), served Kemal's
effort towards the establishment of a homogeneous Turkish nation
state. However, respect for the *status quo* never became an axiom
of Turkish foreign policy, which remained flexible enough in order
to take advantage of favourable international circumstances. This
was demonstrated, still in Kemal's time, by the successful revision
of the Straits regime, in 1936, and the acquisition of the Hatay-
Alexandretta province from French-dominated Syria, on the eve of
World War II.[8]

Despite the repudiation of irredentist trends by official ideology, Kemal's death and the watershed of World War II had facilitated a relative revival of Pan-Turkism. Its proponents aspired to the
eventual union of Turkic populations, 'from the Eastern Mediterranean to Sinkiang, and from the Volga to southern Anatolia'.[9] To them,
Cyprus was a small but accessible piece of former Turkish territory
that was being claimed by an untrustworthy friend and erstwhile

foe. Playing up the spectre of Greek encirclement, Pan-Turkist zealots energetically advocated the recovery of the 'Green Island'.[10] They were active in the Cyprus Turkish Cultural Association (CTCA), which was founded in Istanbul in 1946, and undertook to foster closer links between the minority and the Turkish motherland.[11]

A more important part in public agitation on Cyprus was played by the standard-bearers of Turkish nationalism: the popular press and the university student movement.[12] Even these factors, however, were never allowed to dictate the course of Turkish foreign policy. Rather, the governments of Ankara proved able to exploit and manipulate nationalist and irredentist sentiments at will, while keeping the entire anti-Enosis movement under discreet but effective control.[13]

Early reactions

The periodic outbursts of public interest in the Cyprus question began in late 1948. As Lord Winster's constitutional plan failed amid a wave of Enosis agitation, the press, led by a newly published daily, *Hürriyet*,[14] commenced a campaign asserting the Turkish interest in the fate of the island and vehemently opposing the Greek Cypriot aspirations. Many of the arguments subsequently advanced against the cession of Cyprus to Greece were first articulated in that period. The emphasis was put on the island's importance to Turkey's security due to its geographic proximity, and the danger of its falling under Communist control. In this respect, Enosis was projected as another plot of international communism – a staple of Turkish propaganda over the following years. This campaign was endorsed by leading figures of the opposition, such as Celâl Bayar, the future President of the Republic. Bayar reportedly warned that the Turkish people would not remain indifferent to the fate of Cyprus as it had been the case with the Dodecanese.[15] Student organisations championed the anti-Enosis cause in the streets of Ankara and Istanbul and irredentist slogans were increasingly heard.[16] The ease with which the campaign died down, after Foreign Minister Necmeddin Sadak assured the public that Britain would never consent to give Cyprus away, strengthened suspicions in Greece that the turmoil in the 'closely controlled' Turkish society was inspired

by the British and abetted by the Turkish government.[17]
     Turkish feeling was further aroused after the announcement of
the Ethnarchy's decision to hold a plebiscite. In Cyprus, the spectre
of Enosis apparently prompted the existing two rival Turkish Cypriot organisations to merge into a single Federation. During a mass
meeting on 12 December 1949, the organisation issued an appeal
of protest, which was widely circulated abroad. After calling attention to the Turkish presence in the island, a whole set of arguments
was advanced against Enosis: Greece had never ruled Cyprus; its
'Greek-speaking' inhabitants were not really of Greek origin; the
island was much closer to Turkey than to Greece; speaking of self-
determination, the Greek majority should not be regarded in isolation from the wider context of Turkish Anatolia; Cyprus affected
the security of neighbouring countries; Greece was incapable of
administering and defending it; Enosis agitation was actually a 'Communist manoeuvre'; the *status quo* served both the security of the
island and the protection of its minorities. The protest ended with a
counter-claim: 'if Great Britain ever wish to abandon the island,
then we claim to be returned to Turkey, the ex-suzerain, its nearest
neighbour, and the only state in the Near East able properly to defend Cyprus'.[18]
     In Turkey, there was a new bout of demonstrations and press
polemics against Enosis. This time, Foreign Minister Sadak's assurances to the Grand National Assembly were received amid cries for
the return of Cyprus and the Dodecanese.[19] There is also evidence
that Sadak's appeal for calm was, at least in part, the result of American prodding.[20] At the same time, the Turkish government expressed
its concern to the British. Sadak told the British Ambassador that
his government would not make an issue as long as Britain showed
no intention of handing Cyprus over to Greece and the latter continued to take a 'sensible attitude'. Yet, if a change in the *status quo*
was envisaged, Turkey 'would be fundamentally concerned'. Sadak
justified Turkey's interest mainly on strategic grounds. This statement had a considerable impact on the British. As Ambassador
Charles pointed out, it departed from the British interpretation of
Turkish foreign policy since the end of the war, i.e. that Turkey would
not object the acquisition of territory on her southern flank by a
friendly Greece.[21]

The Menderes government and Cyprus

The government of the Democratic Party, which came to power in May 1950, did not desist from the line of its predecessor. Aspiring to a greater role for Turkey within the Western world, it studiously sought to build up an image as a loyal and energetic ally of the 'Free World' leaders, Britain and the United States. This was reflected in the substantial Turkish participation in the Korean War and the bid for NATO membership. It also provided the context of close co-operation with Greece, and, later, Yugoslavia.[22] With regard to Cyprus, these broader considerations dictated a prudent line.

Thus, during its first four years in office, the Menderes government generally refrained from publicly involving itself in the Cyprus dispute, unless provoked by Greek initiatives or pressed in parliament. On the domestic scene, however, it proved much more tolerant than its predecessor to the incipient Islamic revival and the growth of Pan-Turkist tendencies, which found a convenient outlet in the claim for Cyprus.[23] Although demonstrations and large-scale public events were discouraged, irredentist propaganda freely circulated and the views of Turkish Cypriot activists were regularly reported.[24] Occasionally, the government chose to tighten things up. This happened in the case of the Turkish League for the Protection of Cyprus, an irredentist organisation that was dissolved in late 1950 or early 1951.[25] It countenanced, however, the activities of the more subtle CTCA and the Students' Federation, which undertook to strengthen the links between the minority and the 'mother country' by organising visits and exchanges, particularly of businessmen, students and teachers, and by raising funds. To this worthy end, not only Turkish but also British business concerns in Turkey were required to contribute.[26]

The official silence of the Turkish government was first broken in spring 1951, after Venizelos had openly admitted the Greek claim on Cyprus. Köprülü's statement to *Hürriyet* on 21 April was as much an expression of concern as it was a reminder of Turkey's interest. Its essential message was that, if the question of Cyprus ever arose, his country would seek to participate in any settlement in order to safeguard her rights. At the same time, however, Köprülü was careful to stress the overriding need for Greece and Turkey 'to stand together unreservedly' on international issues, particularly in view of their joint bid for NATO membership.[27] Subsequently, as further proof of goodwill, the Menderes government would discourage the visit of Turkish deputies to Cyprus.[28]

Three months later, the Turkish Embassy in Washington raised the Cyprus question with the State Department, apparently for the first time since Menderes had come to power. Like the British and the Greeks, Ankara attributed particular importance to the potential role of the United States in the dispute. The representation was prompted by an allegation in a semi-official Greek newspaper, that an American diplomat had envisaged twenty years of British administration in Cyprus, after which there could be a bilateral, Anglo-Greek settlement. Ambassador Erkin summed up the views of his government as follows: 'the Cyprus question was an artificial one' since the island was part of the British Empire and Commonwealth; although there was no need for a change in the *status quo*, Turkey reserved her rights; the clamour for Enosis and self-determination was inspired by self-seeking Greek politicians: the Cypriots were not really Greeks, but 'an island people of the Mediterranean who adhere to the Greek Orthodox religion'; by sponsoring self-determination for the Cypriots, Greece invited trouble with her own minorities.[29]

The Turkish government was also concerned with the pro-Enosis activities of the Greek-American lobby. Lacking a comparable ethnic pressure group in the United States, the Turks resorted to the Jewish lobby whose services had been utilised on previous occasions, such as loan raising and the Turkish bid for NATO membership. This sort of tactics paid off. When Greece eventually raised the Cyprus question at the UN, the Turkish government would earnestly seek assistance from the Israeli government in mobilising Jewish-American support against the Greek case.[30]

On the whole, the Menderes government relied on the press for airing its views on the question.[31] Turkish newspapers, of course, tended to go far beyond the official line. From an early stage, *Hürriyet* and its rival *Yeni Sabah* took the lead in giving stories on Cyprus a rabidly anti-Greek tone. Until 1953 such publicity mainly came in response to Enosis flare-ups in Greece. The standard doubts regarding Greece's commitment to the friendship with Turkey were coupled with warnings about the future: Turkish moderation should not be construed as weakness or indifference; the Greeks were wrong to ignore the Turkish views; and, if the question ever arose, Turkey was bound to take an active interest. To all this, more disturbing comment was frequently added, to the effect that no real friendship existed between the two countries, territorial issues such as the Dodecanese could be reopened, the position of minorities should be reconsidered, and so on.[32]

Temporising

During 1953, the formal ties of friendship and alliance between Greece and Turkey appeared to grow stronger than ever. The two countries successfully promoted the conclusion of the Balkan Pact with Yugoslavia and worked together to transform it into a military alliance. Yet, by autumn 1953, renewed press polemics threatened to tarnish this bright picture. A temporary increase in arrivals of illegal immigrants from Western Thrace to Turkey led to recriminations about the alleged ill treatment of the Muslim minority in Greece. This campaign was not unrelated to Cyprus. As the Greeks made their intention to resort to the UN clear, the tone of anti-Greek comment in Turkey grew shriller and increasingly ominous.[33] A section of the Greek press retaliated and the ensuing war of words prompted the British Embassy in Ankara to give some thought to yet another exchange of populations between the two countries. In this connection, the British diplomats observed that the prosperous Greek community of Istanbul had little incentive to emigrate to Greece, whereas Western Thrace Muslims, despite the pretensions of the popular Turkish papers, were not particularly welcome in Turkey owing to their 'reactionary' (i.e. Islamic) outlook.[34]

Whether this clamour was officially inspired or not, the Turkish government successfully used it in order to extract concessions that would strengthen its ties with the minority. In this task, it was greatly aided by Papagos' eagerness to appease Ankara in view of the recourse to the UN. Thus, during 1954, Greece recognised the Turkish ethnic character of the minority and, under the terms of a new cultural convention, Ankara was given considerable control over educational, cultural and religious affairs in Western Thrace.[35]

The hopes and fears of the Turkish government were summarised by the British Embassy in Ankara, in November 1953, as follows:

[the Turks] unquestionably welcome British sovereignty over the island, though they perhaps have little confidence in our management of the Enosis question; indeed, they fear that we may allow ourselves to be pushed off the island, and for that reason do not want their case to go by default. But their desire, nevertheless, is to avoid, for as long as they possibly can, becoming embroiled.[36]

Until August 1954, the attitude of the Menderes government neatly fitted into this pattern. Following the first — and not so effective — representation to the Greek government in March, Ankara avoided further *démarches*. This attitude, which mystified the British and misled the Greeks, was described by the official in charge of Cyprus affairs at the Turkish Foreign Ministry, Orhan Eralp, in the following terms: the Cyprus question was considered an Anglo-Greek problem; no further *démarche* to Athens was desirable; if the issue was raised at the UN, Turkey 'would not wish to take a vigorous line' there, and might even decide to abstain; in view of the sensitivity of the Turkish press on Cyprus, no action should be taken which might incite a campaign against Greece; nothing should be done to endanger the progress of the Balkan alliance, which was 'considered more important than the Cyprus question'.[37] Similar views were expressed to the Americans well into the summer, combined with assurances that inflammatory actions or statements would be avoided.[38]

The reasons put forward by Eralp were more apparent than real. Turkey had no compelling reason to intervene publicly in the dispute, unless the Greeks realised their threat and resorted to the UN — and until well into the summer the Turks appeared to doubt that this would be the case.[39] The negotiations leading to the tripartite Balkan alliance was a further restraining factor. A 'responsible' attitude, Menderes argued on several occasions,[40] served the Turkish case better than any tactics of recrimination. Last but not least, the Turkish government had to look after its interests in Western Thrace, which had a larger Muslim population than Cyprus. Surely, Ankara did not wish to upset Athens pending the realisation of Papagos' pledge to meet Turkish grievances and improve the lot of the minority.[41]

In view of the above, was there any chance of a timely Greek-Turkish understanding on Cyprus? According to Bahcheli, such a thing 'was not inconceivable', if Turkey had been offered strategic facilities and special safeguards for its minority on the island.[42] Clearly, the Menderes government did nothing to encourage such a prospect, although it is equally true that the initiative had to come from the Greek side. In early June 1954, Ambassador Tarray's intervention cancelled the only recorded attempt at broaching the subject. If the Turks had ever contemplated an understanding, the Papagos government failed to cultivate them.

The Turkish press, of course, went on with its anti-Enosis polemics. In the spring, as Turkey went to the polls, the popular press led by *Hürriyet* demanded that the government abandon its 'inaction' and come out in support of the Turkish claim on Cyprus. Failure to do so, it threatened, might cost the party in government many votes.[43] The fundamentals of Greek-Turkish friendship were also cast in doubt. A disquieting feature of this campaign was its thinly-veiled threats against the Greek minority in Istanbul and its institutions. The Patriarchate, in particular, was taken to task for failing to take a stand against Enosis and condemn Makarios' meddling with politics. *Hürriyet* went as far as to allege its involvement in the 'annexationist project'.[44]

Its low profile notwithstanding, the Turkish government on appropriate occasions continued to remind its allies, particularly the British and the Americans, of its views and special interest in Cyprus.[45] The Grand National Assembly publicly reaffirmed this interest, whereas instances of Greek maladroitness, as in the case of the *démenti* of Tarray's representation, served a similar purpose. Ankara would wait to repeat its views more forcefully and widely after the Greek appeal was placed before the UN, on 20 August 1954.[46]

The stirrings of Turkish Cypriot nationalism

Under Winster and his Deputy Turnbull, the colonial administration of Cyprus had become more attentive to the fortunes of the Turkish minority. As a first step, a committee of leading Turkish Cypriots was appointed to prepare a comprehensive report on the minority's long-standing grievances. Although its recommendations were on seemingly 'technical' matters, such as the muftiship, the administration of religious charitable foundations (*evkaf*), family law and education, they bore the marks of a fledgling Turkish nationalism. They called, among other things, for reverence of Turkish national anniversaries and symbols in communal schools and greater control of curricula.[47] The minority's political party, the FTA, increasingly appeared as a counterweight to Greek Cypriot nationalism. On the whole, however, the British administration had a poor opinion of Turkish Cypriot leaders, including the FTA spokesman, Dr Küçük.[48]

For the colonial authorities, the rise in Turkish Cypriot nationalism could be attributed to the fear of Greek domination combined with a number of grievances against the British: (1) the management of *evkaf*; (2) the administration of secondary education and the opening of new schools; (3) tolerance of Enosis agitation; (4) discrimination in civil service appointments; (5) the election of a *Mufti*.[49] Addressing these grievances became the avowed aim of the Turkish National Youth Organisation, which was set up under the aegis of the FTA in July 1953. Its programme also included the cession of Cyprus to Turkey. One of its early successes was the election of the FTA nominee, Mehmet Dana, to the muftiship.[50]

By 1953, conditions in Cyprus and the lax visa policy of the British consular authorities had facilitated the strengthening of ties between the Turkish Cypriot minority and the 'mother country'. Apart from the frequent exchanges and visits organised by educational and religious organisations, state banks, businesses and other interests extended their activities to the island.[51] Only in the second half of 1953, as British policy came under criticism in the Turkish Cypriot press and voices in favour of the island's return to its previous owner were increasingly heard, Governor Wright attempted to put a brake on traffic between Turkey and his colony –

admittedly without much success.[52]

Uncertainty about the future of British rule tended to strain relations between the administration and the minority. In early 1953,
colonial reports acknowledged a crisis of confidence among the Turkish element as a result of the alleged British 'tolerance' towards
Greek nationalist agitation. Wright was also criticised for neglecting the Turkish Cypriot minority and taking its loyalty 'too much
for granted'.[53] Such resentment as it existed was being exploited
by the minority's nationalistic leaders in their effort to project the
re-union with Turkey as the only satisfactory solution.[54]

Further reactions were caused by rumours, fuelled by the arrival of a new Governor, that the British intended to introduce political reform. By spring 1954, Turkish Cypriot newspapers were
warning that the community was 'determined to fight to the bitter
end so that self-government shall not be introduced in Cyprus'.[55]
On 16 July, Küçük, the FTA leader, addressed a letter of protest to
the Colonial Office, while the minority press intensified its clamour
for the return of Cyprus to Turkey. In the event, Hopkinson's announcement on 28 July proved that Turkish fears were quite un-
founded.

Apart from dampening Turkish Cypriot agitation, the Greek recourse to the UN practically pushed the minority leaders into a
common front with the British.[56] Thus, from August 1954 onwards,
Turkish Cypriot leaders actively assisted in the struggle against the
Greek appeal. Küçük sent telegrams to the UN Secretary-General
supporting either the continuation of the *status quo* or the return of
the island to Turkey. He was joined by the *Mufti*, Dana *effendi*, who
claimed that neither Enosis nor self-government based on majority
rule were acceptable because the Greeks hated the Turks and they
would betray them, as had happened in Crete half a century ago.[57]
In September, the Turkish Cypriot delegation, which was destined
for New York under British auspices, set out the conditions under
which a constitution could be accepted. Besides the familiar demands for community control over the *evkaf* and education, the
delegation asked for fair representation in the civil service and the
judiciary and specific safeguards against domination by the Greek
majority.[58] Thus, while the reserve towards the constitutional issue
continued, the colonial authorities could note with satisfaction that

the Turkish Cypriots had become 'very pro-British' since the summer while the slogan of union with Turkey was no longer heard.[59]

Opposing the Greek recourse

As already noted, the Menderes government waited for the conclusion of the Balkan alliance, on 9 August, before concerting openly
with the British against the Greek appeal to the UN. There had already been signs of Greek-Turkish friction in the negotiations leading to the Bled Pact, a fact that both sides had revealed to the Americans and the British respectively.[60] By the time Greece had lodged
its appeal, Turkey had had its response ready. Washington was the
first recipient. A modified version in French was also communicated to most UN members. According to the Foreign Office, this
text was neither 'grammatical' nor respectful of figures, but suited
the British well since it subscribed to their position that Cyprus was
a matter of domestic jurisdiction and commended their efforts to
promote 'a system of autonomous government'.[61]

Above all, the raising of the Cyprus issue at the UN signalled
Turkey's active involvement in what had until then seemed an Anglo-
Greek dispute. Menderes' personal appeal to Dulles on 31 August,
besides asking the United States to oppose the Greek item, was a
forceful presentation of Turkish interest in Cyprus. While the dispute was recognised as being 'formally between the United Kingdom and Greece', Turkey's intervention was justified as follows:

The importance of Cyprus for Turkey is vital from both geographical and
strategical (*sic*) viewpoints. There is an important Turkish minority on the
island in proportion to the total population. The Turkish Government cannot permit this minority to fall into the same plight as the other Turkish
minorities in Greece. In view of all these considerations, the Turkish Government considers that it has a primary right to have a say in the future of
the island.

Finally, Menderes' message struck a note of warning against a possible compromise satisfying the Greeks – Turkey did not intend to
sacrifice her interests in Cyprus 'for political reasons which it cannot explain'.[62]

Following the inscription of the Greek item, the tone of Turkish pronouncements on Cyprus became increasingly assertive. The obvious concern was lest the Turkish case went by default. Now that the genie of internationalisation had been set free, Ankara could not afford to discount the possibility of either the UN taking interest in the matter or the British giving ground to Greek demands. On 26 October, a spokesman of the Foreign Ministry warned that no change in the status of the island could be effected without the 'permission' of his government.[63] In December, on the eve of the debate on the Greek item, Ankara addressed a memorandum to all UN member states with the avowed aim to correct certain 'erroneous interpretations' of its attitude. Neither its 'policy of restraint' nor its full support for the British position should be construed as a lack of interest; on the contrary, Turkey considered herself to be 'the principally interested power' in the fate of Cyprus. An annex attached to this memorandum reiterated the usual argument in support of the Turkish counter-claim.[64]

Of some interest is the interpretation of the principle of self-determination advanced in Turkish diplomatic communications. In determining questions of sovereignty, the wishes of the majority of the population should not be the sole criterion; the 'strict', 'out of context' application of self-determination could lead to 'detrimental results'; like every other principle, self-determination 'should be limited by consideration of equity and realities'; what was more, this particular principle could not possibly override the validity of treaties.[65] The Turks also persistently put forward the claim that the Greek-speaking majority in Cyprus was not of Greek 'origin' but 'of mixed racial background', describing them as 'Levantines' or '*métisses de la Méditerrannée*'. This spurious 'ethnological' formulation, based on discredited perceptions of race and blood purity, reflected a certain ideological predilection,[66] which was not, of course, exclusive to Turkish official circles. As has been noted, racial perceptions were still current among the defenders of British colonialism.

Turkish memoranda on Cyprus rehearsed all possible arguments against Enosis and the Greek recourse, most of which have already been mentioned.[67] Some of them, like those relating to the racial origin of the Cypriots, were too far-fetched to be effective. Others,

however had considerable appeal to third parties. The United States
and most Western powers tended to share those claims relating to
defence and security. Few in Washington or London would doubt
that Cyprus was of greater strategic importance to Turkish rather
than to Greek security, or that the airing of the dispute in the UN
would endanger Western unity and benefit the Soviets. Other important countries, such as India, were impressed by the Turkish interpretation of the Greek recourse as an annexationist design, inspired by self-seeking politicians, communists and the Church of
Cyprus.

The Domestic dimension

While its diplomatic campaign was in full swing, the Turkish government took care to appear moderate in its public pronouncements. The obvious target of such tactics were, of course, the Americans. They were often reminded, lest they had not noticed themselves, that Turkey wished 'to give an example of composure to a
Nation to which it is bound by close ties of alliance and co-operation'.[68] In his message to Dulles of 31 August, Menderes was careful to contrast Turkish restraint and sense of responsibility to the
Greek 'demagogical (*sic*) manoeuvres'.[69]

On the domestic scene, these tactics dictated a ban on public
meetings and demonstrations. The issue arose when nationalist committees planned to hold a rally at Izmir, on 9 September, the anniversary of the Kemalist victory against the Greek army in Anatolia.
Explaining his decision, Menderes stated that it would be a mistake
to commit the same 'fallacious' actions as the Greek government
did.[70] At the same time, he assured that his government was resolved to protect national interests and rights.[71] A fortnight later, as
the inscription of the Greek appeal was being debated at the UN,
the Turkish Prime Minister declared that his country was 'resolved
to prevent anyone having any designs on her territory or interfering
with her interests and rights'.[72] The venue of that speech was hardly
coincidental – Menderes was speaking at Afyon, the place where
the Greek rout had begun in September 1922.

At the same time, the government quietly endorsed the nationalist reaction to Enosis, which was bound to gain new impetus in

the wake of the Greek appeal. On 24 August, press publishers, journalists and representatives of the National Student Federation met in Istanbul and set up the 'Cyprus is Turkish' Committee, which undertook to co-ordinate all Cyprus-related activity and project the Turkish case at home and abroad.[73] Its founding was hailed by the press and, a few days later, its executive council was received by Menderes and other government leaders, who unreservedly gave their blessing. The Committee also enjoyed the support of the opposition Republican People's Party and the trade unions. Despite the government's ban on public demonstrations, which lasted throughout the session of the General Assembly, the organisation was able to extend its activities across the country and, within a year, it claimed a membership of 100,000. The 'Cyprus is Turkish' Committee did not neglect its foreign contacts either. In October, a delegation visited London and handed the Foreign Office a memorandum in which it pledged to 'protest against and combat the Enosis movement' and also to work for the adoption of the new constitution.[74] Significantly, and ominously, one of its first acts was to address a letter to Patriarch Athenagoras, protesting against the involvement of Church leaders in politics.[75]

The calculated hardening of the attitude of the Menderes government and its close connections with the anti-Enosis movement led certain authors to seek an interpretation in the domestic context. The difficult economic situation and the populist proclivities of Menderes and his party, which would be painfully manifested from 1955 onwards, may partly account for its decision to escalate its public opposition to the Greek policy and, eventually, adopt an uncompromising nationalistic rhetoric on the issue.[76]

The seeds of confrontation

Official warnings about the future of Greek-Turkish relations became sterner after the inscription of the Greek item on the agenda. On 30 September, an article was published in the government's daily organ, *Zafer*. The undersigned, 'Fenik', was no other than the Secretary-General of the Turkish Foreign Ministry, Birgi. After hinting at Turkish grudges for the 'loss' of the Dodecanese to Greece and the alleged ill treatment of the Turkish minority in Western

Thrace, Birgi concluded with a note of suspicion: 'Are we observ-
ing a re-creation of the *Megali Idea*? Are we obliged to conclude
that annexation of various islands to Greece, which are very close
to Turkey, now constitute a danger for Turkey?'[77] Such comment
proliferated through the columns of the press as the day of the discussion of the Greek item approached.[78] On 5 October, a *Cumhür-
riyet* leader warned that Greece would eventually realise that there
existed not only a Cyprus question, but also those of the Dodecanese and Western Thrace.[79]

Before long, Greek-Turkish co-operation in NATO began to fal-
ter. During exercise 'Keystone', in early September, difficulties appeared in the relations between officers from the two countries.[80]
Two months later, friction on account of Cyprus came to obstruct
the military planning of the Alliance. Turkey opposed the establishment of a fast patrol base on Leros, on the grounds that Greece was
under treaty obligation to keep the island and the rest of the Dodecanese demilitarised. The Turkish Ambassador in Washington affirmed that his country always felt bitter at the 'loss of these coastal
islands', which it had accepted only because of their demilitarisa-
tion. Erkin further admitted that the Turkish veto on that particular
issue was also in response to the Greek policy on Cyprus. The forti-
fication of Leros, he claimed, would only increase Greek appetite
elsewhere.[81] This incident was perhaps the first in a long series that
would plague NATO's south-eastern flank for decades.

The discussion of the New Zealand procedural motion in the
Political Committee offered the opportunity for the fiercest expression of Turkish opposition to the Greek claim. Sarper's speech
of 14 December was described by the British delegation as 'particularly strong and even menacing'.[82] The Turkish press interpreted
the outcome as a defeat for 'Greek agitators'. The nationalistic press
continued to heap scorn upon Greece and to question her value as
an ally. Taking exception of anti-Turkish manifestations during the
outburst of popular indignation in Athens and Salonika, the leading
opposition paper *Millet* claimed that the time had come for a revision of relations with Greece which should extend over the status
of the Dodecanese and even a further exchange of populations involving the Turks of Western Thrace and the Greeks of Istanbul.
Hürriyet called for vigilance against further Greek designs and a

more assertive policy towards Cyprus. Comment in the government press was more restrained, expressing regret for 'the erroneous course' of Greek policy, which, it warned, only served Soviet designs. The wave of anti-Greek comment was reciprocated from the other side of the Aegean. It was temporarily halted after American prodding which helped produce Menderes' conciliatory statement of 20 December.[83]

Ankara had every reason to be satisfied with the outcome of the UN 'battle'. Not only Greece had failed to advance Enosis, but Turkey's claim to be party to the Cyprus question had widely been recognised, not least by Britain and the United States, both of which clearly indicated that they were unlikely to promote a future settlement without taking Turkey's particular interests into account. The country's sheer geostrategic weight, her growing importance to British and American planning for the Middle East, seemed to guarantee that her interests would not be overlooked. The British had already turned to Turkey as the pivot of a regional pact that seemed to offer the only feasible alternative to their now defunct plans for a Middle East defence arrangement. Ankara had actively promoted these plans, first with the signing of the Turco-Pakistani friendship agreement on 2 April 1954, and later with the Baghdad Pact, which Britain itself would join on 5 April 1955.[84] Although the Americans stayed out, they were known to favour the 'northern tier' concept as part of their strategy of containment. Therefore, by 1955, Turkey had become the 'overlapping link' among three major defence arrangements serving Western interests, NATO, and the Balkan and Baghdad Pacts.[85]

NOTES

1. This is based on the almost identical assessment of a Greek diplomat, a Hungarian-American scholar and a Turkish expert, examining the issue at a distance of several years from each other. Panayotis Pipinelis was one of the few articulate critics of Greek Cyprus policy between 1954-9. Ferenc Vàli wrote a classic analysis of Turkish foreign policy until the early 1970s. Tozun Bahcheli is an authority on Turkish foreign policy. See Pipinelis 1959, 13; Vàli 1971, 47, 242; Bahcheli 1990, 36.
2. Bahcheli 1990, 36-37; cf. Bilge 1975, 142; Vàli 1971, 242, 260-263.
3. *Ibid.*, 36; cf. Mihalopoulos 1989, 44-47; Nachmani 1987, 9; Tachau 1959,

262-264.

4. This was candidly stated in a message sent by Sir Mehmed Munir, Turkish Cypriot representative to the Governor's Executive Council, to the Foreign Office, in early 1950. His community, he claimed, was 'only supporting the regime because they disliked the prospect of union with Greece even more'; quoted in Kelling 1990, 111-112.

5. On the belated development of Turkish nationalism in Cyprus, see Attalides 1981, 419-421; Bahcheli 1990, 27; Hill IV 1952, 350ff., 502ff.; Kitromilides 1979, 25-27.

6. Attalides 1981, 422-423; Crouzet I 1973, 173-177.

7. As early as January 1947, the Cyprus Turkish Minority Association (KATAK), reacting to the recrudescence of Enosis, asked for the return of the island to Turkey: Hill IV 1952, 563-564.

8. Vàli 1971, 55, 69, 353.

9. Landau 1974, 193-194.

10. For the Pan-Turkist claim on Cyprus and Turkish nationalist perceptions of the Cyprus question, see Landau 1981, 115, 118, 127, 131-132; Tachau 1959, 263, 267-268; cf. Ioannides 1991, 63-64, 75-76.

11. Landau 1981, 150; cf. Crouzet I 1973, 301-302, according to whom the CTCA was founded in Ankara, in December 1948.

12. Crawshaw 1978, 42-45; Kelling 1990, 110-111. Regarding the 'strongly nationalistic attitudes' of the student community in Turkey during the 1950s, see Landau 1974, 30 and *passim*. On Turkish nationalism and its variations, see Vàli 1971, 58-60.

13. Crouzet I 1973, 389; Ioannides 1991, 76, 80-83; Landau 1981, 132.

14. *Hürriyet* (Liberty) was founded by Sedat Simavi, a journalist born on Rhodes, and, thanks to its sensationalist and rabidly nationalistic profile, it rapidly gained the largest circulation in Turkey: Alexandris 1988, 495-496.

15. 78420, R9, Kelly to Wallinger, Ankara; 28 Dec. 1948; cf. Crouzet I 1973, 298-301.

16. 78420, R9, Kelly to Wallinger, Ankara, 28 Dec. 1948; R200, FO to H.M. Representatives, 26 Jan. 1949; 849C.00/3-2349, Rankin to Acheson, desp. 224; Crouzet I 1973, 301-302.

17. 849C.00/3-2349, Rankin to Acheson, desp. 224.

18. 78425, R11553, tel. from Küçük to FO, 12 Dec. 1949; cf. Crawshaw 1978, 48; Mihalopoulos 1989, 21-24, who incorrectly dates the Turkish Cypriot appeal in March 1950.

19. Crouzet I 1973, 305-306.

20. 78427, R12052, Rumbold, FO, to Bennett, CO, 2 Jan. 1950; 87716, 1081/45, Charles to McNeil, 25 Jan. 1950.

21. 78427, R11889, Charles to Bevin, 21 Dec. 1949.

22. Holden Reid 1988, 160; Vàli 1971, 36-37, 64, 69-71.

23. Kitromilides 1979, 26; Landau 1974, 173-174, 194, 200-201; Tachau 1959, 267-269.

24. 747C.022/6-252, Carp to State, desp. 649; /12-654, Carp to State, desp.

239; cf. Ioannides 1991, 80-83.
25. 747C.00/1-650, Yost to Acheson, tel. 1040; cf. Bilge 1975, 137-138. That the Menderes government had little difficulty in checking or even suppressing nationalistic organisations, whenever this served wider policy objectives, can be seen in the case of the much more powerful Association of Turkish Nationalists (*milliyetcis*), which was dissolved in 1953: Ioannides 1991, 76, 80-83; Landau 1981, 132. Regarding the restrictive practices of the Menderes government in dealing with 'non-governmental' organisations, see Weiker 1963, 9-10.
26. 747C.00/8-254, Kohler to State, desp. 63. Significantly, as late as August 1954, the American Embassy in Ankara possessed 'no evidence of substantial British assistance' to the anti-Enosis campaign in Turkey other than 'solicited' funding from private sources.
27. 95133, 1081/49, Norton to FO, 25 April 1951; 1081/60, Charles to Morrison, 1 May 1951.
28. 681.82/6-2351, Miner to State, desp. 1977.
29. *FRUS 1951*, V, 534-535.
30. Nachmani 1987, 52-53, 91-92, 100.
31. According to Crouzet, 'it is not impossible that [the Menderes government] was in collusion with [the press and nationalist organisations] and encouraged them underhand, [a tactic that] allowed it to send warnings to Greece, while maintaining an official façade of cordiality on its part': Crouzet I 1973, 389.
32. 107494, 10344/1, Izmir press notes, 29 April-14 May 1953; 10344/2, Istanbul press review, 16 June 1953; cf. Crouzet I 1973, 385-387.
33. 107494, 10344/2, Istanbul press review, 16 June 1953; 107544, 1823/4, British Embassy, Ankara to British Embassy, Athens, 10 Nov. 1954; Hristidis 1967, 4-5, 7-9.
34. 107544, 1823/4, British Embassy, Ankara, to British Embassy, Athens, 10 Nov. 1953.
35. 112835, 10344/2, Chancery, Ankara, to Western and Southern Departments, 26 March 1954; Alexandris 1983, 249, 308-309.
36. 107558, WK 1081/11, British Embassy, Ankara, to Chancery, Athens, 2 Nov. 1953.
37. 112844, 1081/62, Bowker to FO, 30 March 1954.
38. *FRUS 1952-54*, VIII, 680-681.
39. 747C.00/6-2254, Warren to Dulles, tel. 1366; /8-254, Kohler to State, desp. 63.
40. The obvious aim was to take credit from the Americans for being a loyal and responsible ally. See notes 68-69.
41. 747C.00/3-3154, Warren to Dulles, tel. 1024.
42. Bahcheli 1990, 38.
43. 107558, WK 1081/11, British Embassy, Ankara, to Chancery, Athens, 2 Nov. 1953.
44. 747C.00/3-2954, Carp to State, desp. 414.
45. 112843, 1081/28, British Embassy, Ankara, to FO, 24 Feb. 1954. The first

full-length communication of Turkish views was made by Ambassador Erkin on 10 March: *FRUS 1952-54*,VIII, 681-683.

46. 747C.00/8-2054, informal memorandum from the Turkish Embassy to the State Department; 112857, 1081/418, memorandum to Turkish Representatives abroad.

47. 849C.00/3-2349, Rankin to Acheson, desp. 224; Crawshaw 1978, 44. Among the members of the 'Committee on Turkish Affairs' there was Rauf Denktash, the future leader of Turkish Cypriot separatism: Kyrris 1977, 46.

48. '... today it is extraordinarily difficult to find educated and responsible middle-aged Cypriot Turks to take a part in public affairs': 112933, WK1081/5, Colonial Secretary's Office, Nicosia, to Athens Chancery, 19 Feb. 1954; elsewhere, the FTA was described as 'a vocal but irresponsible body, of which the [Cyprus] Administration have a poor opinion': 112848, 1081/177, Scott Fox to Young, 30 June 1954; regarding Dr Küçük himself, it was remarked that he was 'so often inebriated that it is difficult to gauge his exact state of sobriety': 112830, 10110/4, Cyprus Political Situation Report, March 1954.

49. 107501, 1081/38, Colonial Secretary's Office to Chancery, Ankara, 16 June 1953.

50. 107485, 10110/5, Cyprus Political Situation Report, July 1953. Dana was also supported by the Turkish government, which prevented a rival candidate from going to Cyprus, because it considered him 'reactionary': 107558, WK1081/13, Helm to Harrison, 3 Dec. 1953.

51. 107589, WK1741/5, British Embassy, Ankara, to Colonial Secretariat, Nicosia, 21 July 1953.

52. 107589, WK1741/7, FO minute by Maby, 30 Sept. 1954; 107558, WK1081/10, Pearson, CO, to Selby, FO, 24 Oct. 1954.

53. 112848, 1081/177, Scott-Fox to Young, 30 June 1954.

54. 107485, 10110/3, Cyprus Political Situation Report, February 1953; cf. Crawshaw 1978, 55; Crouzet I 1973, 385.

55. 112830, 10110/5, Cyprus Political Situation Report, April 1954.

56. Crouzet I 1973, 448-449; 112830, 10110/11, Cyprus Political Situation Report, Oct. 1954.

57. Crouzet I 1973, 449-450.

58. 112859, 1081/487, Istanbul to FO, 8 Sept. 1954; 112866, 1081/686, Ankara to FO, 24 Sept. 1954.

59. 112830, 10110/11, Cyprus Political Situation Report, Oct. 1954.

60. 747C.00/8-454, Stefanopoulos' reply to Dulles; 112852, 1081/288, Scott-Fox to Young, 12 Aug. 1954.

61. 112857, 1081/418, memorandum to Turkish Representatives abroad; *ibid.*, minutes by Wilding and Buxton, 1 Sept. 1954.

62. Menderes' message remains classified in 747C.00/8-3154, note from the Turkish Embassy to the State Department. Its substance, however, and extensive quotations are given in 747C.00/9-1354, office memo from Howard to Baxter *et al.*.

63. 112874, 1081/987, Ankara to FO, 26 Oct. 1954.

64. 747C.00/12-754, memorandum (and annex) from the Turkish Embassy to the State Department; 112879, 1081/1114, Turkish memorandum on Cyprus, 9 Dec. 1954.
65. 112881, 1081/1195, UKUN Delegation to FO, 15 Dec. 1954.
66. For the racist, Pan-Turkist overtones of this argument and its wide currency in Turkey, see Landau 1974, 194-200.
67. Greece's claim on Cyprus was opposed on the following grounds: historically, the island had never belonged to the Greek state, whereas it had been Ottoman territory for three centuries; geographically, it was 'close enough to Turkey to be considered a part of the mainland'; its 'hundred thousand Turks', who were relatively well off under British rule, were bound to suffer under Greek administration; the latter was unable to guarantee either the economic advance or the security of the island. See the text in French of the memorandum to Turkish Representatives abroad sent by the Turkish Foreign Ministry after the Greek appeal to the UN: 112857, 1081/418, Bowker to Young, 1 Sept. 1954. An extensive recapitulation of Turkish arguments on Cyprus see in Vàli 1971, 241-244.
68. 747C.00/8-2054, informal memorandum from the Turkish Embassy to the State Department; *FRUS 1952-54*, VIII, 952.
69. 747C.00/9-1354, office memo from Howard to Baxter *et al.*.
70. 112856, 1081/407, Ankara, 31 Aug. 1954; 112860, 1081/514, Istanbul, 10 Sept. 1954; 747C.00/8-254, Kohler to State, desp. 63; /9-954, Ankara tel. 268; /9-1354, office memo from Howard to Baxter *et al.*.
71. 112856, 1081/407, British Embassy, Ankara, to FO, 31 Aug. 1954; 112865, 1081/657, Chancery, Ankara, to FO, 22 Sept. 1954.
72. 112865, 1081/657, Chancery, Ankara, to FO, 22 Sept. 1954.
73. According to its charter, the aims of the organisation were 'to acquaint world public opinion with the fact that Cyprus is Turkish, to defend the rights and privileges of Turks with regard to Cyprus and [do it] from every point of view, and to condition Turkish public opinion': quoted in Ioannides 1991, 77.
74. 112870, 1081/859, memo from the 'Cyprus is Turkish' delegation, 7 Oct. 1954.
75. For an anatomy of the 'Cyprus is Turkish' Committee, see Ioannides 1991, 80-91; cf. 747C.022/12-654, Istanbul desp. 239; Alexandris 1988, 496-497; Crouzet I 1973, 689.
76. Crouzet I 1973, 446-447; Holden Reid 1988, 160. In this connection, the experience of the Israeli legation in Ankara may be quite enlightening on 'Turkey's particular touchiness with regard to matters of national pride'. See Nachmani 1987, 60 and *passim*.
77. 112867, 1081/734, British Embassy, Ankara, to FO, 2 Oct. 1954; 747C.00/10-1554, Turkish Embassy note.
78. 112868, 1081/779, British Embassy, Ankara, to FO, 5 Oct. 1954; 112870, 1081/874, British Embassy, Ankara, to FO, Oct. 1954; cf. Crouzet I 1973, 443.
79. 112868, 1081/779, British Embassy, Ankara, to FO, 5 Oct. 1954.
80. 112863, 1081/620, British Factual Note to the State Department, 20 Sept. 1954.
81. 781.022/11-1554, memo of conversation between Erkin and Byroade.

82. 112881, 1081/1181, UKUN Delegation to FO, 14 Dec. 1954. As a Foreign Office official commented upon receiving the text of Sarper's speech, the latter had spoken 'more sharply than we should have wished to speak ourselves': 112881, 1081/1195, minute by Wilding, 16 Dec. 1954.

83. 747C.00/12-2154, Wendelin to State, desp. 276.

84. Holden Reid 1988, 159-179.

85. For the importance of geostrategic factors in the Turkish-Western relationship, see, *inter alios*, Vàli 1971, 372.

7

'ENOSIS AND ONLY ENOSIS': THE POLITICS OF GREEK CYPRIOT IRREDENTISM

Greek nationalism and Cypriot politics

Thriving on a considerable 'demographic and cultural substratum', Greek nationalism had begun permeating the island's Christian Orthodox community since the last decades of Ottoman domination. This process, which was carried on by the schools, cultural associations, and the Greek consulates on the island, accelerated during the period of British colonial rule. The 'nationalisation' of the Orthodox Church, in particular, was complete by the turn of the century. This ensured that nationalist ideology became 'an integral part of the prevailing orthodoxy of beliefs and values' of a population who till then had identified itself in fundamentally religious terms.[1] The result was the complete merging of the Orthodox confession with the Greek national identity. The latter was often disputed by opponents of Enosis on various grounds, but Professor Crouzet formulated an answer which might well stand the test of time:[2] 'Whether one adopts the "French" idea of a nation as a voluntary community or the "German" idea of the *Volk* as immanently given, one has to admit that the Greek Cypriots are Greek. [...] And, in the last analysis, the fundamental fact is this willingness of the Cypriots to be part of the Greek nation.'[3]

By the inter-war period, Greek Cypriot nationalism with its battle-cry of Enosis had proved itself a force to be reckoned with. Yet, to those seeking to fit such phenomena in the pattern of post-war decolonisation,[4] the case of Cyprus might appear as an 'extraordinary and baffling inconsistency'.[5] In fact, the Enosis movement owed more to nineteenth-century European irredentism than to post-1945 anti-colonialism.[6] This antinomy was not without consequence, as the experience of internationalisation would prove.

Since the early twentieth century, the Church of Cyprus had emerged as the rightful champion of the national cause. This was an all important development, for the Church was not simply the spiritual shepherd of some 80 per cent of the Cypriot population but also the single most potent factor in the island's economic and social life. After the 1931 uprising, Church leaders and their lay supporters, many of them living in exile, adhered to the rigid 'Enosis and nothing but Enosis' line, which precluded any thought of constitutional evolution.[7] Their underlying fear was that a more liberal regime might 'naturally' weaken the population's commitment to the national cause and encourage a 'narrow Cypriot patriotism'.[8] While pinning their hopes on Greece, Enosis supporters, especially those connected with the 1931 events, were getting restless over the failure of successive Greek governments, which were engaged in a bitter struggle of survival throughout the 1940s, to advance their cause.

The eventual relaxation of Governor Palmer's repressive regime and the development of a brisk political life, already in the war years, created the conditions for a nationalist revival. This time, however, the traditional nationalist circles had to face a formidable challenge from the Left. AKEL's message of social reform was grasped by the Cypriot peasantry and manual workers, whose position had improved little after decades of British rule. Owing to its effective organisation and active interest in local affairs, AKEL scored impressive victories in successive municipal elections. In 1946-9, AKEL managed to control all major city councils, having secured the cooperation of widely-respected moderates, such as John Clerides, Adamos Adamantos and Lysos Santamas, mayors of Nicosia, Famagusta and Larnaca respectively. Spear-headed by the militant miners' and builders' associations, its influence extended over the trade union movement, managing to attract a significant number of Turkish Cypriot workers as well.[9] As has been noted, the election of Leontios, the moderate *locum tenens*, as Archbishop in summer 1947 was considered the high point of AKEL's remarkable course.

Yet, right after his election, Leontios repudiated his supporters and condemned AKEL's participation in Winster's Consultative Assembly.[10]

The Greek Cypriot nationalists organised themselves around a new leader, Bishop Makarios of Kyrenia, who had been allowed to return to the island in late December 1946. In addition to their fervent irredentism, Makarios and his entourage were imbued with the rabid sort of anti-communism thriving in civil war Greece. Once in Cyprus, the rise of AKEL filled them with insecurity and prompted them to see Cypriot politics in terms of an anti-Communist crusade. Makarios became the obvious choice to lead the struggle. His hour came eight months later with the untimely death of Leontios. It was an opportunity for the Right to redress the impiety of an AKEL-elected Archbishop. Prior to his election, Makarios concentrated his fire upon the Left. On 19 September, he stated that 'the struggle against communism is more pressing for the time being. Britain is one of the main bastions against communism in the Eastern Mediterranean. We shall never attack Britain in order to achieve Enosis'.[11] Upon assuming office, however, he committed himself to an unremitting struggle against both the foreign ruler and the 'atheist' and 'traitorous' AKEL.[12]

Under Makarios II, the role of the Church as the Ethnarchy of the Greek Cypriot community was completely transformed into a factional, political one. Assuming the leadership of the anti-Communist, nationalist faction, the Archbishop brought its various groups together in the Ethnarchy Council, which he set up in January 1948. The co-ordination of day-to-day activity was entrusted to an Ethnarchy Bureau under the newly-elected Bishop Makarios of Kition.[13] Before long, Right and Left had engaged in an all-out struggle for supremacy. Apart from excommunicating the supporters of the Left, the Church and its allies declared economic warfare on 'the enemies of fatherland and faith'. This entailed the boycotting of leftist-owned business and blackleg tactics, as in the case of the two great strikes declared by PEO in the mining and building sectors, in the course of 1948. AKEL retaliated and the division of Greek Cypriot society reached absurd proportions – not only the trade unions but also coffee-shops, cinemas and even football clubs came to be divided along party lines.[14] The effects on the pursuit of the national cause, Enosis, would soon become apparent.

The Ethnarchy's onslaught made things harder for the AKEL leadership, which was already divided over the participation in the constitutional process initiated by Governor Winster.[15] The British failure to offer a wider measure of internal autonomy further weakened the position of the moderates and led the party to withdraw from the Consultative Assembly.[16] Two further factors must account for AKEL's about-face against self-government, which became complete by January 1949. Firstly, the influence of the Greek Communist Party and, through it, Moscow. In October 1948, two leading members of AKEL, Secretary-General Fifis Ioannou and PEO leader Andreas Ziartidis, undertook an adventurous pilgrimage, which, through various Soviet bloc capitals, brought them to Mount Vitsi, the Communist stronghold in civil war Greece. At that time, the KKE was using the Greek government's acquiescence to the British domination of Cyprus in order to offset the adverse impact of its own tortuous policy on the Macedonian question. In this spirit, the KKE Secretary-General, Nikos Zahariadis, urged the AKEL leaders to abandon self-government and revert to Enosis as an immediate target to be achieved, if necessary, by armed struggle.[17]

A second consideration weighing in AKEL's tactics was, of course, its domestic political fortunes. Many in the party felt that support for self-government left them exposed to Ethnarchy attacks and cost votes.[18] This latter fear was partly justified by the municipal election results, in May 1949, when Nicosia was lost to the Ethnarchy candidate.[19] Yet the change in line was not imposed without internal rigours. It alienated prominent moderates, like mayors Clerides and Santamas, while a strong minority inside the party, including former Secretary-Generals Servas and Ioannou, continued to criticise the unconditional reversal to Enosis. In true Stalinist fashion, the dissenters would first be removed from the top party echelons and then purged, in the course of the following three years. The new leadership under Papaioannou proved a staunchly pro-Soviet and durable choice, managing to remain at the helm until the late 1980s.

After AKEL's change of tactics, Left and Right engaged in a relentless contest to outbid each other in nationalist fervour. After the failure of the Consultative Assembly and Winster's resignation, the Ethnarchy sought to draw the line before the arrival of the new

Governor. No offer of self-government, whatever its content, could be accepted. It also urged the population to avoid contact with the colonial administration, except for day-to-day matters. Whether out of fear of excommunication or genuine national feeling, the Greek Cypriots generally complied.[20]

AKEL responded by advancing its proposals for involving the UN in the struggle for Enosis and turning it into an international question of self-determination versus colonial rule. The holding of a plebiscite would be the first step. It is not difficult to see what prompted the party to take this initiative. From the domestic point of view, it would not only counter accusations of being unpatriotic but would also help AKEL to steal a march on the Ethnarchy in the pursuit of the anti-colonial struggle. any subsequent wavering on the part of the Church and the Right would leave *them* exposed to charges of compromise and treason.[21]

Yet, in view of the external circumstances in which internationalisation was launched, it can justifiably be assumed that its objectives far exceeded the narrow context of Cypriot politics. By seeking UN involvement, AKEL would not only pose as an implacable enemy of British colonialism; it would also force a grave dilemma upon Greek 'monarchofascism' whether to enter into a confrontation with Britain or lose the initiative to the Communists. If the first course was chosen, relations between Greece and Britain would deteriorate, the Americans would be seriously embarrassed, while Turkey might also be drawn in. Apparently, the implications of Turkish involvement for Greek Cypriot interests were not fully appreciated at the time. The struggle against Western interests and plans in the Eastern Mediterranean was a definite priority. The transcripts of Radio 'Free Greece' and other Eastern bloc stations, whose broadcasts on the Cyprus question intensified after September 1949, are quite revealing in this respect.[22]

Whether the idea of a plebiscite originated with AKEL or the Ethnarchy is unclear. Upon announcing its intention to hold the plebiscite itself, on 1 December, the Ethnarchy bureau referred to a decision taken by the Holy Synod on 18 November, that is five days before AKEL announced its own project. While that claim is not entirely convincing and cannot be verified, the fact remains that, after its preliminary announcement, the Ethnarchy dispatched an envoy to Athens to ascertain the views of the Greek government.[23] Thus, even if a plebiscite had been envisaged by the hierarchy, there was no decision until after AKEL's initiative forced the hand of the Ethnarchy.[24] The significance of the AKEL-Ethnarchy antagonism in determining the options of the nationalist leadership into the early 1950s cannot be doubted and had momentous consequences for the fate of Enosis and Cyprus itself.[25]

Then, the question arises, whether a recourse to the 'international community' was among the Ethnarchy's original aims or it was adopted at a later stage. Its attitude on this point remained rather ambiguous until the eve of the plebiscite. The fact that it had not pressed for a plebiscite under UN auspices but limited itself to organising a collection of signatures could be interpreted as a sign of caution. The intention was not to discover but to confirm an overwhelming majority in favour of Enosis.[26] The Greek government, which the Ethnarchy had consulted, had just issued three public statements discouraging Enosis agitation, and was subsequently forced to recall its Consul-General from Nicosia. Therefore, Greek Cypriot leaders knew that they could only count on non-official Greek support, for the near future at any rate. Pipinelis, then permanent Under-Secretary for Foreign Affairs, admits that he had encouraged the plebiscite but only as a step towards 'the raising of the question *by the Cypriot people themselves*'.[27] This is in accordance with what the Bishop of Kition would confide to the US Consul *after* the plebiscite. The Ethnarchy, he said, did not propose to go further than announcing the result to the colonial authorities and demand that the latter comply with the 'unanimous will of the Cypriot people'.[28] All this seems to support the view that internationalisation was neither a primary nor an inevitable objective.

Again, there is reason to believe that the Ethnarchy's eventual decision was influenced by yet another initiative of AKEL. On 20 January 1950, AKEL addressed an open letter to the Ethnarchy laying out the course that would be actually followed in the near future: transmitting the plebiscite results to the UN; dispatching a committee to Athens to urge the Greek government to take up Enosis with Britain, and, failing this, to resort to the UN; 'enlightening' public opinion in European capitals and the United States.[29] There followed, on 4 February, Archbishop Makarios' last appeal to the Governor to respect the expressed will of the people. Pending a reply, on 14 February, Makarios of Kition announced the formation of a 'national mission' to travel abroad, warning that the Ethnarchy 'would not hesitate to resort to the UN if it considers such a *démarche* necessary, in case that England would refuse to satisfy our demand of Enosis'.This course was sanctioned by the Holy Synod on 3 March, following Creech Jones' negative reply to the Archbishop's letter. From all this there remains little doubt that the Ethnarchy viewed the UN as the last resort, pinning its hopes on an Anglo-Greek understanding.[30]

As it turned out, AKEL, while always making the first step until after the plebiscite, was subsequently content to leave the first role in the Enosis campaign to the Ethnarchy, intervening only in order to sustain its momentum.[31] AKEL sent its own delegation abroad, after its appeal for a representative mission had been rejected. In Paris, Plastiras tried to dissuade its members from pursuing their internationalisation plans further.[32] Travelling behind the 'Iron Curtain', the Cypriot Communists reportedly asked the assistance of Soviet satellite governments in putting their case at Lake Success. AKEL leaders did their best to fan such speculation, while violently attacking the Greek government for 'betraying' the national cause.[33] In the event, the delegation would be prevented from visiting Moscow, while Eastern bloc interest at the UN would amount to no more than the oblique reference to Cyprus by the Polish delegation.[34] Since AKEL knew what not to expect, its bombastic talk was again little more than a tactical manoeuvre to spur the Ethnarchy and Athens towards the path of internationalisation.

AKEL was probably correct to estimate that the Ethnarchy still needed some prodding, though it was most probably unaware of the fact that certain of its leading figures were talking to the 'imperialists' in private about the prospect of a compromise. Following the plebiscite, the US Consul in Nicosia, Porter, sought a meeting with Makarios of Kition. The Bishop, who normally presided over the Ethnarchy Council, was already seen as future leader of the Ethnarchy.[35] The meeting was arranged at the house of a common friend. Over several glasses of one-star Cypriot brandy, Porter probed into the future tactics of the Ethnarchy. Makarios tendered the outline of a compromise, whereby the British 'would agree to maintain military bases and protect the Island, while permitting the administration and people to become Greek'. Was this acceptable to the Ethnarchy, Porter wondered. It had been put on the table, Makarios replied, 'but was not adopted as an official position' for fear of Communist reactions.[36] This was probably one of the best recorded instances revealing the extent to which AKEL tactics circumscribed the options of the Ethnarchy.

The Ethnarchy mission

The mandate of the Ethnarchy mission to Athens included the pursuit of internationalisation, in case the British refused to enter into talks with the Greek government over the Cyprus question.[37] Yet, with the exception of the Left, no Greek party was prepared to support a recourse to the UN. Getting no satisfaction from the government, the delegation turned to the right-wing opposition, the Church, the student associations and the trade unions, which were also controlled by the Right. US diplomats tended to attribute this predilection for right-wing association to the composition of the mission itself. its head, Bishop Kyprianos of Kyrenia, was an ardent nationalist who was also considered a likely successor to the ailing Archbishop, while its most active member, Savvas Loizidis, director of the Ethnarchy office in Athens, was a lawyer and exile of the 1931 uprising of solid anti-Communist convictions.[38]

As has been seen, despite the stirring up of public feeling and the publicity accorded to its activities, the Ethnarchy delegation left Athens disgruntled – and, with the departure of Rossides, less united.[39] It had failed in its primary task to induce the Greek government to take an active interest in Enosis. As a US Embassy official remarked, Plastiras had shown 'considerable courage' in not paying more than lip service to the Cypriot cause.[40] The resolutions of the Greek parliament, however warm, did not amount to much in practical terms. The only concrete achievement that the delegation could point at with satisfaction was the establishment of PEAEK. The outbreak of the Korean War was, of course, a misfortune. The ensuing atmosphere of crisis led to the cancellation of plans for a more forceful campaign, which would have culminated in mass meetings throughout Greece. It also prejudiced the chances of the mission at the UN seat in New York and the United States.

Yet, upon returning from New York, the Ethnarchy delegation chose to present a quite misleading picture. Thus, it interpreted its reception at the State Department as an expression of sympathy for its cause, whereas the only encouragement it had got was from the Greek-American community and a few Congressmen. Above all, the mission, far from awakening the Ethnarchy to the inherent risks of internationalisation, did its best to reinforce those who preached this particular course as the ante-chamber to Enosis.

Makarios III and the chances of compromise

The elevation of the young Bishop of Kition to the St Barnabas throne inaugurated a new phase in Cypriot politics and the struggle for Enosis. Makarios III would provide leadership and cohesion to the Ethnarchy camp of a kind never experienced before. A charismatic personality, imbued in the tradition of Greek irredentism and versed in the intricacies of ecclesiastical politics, Makarios had also received higher theological education in Athens and Boston. Yet, despite his long spell outside his native island (1938-48), he had little grasp of contemporary international politics.[41] At his enthronement on 23 October 1950, he was quick to reaffirm the 'Enosis and only Enosis' line.[42] Thereafter, he seized every opportunity to rule out any thought of a constitutional compromise and rejected any contact with the 'alien rule'.[43]

Before long, the new Archbishop commenced his activity abroad aimed at bringing pressure to bear on the Greek and British governments and otherwise promoting the internationalisation of the question. Athens became a customary annual destination. His visits there followed a standard pattern: an audience at the palace, 'a round of calls' on the Prime Minister, members of the government and opposition leaders, visits of sympathetic delegations, consequent statements, radio addresses, receptions of honour, resolutions, messages of support, consultation with PEEK[44] and the clandestine Struggle Committee. Makarios' presence never failed to inspire editorials and feature articles reviewing pro-Enosis arguments, as well as student demonstrations which, more often than not, ended in clashes with the police.[45]

Yet Makarios and other Ethnarchy representatives occasionally
indicated, even if not in public, that internationalisation was not an
end in itself and that a gradual evolution towards self-determination could be accepted. As has been seen, before his election,
Makarios had spoken to Porter of something like an Anglo-Greek
condominium.[46] In March 1951, Carl Bartch, the US Vice-Consul,
reported that nationalist leaders had 'repeatedly' told him in private that the Ethnarchy might accept a British promise for self-determination 'within a given number of years'; this would enable
them to co-operate in the running of the island's affairs and even
accept a period of self-government to be followed by a plebiscite.[47]
As has been seen, Makarios, during his first visit to Athens as Archbishop, spoke along similar lines to Peurifoy[48] and even hinted at
the possibility of a compromise to the British Ambassador.[49]

It is not clear to what extent Makarios and the Ethnarchy were
prepared to work for a compromise solution, even if the British had
responded. The promulgation of the anti-seditious measures in early
1951 had reinforced the proponents of internationalisation. Moreover, having enticed the Americans to take up his ideas with the British, it was Makarios who publicly repudiated any prospect of compromise. His tendency to go back on his own words would hence
undermine his reliability outside Cyprus.[50]

Still, there would be further signs that the Ethnarchy might have
taken its chances had the British shown any measure of flexibility at
all. The Financial Secretary of the colony revealed to the US Consul
that certain 'political figures', while asking permission for public
meetings, intimated that they would 'not be too concerned' if they
were refused.[51] During late 1951-early 1952, according to the colonial authorities, a moderate trend seemed to prevail within the
Ehnarchy camp, which was reflected in the waning of Enosis agitation.[52] Perhaps, a safer explanation is that Makarios was still busy
reorganising his basis of support. During his long visit to America,
in the winter of 1952-3, he would repeat to Porter his earlier views
in favour of a compromise, provided there was a 'definite and clear'
British undertaking to hold a plebiscite after a few years.[53] More
intimations of this sort would emanate from Ethnarchy sources during Makarios' visit to Athens, in early spring 1954.[54]

Hard-liners, Communists and 'Constitutionalists'

Throughout this period, Makarios' public rhetoric sounded as un-compromising as ever. He would use every suitable occasion to raise the battle cry for the 'sacred and holy' cause of union with Greece. As before, domestic considerations remained paramount in deter-mining the agenda. Enosis proved the most effective platform on which to unite the Ethnarchy camp and silence critics. For the Arch-bishop faced serious challenges from within. Kyprianos of Kyrenia, who saw Makarios' elevation to the throne thwarting his own ambi-tions, and the extreme nationalists around him were never more than fair weather companions.[55] Always on the guard against signs of 'compromise', they already pressed for more forceful methods in pursuing Enosis.[56] Other issues, like the composition of the delega-tion to the Sixth session of the General Assembly or the appoint-ment of a new bishop in Paphos, continued to bring rivalries to the fore.[57] This internal struggle for power persisted until the spring of 1952, at least according to the reports of the US Consulate, which kept a close watch on the situation.

In the event, of course, Makarios emerged as the undisputed leader of the nationalist camp. He felt no qualms about using the pulpit to get his political messages through. In addition to the po-tent ideological assets of religious faith and nationalism, the Arch-bishop could also draw on the very substantial role of the Church in the island's economic life – its land and other real property were estimated at several million pounds, while its multifarious activities rendered it a major employer.[58] What was more, Makarios' success owed much to his personal charisma, his impassioned oratory and commanding presence easily inspiring the faithful with enthusiasm and devotion.[59] Last but not least, his ascent was aided by what the US Consul described as the 'political weakness and inconstancy' of secular politicians.[60]

In reorganising the Ethnarchy-affiliated bodies and setting up new ones, Makarios sought to secure ultimate control of nationalist politics into his own hands. He reorganised the Ethnarchy Council to ensure a majority loyal to himself; critics like mayor Dervis of Nicosia or Bishop Kyprianos were held at bay. He gained hold of the powerful farmers' union, PEK, through the appointment of a per-

sonal supporter, Andreas Azinas, as Secretary-General. Recognising
the potential of the youth movement, he tapped the resources of
Sunday schools and secondary education – itself virtually under
Church control – in order to set up the Pancyprian National Youth
Organisation (PEON), in January 1952.[61] What Makarios referred
to as the 'disciplined and organised ranks of our youth' would become the vanguard of the Enosis movement and a reservoir of dedi-
cated future fighters.[62] After its dissolution, in June 1953, its members were induced to join the pre-existing Orthodox Christian Union
of Youth (OHEN), which then assumed a more militant character.[63]

In order to be able to claim popular backing for his policies and
to offset internal criticism, especially from the Kyprianos group,
the Archbishop twice convened the so-called Pancyprian National
Assembly. While AKEL members were excluded, an effort was made
to meet criticism of the Ethnarchy leadership as being an 'urban'
body by assembling delegates from rural districts. Yet National Assemblies did little more than endorse decisions already taken and
Makarios' proposal to have them convened on a regular basis was
not followed up.[64]

In claiming the allegiance of the entire Greek Cypriot population, Makarios still had to reckon with the challenge from the Left.
Ever present was the fear that AKEL would be quick to exploit any
sign of compromise and pose itself as the champion of the national
cause. AKEL never ceased denouncing the Ethnarchy as a tool of
Anglo-American imperialism, while, upon occasion, it would offer
to join forces with its rival in a common front against British rule.
These offers rather than outright hostility were a real embarrassment. If accepted, they would not fail to compromise Makarios in
the eyes of his nationalist rivals at home and anti-Communist opinion abroad. Even when British tactics, such as the anti-seditious
measures of early 1951 or the threat to enforce them in August
1954, seemed to encourage a united front, AKEL's overtures would
steadily be rejected. Instead, the Archbishop sought to take the wind
out of his opponents' sails by declaring his intention to accept help
from 'East and West' in the pursuit of internationalisation.[65]

It is also true that Makarios never adopted the brand of strident
anti-communism practised by his predecessor or other ecclesiastic
figures, such as Kyprianos. Rather, as the 'battle of the UN' ap-

proached, he would seek to downplay the theme of the Communist menace, particularly with an eye to reassuring American opinion. AKEL, he would claim, was 'mainly interested in agrarian reform',[66] and, in the final analysis, Enosis would result in the outlawing of AKEL and the dissolution of its trade unions.[67]

Regarding AKEL tactics, the political resolution of the its Seventh Congress in December 1951 is quite telling. The party 'should continue its pressure on the Ethnarchy and the Right, by calling upon them to embark on joint action insofar as the people's economic and political problems are concerned and by unveiling to the masses of the people their negative disruptive attitude'. With regard to Enosis, the party was 'firmly standing on its line' for 'a free Cyprus in a free Greece' and was 'unveiling all constitutional manoeuvres'. At the same time, however, it 'should clearly distinguish between what is on the one hand a firm and immutable line and on the other a flexible tactic'.[68] Yet the party never became explicit about how to achieve its 'free Cyprus in a free Greece' goal.[69] It would explicitly oppose the acceptance of a constitution, even if it was coupled with a promise of future self-determination,[70] while it was always ready to denounce any 'bargain' that provided for the granting of military rights and bases to the 'imperialists'. Such pronouncements, of course, played directly into British hands.[71]

On the whole, AKEL proved unable – or perhaps unwilling – to dispute Makarios' leadership of the Enosis movement in any effective way. Besides, it had to face its own internal divisions. The crisis culminated in mid-August 1952, with the expulsion of leading members, including former mayors Adamantos and Servas, who questioned the realism and expediency of the party's pro-Enosis line.[72] The loss of some of its most able and charismatic members and the consolidation of an uninspiring leadership under Secretary-General Papaioannou, ever anxious to conform to guidance from Moscow,[73] apparently contributed to the party's eventual inability to influence the train of events, which its own initiatives had set in motion in 1949-50.[74] Afterwards, it largely concentrated on local politics and the labour movement, in an effort to preserve its power base.[75] Yet, by 1953-4, the colonial authorities repeatedly estimated that its influence was ebbing exactly because the party had lost the initiative on the national question to the Ethnarchy.[76]

The emergence of a moderate, 'constitutional' faction in Cypriot politics was never a serious possibility. This was not due to lack of potential leaders. Rather, it seems that Clerides, the former mayor of Nicosia, and Hryssafinis, a prominent lawyer and former member of the Executive Council, did try to do some groundwork for the return of the island to constitutional life.[77] They were joined by purged members of AKEL, such as Ioannou, its former Secretary-General and newspaper publisher, and, on 30 March 1953, they even managed to hold a small pro-constitution meeting at Limassol.[78] Their efforts failed as a result of, firstly, the British failure to produce a credible and workable proposal for constitutional advance, and, secondly, the relentless hostility of the Ethnarchy. Like his predecessors, Makarios feared that the introduction of a constitutional regime, unless coupled with a clear and short timetable for a plebiscite, would lead to the formation of political parties, which 'would tend to neglect [the] national struggle' in their pursuit of parochial political goals.[79] The Archbishop used every opportunity, be it the plebiscite anniversary or his periodic sermons at Faneromeni, to warn against any constitutional 'deviation' from nationalist orthodoxy.[80] Under the circumstances, those who dared defy such warnings and threats never managed to attract enough popular support.

A matter of urgency

By 1953, the Ethnarchy leaders had enough reasons for concern about the prospects of their campaign. Four General Assembly sessions had passed since the 1950 plebiscite without the Cyprus question being formally raised. There was an acute feeling among the Cypriots of being made an exception at a time when, as Makarios put it to Papagos, they failed 'to achieve whatever the semi-civilised peoples of today are achieving by their perseverance'.[81] There were also signs, according to diplomatic sources at least, that Cypriot opinion had begun to show 'a surprising lack of sincere interest' in Enosis. Wagner, the US Consul, continued to speak of a, however latent, constitutionalist current of opinion. In October 1953, he appeared to believe that a timely British offer might induce a sufficient number of influential Cypriots to accept it 'out of political desperation or in self-interest'.[82] Georgios Seferiadis, Greek Ambassador in Beirut, confirms that this prospect deeply concerned the Archbishop. After meeting with Makarios on 7 November, he noted in his diary that 'the Ethnarchy, despite its best efforts, cannot keep people's feeling on its side. The fear was that the prolongation of the present regime might prejudice the outcome of a plebiscite, even if it was held after two or three years.' In view of all this, Seferiadis concluded, 'something had to be done soon'.[83]

Makarios' first reaction was to try to galvanise the faithful with ever more combative rhetoric. Preaching at Faneromeni on 28 June 1953, he braced his flock for sacrifices, arguing that Britain never set any people free unless forced to do so by violent means. He also sent a clear warning to the Greek government, when he exclaimed that the Cypriots would 'stretch out both our right and our left hands to accept help from the East as well as the West' in pursuing their cause.[84] After addressing his petition to the UN Secretary-General, on 10 August 1953, Makarios authorised his envoy to New York, Savvas Loizidis, to solicit the support of members of the African-Asiatic group. Loizidis was able to report that the Thai representative was being sympathetic.[85] Although this did not amount to much, the Archbishop, in his subsequent appeal to Papagos for sponsorship, once more referred to resorting 'to every means' and 'the affections of foreigners'.[86] Perhaps, Makarios did not as yet know that Papagos' mind was evolving towards the UN option.

By early 1954, the initiative in the pursuit of Enosis had passed from Nicosia to Athens.[87] Kyrou told the US Ambassador in March 1954 that Makarios' visit and activities in the Greek capital were 'of quite secondary importance', since the government had already decided to resort to the UN.[88] From then on, Makarios concentrated on sustaining that decision against any slackening or sign of compromise. His repudiation of Stefanopoulos' acceptance of a constitution cum eventual self-determination in late April, and Papagos' subsequent reaffirmation of the UN course proved that his reactions could not be ignored by Athens. That particular intervention becomes more significant with hindsight, as it came exactly when the British Foreign Office was close to endorsing a formula similar to that envisaged by Stefanopoulos. Of course, the Archbishop could have no idea about deliberations behind Whitehall walls. Once again, the reasons of his reaction were mainly internal – official references

to a compromise tended to 'dismay and confuse' the Ethnarchy camp
and exposed it to AKEL polemics.[89]

Similar considerations probably led Makarios to oppose an effort by Tom Driberg, a Labour MP, to convene an all-party political
debate in Nicosia, in early September 1954. Driberg persuaded
Mayor Dervis to invite some 250 prominent Greek Cypriots of every
political persuasion as well as Turkish Cypriots to attend the meeting. The agenda included all aspects of the island's political problem,
from the British constitutional offer to self-determination. The Archbishop found himself in an awkward position from which he was
extricated thanks to the short-sightedness of the colonial authorities. The insistence of the police to be present and able to dissolve
the gathering, if it turned 'seditious', led Dervis to have it cancelled.
Driberg left Cyprus in frustration and anger, comparing the colonial regime to a 'fascist and police state'.[90]

The use of force

The price Makarios would ultimately have to pay for his ascendancy
was his sliding into the hard line advocated by his fair weather companions in the struggle for Enosis. From 1951 onwards, resort to
forceful methods was advocated by irredentists such as Kyprianos
of Kyrenia and the quasi-professional Enosist circle in Athens. Prominent among the latter were Georgios Stratos, a former Minister for
War, Law Professor Dimitrios Vezanis, a former theoretician of General Metaxas' inter-war authoritarian regime, and the expatriate
Loizidis brothers, Savvas and Sokratis. In May 1951, these men solicited the services of retired Colonel Georgios Grivas, a seasoned
warrior and die-hard nationalist of Cypriot descent.[91] According to
Savvas Loizidis, the prospect of armed struggle had the blessing of
Archbishop Spyridon of Athens, while Makarios himself had appeared willing to discuss it. Exactly a year later, while in Athens,
Makarios came under pressure to sanction a concrete plan of action. In the event, a Struggle Committee was formed and organisational groundwork commenced.[92]

Yet Makarios' attitude to the use of force remained ambiguous
even after Grivas' plans got under way. At the same time, he proved
unwilling or unable to distance himself from the ring of extremists

in Athens, possibly because he wanted to retain a measure of control over their actions too. Thus, in March 1953, Makarios joined
the other members of the Struggle Committee in taking an oath to
support Enosis unto death, in the fashion of nineteenth century secret societies.[93] At that point, Grivas was appointed military chief
of the struggle, but the Archbishop reserved the last word for himself.[94] Makarios' conversion to the use of force appeared complete
by June 1953, but he would continue to disagree with Grivas and
his associates over the scale of the operations, which he wanted
limited to acts of sabotage.[95]

The plans for armed struggle in Cyprus had been known to
Papagos since their inception, as some of those involved, like General Georgios Kosmas, belonged to his entourage. Colonel Grivas
claimed that the Field Marshal had never given any encouragement,
while, after his coming to power, he sought to stop the Colonel's
scheming through various intermediaries, at one point threatening
him with arrest.[96] Yet the fact remains that Papagos and his government raised no obstacles to the illicit activities of Grivas and his
associates in the Struggle Committee.[97] His sole concern, as Grivas
notes, was to ensure that his personal knowledge of the plot remained secret. At the same time, he turned a blind eye to the collusion of Greek officials with the preparation of the struggle.[98]

By the time the Greek government decided to raise the Cyprus
question at the UN, Greek foreign policy-makers envisaged some
show of force in Cyprus as a last resort. By way of contrast, Colonel
Grivas and the Struggle Committee insisted that the diplomatic effort should be complemented by dynamic methods. Makarios had
also come to share this view, although he continued to insist that
operations be limited to sabotage. However, although he was recognised as supreme authority of the future struggle, he had little control over Grivas' planning. Thus, on 2 March 1954, the first ship-
load of arms and explosives safely landed on an isolated Cyprus
beach.[99]

Following Armitage's anti-seditious pronouncements in August,
Makarios asked Grivas to step up preparations. Then, the dilemma
arose whether to sanction the use of force pending the discussion of
the Greek item at the General Assembly or to await its outcome. In
Makarios' view, some acts of sabotage might prove sufficient to im-

press foreign opinion, particularly in the United States, that the prolongation of British rule in Cyprus was fast leading to a new crisis in
the Middle East. On his way to New York in early October 1954,
Makarios saw Grivas in Athens and asked him to wait for his signal.
At the UN seat, however, he found Kyrou still hopeful that a change
in US attitude could be achieved without resort to violent means.
Thus, it was decided to postpone action until after the Assembly.[100]

Nonetheless, Grivas embarked for Cyprus in late October. He
arrived there on 10 November and methodically set about organising small guerrilla groups, which he trained in the use of arms and
explosives. For manpower, Grivas tapped the reservoir of former
PEON members. At the same time he set up an effective network
of intelligence and couriers in villages and towns. To this end, he
relied on the loyal co-operation of Azinas and his associates in PEK.[101]

Back in Cyprus after the General Assembly, the Archbishop met
Grivas on 11 January 1955 and gave him the green light. According
to Makarios, Kyrou had advised action right after the UN debacle,
while Papagos had come round the idea too.[102] D-day was set for 25
March, Greek Independence Day.[103] The capture of 'Agios Georgios'
with its cargo of explosives and other difficulties only caused a slight
delay. On Makarios' insistence, there would be only acts of sabotage against military targets.[104] Eventually, during the night of 31
March-1 April, EOKA would enter the stage with blasts that rocked
the island.

From the outset, AKEL would come out against the use of force.
In his *Reminiscences*, Secretary-General Papaioannou claims that,
as early as mid-1954, he had been warned by an unnamed Greek
officer to 'keep out of the struggle'.[105] In December, the party condemned as provocative the violent incidents which took place in
the aftermath of the Greek failure at the UN and threatened to
undermine inter-communal relations. On 13 January 1955, its Central Committee denounced the allusions of the Athens radio broadcasts to violence and declared its commitment to a struggle by peaceful means.[106] Equally damning was the party's first reaction to the
EOKA explosions of 1 April 1955.[107] Having helped to set the genie free by commencing the drive towards internationalisation, the
Communist Party of Cyprus had by then forsaken its ability to influence the course of events.

NOTES

1. On the domestic and external factors that helped foster the Greek nationalist ideology in Cyprus, see Kitromilides 1979, 18-24; *idem* 1990a, 4, 6-17. On the role of the Church, see also Crouzet 1973, 101-107.

2. Particularly in view of the 'startling' developments in the study of nationalism since the 1970s, as Benedict Anderson observes in his celebrated work: Anderson 1991, xi-xii.

3. Crouzet I 1973, 96-100. The same voluntaristic approach was expressed by E.L. Mallalieu, Labour MP for Brigg, in the House of Commons, where the tendency of disputing the ethnic character of the Greek Cypriots was not uncommon. During the debate of 2 November 1954, he remarked: 'It is quite foolish to say that 80 per cent of the Cypriots are not really Greeks. What does it matter, whether they are or not Greeks by race or origin, since they regard themselves as Greeks and want to be regarded as such by others?': Kyrou 1955, 368-371, n. 1.

4. On the dubious value of comparative analyses of anti-colonial movements in search of patterns and typologies, see Darwin 1988, 17-25, 170-171; Smith 1978, 83-84.

5. Darwin 1984, 190.

6. Crouzet I 1973, 95; Kitromilides 1979, 27-29; *idem* 1981, 454.

7. Kitromilides 1981, 452-454; *idem* 1990a, 12-14.

8. Loizidis 1980, 53; Pikros 1980, 100, 102; Pipinelis 1959, 17.

9. Adams 1971, 25-28, 43-45; Attalides 1981, 424; *idem* 1986, 145; Kyrris 1977, 80-89.

10. Papaioannou 1988, 79-81.

11. *Eleftheria* (Nicosia), 19 Sept. 1947; quoted in Fantis 1993, 87.

12. 849C.00/4-1849, Porter to State, A-35; Crawshaw 1978, 41.

13. Crouzet I 1973, 101-107; Mayes 1981, 35.

14. Adams 1971, 29-31, 33; Papapolyviou ms, 3-5.

15. Servas I 1985, 127-132.

16. Servas, Adamantos and three other members of the Central Committee had supported the continuing participation of AKEL in the Consultative Assembly against a majority of twelve: *ibid.*, 132.

17. In dismissing self-government, Zahariadis boasted before the Cypriot leaders that the Communist Democratic Army would win the war: Papageorgiou 1984, 177-187; Servas I 1985, 133; Servas I 1989, 24-25. Both authors quote from Ioannou's account of the trip to 'Free Greece' in the Cypriot daily *Apoyevmatini* (26 March 1976-ff). See also 78420, R848, Political Situation Report, December 1948; 78421, R2794, Political Situation Report, January 1949; Crawshaw 1978, 41; Crouzet I 1973, 253-254.

18. Crawshaw 1978, 41; Papageorgiou 1984, 213; Papaioannou 1988, 88; Servas I 1989, 23.

19. In those elections, AKEL kept its lead in the three major cities, Famagusta, Limassol and Larnaca. Nicosia was lost partly because the party had alienated former mayor Clerides, a supporter of constitutional evolution. See the comparative electoral results for 1946 and 1949 in 747C.00/7-3153, Wagner to State, desp. 11. Papaioannou also admitted that AKEL polled better than anticipated: Papaioannou 1988, 92.
20. 849C.00/6-1049, Bartch to State, A-51; 78423, R7440, Turnbull to CO, 21 July 1949.
21. Crouzet I 1973, 148. The same author also assumes that AKEL leaders were 'no doubt deeply convinced' that the British were serious about staying in the island, and thus could afford crying for Enosis 'without the risk of falling under the "monarchofascist" regime of Greece'. It is quite significant that Secretary-General Papaioannou in his *Reminiscences*, while confirming AKEL's initiative in proposing a plebiscite (p. 88), has absolutely nothing to say about the party's policy between its Sixth Congress, in August 1949, and the outbreak of violence nearly six years later. See Papaioannou 1988, 93-95.
22. 87717, 1081/65, BBC Monitoring Service, 14-18 Jan. 1950; see also Woodhouse's assessment of Communist tactics in 'Greece's "Great Idea"', *Spectator*, 27 Jan. 1950, in 87716, 1081/50; cf. Mihalopoulos 1982, 573; Vlahos 1980, 18-19. The Greek government itself had expressed anxiety to the Americans about Cominform enthusiasm with Enosis and the plebiscite: 747C.00/1-1250, memo of conversation between Cromie and Economou-Gouras.
23. 747C.00/1-2550, Porter to State, desp. 10. The envoy was, perhaps, Makarios of Kition, who often travelled to Athens to promote public awareness of the Cyprus question. This could be surmised from Loizidis' account of a meeting with Makarios and Law Professor Vezanis, during which the plan for a plebiscite was discussed. Although Loizidis gives no date, he states that, after returning to Cyprus from Athens, Makarios put the matter to the Ethnarchy Council, which decided to announce and organise the plebiscite: Loizidis 1980, 54-56.
24. Crouzet, though inclined towards the view that the idea of a plebiscite had been maturing in ecclesiastic minds, that of Makarios in particular, agrees that 'the initiative of the Communists, which threatened to outstrip [the Ethnarchy], precipitated its decision': Crouzet I 1973, 268-269; cf. Mayes 1981, 37.
25. The significance of the AKEL-Ethnarchy antagonism in determining the options of the nationalist leadership into the 1950s and the grave consequences thereof are noted in Kitromilides 1981, 457-458.
26. This point is correctly made by Mihalopoulos 1982, 575.
27. Emphasis in the original: Pipinelis 1959, 21.
28. 747C.00/1-2550, Porter to State, desp. 10; cf. Vlahos 1980, 23.
29. 747C.00/1-2550, Porter to State, desp. 10; Crouzet I 1973, 275.
30. Crouzet I 1973, 270, 275-276. Crouzet maintains that, 'from the outset, the ultimate aim of the Ethnarchy was to 'utilise the plebiscite as a basis for an appeal to the United Nations'. In this case, too, it does not seem unreasonable that the timing was dictated by AKEL's initiative. Besides, he himself argues

that 'many nationalists were at first convinced that it would suffice for Greece to present the enosist claim officially to England in order for the latter to accept it': *ibid.*, 341.

31. 747C.00/1-2550, Porter to State, desp. 10.
32. Mihalopoulos 1989, 37-39.
33. 87723, 1081/187, extract from Czechoslovak News Bulletin, 31 Aug. 1950; Crawshaw 1978, 49, 51-52.
34. 747C.00/1-1452, office memo from Howard to Porter.
35. This was Governor Wright's assessment: 87716, 1081/39, Wright to Creech Jones, 18 Jan. 1950.
36. Porter concluded his report of that memorable meeting as follows: 'We were alone during this conversation, and I knew better than to try to match (Makarios) drink for drink, especially with only that one-star concoction available. His Grace told me that when he went to college in Boston his fellow students called him "Mak". I almost did myself by the time we finished, and I must confess I am not feeling too vigorous this morning': 747C.00/1-2550, Porter to State, desp. 10. This is probably the same story related in Sulzberger 1969, 510-511.
37. Crawshaw 1978, 58-59; Vlahos 1980, 30.
38. According to an American report, Loizidis was suspected of collaboration with the German occupation authorities in Athens, during the war: 747C.00/ 7-650, Memminger to State, desp. 27. Loizidis himself admits that the Germans had approached him on account of his anti-British record, but he had declined the offer. He had served, however, as defence attorney at the German military tribunal of Athens: Loizidis 1980, 47-48.
39. As has been noted in Chapter 1, Rossides chose not to follow the delegation to London and, then, to New York, arguing that the Korean invasion and the ensuing international crisis had rendered its mission inopportune.
40. 747C.00/6-2150, Memminger to State, desp. 976. In October, Plastiras, then out of office, travelled to Cyprus. There, he was visited by local activists, to whom, according to British information, he repeated the same view he had expressed to the Ethnarchy delegation in Athens, i.e. the time was not opportune for raising the issue. Governor Wright described the General's behaviour as 'at all times proper and discreet': 87723, 1081/210, Wright to Griffiths, 25 Oct. 1950; cf. Servas I 1985, 153.
41. Nikos Kranidiotis, who served the Archbishop first as Secretary of the Ethnarchy and, after independence, as Ambassador to Greece, gives a surprisingly candid picture of Makarios' background and personality: Kranidiotis 1981, 44-47. This is not at variance with the assessment of Stanley Mayes, the British journalist who had been a sharp critic of Makarios in the 1950s and '60s and subsequently produced a studiously balanced political biography of the Archbishop: Mayes 1981.
42. Crawshaw 1978, 51; *Makarios III*, 66.
43. 'Encyclical on the anniversary of the annexation of Cyprus to the British Crown', 5 Nov. 1950, in *Makarios III*, 71-72; 'Encyclical on non-participa-

tion in the elections for area improvement boards', 13 Dec. 1950, *ibid.*, 73-75.
44. Panhellenic Committee for the Union of Cyprus, as PEAEK was renamed.
45. 747C.00/8-1452, Memminger to State, desp. 190; /3-2353, Memminger to State, desp. 1089.
46. 747C.00/1-2550, Porter to State, tel. 10.
47. 747C.00/3-1451, Bartch to State, desp. 155.
48. *FRUS 1951*, V, 529-531.
49. 95133, 1081/39, Norton to Morrison, 28 March 1951.
50. See below, note 254.
51. 747C.00/1-1152, Wagner to State, desp. 194. Maurice Cardiff, director of the British Council in Cyprus, speaking to his friend Seferiadis (Seferis), the Greek diplomat and poet, referred to the 'lukewarm' nationalists, who, despite their rhetoric, secretly showed readiness to co-operate with the British: Seferis, *Meres* VI, 111; cf. Durrell 1957, 124-125, 148.
52. Wagner referred to a discussion with Zinon Pierides, Cypriot businessman and Ethnarchy supporter: *FRUS 1951*, V, 541-542.
53. 747C.00/2-1253, memo of conversation between Porter and Makarios.
54. 747C.00/5-1354, Schnee to State, desp. 1054.
55. Crawshaw 1978, 51; Kelling 1990, 122. Kyprianos would always bear Makarios a grudge for his election to the St Barnabas throne, while the former was still on the Ethnarchy mission abroad. The Bishop of Kyrenia decided not to enter the contest after an 'agonising process' described in Loizidis 1980, 75. Some two decades later, Kyprianos would attempt to have Makarios dethroned for holding both ecclesiastical and secular high office as President of the Republic of Cyprus.
56. Grivas *Memoirs*, 13, 16-17.
57. 747C.001/10-351, Wagner to State, desp. 91. Dervis, the mayor of Nicosia, was reported as being at odds with Makarios over the appointment of Fotios Koumidis as bishop of Paphos: 747C.00/1-1652, Wagner to State, desp. 196. The Enosist movement in Greece was not immune from internal discord either. The prominence which the Ethnarchy Bureau in Athens sought in the conduct of the campaign and its policy of high profile antagonised Archbishop Spyridon, head of PEEK, and threatened to strain relations with Nicosia. Thus, in March 1954, Makarios would have to close the Bureau: 112830, 10110/4, Cyprus Political Situation Report, March 1954.
58. Crouzet I 1973, 105.
59. Mayes described Makarios' 'free-verse-like' sermons: 'The passion was always controlled and the speech the more compelling because of it': Mayes 1981, 41-42. He also acknowledged the Archbishop's great personal charm and genuine consideration for others.
60. 747C.03/5-152, Wagner to State, desp. 275.
61. Crawshaw 1978, 52-54; Crouzet I 1973, 324-330; Kelling 1990, 122-123; Kranidiotis 1981, 47-48; Mayes 1981, 43-44.
62. See the Archbishop's message on the founding of PEON, on 4 January 1952,

in *Makarios III*, 133-134.

63. Mayes 1981, 44.
64. 112830, 10110/5, Cyprus Political Situation Report, April 1954; 747C.00/6-354, Wagner to State, desp. 84. See also Mayes 1981, 42.
65. Crouzet I 1973, 149; Kranidiotis 1981, 50.
66. 112830, 10110/11, Cyprus Political Situation Report, Oct. 1954.
67. Crawshaw 1978, 86. A similar view was conveyed to the Americans by the Ethnarchy's foreign adviser, Zinon Rossides: 747C.00/8-1154, memo from Rossides to Wagner.
68. 747C.00/1-1652, Wagner to State, desp. 196.
69. Crouzet I 1973, 253-4; Servas I 1985, 135.
70. 112830, 10110/6, Cyprus Political Situation Report, May 1954.
71. 112870, 1081/865, Nicosia, 15 October 1954; Crawshaw 1978, 53-54; Vlahos 1980, 41.
72. 747C.00/8-1852, Wagner to State, desp. 20; /8-2852, Wagner to State, desp. 48; /8-2952, Wagner to State, desp. 49; Crawshaw 1978, 53; Papageorgiou 1984, 188, 190.
73. This was reflected in the frequent visits of AKEL leaders to Eastern European capitals throughout the period discussed here. Party congresses and festivals provided ample opportunities for such visits, while several AKEL youths benefited from state scholarships for higher studies. While keeping a watchful eye on this traffic, the colonial authorities did little to prevent it: Crawshaw 1978, 51; 112933, WK1081/5, Colonial Secretary's Office to Chancery, Ankara, 19 Feb. 1954.
74. This makes nonsense of Papaioannou's claim that, by embracing the 'solidly anti-imperialist slogan' of Enosis, the party prevented 'the reactionary Right from taking the lead in our national liberation struggle': Papaioannou 1988, 88. His *Reminiscences* is riddled with inconsistencies of this sort and given an easy target to criticism: Servas I 1989.
75. Crawshaw 1978, 53; Crouzet I 1973, 335-338. In early 1954, AKEL dissolved its front organisation, EAS, and replaced it with a more tightly controlled body, the United National Front of Action, which never attracted any serious following: 747C.001/2-254, Wagner to State, desp. 57.
76. 107485, 10110/4, Cyprus Political Situation Report, March 1953; 112933, WK1081/5, Colonial Secretary's Office to Chancery, Ankara, 19 Feb. 1954. As was aptly remarked, 'AKEL preserved its power, but lost its influence over the course of events': Crouzet I 1973, 338.
77. 747C.03/4-1852, Wagner to State, desp. 268; cf. Kelling 1990, 102.
78. Crouzet I 1973, 260-261; 747C.00/4-153, letter from Wagner to Porter. The US Consul suspected that the British were secretly subsidising Ioannou's paper *To Fos* to promote the constitutional cause.
79. 747C.00/6-2852, Yost to Acheson, tel. 5512. Makarios' fears mirror-imaged the wishes of those who had supported constitutional evolution in Cyprus since 1946: Louis 1984, 221-222.
80. 747C.00/4-2552, Wagner to State, desp. 272.

81. 747C.00/9-953, Anschuetz to State, desp. 262.
82. 747C.00/10-1653, Wagner to State, desp. 32; /1-454, Wagner to State, desp. 49; /2-254, Wagner to State, desp. 56.
83. Seferis, *Meres* VI, 100.
84. *Makarios III*, 198-202; 747C.00/7-1353, Wagner to State, desp. 1; Linardatos II 1978, 85; Vlahos 1980, 62-63.
85. Loizidis 1980, 86.
86. 747C.00/9-953, Anschuetz to State, desp. 262.
87. 112830, 10110/5, Cyprus Political Situation Report, April 1954.
88. 747C.00/3-1754, Cannon and Axelrod to State, desp. 860.
89. 747C.00/6-354, Wagner to State, desp. 84.
90. 747C.00/9-554, Sprecher to State, tel. 18; /9-954, Sprecher to State, desp. 19; cf. Crouzet I 1973, 437.
91. Grivas *Memoirs*, 17. For a succinct account of Colonel Grivas' background and activities until 1954, see Crawshaw 1978, 90-99.
92. Grivas *Memoirs*, 17-18; cf. Crawshaw 1978, 94; Foley-Scobie 1975, 15-16; Kranidiotis 1981, 57-58.
93. Among the ten men who, like Makarios, signed the oath were Stratos, General Nikolaos Papadopoulos, Colonels Grivas and Ilias Alexopoulos, University Professors Vezanis and Gerasimos Konidaris, the Loizidis brothers, and two obscure lawyers, Antonios Avgikos and D. Stavropoulos: Grivas *Memoirs*, 19-20, n. 1; Konidaris 1964, 253-254; Loizidis 1980, 100-101. In the following year, General Papadopoulos ('Pappous'), who had originally been one of the candidates for the military leadership, disagreed with Vezanis' proposal that all British-decorated officers return their medals and left the Committee: Konidaris 1964, 257.
94. Grivas *Memoirs*, 20; Foley-Scobie 1975, 20; Kranidiotis 1981, 73-74.
95. Grivas *Memoirs*, 20-21; Crawshaw 1978, 96; Foley-Scobie 1975, 20-21; Konidaris 1964, 255; Mayes 1981, 49, 51-52.
96. Grivas *Memoirs*, 21, where he claims that, on 28 September 1953, he 'was called to the office of a Government Minister' and warned that, unless he dropped his plans, the Minister 'would "unhappily" have to arrest' him.
97. Loizidis, a close associate of Grivas, states that Papagos 'showed understanding and sympathy once he became aware of preparatory moves'. He also argues that no such moves, especially the procurement and shipment of arms and explosives to Cyprus, could have been effected unless the government had sanctioned the involvement of state officials: Loizidis 1980, 92; cf. Linardatos II 1978, 221-222.
98. Grivas *Memoirs*, 20; cf. Crawshaw 1978, 96-97.
99. Grivas *Memoirs*, 21-22; cf. Crawshaw 1978, 96-97; Mayes 1981, 51-52; Xydis 1966, 9-10.
100. Grivas *Memoirs*, 23-24; Kranidiotis 1981, 79-81.
101. Grivas *Memoirs*, 24-28; cf. Crawshaw 1978, 100-102.
102. On that day, commenting on Papagos' attitude, Grivas noted in his diary: 'What a terrible thing it is when politicians and, worse still, men in charge of

governments, react in this manner to matters of national importance and make use of them for their own party interests. Instead of Papagos support-ing us – behind the scenes at any event – he has been restraining us until today. …When Papagos was put before the accomplished fact of all that had been done and when he was faced with the impasse of the UNO decision, he was forced to change his mind. But what help has he given us? None.': *Captured Documents*, 5.

103. *Ibid.*, 7; cf. Crawshaw 1978, 105; Xydis 1966, 17-18.
104. Crawshaw 1978, 107.
105. Papaioannou 1988, 94-95.
106. Kranidiotis 1981, 75-76; Linardatos II 1978, 281-282.
107. Adams 1971, 45-46; Papaioannou 1988, 95.

8

TREADING THE TIGHTROPE: THE FORMULATION OF GREEK POLICY

Post-war irredentism and Cyprus

Besides triggering a multifaceted domestic crisis, which culminated in a bloody civil conflict, the bitter experience of World War II spurred a resurgence of Greek irredentism. Having dominated the political discourse of the Greek state for nearly a century, this all-permeating ideological phenomenon had receded following the Asia Minor catastrophe in 1922. The war, however, helped to foster the belief that the nation's gallant record of resistance and its sufferings under enemy occupation entitled it to a new, perhaps the final, bout of national restitution. This belief was shared and cultivated by the country's political leadership. Barring the most extreme pretensions, emanating from both the extreme Left and Right, Greek *irredenta* were limited to the Dodecanese Islands, Northern Epirus and Cyprus – all three being areas with compact Greek populations. Only the first of these claims was to be satisfied by the Peace Settlement: the Dodecanese, scattered in the southeastern Aegean, had belonged to a former enemy state, Italy, and had an overwhelmingly Greek population, while the only possible rival claimant, Turkey, chose to acquiesce. The other complicating factor was Great Power rivalry, which proved an insuperable obstacle in the case of Northern Epirus (or Southern Albania). Rival Albanian nationalism and the fact that Albania had also been an occupied state, but above all her place within the Soviet sphere of influence effectively cancelled the Greek claim. [1]

While the Dodecanese happily joined the fold of mother Greece and Northern Epirus was indefinitely sealed behind the Iron Cur-

tain, Cyprus, despite the apparent odds, still appeared as a tempt-
ing bait for Greek irredentism. It was an island inhabited by a four-
fifths Greek majority which time and again manifested its desire for
Enosis. Unlike the Dodecanese, however, Cyprus belonged to a
friendly power, indeed the power that held sway in Greece till 1947;
nor was it possible to advance a claim against a victorious Great
Power at the Peace Conference. The only way in which Greek leaders had felt able to put the question to the British since the war,
however tentatively and discreetly, was through bilateral diplomatic
channels.

Regent Damaskinos' approach to Bevin in 1945 was the first
clear proposal for a settlement,[2] and King Paul repeated it in public, three years later. In an interview with Sulzberger, the *New York
Times* editor on 27 July 1948, he stated the Greek position as follows:

> Greece certainly desires and will continue to desire the union of Cyprus
> to the rest of Greece. It is difficult to understand why this has not yet been
> effected. The argument that this might interfere with British security pro-
> visions is not valid. Were Cyprus to be given to Greece, as the vast major-
> ity of its population desires, this would in no way interfere with any mili-
> tary or other bases Britain has established there.[3]

This statement was all the more remarkable in coming at the height
of the civil war, and only a year after Greece had passed from British
to American tutelage. Throughout this period, the issue of Cyprus
was kept alive thanks to the interest of the press, fuelled by Greek
Cypriot activities and occasional official expressions of the entire
nation's keen interest in the 'fulfilment of the national destiny of the
people of Cyprus'.[4] What was more, the Communists, outlawed
since 1947, never ceased championing Enosis and charged their opponents with betraying the cause.

On the whole, however, Greek governments until after the civil
war bowed to British pressure and exercised self-restraint. Foreign
Minister Tsaldaris' request to the British Ambassador, in December
1949, 'to draft something [i.e. a statement discouraging Enosis] and
let him have it', was indicative of the prevailing frame of mind at the
time.[5] On the occasion of the Ethnarchy delegation's visit to Ath-

ens, official Greek reticence towards the Enosis movement was epito-
mised by Deputy Prime Minister Papandreou in his usual epigram-
matic way: 'Greece breathes with two lungs, one British and one
American. Therefore, she is unable for the sake of Cyprus to suffer
suffocation'.[6]

Yet successive Greek governments were to be subjected to the
tactics of pressure, initiated by the Ethnarchy delegation and later
perfected by Archbishop Makarios III. In this effort, the Church of
Greece proved a powerful ally, willing to keep the flames of Enosis
burning in the hearts of its flock.[7] Its motives can be surmised in
that by assuming the leadership of an irredentist cause, the Church
posed as champion of the national aspirations of Hellenism – a role
that owed more to a latter-day ideological construction than to the
historical record.[8] Again, it was only natural that the Church of
Greece should wish to assist its sister Church of Cyprus to maintain
its leading role against the challenge from the Left. Perhaps, in championing a 'just' and, above all, popular cause, the Greek hierarchy
saw a good means for buttressing its own position in Greek society.
Greece, like most countries in Europe, had not been spared a certain alienation from religious faith during and after the war, although
the extent of that phenomenon is not easy to verify.[9] That was also
a period when various para-ecclesiastical organisations flourished,
partly as a response to the powerful grassroots movement of the
Left. These organisations, whose relations with each other and the
official Church were not always harmonious, acquired considerable
political patronage, which made them particularly hard to ignore.
Enosis offered a rallying point which the Church successfully used
in order to mobilise the support of these later-day zealots.

Similar considerations of capitalising on a good, popular cause
must have led the GSEE to jump on the bandwagon.[10] In fact, it had
been the populist right-wing leaders of the 'official' trade unions,
who, prompted by their Cypriot counterparts of the SEK, had advanced the formation of the PEAEK under Church leadership.[11]
With regard to the student unions, the Cyprus question would permit them, besides manifesting their patriotic exaltation, to extend
their activity beyond the relatively regimented university politics.

Quite revealing of the early objectives of the Enosist movement
in Greece was the declaration approved at the mass meeting held by

PEAEK in Athens on 21 July. The text called upon the government to 'leave aside all diplomatic reserve' and take the Cyprus question up with Britain; if the government was not forthcoming, then the members of parliament should raise it themselves before the parliament and public opinion of Britain and, 'if necessary, before world opinion'. In any case, Archbishop Spyridon interjected, the Church was 'determined to assume its responsibilities for Cyprus'. This declaration is quite a typical example of the nationalist rhetoric which was bound to dominate the public discourse on Cyprus over years to come. It not only proclaimed the union of Cyprus with the 'mother country' to be an incontestable right of the Greek people; it also alluded to an irredentist programme, reminiscent of the *Megali Idea*, when it spoke of the 'sacred duty' of all Greeks to 'complete the liberation and reinforce the independence of Hellenism', which included Cyprus and Northern Epirus.[12]

The claim becomes official

Rather unwittingly, Venizelos became the first post-war Greek Prime Minister to publicly express the demand for the union of Cyprus with Greece. He probably did so against his own better judgement in order to extricate himself from a difficult situation in parliament. As has been seen, his minority government came under pressure from its supporters to reply to Younger's provocative statement in the House of Commons on 14 February 1951.[13]

Venizelos was also the first Greek Premier to experience the stresses of Archbishop Makarios' long visits to Athens, which invariably provoked Anglo-American counter-pressures. In this case, his government managed to secure the broadest possible consensus upon a common line. Those present at the all-party council of 21 March 1951 seemed to realise the fundamental dilemma of all Greek governments, namely their inability to ignore the strength of public feeling which Enosis – or its champions – could arouse, at the same time, to preserve the traditional Anglo-Greek relationship intact. The government was given a mandate to explore any solution, which would satisfy the desire of the majority of the Cypriots, would safeguard British strategic interests and respect the rights of the Turkish Cypriot minority. The council also consented to a compromise, pro-

vided the British would pledge to respect the right of the Cypriot
people to self-determination 'within a reasonable period of time' –
a sort of 'Balfour Declaration' for Cyprus. Significantly, a recourse
to the UN was rejected as impracticable. Instead, the government
was authorised to do everything in its power to dissuade the
Ethnarchy from soliciting third-party support to that end.

Accordingly, on 9 April Venizelos informed the Greek Ambassador in London of his intention to raise the question with the British
government. The timing of the Greek *démarche* was itself a matter
of serious concern. As the Premier explained to Melas, he would
rather wait until after Greece's admission to NATO looked reasonably secure. He feared, however, that Turkey, whose admission to
the Alliance was also pending, might seek a guarantee that there
would be no change in the status of Cyprus. Thus, Venizelos opted
for a relatively early approach. Melas was instructed to convey the
proposals of the all-party council in any way he might deem most
opportune.[14] This Greek approach, the first since the one of Regent
Damaskinos six years earlier, met with rejection.

In June 1951 Greece entered a period of political uncertainty,
which made politicians and diplomats quite reluctant to pursue the
Cyprus claim further. It was no coincidence that the statement of
policy of the Plastiras-Venizelos coalition, which was able to muster a thin majority in October, contained no reference to the matter. This omission was not fortuitous. Greece had just been invited
to join NATO and her admission had to be sanctioned by the legislature of every member state, including Britain. She was also seeking election to a non-permanent seat of the UN Security Council.
In that effort, Greece could count on American support, but the
position of Britain and the Commonwealth was far from encouraging. What was more, the government could ill-afford to ignore the
expressed American opposition to the raising of the Cyprus question, at a time when it was desperately fighting to avert a dramatic
reduction in the level of US aid.

During the same period, the rise of Field Marshal Papagos as
leader of the strongest party in parliament seemed to undermine
the consensus expressed by the all-party council of the previous
March. Although his lieutenants, Kanellopoulos and Stefanopoulos
had been present, Papagos did not feel himself bound by its deci-

sions. Yet he avoided making an issue out of Cyprus while in opposition and intended to handle the matter himself after coming to power. For this reason, he would refuse to join the government in a new attempt to work out a common line. In the event, it was criticism from within its own ranks that eventually compelled the government to display some interest in Cyprus during the Fifth UN General Assembly in Paris. Mavros' statement at the Fourth Committee, in particular, was actually the first instance that the Cyprus question was explicitly raised by a Greek delegate in a UN forum. According to Mavros' own account, he had done so largely on his own initiative and against instructions from Athens.[15]

Venizelos' decision to defy Makarios' pressures and not to resort to the UN in the summer of 1952 was undoubtedly influenced by the sharp deterioration of Anglo-Greek relations. The palace was also known to oppose internationalisation, while King Paul had repeatedly expressed to the British Ambassador his discomfort with Makarios's visits.[16] Although for different reasons, Kyrou, the permanent representative to the UN, also advised against a recourse. The thinly-veiled American opposition was also a potent consideration. What might have weighed more on Venizelos' mind, however, was the sheer uncertainty of the government's future. With Prime Minister Plastiras still incapacitated, the coalition was subjected to relentless pressure from both the opposition and the Americans to step down and clear the way for new elections – the third in three years. Therefore, it was a matter of elementary sense of duty not to open a new front in the country's foreign relations, however strong the popular feeling on Cyprus might have been.

As it happened, Venizelos was out of office before the opening session of the Seventh General Assembly. The caretaker government, which took office on 10 October, simply lacked the mandate to pursue any major issue of foreign policy. On the question of Cyprus, Filippos Dragoumis, Venizelos' successor in the Foreign Ministry, chose to rely on the counsel of Ministry officials. According to British sources, the latter suggested that UN tactics ought not to disturb Anglo-Greek relations or jeopardise other national objectives, citing Greece's exclusion from MEDO as an instance. Indeed, Kyrou, who headed the Greek delegation to the General Assembly, was instructed to avoid provoking the British at the various committees. He was also told to be 'very cautious' in his contacts with Archbishop Makarios, who travelled to New York in search of international support.[17]

Papagos and the Cyprus question

While in opposition, Papagos and his party had cultivated a markedly pro-American outlook, often working hand-in-glove with the US Embassy in Athens on domestic issues. On the other hand, Ambassador Peurifoy had been instrumental in bringing the Greek Rally to power, by exercising relentless pressure on both the government and the palace. After victory, the alignment of the new government with US policy was almost complete. Anti-communism once more became the order-of the day. Economic stabilisation continued along the lines drawn by the American mission. Despite the diminishing volume of aid, defence expenditure and the strength of the armed forces were maintained at high levels. The government fulfilled its obligations to NATO, offered additional forces for service in Korea, concluded the treaty of friendship with Turkey and Yugoslavia and actively promoted its upgrading to a military alliance. On 12 October 1953 an agreement was signed giving the US air and naval bases and other facilities on Greek territory. The government also took steps to ease friction in Anglo-Greek relations, to the point that by August 1953 the British Embassy observed 'signs' of a willingness to establish a 'closer working relationship' with Britain.[18]

Thus, it might seem a paradox that Papagos of all Greek leaders would decide to 'activate' the Cyprus question and, thus, threaten to upset allied relations in the wider region. What British and American diplomats, among others, overlooked was the strong nationalistic undercurrent which crosscut political loyalties and formed an integral part of Greek official ideology. According to Markezinis, even before he came to power the Field Marshal 'was burning ... to connect his name with Cyprus'.[19]

To be sure, the government's early record contained few signs of this. The foreign policy section of its inaugural statement in parliament, drafted by Mostras, then director of Soviet and Balkan Affairs, contained only a brief reference to Cyprus, to the effect that the government would deal with the question 'within the frame-

work of present realities'. While not mentioning Anglo-Greek friendship as the proper framework for a future solution, the government's
statement was denounced by the opposition as being too vague or
even oblivious of the 'just' aspirations of Hellenism.[20]

The interest of the Papagos government in Cyprus was first manifested in its attempt to link Greece with Western plans for Middle
East defence, where the island was expected to play an important
role.[21] In fact, the initiative belonged to the previous government
as, in August 1952, the Greek Ambassador in Washington had already approached the State Department regarding participation in
the projected MEDO. Revealing the motives of this move, Ambassador Politis referred to 'the Greek islands of Cyprus and the Dodecanese' as part of his country's contribution to the planned organisation.[22] The State Department was inclined to discourage the
Greek interest, when on 19 September, Athens formally requested
participation in the planned organisation. Upon taking office, Papagos
reaffirmed this request.[23] Before long, it became evident that six
out of the seven sponsoring powers were opposed.[24]

The fact that MEDO was a British-sponsored project did not
augur well for the Greek bid. Eden was particularly averse to the
idea, fearing Greek infiltration into Cyprus.[25] It was also feared lest
the admission of Greece provoked a similar demand from Italy and
thus distract the plan from its original aim, which was to secure the
participation of Egypt and Arab states. For these reasons, in March
1953 the Foreign Office, with US approval, informed the Greek
Embassy that it was 'altogether premature' to consider any arrangement for Greece at that point.[26] The Greek government did not
lose hope. In May 1953 Papagos raised the matter with the US Secretary of State. While quoting strategic and psychological reasons,
the Field Marshal made it clear that it was the possibility of the
MEDO headquarters being established in Cyprus that motivated
Greek persistence.[27] As it happened, the Greek request was never
given a formal reply until it became evident that MEDO did not
stand much chance of being realised.[28]

In spring 1953 Papagos had communicated to his inner Cabinet
his decision to raise the question of Cyprus with the British Foreign
Secretary, Eden, who was expected in Athens in April.[29] That visit,
of course, did not take place and Papagos had to wait until Septem-

ber. His intention apparently was to exhaust the time limits of direct negotiations with Britain, before taking the next step – a recourse to the UN. In contemplating internationalisation, Papagos
decisively departed from the line of his predecessors. In this respect, Makarios' pressures at best played a secondary role.

Eden's rebuff of Papagos on 22 September 1953 widely came to
be regarded as the death-knell for the concept of Anglo-Greek friendship as the proper framework for the solution of the Cyprus question. To many it also signified the 'decisive moment' in the evolution
of Greek policy towards internationalisation.[30]. Of course, the Greek
Premier had envisaged this latter prospect at least since spring 1953,
and Eden's discourtesy only served to add a sense of personal offence to his motives.[31] From then on, Papagos came to regard his
personal prestige as being involved in the matter. This in part explains the repeated statements to the effect that he personally handled the Cyprus question; further explanation can be sought in his
image as 'paladin of Greek nationalism'.[32]

Architects and critics

Although Papagos had the final word, the formulation of the Cyprus policy was the work of a small circle of diplomats. A key role
was undoubtedly played by Alexis Kyrou, the Greek Permanent Representative to the UN and, from February 1954 Director-General
of the Foreign Ministry. His family, of Cypriot origin, owned the
daily *Estia* which supported the Greek Rally. Kyrou enjoyed a personal acquaintance with Field Marshal Papagos from the time of the
enemy occupation.[33] He was also on close terms with the Minister
of Co-ordination, Markezinis. His active involvement in the Cyprus
question dated back to 1930-1, when, as Consul General in Nicosia,
he had played a crucial part in the Greek Cypriot uprising.[34] During his term at the UN in 1947-54 Kyrou came to be regarded as
ever ready to push the case of his ancestral island 'with or without
instructions' from Athens.[35] Underestimating the external obstacles,[36] he sincerely believed that a strong and stable government in
Greece was a necessary *and* sufficient condition for the successful
raising of the Cyprus question.[37] In his view, this condition had been
met after Papagos' coming to power in November 1952 and the

opportunity had to be seized during the government's four-year term, since it might not offer itself again. No wonder that he was regarded by his contemporaries as the mastermind of Cyprus policy. Perhaps, his role can be more accurately described as that of chief tactician, a sort of head of operations under Papagos' high command.

There is little doubt that, in the handling of this question, Kyrou clearly overshadowed Foreign Minister Stefanopoulos. According to the latter's account, he had initially favoured a step-by-step solution to the problem, including a stage of self-government. Stefanopoulos, however, was not a forceful personality. Having failed to carry Papagos along with him, he lined up with the 'Cypriot lobby' in order not to be branded a traitor.[38] Thereafter, his role was largely limited to receiving and replying the *démarches* and representations of the British and American Ambassadors. Most of these replies were drafted by Kyrou and his aides. Kyrou was substantially aided by Ambassador Georgios Koustas, Director of Political Affairs, who was considered 'a sharp critic of British policy' owing to his nine-year experience in Iran, and an ardent advocate of a vigorous line on Cyprus.[39]

Papagos' other lieutenant, Defence Minister Kanellopoulos, was reported as having 'strong feelings' about Cyprus, although his direct involvement was limited.[40] Markezinis, on the other hand, did aspire to a greater role in the handling of the issue. From mid-1953 he keenly aimed at replacing Stefanopoulos as Foreign Minister. This was not to be, as he rapidly fell from Papagos' grace in the following year. His views on the Cyprus question had not been stated openly at the time,[41] and his attitude was anything but predictable. In March 1954 he did encourage Papagos to pursue the Cypriot cause, though, according to his own account, he counselled 'great caution'.[42] Of course, his connections with the Kyrou brothers, ardent proponents of internationalisation, were well known.[43] This, coupled with his West German dealings, led some to allege a British role in his eclipse[44] – an obvious overestimation of British influence under the circumstances.

Until after the recourse to the UN, criticism of the government's handling of the Cyprus question, however muted, emanated not so much from the opposition as from within the diplomatic service, the palace and its entourage. Surprisingly, for the execution of its

policy in London and Washington, two capitals of utmost importance, the government relied on persons who did not enjoy its confidence. Ambassador Politis in Washington was overshadowed by
Kyrou, whenever the latter happened to be in NewYork. Besides, as
early as July 1953 Papagos had revealed to the Americans that he
did not trust Politis and intended to replace him.[45] No wonder,
then, that his advice was habitually ignored.

According to his own account, Mostras, the Greek Ambassador
in London since 1953 was in disagreement with Cyprus policy in
almost every crucial respect. In his view, the only realistic course
would have been to promote an understanding between the British
and the Cypriots.[46] Mostras complained that his reports 'counsel-
ling moderation' went unheeded and he was often kept in the dark
about shifts in the Greek tactics and. other crucial information.[47]
The frustrated Ambassador did not care to conceal his discomfort
with Greek policy from his hosts. As he was later to tell a British
official, he was 'suspect' to his own Ministry owing to 'his well-
known British sympathies'.[48] Indeed, the records of his contacts at
the Foreign Office are replete with references to his 'apologetic
manner' in carrying out his representations on Cyprus.[49] On an
informal occasion, he appeared to deplore that policy, which he
attributed to Kyrou.[50] He would also assure the British that he 'did
his utmost' to persuade his government to let a back door open out
of the UN recourse[51] – which, of course, he did.[52] The Ambassador
was not alone in his sympathies. The Counsellor of the Greek Embassy, Ioannis Phrantzes, was described by Foreign Office diplomats
as a 'die-hardTory' and a 'good chap ... absolutely to be trusted'.[53]

The palace was also against internationalisation. Moreover, it was
probably the only state institution to remain in touch with the British Embassy in Athens throughout the Anglo-Greek confrontation
at the UN. In May 1954, King Paul told Sulzberger that Papagos had
taken a great risk and 'would only get embarrassment' if he persisted in the recourse to the UN.[54] On the eve of the General Assembly, the King would complain to the British Ambassador of
Kyrou's 'mischievous' role.[55] His unofficial diplomatic adviser,
Pipinelis, was at daggers drawn with Kyrou and would later distinguish himself as the foremost critic of internationalisation.

Among Greek political leaders only Venizelos was critical of

Papagos' decision to raise the Cyprus question at the UN – although not in public. At one point, he assured the British Ambassador that 'he would never have done such a thing himself'.[56] Following the inscription of the Greek item, he was reported by an official of the BIS in New York as deploring Papagos' weakness 'in allowing himself to be stampeded by popular outcry'. He also criticised Makarios for inadvertently lending himself to Communist designs. Venizelos implied that the Greeks only needed to be patient, since 'one day' the British would give them Cyprus, anyway.[57] Yet he was careful never to express these views in public.

In fact, with the exception of Venizelos and figures of the extreme Right with a background of Anglophilia, like Maniadakis and Zervas, the opposition normally sought to outbid the government in patriotic fervour. When Papagos made his 'final word' statement on Cyprus in early May 1954, Papandreou, then leader of the Liberal Party, approved and added that Enosis was the demand 'of the entire Nation and its representatives, the sacred demand of the Greek race as a whole'. Only the extreme Left, in its effort to monopolise patriotism, continued to accuse the government of defeatism and 'treachery'.[58]

The objectives of internationalisation

Despite public rhetoric, the recourse to the UN was not an end in itself. The Greek government endorsed it in order to enhance its bargaining position *vis-à-vis* the British, hoping that the latter would feel the sting and relax their attitude before the matter reached the General Assembly. Between November 1953, when it first revealed its intentions, and March 1954, the government kept its public pronouncements on Cyprus at a low key. At the same time, it sought to assure the British of its intention to avoid provocative actions and exhaust the time limit before resorting to the UN.[59] Clearly, at that stage, the Greek government had not entirely lost hope in some relaxation of the British position. From London, Mostras encouraged this trend. After meeting with Harrison on 1 March, he cabled to Athens that, while there was no immediate prospect of change in British policy, he had been told in confidence that the British were prepared to offer self-government 'through which the Cypriots could find it possible to determine their own affairs after 10 or 15 years'. Although this statement could not be repeated in public, Mostras believed that it offered a way out from internationalisation.[60] Of course, such hopes were bitterly disappointed by Eden's statement in the Commons on 15 March, which explains the vehemence of subsequent Greek reactions.

Subsequently, the Greek government enunciated what was described in Papagos' message to Eden of 6 April as 'firm and conciliatory policy'. It was elaborated nine days later, at a meeting attended by the Prime Minister, Stefanopoulos, Kyrou, Mostras and Koustas. Kyrou's formulation aimed at shifting responsibility for the Greek recourse on to British shoulders. The latter would be arraigned before the international community for refusing the Cypriots' right to self-determination. According to Mostras' account, Papagos appeared convinced that the British were so fearful of that prospect, that, at the eleventh hour, they would accept bilateral talks; nor did he seem particularly concerned with American attitude or Turkish reactions, which his principal adviser tended to attribute to a British 'policy of intimidation'.[61]

Still the Greek government would repeatedly put out feelers to the British regarding a compromise that would allow it to go back on its decision. Even after the announcement of the British constitutional offer on 28 July and amid the furore created by Hopkinson's 'never', Papagos continued to sound out the British Embassy about either secret consultations or a Council of Europe mediation.[62] After 20 August, Athens would turn to the Americans for mediation.[63] An acceptable compromise might consist of a British promise to acknowledge the problem and agree to discuss it with Greece or, alternatively, to recognise the right of the Cypriot people to self-determination after a number of years. Of course, there should be a clear and public undertaking for the compromise to look binding enough and justify its acceptance in the eyes of Greek opinion. As time passed, it became increasingly difficult for the Greek government to settle for less, for the price went up 'every time the issue [was] bandied about in the press'.[64] The government also needed to appear firm, until the British gave ground or the matter reached the UN floor. For these reasons, Papagos could not have pursued vague and informal British overtures of the kind referred to by Mostras[65] or Pipinelis[66] in their later accounts. Moreover, he had to take Makarios' reactions into consideration. As has been noted, the Archbishop appeared prepared to discuss only a temporary extension of British rule for two or three years to be followed by a plebiscite.

Failing in its principal aim, that of bending British intransigence, the Greek government ought to re-evaluate its tactics and define its further objectives. Otherwise, its appeal to the UN might well end up an 'empty threat'.[67] There is little evidence that this was done in a realistic way. Statements to the effect that Greece expected to find 'justice and freedom' for the Cypriots in the UN, while suitable for domestic consumption, showed little grasp of reality. Yet this was exactly the position expressed in the text of the Greek appeal and subsequently repeated on several occasions. The 'new order established by the Charter', it was often claimed, allowed Greece to resort to the UN as a kind of 'judge' or 'arbiter' in search of justice.[68] This highly idealistic formulation ignored the primarily political character of the UN, in general, and of the General Assembly, in particular. The latter was no 'court' but rather a 'talking shop', whose resolutions on matters other than those prescribed in the Charter[69] were not considered binding.[70] Equally utopian was to claim self-determination 'an integral part of the Law of the UN', as Kyrou did before the Political Committee; rather, the prevailing interpretation of Articles 1(2), 55 and 56 of the Charter at the time stressed the programmatic character of self-determination as one of the Organisation's 'many lofty goals', which 'did not impose direct and immediate legal obligations on Member States'.[71] It was no coincidence that, until 1954 the General Assembly had never adopted a resolution on the basis of that principle.[72]

There were, however, more modest propositions. Apparently, there were those who believed that by resorting to multilateral 'parliamentary diplomacy', Greece could improve her diplomatic standing. As early as 30 March Kyrou's mouthpiece, *Estia*, claimed that, although a 'Greek victory' was far from certain, 'total failure' need not be feared either – even the inscription of the Cyprus issue on the UN agenda, it was claimed, 'would be a step forward'.[73] On the day that the Greek appeal was filed, Kyrou stated that the aim was to 'ascertain that Cyprus constitutes an international problem'.[74] Papagos would later reiterate this position in parliament, adding

the projection of the Greek case abroad as a complementary objective.[75] *Ex post facto*, Stefanopoulos would claim that 'only a moral
gain' had been expected, which, however, was 'necessary for the
natural solution of the question'.[76] Regarding the prospects of international support, Kyrou claimed that Greece could count on most
Latin American countries, the Arab-Asian and the Soviet blocs and
Yugoslavia.[77]

In submitting its appeal on Cyprus, the Greek government invoked a threat to 'the friendly relations' between Greece and Britain and 'the general welfare of the international community'. The
Arab states had done likewise in attempting to raise the questions of
Morocco and Tunisia.[78] Yet this formulation posed certain problems,
which were not missed by Greece's opponents. For one thing, it
appeared to imply that whenever self-determination was involved,
then the issue could automatically be referred to the UN under
Article 1(2). This was objected to not only by the British but also by
the Americans as bound to create an unwelcome precedent with
'chaotic' effects.[79] Secondly, the explanatory memorandum of the
appeal, while elaborating on the historical and ethnological ties between Cyprus and Greece,[80] Britain's responsibility for the problem[81] and the state of public feeling in Greece, failed to focus on
the quest of self-determination of the people involved. The result
was that the problem was understood by certain anti-colonial UN
members, such as India, as a territorial dispute between two states
and not as a clear case of colonial emancipation.[82] What was more,
the memorandum failed to address the question of the Turkish minority.

Last but not least, in defining Cyprus policy, Papagos and his
aides appeared to exaggerate Greece's strategic importance to the
West in comparison to her two, clearly bigger and more powerful,
rivals, Britain and Turkey.[83] The inference was that her interests
could not be lightly overlooked. The description of Greece as '*le
concierge de l'Europe*' expressed this trend of thought.[84] The Greek
press often argued that Greek contributions to the mutual security
of the 'Free World' should be used as a lever in order to extract
support, from the United States in particular.[85] This position went
in tandem with the highly idealistic notion that Greece, in view of
her past glory or her more recent sacrifices to the common cause of

freedom, was 'entitled to expect a different treatment' from her great allies.[86] The most disturbing tendency, however, of Greek policy-makers was their persistent inability to appraise the attitude and antici-pate the reactions of friend and foe alike.

The Turkish factor

Greek opinion, both in Greece and Cyprus, had been led to under-estimate the Turkish factor. From late 1948, when the first signs of Turkish interest in the fate of Cyprus were manifested, the Greek press tended to attribute them to British 'machinations'.[87] Yet the first Turkish diplomatic approach to Athens against the raising of the issue at the UN dated from November 1951.[88] Further early warn-ings could be found in abundance in the press and the statements of official spokesmen and officially connected activists. The press cam-paign over the alleged maltreatment of the Muslim minority in Western Thrace, which culminated in the autumn of 1953,[89] should have made it apparent that Turkish opinion would not tolerate the transfer of another kindred minority under Greek rule. All along, lesser points of friction, from football matches to the frequent inci-dents between Greek fishing vessels and Turkish patrol boats in the Aegean, should have served as adequate warnings.[90]

A further factor, which the Papagos government apparently over-looked, was Turkey's importance to Western and, particularly, Brit-ish strategy in the Middle East. There should have been no doubt that Turkish views on the Cyprus question would weigh consider-ably in the eventual attitude of the Western powers, not least the United States. This was duly noted by Greek representatives abroad. From London, Ambassador Mostras repeatedly warned that, in case of inter-governmental discussions on the future of Cyprus, Turkey was certain to be involved, with serious repercussions for Greek-Turkish relations as a whole.[91]

Similar warnings emanated from special emissaries to Turkey, who were able to ascertain Turkish views at first hand. After a long visit to Istanbul in December 1953, Hristoforos Hristidis, adviser to the Press Directorate-General, presented the state of local opin-ion in its true light and warned that Turkey was bound to be 'the *main* obstacle' to the Greek claim on Cyprus. His recommendation was that, before raising the issue at the UN, the Greek government ought to prepare the ground for some sort of understanding with Ankara. To this end, it should discourage public agitation and reassure Turkish opinion with concrete gestures, such as the improvement of conditions for the minority in Western Thrace. Then, there should follow a 'frank explanation' between the two governments.[92] Hristidis' assessment was shared by Vassos Vassiliou, a journalist whom the government had asked to gauge official Turkish reactions. After visiting Ankara in early 1954, Vassiliou confirmed that the Turkish government was simply determined 'not to let Cyprus become Greek'.[93]

Far from appreciating the risks, Papagos and his advisers appeared confident that, in the end, the Turks were going to accept whatever solution the Greeks and the British might agree to. In the memorandum, which accompanied Kyrou's intimation of Greek intentions to Lodge in November 1953, it was claimed that 'the relations of close friendship and Alliance uniting Greece with Turkey can vouch for the fact (*sic*) that, were a satisfactory *modus vivendi* to be worked out between Great Britain and Greece, the Turkish minority would not have to face any serious problem in adjusting itself to the new conditions'.[94] A few months later, Kyrou assured a Western ambassador that he had 'every reason to think that Ankara would let the Greek government free to act at will in the Cyprus question'.[95] In early March, the Greek Ambassador in Ankara, Ioannis Kallergis, told an American diplomat that Turkey 'would not object on [the] official level' to the union of Cyprus with Greece.[96] Kyrou and the Foreign Ministry systematically played down Turkish reactions to the point of self-deception, as shown by the denial of the first Turkish representation, in April 1954.[97] At that time, Kyrou was inclined to attribute the reactions from Ankara to the exigencies of Menderes' electoral campaign, a trend of thought that reverberated in the Greek media.[98]

The Turkish factor was in fact discussed at the meeting of 15 April, where the Cyprus policy was finalised. According to Mostras' account, the prevailing view was that some plain talking would suffice to remove any difficulties.[99] The ties of alliance between the two countries were one cause for optimism; the satisfaction of Turkish grievances concerning the minority in Western Thrace was another.

In early March, Kyrou had told the Turkish Ambassador that the government intended to reverse discriminatory practices of the past.[100] Later on, Papagos, in an interview to the Anatolian Agency, committed himself to improving the lot of the minority.[101] In a further move of good will, the Greek authorities started referring to the minority as 'Turkish' rather than 'Muslim', in recognition of its ethnic character. There followed a new Greek-Turkish educational convention, which largely satisfied Turkish objectives in that field.[102] At the same time, however, the government's complacency left little scope for concern with the signs of Turkish ill-feeling against the Greek minority and the Orthodox Patriarchate in Istanbul.[103]

The question remains as to why the Greek government failed to have its 'plain talking' with the Turks before going to the UN. To be sure, after its first lukewarm representation in March, the Turkish government did not raise the subject again. This undoubtedly contributed to Greek wishful thinking, as did the attitude of Ambassador Tarray, who, according to the Director-General of the Turkish Foreign Ministry, 'tended to be rather timid in his dealings with the Greek Government on Cyprus'.[104] The Turkish elections in May were a further delaying factor. Yet, after Menderes' re-election, Papagos could have raised the Cyprus question when his Turkish counterpart stopped over in Athens on his way home from a state visit to the United States on 7 June. Kyrou and Stefanopoulos confirmed that, although Papagos had intended to do so, the subject was not brought up on the insistence of the Turkish ambassador.[105] According to Birgi, Menderes had 'expected' to discuss the Cyprus question, in case the Greeks raised it first; as they did not, the Turkish party had no reason to take the initiative.[106] The two versions are hardly incompatible, provided Tarray had acted on his own initiative.[107] That, of course, was not the only opportunity: well into August, the Greeks could have taken advantage of the frequent diplomatic contacts between the two countries, not least the ongoing talks on the Balkan Alliance, and take the Turks into their confidence.[108]

In the event, the government conveniently entrenched itself behind the position that Turkey had no business in Cyprus and was painfully surprised when other powers, the United States in particular, turned out to be thinking otherwise. Stefanopoulos' message to Dulles on 3 August, for example, was a bitter denunciation of Turkish involvement in the Cyprus question. Pointing at Turkey's 'treacherous attitude' during World War II, he spoke of the negative 'psychological' impact of the 'strange diversions' of Turkish policy upon Greek opinion.[109] Even after several months of press polemics, public statements and, finally, Sarper's speech in the UN, Greek officials would still interpret Turkish reactions as the result of British machinations or, indirectly, of American manoeuvres.[110]

Equally pointless proved the effort to forestall Turkish involvement by invoking the Lausanne Peace Treaty. Indeed, under Article 20, Turkey had recognised the annexation of Cyprus by Britain, while, under Article 16, she had renounced 'all rights and title' on former Ottoman territories outside her present frontiers; the future of those territories was or would be 'settled by the parties concerned'. Mostras had warned that the treaty offered no solid ground and a reference to it could backfire.[111] Indeed, when Stefanopoulos invoked it at the UN, both the British and the Turks retorted that it was Greece which was seeking to violate the Lausanne territorial settlement. Although the accusation was quite far-fetched, it did succeed in putting the Greek delegation on the defensive. Kyrou must have felt the awkwardness of his argument, when he claimed that, by signing that treaty, Greece and the other signatories had certified Turkey's recognition of the annexation of Cyprus by Britain but had 'recognised nothing directly for themselves'.[112]

As a postscript, it should be noted that, after the inscription of the Greek item, the Turks informed the British delegation to the UN of a Greek approach regarding two possible alternatives: one calling for bilateral talks between Greece and Britain, and another inviting all parties concerned, including Turkey, to discuss the problem. The Turks said that they had rejected them both.[113] It seems unlikely, however, that the Greeks might have wished to acknowledge Turkey's interest at that point. Yet, following the conclusion of the General Assembly, the Greek Ambassador in Ankara, Kallergis, was reported as being in favour of a tripartite conference,[114] a step that would eventually be taken in summer 1955.

The American factor

Greek opinion, from politicians and journalists down to the man in the street, had been accustomed to seeing the United States as holding the key to the solution of the Cyprus question.[115] Several months before the Greek recourse, *Estia* declared that the outcome of 'the battle of Cyprus (would) mainly depend on the point up to which the American attitude will be advanced'.[116] The implication was that US policy could be influenced in favour of the Greek position. For one thing, there was a widely held assumption that the United States was sympathetic to the cause of Enosis. Optimistic assessments of this sort, which were repeated every time Makarios and other figures visited the United States,[117] simply reflected wishful interpretations of the official, non-committal attitude of the US government. This tendency abetted an undercurrent of false expectations among the public, which, once bitterly disillusioned, would produce a violent backlash.

The Papagos government, while better informed than the average observer, was itself caught in this general climate of opinion. In November 1953, Peake found Papagos hopeful that the US government 'would not be averse to Enosis'.[118] Until April 1954 at least, Kyrou appeared to believe that Dulles himself was 'favourably disposed'.[119] Following the American Secretary's warning of 28 July, Stefanopoulos still expressed his conviction 'that the United States will stand by the side of Greece'.[120] When embarking on its course to the UN the Greek government, against mounting evidence to the contrary,[121] believed that the United States would not oppose its efforts to obtain a resolution.[122] Even the abstention from the inscription vote was interpreted by Papagos' advisers as 'strict neutrality'.[123] The Greek view of Washington as an 'honest broker' was also reflected in the repeated requests for American 'good offices'.

In all this, Papagos and his advisers appeared to underrate several factors influencing US policy, above all the strength of the 'special relationship' with Britain and the exigencies of containment. Instead, they were unduly impressed by real or perceived Anglo-American differences in the Middle East. Moreover, Greek policy-makers seemed to count excessively on the American tradition of anti-colonialism and support for self-determination, appearing ob-

livious to the fact that traditions and lofty principles are inevitably
mitigated by national interest. Somehow, the Greek government
thought it would be able to 'help' Washington resolve its dilemmas
to the advantage of Greek interests by sheer argumentation and ap-
peals to high principles. Thus, a whole set of arguments was advanced in order to meet the central theme of US criticism that, by
raising the Cyprus question at the UN, the Greeks would upset allied relations and play into the hands of the Soviet bloc.

First, the recourse to the UN might create a favourable atmosphere for the further handling of the problem. If Greece desisted,
then, under the impact of popular reactions, Greek relations with
Britain and Turkey would definitely deteriorate and the outcome
would be a great moral victory for Moscow.[124] Secondly, British
intransigence left no other course open to Greece than to resort to
the UN. According to Kyrou's uncanny formulation, British policy
was itself 'anti-British',[125] while the Greek recourse was 'designed
to prevent the poisoning of Anglo-Greek relations'[126] or 'a still further dangerous intensification of anti-British feeling in Greece'.[127]
Thirdly, Turkish public reactions and official statements on Cyprus
were the result of British 'machinations'. As in the case of Anglo-
Greek relations, failure to raise the issue at the UN would create
more mistrust between Greece and Turkey.[128] Fourthly, if the Greek
government failed to raise the Cyprus question in the UN, then
both the Cypriot and Greek public would become easy prey to
Communist blandishments.[129] Moreover, the colonial administration of Cyprus had been using the Communists in order 'to break
up the national front for Enosis and to discredit it abroad'.[130] And
finally, in reply to the British strategic imperative, it was argued that
the place of Cyprus in Western defence planning and the particular
strategic interests of Britain could always be safeguarded through
base rights and, above all, a friendly population. In this respect, the
analogy of the 1953 Greek-American base agreement was often
quoted.[131]

Although the Greek case had its merits, the methods of putting
it across to the Americans were not particularly successful. For one
thing, Greek communications on the matter were considered particularly unappealing, taking the form of lengthy historical accounts,
laden with emotion and couched in awkward English. Stefanopoulos'

ten-page reply to the message from Dulles of 28 July astonished a State Department official by its 'almost hysterical vein'.[132] The Counsellor of the British Embassy in Ankara, who was shown the text, found it a 'curious document', written in 'extravagant and emotional language'.[133] Similarly, Papagos' letter to Eisenhower of 23 October was accompanied by an eight-page memorandum, replete with references to common ideals, traditions and struggles, which ended by appealing to the 'wisdom and sentiments' of US leaders.[134]

Realising the ineffectiveness of its American campaign, the government reacted by replacing the Ambassador in Washington only days before the Greek item was due to be discussed at the UN.[135] This turned out to be a reflex action of no avail. Politis' successor, Georgios Melas, was a retired diplomat and former minister who had been actively committed in the campaign for Cyprus. He would tirelessly remind his hosts of the high principles of US foreign policy before expanding on the 'just and lawful basis' of post-war international relations, Greece's record of 'love of liberty and defense of freedom', or the cultural superiority of the Greeks of Cyprus, who, being 'neither Zulus nor Sudanese', could not be treated as 'colonials'.[136] Unfortunately, the State Department found this sort of language most unappealing.

Opposition in Britain

Misperceptions and wishful thinking were also present in the government's appraisal of British attitude. Criticism of Cyprus policy in the British parliament and press fuelled exaggerated hopes in Athens and Nicosia. The line taken by leading newspapers in favour of a compromise contributed to a belief that British rule continued in order to 'meet the requirements of some passing phase in international relations'.[137] By summer 1954 the US Embassy in Athens reported a widespread feeling that Enosis came closer with every British 'blunder', such as Hopkinson's 'never' or the anti-sedition measures.[138] The resolution of the Labour Conference at Scarborough in October 1954 which urged the Party to oppose the Tory policy on Cyprus, was enthusiastically received in Greece. The British Embassy reported Papagos to be 'beside himself with joy' and convinced that 'Enosis was just round the corner'.[139]

From London, Mostras tried in vain to dispel undue optimism.
Since early 1954 he had steadily sought to explain that consensus on
imperial issues in Britain went beyond partisan lines and no 'enlightenment' effort on the Greek part could possibly shake it.[140]
Criticism in the Commons or on party occasions, he cautioned,
largely came from the 'fellow-travelling', left wing of the Labour
Party and was not shared by its leadership. Besides, what most critics of government policy had in mind was not Enosis but a negoti-
ated settlement between Britain and the Cypriots – not Greece.
Finally, Mostras argued that, opposition tactics notwithstanding,
Labour had proved that, once in office, it always left 'the last word
to the Imperial Staff'.[141] The Greek Ambassador did not hesitate to
warn the British Foreign Office against the tendency of some opposition leaders to encourage visitors like Makarios in their interpretations.[142] Such ill-founded optimism, Mostras warned, would make
'Kyrou and his associates more intransigent than ever', sowing 'seeds
for future trouble'.[143] He also went as far as to suggest a stronger
British reaction against inflammatory Greek broadcasts, in an effort
'to impress upon his Government the need to be sensible and exercise self-restraint'.[144]

The projection of the Greek case

The pressure of public opinion in support of Enosis was indeed one
of the standard arguments used by successive Greeks governments
in order to justify their attitude towards the Cyprus question since
1949.[145] Much more than its predecessors, however, the Papagos
government did not limit itself to reacting to pressure from below.
Once it had decided to raise the issue at the UN, it did much to
mould public opinion. This interactive process,[146] however, could
easily turn into a stranglehold. By summer 1954, the US Embassy
in Athens estimated that no Greek government could stay in power
if it ignored popular feeling and reversed its course.[147]

What was more, the tenor of publicity about Cyprus, while
mainly intended for consumption in Greece and Cyprus, threatened to compromise the Greek campaign in Western eyes. Despite
the repeated assurances of the Greek government that it would avoid
all provocation,[148] broadcasts to Cyprus assumed a virulently anti-

British tone. Their references to the Greek nation's record of struggles and sacrifices were combined with more explicit allusions to violence.[149] When the Foreign Minister was confronted with Anglo-American representations, he tried to deny government complicity,[150] only to be subsequently belied by a special bulletin, issued by the Prime Minister's office and aired on 29 October – which reproduced the standard language of broadcasts to Cyprus, denouncing, among other things, British 'slavery', 'chicanery', 'perfidy' and 'craftiness'.[151] No more successful was the Greek effort to use the postal service in order to denounce British intransigence world-wide. One stamp which intended to stigmatise Hopkinson's 'never' by blotting the relevant excerpt from *Hansard* received particularly unfavourable attention.[152]

Self-defeating verbosity was also evident in the reactions of the religious and academic milieu. In May, the University of Athens adopted a resolution proclaiming 'the absolutely Hellenic character of Cyprus' and denouncing the attempt of the colonial administration to exercise control over secondary education as 'violating the elementary rights of the man and the citizen and leading humanity back to the dark ages of oppression and barbarism'. Its intellectual relations with Britain, the University declared, would henceforth be dependent upon the issue of Cypriot emancipation.[153] The most extreme case undoubtedly was the address of rector Apostolos Daskalakis to a student meeting on 15 August. In what was then dubbed a 'preaching of hate', Daskalakis urged his colleagues to turn Anglo-Greek friendship to ashes and to inspire the Greek youth with hostility against Britain.[154]

Daskalakis, of all others, was selected as member of the committee, which the government sent to the United States in order to 'enlighten' American opinion on Cyprus. It was a half-hearted initiative, which, as Papagos admitted to the US Ambassador, had been motivated by domestic considerations.[155] The committee consisted of seven middle-ranking politicians, plus Daskalakis.[156] The fact that some of its members could not even speak English narrowed its scope largely to preaching to the converted: the Greek-American community.[157] The latter once more engaged in extensive lobbying of Congressmen, Governors, other prominent citizens and the State Department. Following the Greek recourse, the various Greek-

American organisations and the press of the community set up a joint 'Justice for Cyprus Committee', which undertook to stir official interest. By December 1954 its 'National Advisory Board' – American politicians who, one way or another, had subscribed to the Committee's cause – included a long list of names, from Senator Barry Goldwater of Arizona to Representative Tip O'Neill of Massachusetts and Governor Averell Harriman of New York.[158]

Kyrou also enlisted Archbishop Makarios in projecting the Greek case at the UN. After coming to New York in October, the Archbishop engaged in extensive public relations. In his foreign contacts he was careful to avoid the 'Enosis and only Enosis' slogan and to speak only of self-determination. Yet, despite his best efforts, he failed to attract any sympathetic attention from American officialdom. Since 1953 at least, Makarios had built up in Washington a reputation as not only a dynamic and tenacious leader, but also something of a firebrand and, still worse, a volatile and indiscreet negotiator. Therefore, US diplomacy was inclined to treat Makarios with utmost reserve and to avoid contact, whenever possible. As a result, messages from the Archbishop to the US President were left unreplied, and it was the State Department's view that his Beatitude 'should not be given the slightest encouragement'.[159]

Indicative of the makeshift character of Greek publicity on Cyprus was the fate of the White Book, which was issued by the Foreign Ministry pending the discussion of the Greek item at the UN. The Book was first widely distributed and then it was realised that it did not serve its purpose: it focused on Enosis rather than self-determination, in contrast to the line at the UN.[160] Yet, as Stefanopoulos would admit in parliament, Greece, 'armed only with her faith in right and freedom', relied on such 'leaflets and memoranda', distributed through embassies and the UN delegation, as 'the most effective and expedient' means of projecting her case.[161]

While castigating Britain for her illiberal practices in Cyprus, the Papagos government appeared intolerant to domestic criticism, which in this case emanated from a kindred, right-wing source. The publication in April of a long unsigned article in an obscure police weekly, *Astynomika Nea*, which denounced internationalisation as 'the grave for the Cyprus question' and criticised Makarios for his political role, infuriated the government and provoked a small scale witch-hunt. The journal's editor and a journalist were taken to court and sentenced to four and a half month's imprisonment for spreading false reports; right-wing politicians, known for their British connections, such as Maniadakis and Zervas, were implicated by the defendants, as was the chief of the Police, Angelos Evert. There followed a special investigation in the activities of 'foreign agents' in the state services. Evert was placed *en disponibilité* pending the result of a further inquiry. The epilogue of this affair was written in January 1955 when the results of the investigation were handed to Papagos. Other than Evert's resignation, nothing concrete came out of what the British Embassy described as a 'storm in a teacup'.[162]

The 'keystone' of Greek foreign policy?

By the autumn of 1954 Cyprus had clearly become the dominant issue in Greek politics. This was definitely how Kyrou and other officials saw things, when they proclaimed this question to be 'the keystone' of Greek foreign policy.[163] The logical outcome of this approach was that Greece's policy might have to be modified to the extent that her Western allies failed to appreciate her case on Cyprus. Fomented by Makarios' rhetoric,[164] revisionist tendencies soon became commonplace in the press. Even pro-government papers, like the leading daily *Kathimerini*, increasingly demanded a more independent and assertive attitude *vis-à-vis* the United States and the West as a whole. Greece's relations with her allies, it was argued, should be reappraised on a *quid pro quo* basis – no more sacrifices, like the sending of troops to Korea, or concessions, such as the bases agreement with the United States, without something concrete in return.[165] The Foreign Ministry was not immune to this trend either.[166]

These pronouncements were combined with warnings about the future of Greek-American relations.[167] It was an officially-inspired effort which stemmed from the realisation that the US attitude in the UN was hardly compatible with the Greek interpretation of 'strict neutrality'.[168] From New York, Kyrou was often quoted as referring to 'unpleasant signs of backstage' American activities.[169] In a cable to Athens, dated 12 October, he argued that the government ought to adopt a more decisive attitude towards the Americans or else start considering the prospect of 'not having the Cyprus question discussed' during the current session of the General Assembly.[170] In the event, Kyrou's suggestion for a more 'straightforward' language was reflected in the notes handed by Papagos to Dulles in Paris. References to 'the dangers of a mounting pressure of Greek public opinion' upon the government's foreign policy were clearly designed to serve as a warning.[171] On 28 October, a special official bulletin on the anniversary of Greece's entry in World War II expressed 'Greek bitterness over the attitude of these two old and dear Allies', Britain and the United States.[172]

The US Embassy in Athens was inclined to see in all this a tactical manoeuvre rather than a genuine 'new look' in Greek foreign policy. Indeed, as Kyrou was feeding the press with comment critical of US policy, Stefanopoulos sought American 'ideas and guidance' on the Greek moves in the General Assembly.[173] What was more, while conveying his strongly-worded notes, the Greek Premier was discussing the possibility of a postponement with Dulles, perhaps in accordance with Kyrou's proposals.[174] The eventual failure of both Papagos and Stefanopoulos to join the battle in New York raised further doubts regarding the government's sincerity in proclaiming Cyprus the pivot of its foreign policy.[175]

If there was an area where Greek policy was actually – and understandably – revised, this was the colonial issue at the UN. Until 1953 Greece had largely fallen into line with the rest of NATO members voting against or, by the Eighth session, abstaining on colonial questions.[176] Following the inscription of the Greek item, Kyrou hastened to declare that Greece 'would henceforth maintain an attitude of unreserved support to anti-colonial powers'.[177] It was not just a matter of consistency; there was the practical aim of securing the goodwill of the anti-colonial group in the General Assembly, certain members of which, such as India or Ethiopia, had failed to support the inscription of the Greek item. This tactic, of course, placed Greece at odds with her Western allies on a number of roll-call votes.[178]

Having secured inscription, the Greeks had to devise a resolution likely to attract enough support in the General Assembly and, above all, to obtain at least the neutrality of the United States. This precluded a thorough 'interventionist' text of the kind the British

secretly wished to confront and defeat. At the same time, Kyrou
and the Foreign Ministry anxiously sought to salvage at least part of
the original appeal. Thus, they repeatedly revised their drafts, end-
ing up with a text simply recognising the right of self-determination to the people of Cyprus.[179] This meant that, despite clear warnings, those in charge of the Greek effort at the UN were unable or
unwilling to understand that by the term 'substantive' the Americans meant *any* reference to the content of the Greek appeal. Kyrou's
professed optimism was unshakeable as it was misleading.[180] Of
course, he would later claim that his attitude was dictated by the
need to combat defeatism at home.[181] Indeed, having consulted the
Ministry files, Markezinis would later speak of baffling 'transitions
from optimism to pessimism'.[182] This, however, hardly contributed
to an effective course in the UN; instead, until the eleventh hour,
the delegation would persist in sterile draft revising.[183]

Dulles' letter of 16 November also forced the Greek government to address the US position that the Cyprus problem could be
best settled between the British and the Cypriots themselves in
stages, and that Athens should encourage that prospect. Papagos
and his advisers insisted that the dispute was not an Anglo-Cypriot
but 'essentially' an Anglo-Greek one. That this could well cast doubt
on the sincerity of their commitment to Cypriot self-determination was apparently disregarded.[184]

That the Greek effort at the UN did not stand a chance of American neutrality should have become plain by 11 December, when
Cannon so informed Stefanopoulos, or, at the latest on the following day, with Dulles's message to Papagos. Yet that critical weekend
passed without any attempt to revise tactics. It was only in the evening
of Monday, 13 December, after the *New York Times* had revealed
the substance of Dulles' message, that Stefanopoulos, already in Paris,
faced that prospect.[185] From Washington, Melas realised that the
situation was desperate and advised that the Greek draft be withdrawn.[186] Kyrou, however, who until then counted on 37 or 38 votes
in favour, was in a combative mood and insisted on discussion.[187]
Eventually, the Foreign Ministry authorised him to press for a vote
on the Greek resolution at the Political Committee and then seek a
way out in the plenary.[188] This was not to be. As the New Zealand
motion took precedence, the Greek draft was doomed. Subsequently,

Kyrou concentrated on promoting amendments. His aim was twofold: first, to secure some allusion to the substance of the problem
or, failing this, a, however indirect, acknowledgement of UN competence; second, to limit the effect of the resolution only to the
current session of the General Assembly, thus leaving the door open
to a future appeal. The first aim, advanced as a preambular reference to 'the principles and purposes of the Charter', was not
achieved. More successful was the effort that resulted in the 'for the
time being' clause.[189]

Domestic reactions

Despite the government's efforts to present the outcome of the
'UN battle' as a qualified success, it was clear that the Greek recourse had come to naught. The most disturbing side-effect was not
the criticism of the opposition, since the government still had an
overwhelming majority in parliament, but the reactions of a public
which for months had been nourished with illusions and high expectations. Given the addiction of nearly everyone to the alleged
key role of the United States, the subsequent outbreak of anti-American feeling was only to be expected. Yet the government reacted in
a disconcerted way, seeking at first to defuse some of the pressure
by criticising the attitude of its Western allies'; then, confronted
with the violent outburst of popular indignation, it became more
circumspect and apologetic.[190]

With regard to the opposition, the Centre leaders concentrated
their fire against the government's handling of the issue. Papagos
and Kyrou became the main targets. During the parliamentary debate of 7 February, Venizelos pointed out that the General Assembly
resolution would hardly make future attempts to raise the issue any
easier. Papandreou warned that the pursuit of the Cyprus cause
should not isolate the country from her 'natural allies' – otherwise,
'in the name of Cyprus, Greece would be lost'. Both these leaders
and Markezinis agreed that it was the attitude of the United States
on which the government had committed 'its gravest misjudgement'.
Venizelos, in particular, dismissed as 'childish' the contention that
the American opposition could ever remain secret.[191] Further to
the Left, the entire concept of Greek foreign policy came into ques-

tion. Georgios Kartalis, the leader of the Centre-Left Democratic Party, accused the government for adhering to a policy of unconditional attachment to the West, whereas it should have made it clear that 'a vote against Cypriot rights ... would be inconsistent with its participation in NATO'. This analysis was subscribed by pro-Communist EDA.[192] On the Right, Tsaldaris, leader of the defunct People's Party, professed relief for the outcome, while Pipinelis, the King's confidant, argued that, in view of the international situation, the Greek government ought not to have raised the issue and, having done so, not to expect American support.[193] Significantly, all sides chose to downplay the role of Turkey. For the government, at least, the need to salvage Greek-Turkish relations was an important afterthought.

After the UN, what?

After the recourse, the Greek government found itself in search of a Cyprus policy. In public, it reaffirmed its determination to stick to its course and return to the UN if necessary. Makarios kept up the pressure stating that the Cyprus question was the 'main factor' in the foreign policy of Greece and the touchstone in her relations with 'the so-called friends and allies'. This meant that the Greek government should keep on bringing the question before the UN, year after year, until there was a solution, which, in Makarios' view, could only be Enosis.[194]

Yet the bitter experience of the first recourse did not fail to generate second thoughts. Kyrou's removal might herald a shift in tactics at least. According to British reports, there were Greek leaders willing to seize a suitable opportunity to extricate the country from the Cyprus tangle. King Paul gave expression to this trend, when, in his public message of 20 December, he urged the mending of Greece's relations with her allies.[195] The reply of the Foreign Ministry to Mostras' request for guidance clearly indicated that government policy was in a state of flux: 'press reports are in accord with the government's decision (to resort to the UN), which will be revoked if events intervene dictating a change of direction'.[196]

The pretext that might help the government to change course could well be a new British offer of a liberal constitution with an

elected majority. As much was stated by Pipinelis, known to express the views of the palace,[197] to Patrick Maitland, who visited
Athens in January 1955. Maitland was also told by the King that
both he and Papagos had advised Makarios to accept a liberal constitution if it were offered. When he saw the Archbishop in Cyprus
later in January, Maitland found him 'in an inquisitive frame of mind'
regarding the constitutional proposal. Powerful counter-influences,
however, were at work, as Maitland realised, and narrowed Makarios'
scope of action.[198] In public, he continued to warn against the 'constitution trap'[199] and to declare that the Ethnarchy would only agree
to sit down with the British 'around the round table which will
recognise our right of self-determination'.[200] In reality, the Archbishop had already moved down the path to armed struggle.[201]

The Greek government would be disappointed by the absence
of any visible change in British attitude, four months after the end
of the UN debate.[202] Moreover, uncertainty crept in about its own
future. To be sure, despite the defection of the Markezinis group, its
parliamentary majority remained comfortable. Papagos' leadership,
however, was on the wane. Although, with the partial exception of
defence and foreign affairs, the Field Marshal had never been particularly active in the running of the country's affairs, his role as a
symbol of unity of the conservative camp was unquestionable. By
February, the opposition press and foreign observers were widely
reporting his deteriorating health. His admission to a Swiss clinic in
early March seemed to confirm the worst and further contributed
to the climate of uncertainty.[203]

Two years later, in July 1957, a State Department report would
observe that, having been 'the dominant issue in Greek politics and
foreign policy' since 1954, the Cyprus question had 'absorbed the
energies of the Greek government, diverted attention from the problems of economic development, and caused the rigidity of Greece's
foreign policy and serious strains with its major allies'.[204] But this
was something Greek leaders were unable or unwilling to foresee
and change course.

NOTES

1. Crouzet I 1973, 343-346.
2. This approach had been recommended by Damaskinos' *chef de cabinet*, Seferiadis (Seferis): Seferis *Diary* II, 26-30; cf. Vlahos 1980, 15. By way of contrast, Alexis Kyrou, the future sponsor of the first Greek recourse to the UN, had opposed the raising of the question in view of the country's domestic and external difficulties: Xydis 1963, 582, n. 80.
3. 87715, 1081/10, 'Cyprus', FO minute from Rumbold to Bevin, 16 Dec. 1949. The offer of base rights had been complementing the Greek claim on Cyprus at least since the time of the 1931 revolt: Pikros 1980, 99.
4. As much was stated by Prime Minister Diomidis after his meeting with Bishop Makarios of Kition in Athens, in September 1949: 78424, R9209, Chancery to Southern Department, 22 Sept. 1949.
5. 78425, R11622, Norton to FO, 14 Dec. 1949.
6. *GPR*, meeting of 25 April 1956, 288.
7. There were exceptional cases among the Greek hierarchy, like Panteleimon of Salonika, who was privately against agitation in Greece and in favour of a 'truce of God' in Cyprus for a period of time: 107502, 1081/67, Peake to Cheetham, 1 Dec. 1953; 112843, 1081/6, Peake to Cheetham, 23 Jan. 1954.
8. Kitromilides 1990a, 51-59.
9. Crawshaw 1978, 61; Crouzet I 1973, 346-347.
10. Crawshaw 1978, 63.
11. Mayes 1981, 45-46.
12. 747C.00/7-2150, Memminger to State, desp. 155; Vlahos 1980, 34.
13. 95132, 1081/10, Norton to FO, 16 Feb. 1951; Linardatos I 1977, 186-187.
14. Vlahos 1980, 47-54.
15. Linardatos I 1977, 355-357.
16. 101812, 1081/46, Peake to Eden, 14 July 1952; 1081/51, Peake to Harrison, 31 July 1952.
17. 101812, 1081/61, Galsworthy to Barnes, 4 Nov. 1952.
18. 107483, 1017/24, Galsworthy to May, 21 Aug. 1953.
19. *GPR*, meeting of 7 February 1955, 686; Markezinis 1994, 48.
20. 781.21/12-2352, Anschuetz to State, desp. 736.
21. Devereux 1990b, 245.
22. *FRUS 1952-54*, IX, 281.
23. *Ibid.*, 281-2; 107483, 1017/1, memo by Murray, 29 Dec. 1952.
24. France was the only exception: *FRUS 1952-54*, IX, 282-3, and n. 3.
25. 107483, 1017/1, comment by Eden on memo by Murray, 29 Dec. 1952; 107500, 1074/1, brief for the visit of the Secretary of State to Greece, 19 March 1953.
26. 107500. 1074/1, Eden's brief, 19 March 1953; *FRUS 1952-54*, IX, 283, n. 3.
27. *FRUS 1952-54*, IX, 156-7; VIII, 834-837.

28. The State Department so informed the Greek Embassy in Washington on 17 July 1953: *FRUS 1952-54*, IX, 282-3, n. 3; *FRUS 1952-54*, IX, 389-390.
29. Crouzet I 1973, 378.
30. 117624, 1081/100, Lambert to Eden, 9 Feb. 1955.
31. 747C.00/3-1754, Cannon and Axelrod to State, desp. 860; /5-1354, Schnee to State, desp. 1054; *FRUS 1952-54*, VIII, 685; 747C.00/8-1154, Schnee to State, desp. 121; 112845, 1081/71, Peake to Eden, 3 April 1954.
32. *FRUS 1952-54*, VIII, 677; cf. Crouzet I 1973, 376; Xydis 1967, 29.
33. According to Kyrou, Papagos had offered him the position of Director-General immediately after his electoral victory in November 1952: Kyrou 1972, 369.
34. Then, Kyrou had joined forces with nationalist circles in Cyprus against the policy of the Eleftherios Venizelos government: Pikros 1980, 86, 99ff.
35. 747C.00/7-952, Acheson to US UN Delegation, tel. 28.
36. Ambassador Vyron Theodoropoulos, who had served as secretary of the Greek delegation to the UN in 1950, recalls Kyrou lightly dismissing the prospect of Turkish reactions: Alexandrakis *et al* 1987, 97.
37. Kyrou 1955, 272; cf. Markezinis' admission in *GPR*, meeting of 7 February 1955, 684; Xydis 1967, 30.
38. *GPR*, meeting of 25 February 1959, 322-323; cf. Mostras ms, 82. Still, Stefanopoulos would not avoid taking the brand of compromise and irresoluteness. See the caustic assessment of his role in Hristidis 1967, 39-40.
39. 747C.00/3-1754, Cannon and Axelrod to State, desp. 860; Mostras ms, 3.
40. 747C.00/3-1754, Cannon and Axelrod to State, desp. 860.
41. According to the US Embassy, he was expected to favour anything that contributed to the government's popularity: 747C.00/3-1754, Cannon and Axelrod to State, desp. 860; cf. Linardatos II 1978, 134.
42. Markezinis 1994, 53. According to Vlahos, Markezinis had encouraged Papagos' decision to raise the Cyprus question: Vlahos 1980, 76.
43. In his own account of the period, Markezinis attempts to take credit for Kyrou's transfer to the Foreign Ministry in early 1954: Markezinis 1994, 50.
44. Linardatos II 1978, 158, 160.
45. He had so informed Peurifoy: *FRUS 1952-54*, VIII, 841.
46. Mostras ms, 48.
47. *Ibid.*, introductory note and *passim*.
48. 112844, 1081/57, record of conversation between Cheetham and Mostras 'at a party', 23 March 1954.
49. 112845, 1081/72, record of conversation between Eden and Mostras, 6 April 1954; 112848, 1081/182, record of conversation between Harrison and Mostras, 9 July 1954.
50. 112844, 1081/57, record of conversation between Cheetham and Mostras, 23 March 1954.
51. 112846, 1081/125, record of conversation between Nutting and Mostras, 14 May 1954.
52. Impressed by British arguments, Mostras considered that a settlement through backstage activity ought to take into account British prestige, to be compat-

ible with the gradualist line adopted in similar colonial problems (i.e. self-
government, etc.), and to avoid establishing a precedent that might harm 'vital British interests in other fields'. Needless to say, advice of this kind could
hardly appeal to Kyrou and his associates: Mostras ms, 53-54.

53. 112854, 1081/344, minutes by Grady and Wilding, 24 Aug. 1954.
54. 'Papagos had bitten off more than he could chew in the way he was handling
the Cyprus business' was the King's remark: Sulzberger 1969, 1009.
55. 112860, 1081/520, Peake to FO, 12 Sept. 1954.
56. 112847, 1081/144, Peake to Cheetham, 1 June 1954.
57. 112874, 1081/998, Russel, B.I.S., New York, to Makins, 12 Nov. 1954.
58. 747C.00/6-154, office memo from Howard to Wood; /8-1154, Schnee to
State, desp. 121.
59. 112843, 1081/25, record of conversation between Harrison and Mostras, 20
Feb. 1954; 1081/26, record of conversation between Selwyn Lloyd and
Mostras, 23 Feb. 1954; 112844, 1081/32-33, record of conversation between
Harrison and Mostras, 1 March 1954.
60. Mostras quotes tel. 773 from the London Embassy to Athens: Mostras ms, 45.
Yet there is no reference to such statement in the British record of the conversation: 112844, 1081/32-33, record of oral communication by the Greek
Ambassador to Harrison, 1 March 1954.
61. Mostras ms, 3-4.
62. 112851, 1081/264, Lambert to Eden, 6 Aug. 1954.
63. *FRUS 1952-54*, VIII, 691; 112860, 1081/520, Peake to FO, 12 Sept. 1954;
1081/534, minute by Hopkinson, 2 Sept. 1954. Greek requests for US mediation were made on 21 April (Kyrou to Cannon), 17 and 24 June (Politis to
Merchant and to Byroade). Mostras also mentions an informal meeting between Georgios Exintaris, the Greek representative to NATO, and Harold
MacMillan, the British Defence Secretary, after the inscription of the Greek
appeal: Mostras ms, 69.
64. 781.00/5-2854, letter from Mann to Wood; cf. 747C.00/8-1154, Schnee to
State, desp. 121.
65. Mostras ms, 46-47. From his own account it appears that Mostras was not
informed of his government's approaches to the Americans regarding a compromise.
66. Pipinelis refers to an 'indirect sounding' through an unnamed British journalist to himself, in September 1954, which he duly passed on to Papagos without effect. He also mentions a secret approach from a 'higher official of the
British Embassy in Athens' to the Premier through Maniadakis, allegedly in an
attempt to bypass the Greek Foreign Ministry. According to Maniadakis, the
British offered a liberal constitution for Cyprus which should be approved by
the Greek government and a promise of self-determination to be effected
according to an agreed timetable: Pipinelis 1959, 31-33. These contacts were
disputed by people close to Papagos, like Stefanopoulos and Merkouris. What
is more, the alleged proposals were entirely incompatible with the line of the
British government at the time. Pipinelis quotes no testimony other than
Maniadakis' personal recollection, nor is there any hint in the Foreign Office

or State Department records.

67. Mostras ms, 67.

68. 747C.00/8-1754, translation of Greek Appeal to UN. Kyrou would repeat this approach in his book: Kyrou 1955, 321-323; cf. Mostras ms, 46; Xydis 1967, 34. In his account of the first Greek recourse before the Chamber of deputies, in February 1955, Stefanopoulos invariably referred to the UN as a sort of 'international tribunal' or 'international conscience'. Yet, at some point, he contradicted himself by admitting that he did 'not ignore [the fact] that the United Nations are not a tribunal but a political Organisation'. See *GPR*, meeting of 7 February 1955, 673-674, 679-680.

69. As, for example, in the cases of the admission of new members (Article 4), or the approval of Organisation's budget (Article 17).

70. Calogeropoulos-Stratis 1973, 127-133; Nicholas 1971, 104, 112-114; Shaw 1991, 93-94; cf. Tenekidis 1981, 195-196; Xydis 1967, 33-34 and notes 126, 127.

71. Cassese 1995, 38-43; cf. Calogeropoulos-Stratis 1973, 110-111, who, however, supports the law-making potential of the General Assembly.

72. Xydis 1967, 34.

73. 747C.00/5-554, office memo from Howard to Baxter; /8-1154, Schnee to State, desp. 121.

74. Pipinelis 1959, 27.

75. *GPR*, meeting of 7 February 1955, 673.

76. *Ibid.*, 680. The Foreign Minister's claim that 'the [government's] position was to bring before the civilised world the grief and the voice of the martyr Island in order to let free men know that in mid-20th century, in the middle of the Mediterranean, there still is a white people, a civilised people, who, however, is treated as a colonial people', was indicative of a line of argument, which was not intended for domestic consumption only: *ibid.*, 677. See also the speech of Theodoros Havinis, Liberal deputy and member of the Greek delegation to the Ninth General Assembly: *ibid.*, 680.

77. 747C.00/4-654, office memo from Howard to Baxter; Mostras ms, 61, n. 1; 747C.00/8-454, personal message from Stefanopoulos to Dulles, 3 Aug. 1954.

78. 101811, 1081/30, minutes by Dunnett, 20 June 1952.

79. 112857, 1081/429, Makins to FO, 3 Sept. 1954.

80. The text began as follows: 'Cyprus is a Greek island, inhabited by Greeks for thousands of years. When for the first time the name of Cyprus appears in history it is accompanied by the affirmation that both the divinities and the inhabitants of the island are Greek. No change has occurred since. The foreign dominations which have succeeded each other in the course of three thousand years of History have invariably been a passing, temporary and transitory element. Greece alone has been the lasting element, the inalterable factor, the only permanent reality in the island of Cyprus. It would be an understatement to repeat once again that Cyprus belongs to the hellenic world; Cyprus is Greece herself'.

81. Hopkinson's statement in the Commons containing the notorious 'never' was given verbatim.

82. Cf. Terlexis 1971, 162-164. For a defence of the Greek appeal, see Kyrou

1955, 280-282.
83. Mostras ms, 4, 9.
84. 747C.00/8-3054, memo of conversation between Howard and Maccas.
85. 747C.00/10-1954, Schnee to State, desp. 336.
86. 112873, 1081/969, BBC Monitoring Service, 29 Oct. 1954.
87. 78420, R200, FO to H.M. Representatives, 26 Jan. 1949.
88. 95134, 1081/105, FO minute, 26 Nov. 1951; 101811, 1081/37, Scott Fox to Cheetham, 23 June 1952.
89. Andreadis 1956; Hristidis 1967.
90. 681.82/6-2351, Miner to State, desp. 1977; 107494, 10344/4, Chancery, Ankara, to FO, 13 Aug. 1953.
91. Mostras ms, 1-2, 8, 54.
92. Hristidis submitted his assessment in three memoranda, dated 12 February, 24 and 29 March 1954. His third text exclusively dealt with the Cyprus question: while expressing himself in favour of a Greek recourse to the UN, Hristidis clearly foresaw the pitfalls ahead: Hristidis 1967, 29-37.
93. Linardatos II 1978, 165-166.
94. 747C.00/11-1653, Lodge to Dulles; *ibid.*, Greek memorandum. It seems that Kyrou repeatedly stated this view to Western Ambassadors: Pipinelis 1959, 25.
95. Mostras ms, 6; Pipinelis 1959, 25.
96. *FRUS 1952-54*, VIII, 683-684.
97. In the same spirit, the Foreign Ministry did not communicate this approach to the Ambassador in London: Mostras ms, 4-5.
98. Mostras ms, 3; 112845, 1081/94, BBC Monitoring Service, April 1954; 747C.00/5-1354, Schnee to State, desp. 1054.
99. Mostras ms, 3.
100. 747C.00/3-554, Warren to State, tel. 928; cf. Pipinelis 1959, 36.
101. 112835, 10344/2, Chancery, Ankara, to Western and Southern Departments, 26 March 1954; 747C.00/4-3054, Cannon to Dulles, tel. 2593; Hristidis 1967, 27.
102. Alexandris 1983, 249, 308-309.
103. Mostras ms, 58, n. 2.
104. 117621, 1081/26, Bowker to Young, 31 Dec. 1954.
105. Kyrou 1955, 279-280; Linardatos II 1978, 197-198.
106. 747C.00/6-2254, Warren to State, tel. 1366.
107. This is, in fact, what Kyrou and Stefanopoulos implied.
108. Kanellopoulos' claim that Stefanopoulos had unsuccessfully attempted to raise the question with Köprülü at Bled, where the Balkan Pact was signed on 9 August, does not appear particularly convincing: *GPR*, meeting of 12 Dec. 1958, 298-299. According to another source, most probably Stefanopoulos himself, the Greek Foreign Minister had 'presented' to both his Yugoslav and Turkish colleagues the Greek position on the Cyprus question: Iatrides 1968, 137. After the raising of the issue at the UN, some thought was given to a trip of the Greek Foreign Minister to Ankara, but nothing came out: Mostras ms, 8. Only Kyrou, according to his own account, tried to reach a gentlemen's agreement with the Turkish Permanent Representative to the UN, Sarper, to

proceed while keeping in mind the need to 'preserve the friendly relations between [their] two countries intact': Kyrou 1972, 355.

109. 747C.00/8-454, personal message from Stefanopoulos to Dulles, 3 Aug. 1954.

110. Kyrou's 'apology' exemplifies this trend: Kyrou 1955, 309-310, 390ff. Ambassador Melas also indulged in this interpretation: *FRUS 1952-54*, VIII, 751; cf. Mostras ms, 8.

111. Mostras ms, 12, n. 1.

112. Kyrou 1955, 352-357. Melas would also have to defend Greek policy on this score before State Department officials: 747C.00/1-2555, memo of conversation between Allen, Wood and Melas; cf. Terlexis 1971, 170-173.

113. 112867, 1081/741, minute of conversation between Eden and Dulles, 2 Oct. 1954; *FRUS 1952-54*, VIII, 717-718; 112868, 1081/783, Commonwealth Relations Office to Ottawa, 6 Oct. 1954. The Foreign Office had actually envisaged such a course as part of the Greek effort to secure the passing of a 'benign' resolution: 112867, 1081/735, FO to various Missions, 2 Oct. 1954.

114. 117621, 1081/26, Bowker to Young, 31 Dec. 1954.

115. 747C.00/6-2452, Peurifoy to Acheson, tel. 5449; /7-552, Peurifoy to Acheson, tel. 51.

116. *Estia* editorial, 30 March 1954, quoted in 747C.00/5-554, office memo from Howard to Baxter.

117. 95132, 1081/3, Norton to Bevin, 2 Jan. 1951; 107485, 10110/3, Cyprus Political Situation Report, February 1953.

118. 107502, 1081/56, Peake to FO, 10 Nov. 1953.

119. Kyrou 1955, 277.

120. 747C.00/8-454, personal message from Stefanopoulos to Dulles, 3 Aug. 1954.

121. American warnings apart, Ambassador Politis had 'clearly and amply informed the Greek government as to what it could not expect': Mostras ms, 34. Stefanopoulos himself admitted in parliament that, 'right from the outset America was dissuading us from resorting to the UN': session of 7 Feb. 1955.

122. Kyrou 1955, 277.

123. Kyrou 1955, 278; Mostras ms, 35-36.

124. 747C.00/8-454, personal message from Stefanopoulos to Dulles, 3 Aug. 1954.

125. This term, it was noted, was 'incidentally' used by *Estia*: Mostras ms, 52.

126. See Papagos' statement on Cyprus policy of 3 May 1954; cf. Kyrou 1955, 274-275.

127. 112845, 1081/72, record of conversation between Eden and Mostras, 6 April 1954. The same formulation was repeated in the text of the Greek appeal to the UN; cf. Mostras ms, 66.

128. 747C.00/8-454, personal message from Stefanopoulos to Dulles, 3 Aug. 1954.

129. 747C.00/11-1653, Greek memorandum, in Lodge to Dulles; /8-454, personal message from Stefanopoulos to Dulles, 3 Aug. 1954.

130. 112855, 1081/395, UKUN delegation to FO, 26 Aug. 1954; 747C.00/8-1154, memo from Rossidis to Wagner.

131. 747C.00/11-1653, Greek memorandum, in Lodge to Dulles.

132. 747C.00/8-1254 CS/MDR, office memo by Hamilton. Commenting on

the same text, Pipinelis quipped that it was 'drafted in the tenor of an *Estia* article' – which was probably accurate owing to the Kyrou connection: Pipinelis 1959, 40.

133. 112852, 1081/288, Scott-Fox to Young, 12 Aug. 1954. Here is a typical passage from page 7 of Stefanopoulos' message: 'Now, I consider it my duty to draw most seriously Your Excellency's attention upon the more than disastrous consequences which would fatally follow a declaration on this very last moment of a change in the decision of the Greek Government to bring the Cyprus question before the General Assembly of the United Nations during its next Regular Session'.

134. 747C.00/10-2354, letter from Papagos to Eisenhower; *ibid.*, memorandum from Papagos to Dulles, 23 Oct. 1953.

135. Ambassador Politis himself interpreted his removal as a result of the government's belief that he had 'failed in his mission to persuade the United States to support Greece': 747C.00/11-954, memo of conversation between Hoover, Baxter and Politis. This interpretation was shared by the State Department: *FRUS 1952-54*, VIII, 725.

136 *FRUS 1952-54*, VIII, 744; 750-753; 747C.00/1-2555, memo of conversation between Allen, Wood and Melas.

137. Yet, according to the deputy Mayor of Nicosia, the Archbishop had become fully aware that, for the time being, Enosis did not stand much chance of international support: 107485, 10110/4, Cyprus Political Situation Report, March 1953.

138. 747C.00/8-1154, Schnee to State, desp. 121.

139. 112874, 1081/990, Peake, 4 Nov. 1954.

140. Mostras ms, 42-43.

141. *Ibid.*, 16-21.

142. 112871, 1081/910, minute of conversation between Harrison and Mostras, 18 Oct. 1954. When, in November, Labour MP Driberg, an ardent supporter of Enosis, visited Mostras to inquire about the Papagos-Eden episode of the previous year, the Ambassador reported this to the British Foreign Office: 112874, 1081/1001, minute by Young, 10 Nov. 1954.

143. 112871, 1081/910, minute of conversation between Harrison and Mostras, 18 Oct. 1954; 112874, 1081/1001, minute by Young, 10 Nov. 1954.

144. 112873, 1081/954, minute of conversation between Young and Mostras, 2 Nov. 1954.

145. 78425, R11316, Norton to FO, 2 Dec. 1949; R11485, Norton to FO, 9 Dec. 1949.

146. Xydis 1967, 30.

147. 747C.00/8-1154, Schnee to State, desp. 121.

148. 112843, 1081/25, record of conversation between Harrison and Mostras, 20 Feb. 1954; 112845, 1081/72, record of conversation between Eden and Mostras, 6 April 1954; 747C.00/4-2154, 'memorandum on the Cyprus Question' (by Kyrou), in letter from Cannon to Baxter; cf. Mostras ms, 66.

149. Such rhetoric became more common following the threat of the Cyprus administration to apply its anti-seditious legislation: 112848, 1081/175, FO

to Peake, 21 July 1954; 112852, 1081/303, Peake to FO, 19 Aug. 1954; 747C.00/8-1154, Schnee to State, desp. 121; cf. Crawshaw 1978, 100; Crouzet I 1973, 438-439; Durrell 1957, 140-141.

150. 112873, 1081/959, Peake to FO, 3 Nov. 1954.
151. 112873, 1081/969, BBC Monitoring Service, 29 Oct. 1954; cf. Crawshaw 1978, 81-82.
152. Mostras ms, 59, n. 2.
153. Crouzet I 1973, 428-429.
154. Daskalakis' address contained the following passage:

> And we are forced to remind [the Britons] that, in the age when the ancestors of today's Cypriots and the rest of the Greeks built up Parthenons ... those who lived in [the British] Isles, and whom (the Britons) call their ancestors, had as sole occupation the jumping from tree to tree in order to pick up their food, while their spiritual condition was no better than that of the Mau-Mau ... As long as Cyprus remains under British oppression there can no longer be any question of intellectual friendship and co-operation between the British and the Greeks because we, the intellectual leaders of the Greek people, will soon turn this friendship into ashes ... we will not refrain from inspiring the Greek youth with wrath and rancour against Great Britain ... During morning prayers in every school there will be heard the voices of hatred and curses coming from the depths of the hearts of the Greek youth against the foreign oppressor of the Cypriot people.

Quoted in 112852, 1081/303, Peake to FO, 19 Aug. 1954; cf. Crouzet I 1973, 429; Hristidis 1967, 44. Significantly, Kyrou praised Daskalakis' activity as 'a brilliant example for imitation', and lamented his successors' decision to discontinue such methods: Kyrou 1955, 437.

155. 747C.00/8-1154, Cannon to State, tel. 344; 747C.03/8-1154, Schnee to State, desp. 121.
156. 747C.03/8-1154, Schnee to State, desp. 121; Hristidis 1967, 44-45; Mostras ms, 60. The members of the 'committee' were Rally deputies Leon Maccas, Dimitrios Babakos and Dimitrios Londos, independent opposition deputy Ioannis Zigdis, EPEK deputy Loukis Akritas, Lena Tsaldaris, widow of the pre-war leader of the People's Party, and Daskalakis.
157. Hristidis 1967, 45, 119; Mostras ms, 60; 112857, 1081/433, Chancery, Washington, to UN (Political) Department, 1 Sept. 1954; 747C.00/8-1754, memo of conversation between Maccas, Cavalierato and Richards; /8-3054, memo of conversation between Maccas and Howard; /9-454, memos from Melas to Jernegan. There were further initiatives aimed at disseminating Greek publicity material abroad. The State Department files preserve several copies of pamphlets issued by the National Council for Public Enlightenment at Home and Abroad, an organisation chaired by Eirenaios, Bishop of Samos: 747C.00/8-2554.
158. 747C.00/12-954, Andrew Vozeolas, National Director of 'The Justice for Cyprus Committee', to Dulles.
159. *FRUS 1952-54*, VIII, 677; 747C.00/7-554, office memo from Richards to

Scott.

160. Mostras ms, 60-61; Pipinelis 1959, 28.

161. *GPR*, meeting of 7 February 1955, 674; cf. Mostras ms, 52.

162. 112846, 1081/113, Lambert to Cheetham, 5 May 1954; 747C.00/5-1554, Schnee to State, desp. 1067; /9-2954, Schnee to State, desp. 259; *Astynomika Nea*, 20 April 1954; Hristidis 1967, 43; Linardatos II 1978, 168-172. The alleged infiltration of Greek public life by agents of the British Intelligence was projected as one of the reasons for the failure of the first Greek appeal: Kyrou 1955, 272.

163. 747C.00/11-1754, Schnee to State, desp. 446; Mostras ms, 58, n. 1; Pipinelis 1959, 29.

164. Before departing from Athens in late September 1954, the Archbishop questioned the expediency of what he saw as unconditional alignment with the West, and asked for a foreign policy putting Greece's interest first: Linardatos II 1978, 220.

165. 747C.00/11-1754, Schnee to State, desp. 446.

166. Mostras ms, 57, n. 3.

167. 747C.00/8-3054, memo of conversation between Howard and Maccas.

168. 747C.00/10-1154, memo of conversation between Politis and Byroade; *FRUS 1952-54*, VIII, 721, n. 4.

169. 747C.00/11-1754, Schnee to State, desp. 446.

170. Kyrou 1955, 298.

171. 747C.00/10-2354, message from Papagos to Eisenhower.

172. 112873, 1081/969, BBC Monitoring Service, 29 Oct. 1954.

173. *FRUS 1952-54*, VIII, 731.

174. *FRUS 1952-54*, VIII, 719-720.

175. Hristidis 1967, 122-123.

176. 747C.00/7-1052, Tibbetts to State, desp. 155; Xydis 1967, 595, n. 34.

177. 747C.00/11-1754, Schnee to State, desp. 446; cf. Pipinelis 1959, 29.

178. 117622, 1081/66, UKUN Delegation to FO, 19 Jan. 1955; Kyrou 1955, 296-297; Xydis 1967, 595, n. 34.

179. *GPR*, meeting of 7 February 1955 [Stefanopoulos], 675. A resolution like this, Kyrou claimed, might even help the British 'by providing an honourable issue out of the deadlock in which they (had) welled themselves': 747C.00/10-2354, memorandum from Papagos to Dulles, 23 Oct. 1953.

180. *FRUS 1952-54*, VIII, 723; 747C.00/12-2054, Schnee to State, desp. 576.

181. Kyrou 1955, 295-296. This tactic continued even after US opposition had become plain on the eve of the discussion at the Political Committee: *ibid.*, 301; Stefanopoulos' speech in *GPR*, meeting of 7 Feb. 1955, 697-699; cf. Hristidis 1967, 125.

182. *GPR*, meeting of 7 February 1955, 686.

183. *Ibid.* [Stefanopoulos], 675; Kyrou 1955, 299-301. According to Xydis, the final draft was prepared with a view to attracting as many votes as possible from non-European and anti-colonial member states, *in spite of* US opposition: Xydis 1967, 599, n. 78.

184. *FRUS 1952-54*, VIII, 733.
185. *GPR*, meeting of 7 February 1955 [Stefanopoulos], 675-676.
186. *Ibid.*, 676. As Ambassador Melas told US officials right after the end of the debate in the General Assembly, it was not until the day that the *New York Times* reported the US position that 'he realized the United States would accept only a purely procedural motion without even any slight reference to principles enunciated in the Charter and so frequently repeated in other statements': *FRUS 1952-54*, VIII, 744.
187. *GPR*, meeting of 7 February 1955 [Stefanopoulos], 676; Kyrou 1955, 297.
188. *Ibid.* [Stefanopoulos], 676; cf. Xydis 1967, 599, n. 79.
189. Kyrou 1955, 301-308.
190. This apparent flaw in the government's posture was widely criticised by the opposition papers, whereas the pro-government press exhausted itself in vituperations against US policy: 747C.00/12-2054, Schnee to State, desp. 576.
191. *GPR*, meeting of 7 February 1955 [Venizelos], 681-683; [Markezinis], 683-689; [Papandreou], 695-698.
192. 747C.00/12-2054, Schnee to State, desp. 576; Linardatos II 1978, 255, 264; Xydis 1967, 16-17.
193. 747C.00/12-2054, Schnee to State, desp. 576.
194. 117220, 1081/13, *Daily News Bulletin*, Prime Minister's Office, Department of Information, Athens, 3 Jan. 1955; Linardatos II 1978, 260, 262.
195. 112884, 1081/1273, BBC Monitoring Service, 20 Dec. 1954. At that point, Peake reported that the King's 'heart is in the right place over all this business and he is ploughing a rather lonely furrow': 117620, 1081/1, Peake to Young, 29 Dec. 1954.
196. Mostras ms, 71.
197. Pipinelis publicly argued in favour of a gradual political evolution in Cyprus in two articles published in the leading pro-government daily, *Kathimerini,* on 5-6 February 1955: Pipinelis 1959, 45-46.
198. 117624, 1081/89, letter from Maitland to Eden, 3 Feb. 1955.
199. Zinon Rossides wrote in *Kathimerini* on 23 March 1955 that 'the proposed constitutional advance can never lead to self-determination': quoted in Kyrou 1955, 328.
200. 747C.00/1-2055, Courtney to State, desp. 62.
201. Regarding the evolution of Makarios' attitude towards the prospect of violence, see Crawshaw 1978, 98-99; Kranidiotis 1981, 58-59, 81.
202. *FRUS 1955-57*, XXIV, 533.
203. *Ibid.*, 528-531; Linardatos II 1978, 277-278.
204. *FRUS 1955-57*, XXIV, 587.
205. Paragraph 1 of Article 33 of the UN Charter reads as follows: 'The parties to any dispute, the continuation of which is likely to endanger the maintenance of international peace and security, shall, first of all seek a solution by negotiation, enquiry, mediation, conciliation, arbitration, judicial settlement, resort to regional agencies or arrangements, or other peaceful means of their own choice'.

EPILOGUE

Having followed the political and diplomatic process that embittered relations between four allied powers and led to a crisis on the island of Cyprus, one is struck by the apparent failure of leadership, particularly on the part of the post-war British cabinets, the Papagos government and the Greek Cypriot leaders. This failure becomes all the more flagrant if one evaluates their decisions not only against the outcome but also against the criteria of rationality. While, of course, decision-making bodies seldom conform to the high standards of reason, a comparison of the actual decison-making processes examined in the previous chapters against the classical 'rational actor model'[1] might serve to present our conclusions in a more systematic way.

First, all four governments professed commitment to a number of shared *values*, such as those embodied in the UN Charter as well as the standard 'Free World' ideals: some type of liberal democracy, security and allied unity, anti-communism, economic development. There were, however, other important, often contradictory values. Perceptions of an imperial mission were still part of the British worldview; anti-colonialism clashed with more mundane values in the case of the United States; nationalism was a core value of both Greek and Turkish political systems and their respective communities in Cyprus. In ranking these values, the British emphasised their imperial and strategic role; the Americans opted for anti-communism and allied unity; and Greek attitudes eventually bowed to irredentism, while the Turks also veered towards an equally assertive type of nationalism.

Secondly, in specifying *objectives* compatible with its values, no government was immune to ambiguities and inconsistencies. For Britain, security priorities, in this case the preservation of its great power status in the Middle East, antagonised loftier objectives, such as the orderly emancipation of colonial peoples.[2] By supporting the British position in Cyprus and elsewhere in the Middle East, US

policy-makers tended to undermine American influence in that region and its ability to intervene and contain local crises effectively.
The Greek government of Field Marshal Papagos failed to realise
the essential incompatibility between the need to foster the country's security and economic recovery and the pursuit of nationalist
goals in that particular conjunction. In the case of Turkey, the twofold objective of arresting Enosis and gaining international recognition as a party to the dispute[3] militated against the concept of Greek-
Turkish partnership.

Thirdly, while the governments and the other groups involved
in the dispute were able to identify a wide range of *options* for
achieving their objectives, they often failed to calculate and evalu-
ate the consequences properly. Until very late, the British regularly
dismissed any option that might open even a slight prospect of change
in the status of Cyprus. Thus, they limited themselves to a largely
negative, reactive stand. In this context, the deterioration of Anglo-
Greek relations was foreseen and accepted as inevitable. The Americans chose to avoid becoming publicly involved in the dispute while
they discreetly supported the British and persistently discouraged
Greek ambitions. This was done, however, at the expense of their
ability to play a mediating role, an objective further compromised
by their choice of low-level or non-diplomatic channels. The decision of the Papagos government to pursue internationalisation not
only revealed a poor sense of timing but also undermined an essential Greek objective – to keep the Cyprus question as a bilateral
Anglo-Greek dispute. As a result, internationalisation became a sort
of strait-jacket that limited Greek options for years to come. The
'Enosis and only Enosis' line of the Greek Cypriot leadership, even
if it is viewed as a reaction to British intransigence, dramatically
narrowed its scope of tactical manoeuvring and ruled out the prospect of a British-Cypriot bargaining process. The Turkish government,
for its part, skilfully temporised until it was able to benefit from Greek
moves in order to promote its afore-mentioned goals.

Fourthly, in selecting the final option or combination of options,
none of the parties, with the partial exception of Turkey, succeeded
in promoting their original objectives:
- In the short term, the British government failed either to avert the
Greek recourse to the UN or to deflate the Enosis campaign and

prevent its escalation to violence. In the longer-term, it would fail to maintain British sovereignty over Cyprus and would be obliged to resort to a number of previously discarded options: talks on Cyprus with a foreign power (at the London Tripartite Conference of 1955); self-government combined with a, however indirect, recognition of the Cypriot people's right to self-determination (during the talks between Makarios and Governor Harding in early 1956 and later, in June 1956); repression (in response to the EOKA struggle but also against the Communist AKEL); the termination of British rule and partition (from December 1956 onwards); a tripartite condominium (according to the MacMillan plan, in June 1958); and, finally, the retention of sovereign bases (by the London agreement, in February 1959).[4]

- The Americans failed to prevent a public controversy between their allies, particularly on the UN floor, and, subsequently, to act as an 'honest broker' and deflate the crisis. Instead, they were increasingly drawn into the Cyprus quagmire. In the longer-term, the damage to allied unity and US strategic planning would not be averted, as shown by the steady deterioration of Anglo-Greek and, particularly, Greek-Turkish relations, the dislocation of NATO's south-eastern flank, and the eclipse of the Balkan Pact.

- By making Cyprus an international issue, the Greek government failed to secure its original aim, that is to expedite a change in British attitude and initiate a process that could lead to Enosis. In the longer run, it would have to face a whole range of undesirable (and unforeseen?) consequences: the demise of Greek-Turkish friendship, the deterioration of relations with its most important allies, the recognition of Turkey as a legitimate party to a settlement, the destruction of the Greek minority in Istanbul, political difficulties at home, and, eventually, the abandonment of Enosis in favour of independence.

- With regard to the Greek Cypriot Ethnarchy, it not only failed to achieve Enosis through internationalisation and, later, armed struggle, but it was gradually forced to accept alternatives previously condemned as treason: talks with the colonial ruler and independence within the Commonwealth, a status of political parity to the Turkish Cypriot minority and a say for Turkey in the affairs of the new Republic. The Communist AKEL, for its part, while succeed-

ing in its presumed aim, i.e. to turn Cyprus into an international
problem and thus disrupt relations between four Western allies, never
came near its professed goal of a 'Free Cyprus in a Free Greece'.
- Turkey did gain international recognition as a party to the dispute
as well as succeeding in forestalling Enosis, and securing a privi-
leged position for the Turkish Cypriot minority in the eventual settlement. She would fail, however, to promote a *de jure* partition of
the island, an objective adopted in late 1956 and abandoned at the
time of the Zurich-London compromise two years later. Future
Greek and Greek Cypriot initiatives would permit her to revive
this aim and ruthlessly accomplish it in 1974.

Part II focused on the role of individuals (government and community leaders or high officials) and 'organisational units' (government departments as well as political parties and pressure groups)
in the policy-making process of each party. The evidence assembled
helps to illustrate the limitations of that process and explain the
outcome:
- The fact that the Cyprus question cut across the lines of foreign,
defence and colonial domains tended to make British policy a bit of
a puzzle. While the colonial and military bureaucracies economised
on searching out alternatives and largely clung to a set of standard
responses, the diplomats did not shy from venturing new approaches,
involving a fairly open-minded discussion of values and the revision
of objectives.[5] At a higher level, there was a distinct sense of 'mud-
dling through', an extreme instance being Churchill's confession of
the way the ill-fated Cabinet Paper on Cyprus became official policy
in July 1954.[6] Yet it was not so much competition among the different parts of the bureaucracy which accounted for the course of
Cyprus policy, particularly after 1947. Rather, government leaders,
both Labour and Conservative, appeared impervious to fresh ideas
which might allow for beneficial adjustments of policy – with the
partial exception of the cosmetic constitutional devices. Instead,
they stuck to the old ways and slid into a rigid and sterile stance –
the retention of sovereignty over Cyprus as long as this was deemed
to serve wider British objectives in the Middle East.[7] As has been
aptly observed, the resulting policy 'did not succeed either to frighten
or to seduce, but it offended, irritated, accelerated the process of
aggravation of the conflict'.[8]

- The American case fits more neatly into what Graham Allison, the American specialist in decision-making theory, describes as 'bureaucratic politics'[9]: policy options were defined, evaluated and all but finalised among various branches of the bureaucracy at home and diplomatic representatives abroad, more often than not after some inter-departmental 'wrangling'. Conflicting values and outside pressures, from, for example, Congress and the Greek-American lobby, were more or less effectively streamlined in the process. Until the Greek recourse, the role of the political leadership, the Secretary of State and the President in particular, was largely limited to rubber-stamping the recommended options. When the threat of a fall-out between allies and substantial damage to US interests became obvious, the role of the administration was exhausted in ineffective, piece-meal initiatives.

- The early phase of Greek policy on the Cyprus question, which adhered to the concept of Anglo-Greek relations as the proper framework for a settlement, was as much the outcome of external pressures as that of more or less rational policy-making. This latter aspect was exemplified in Venizelos' achieving an all-party consensus in March 1951. The eventual decision to turn Cyprus into an international problem owed less to outside pressures, in this case from the Ethnarchy and its supporters, and even less to any bureaucratic competition; rather, it reflected the fact that political elites in Greece and Cyprus acted both as advocates of and hostages to a single value: nationalism. In opting for internationalisation, Papagos and his chief advisers, like the Ethnarchy leaders before them, simplified a complex issue 'by eliminating variety, ignoring elaborate calculations concerning the environment' and the possible outcomes, while committing themselves to 'abstract beliefs' which proved of little relevance to harsh and changing international realities.[9] This was what Ambassador Mostras and others criticised as going 'into battle without a plan of operations',[11] and his British counterpart euphemistically described as 'the known capacity of the Greeks for not counting the costs, if they believe that they are acting in a just cause'.[12] The long-term consequences, which were largely the price of overlooking Turkish opposition to Enosis, would be disastrous.[13]

- In the absence of detailed documentation, it might be too risky to attempt to generalise about the Turkish policy-making process. It seems, however, that the Turkish government succeeded where its Greek counterpart failed: by not subordinating its foreign policy to either ideological precepts or domestic political expediency. Thus, it was able to choose the most efficient options and make the best of its originally weak political and legal position.[14] Of course, it was greatly aided by objective factors, such as the country's sheer size and geostrategic importance to its major allies, as well as by the gross ineptitude of its rival.

A few words remain to be said about the role of the United Nations. The Organisation, dominated as it was till 1955 by the Western European powers and the United States, offered little more in practical terms than a *forum* for the disputing parties to air their differences. Ironically, the policies of the 'actors' involved were to a considerable extent influenced by the perceived political authority of the UN and its potential to initiate change.

When all has been said, one is tempted to speculate on what were the chances of a timely accommodation, which might have prevented the aggravation of the problem to intractable proportions. The only real opportunity for a settlement, whereby the British could have ceded Cyprus to Greece on mutually acceptable terms without provoking undue Turkish reactions, passed in 1945-6 when the Foreign Office lost against the combined reaction of the colonial bureaucracy and the military. A second opportunity, this time for containing the problem between the British and the Cypriots without prejudice to future options, was missed in 1947-8, when the Greek Cypriot leadership rejected the Winster Constitution. From then on, the British consistently ruled out the prospect of change, while Turkish opposition to Enosis or meaningful concessions to the Greek majority stiffened. British rigidity matched the futility of the Greek Cypriot 'Enosis and only Enosis' line. These two factors worked to limit drastically both the room for manoeuvre of successive Greek governments and the chances of American attempts at mediation. Once it had decided to resort to the UN, the Greek government found itself locked in a zero-sum contest against the British and subsequently the Turks, from which no party felt able to withdraw without suffering what it perceived as severe losses. Even then, Greek readiness to de-escalate was offset by British inflexibility and Ethnarchy maximalism. The aftermath of the first

Greek recourse might also have opened the way to a compromise with honour. Yet the revision of British policy towards accepting the prospect of self-determination proved a slow process, and remained unknown to both the Greek government and to those who eventually mounted a campaign of violence in Cyprus. From this point of view, both parties showed a poor sense of timing which was to cost the people of Cyprus decades of tribulation.

NOTES

1. Realising the hermeneutic limits of the the 'classic' or 'rational actor' model, contemporary decision-making theorists have come up with various conceptual models (or 'paradigms'): the 'bounded rationality' model, the 'organisational process model', the 'bureaucratic politics model'. See Couloumbis-Wolfe 1990, 126-134; Dougherty-Pfaltzgraff 1981, 476-483; Frankel 1973, 64-71. For the merits of the 'rational actor' (or 'rational comprehensive', as he defines it) model as an analytical device, see Lindblom 1959.
2. Cf. Darwin 1988, 145. The same author speaks of British policy in Cyprus 'as a striking anomaly alongside the rapid preparation for Ghanaian independence and Nigerian self-government': *ibid.*, 215.
3. Bilge 1975, 140.
4. A comprehensive account of British policy on Cyprus between 1955-9 see in Hatzivassiliou 1997.
5. The result, as Ambassador Norton pointed out in late 1949, was the treatment of the problem in a fragmented way, which was presumably preserved at the highest level: Chapter IV, note 42. This remark would definitely appeal to exponents of organisational behaviour theories on the conduct of foreign policy: Dougherty-Pfaltzgraff 1981, 483-485.
6. CO 926/499, Churchill to Lennox Boyd, 11 Aug. 1954. Cf. Macmillan's warning about how misleading Cabinet minutes can be: Adamthwaite 1988, 2-3.
7. According to Holland, 'the peculiar sensitivity and tenacity which British policy (in both its local and metropolitan forms) displayed in the case of Cyprus may be explained as much by the island's location on the emotional and ideological map of British power overseas as by any strategic considerations arising from its physical situation in the eastern Mediterranean': Holland 1993, 150-151.
8. Crouzet I 1973, 412.
9. This model has been developed on the basis of the American experience by Graham T. Allison: *idem* 1971, 144ff.; see also Allison-Halperin 1972.
10. Dougherty-Pfaltzgraff 1981, 484.
11. Mostras ms, 9. Papagos' successor, Konstantinos Karamanlis, would later comment on the the Field Marshal's decision as follows:

It is certain that, when Field Marshal Papagos decided to internationalise the

Cyprus question by raising it at the United Nations, unlike his predecessors, he did not sufficiently appreciate the terrible impact on the country's external relations. Of course, there was the provocative behaviour of the British as well as the pressure of public opinion, but as a political act it was certainly unfortunate.

Quoted in Kranidiotis 1981, 72.

12. 112843, 1081/6, Peake to Cheetham, 23 Jan. 1954.
13. This seems to confirm those who proclaim Greek Cypriot nationalism 'an irrational force' which has proved incompatible with the standards of rational decision-making: Mavratsas 1996, 93-94.
14. Cf. Vàli 1971, 356-357.

SOURCES

UNPUBLISHED

United Kingdom, Public Record Office:
CAB 128-129: Cabinet Papers
CO 67, 926: Colonial Office Papers
DEFE 5: Ministry of Defence, Papers of the Chiefs of Staff
FO 371: Foreign Office Papers

United States, National Archives:
Record Group 59: General Records of the Department of State, decimal files
Record Group 218: Records of the US Joint Chiefs of Staff

Greece, private:
Mostras ms: Mostras, Vasilios, «Επί του Κυπριακού Ζητήματος» (On the Cyprus Question), 99 pp.
Papapolyviou ms: Papapolyviou, Petros, «Ο αντίκτυπος του Μακεδονικού ζητήματος στην Κύπρο στα χρόνια του ελληνικού εμφυλίου και οι επιπτώσεις του στο κυπριακό ενωτικό ζήτημα» (The Effect of the Macedonian Question in Cyprus during the Greek Civil War Years and its Impact on the Cypriot Question of Enosis), 17 pp.

PUBLISHED

Documents

Captured Documents : *Terrorism in Cyprus. The Captured Documents* (Papers of the EOKA organisation, including General Grivas' diary, seized by the British security forces), HMSO, London 1956
'Documents: Cyprus, 1950-1954; The Prelude to the Crisis', Parts I ('1950') - II ('The View of the United States'), edited by Alexander Kitroeff, *Journal of the Hellenic Diaspora*, XIV-XV (spring-summer 1988, autumn-winter 1988)
FRUS : *The Foreign Relations of the United States*, Government Printing Office, Washington DC
GDR, 1940-41 : *Ελληνικά διπλωματικά έγγραφα* (Greek Diplomatic Records), Ministry for Foreign Affairs, Athens 1980

GPR (Greek Parliamentary Records): *Επίσημα Πρακτικά των Συνεδριάσεων της Βουλής* (Official Records of the Sessions of Parliament), Sessions I-XL, Athens, 1956
Makarios III : *Άπαντα Αρχιεπισκόπου Κύπρου Μακαρίου Γ´* (Complete Speeches of Makarios III, Archbishop of Cyprus), I (1948-1954), Nicosia, January 1991
YUN : *Yearbook of the United Nations*, Department of Public Information, United Nations, New York

Books and Articles

Adamthwaite 1988: Anthony Adamthwaite, 'The Foreign Office and Policy-making', in Young (ed.) 1988, 1-28
Adams 1971: T.W. Adams, *AKEL: The Communist Party of Cyprus*, Stanford, Ca.
Aldrich-Hopkins (eds.) 1994: Richard Aldrich and Michael Hopkins (eds.), *Intelligence, Defence and Diplomacy: British Policy in the Post-War World*, London
Alexander 1979: George M. Alexander, 'British Policy on the Question of Enosis, 1945-1946', *Kypriakai Spoudai* 43 (1979), 79-94
Alexandrakis *et al.* 1987: M. Alexandrakis, V. Theodoropoulos and E. Lagakos, *Το Κυπριακό 1950-1974. Μια ενδοσκόπηση* (The Cyprus Question 1950-1974. An Introspection), Athens
Alexandris 1983: Alexis Alexandris, *The Greek Minority of Istanbul and Greek-Turkish Relations 1918-1974*, Athens
_____ 1988: Alexis Alexandris, «Το μειονοτικό ζήτημα, 1954-1987» (The Question of Minorities), in Alexandris-Veremis *et al.* 1988, 493-552
Alexandris-Veremis *et al.* 1988: Alexis Alexandris, Thanos Veremis, *et al.*, *Οι ελληνοτουρκικές σχέσεις 1923-1987* (Greek-Turkish Relations, 1923-1987), Athens
Allison 1971: Graham T. Allison, *The Essence of Decision: Explaining the Cuban Missile Crisis*, Boston Mass.
Allison-Halperin 1972: Graham T. Allison and Morton H. Halperin, 'Bureaucratic Politics: A Paradigm and Some Policy Implications', *World Politics* 24 (Spring 1972), Supplement
Anderson, B., 1991: Benedict Anderson, *Imagined Communities: Reflections on the Origin and Spread of Nationalism*, London-New York
Anderson, D., 1994: David M. Anderson, 'Policing and Communal Conflict: The Cyprus Emergency, 1954-60' in Holland (ed.) 1994, 177-207
Andreadis 1956: K.G. Andreadis, *Η μουσουλμανική κοινότης της Δυτικής Θράκης* (The Muslim Community of Western Thrace), Thessaloniki
Ansprenger 1989: Franz Ansprenger, *The Dissolution of the Colonial Empires*, London
Attalides 1979: Michael Attalides, *Cyprus: Nationalism and International Politics*, Edinburgh
_____ 1981: Michael Attalides, «Οι σχέσεις των Ελληνοκυπρίων με τους

Sources   305

Τουρκοκυπρίους» (Greek Cypriot Relations with the Turkish Cypriots), in Tenekides-Kranidiotis (eds.) 1981

_____ 1986: Michael Attalides, «Τα κόμματα στην Κύπρο» ([Political] Parties in Cyprus), *Kypriaka 1878-1955*, Nicosia, 1986, 123-152

Averof I 1982: Evangelos Averof-Tosizza, *Ιστορία χαμένων ευκαιριών (Κυπριακό, 1950-1963)* (A History of Missed Opportunities: The Cyprus Question, 1950-1963), vol. I, Athens (publ. in English as *Lost Opportunities: The Cyprus Question, 1950-1963*, New York, 1986)

Bahcheli 1990: Tozun Bahcheli, *Greek-Turkish Relations since 1955*, San Francisco-London

Bilge 1975: Suat Bilge, 'The Cyprus Conflict and Turkey', in Karpat (ed.) 1975, 135ff.

Blinkhorn-Veremis 1990: Martin Blinkhorn and Thanos Veremis (eds.), *Modern Greece: Nationalism and Nationality*, Athens

Bolukbasi 1988: Suha Bolukbasi, *Turkish-American Relations and Cyprus*, Lanham, Md.

Bull 1995: Hedley Bull, *The Anarchical Society. A Study of Order in World Politics*, 2nd edition, Houndmills-London

Calogeropoulos-Stratis 1973: Spyridon Calogeropoulos-Stratis, *Le droit des peuples a disposer d'eux-memes*, Brussels

Calvocoressi 1987: Peter Calvocoressi, *World Politics since 1945*, 5th edition, London

Campbell 1960: John C.Campbell, *Defence of the Middle East*, 2nd edition, New York

Cassese 1995: Antonio Cassese, *Self-Determination of Peoples: A Legal Reappraisal*, Cambridge

Choisi 1993: Jeanette Choisi, *Wurzeln und Strukturen des Zypernkonfliktes 1878 bis 1990. Ideologischer Nationalismus und Machtbehauptung im Kalkuel konkurrierender Eliten*, Stuttgart

Clerides 1989: Glafkos Clerides, *Cyprus: My Deposition*, vol. I, Nicosia

Couloumbis-Wolfe 1990: Theodore A. Couloumbis and James H. Wolfe, *Introduction to International Relations: Power and Justice*, 4th edition, Englewood Cliffs, NJ

Crawshaw 1978: Nancy Crawshaw, *The Cyprus Revolt: An Account of the Struggle for Union with Greece*, London

Crouzet I 1973: François Crouzet, *Le conflit de Chypre 1946-1959*, vols. I-II, Bruxelles

Darwin 1988: John Darwin, *Britain and Decolonisation: The Retreat from Empire in the Post-War World*, London

Deighton (ed.) 1990: Anne Deighton (ed.), *Britain and the First Cold War*, London

Devereux 1990a: David Devereux, *The Formulation of British Defence Policy towards the Middle East, 1948-56*, London

_____ 1990b: David Devereux, 'Britain and the Failure of Collective Defence in the Middle East, 1948-53', in Deighton (ed.) 1990, 237-252

Dougherty-Pfaltzgraff 1981: James E. Dougherty·and Robert L.

Pfaltzgraff Jr., *Contending Theories of International Relations. A Comprehensive Survey*, 2nd edition, New York

Durrell 1957: Durrell, Lawrence, *Bitter Lemons*, London

Eden *Memoirs* III: Anthony Eden, *The Memoirs of Anthony Eden: Full Circle*, London, 1960

Evryviades 1987: Marios Evryviades, 'Greek Policy and Cyprus: An Interpretation', *Journal of the Hellenic Diaspora*, XIV.4 (1987), 25-48

Fantis 1993: Andreas Fantis, *Η Διασκεπτική. Η πρώτη χαμένη ευκαιρία στο Κυπριακό* (The Consultative Assembly. A First Missed Opportunity in the Cyprus Question), Nicosia 1993

Foley-Scobie 1975: Charles Foley and W.I. Scobie, *The Struggle for Cyprus*, Stanford, Ca.

Frankel 1973: Joseph Frankel, *Contemporary International Theory and the Behaviour of States*, Oxford

Frederica 1971: Queen Frederica, *A Measure of Understanding*, London

Georghallides 1985: G.S. Georghallides, *Cyprus and the Governorship of Sir Ronald Storrs*, Nicosia

Grivas *Memoirs*: Georgios Grivas (*Digenis*), *The Memoirs of General Grivas* (edited by Charles Foley), London 1964

Hatzivassiliou 1994: Evanthis Hatzivassiliou, 'The Cyprus Question and the Anglo-American Special Relationship, 1954-58', in Aldrich-Hopkins (eds.) 1994, 149-168

_____ 1997: *Britain and the International Status of Cyprus, 1955-59*, Minneapolis, Minnesota

Holden Reid 1988: Brian Holden Reid, 'The 'Northern Tier' and the Baghdad Pact', in Young (ed.) 1988, 159-179

Holland 1993: Robert Holland, 'Never, Never Land: British Colonial Policy and the Roots of Violence in Cyprus, 1950-1954', *The Journal of Imperial and Commonwealth History*, 21.3 (1993), 148-176

_____ (ed.) 1994: Robert Holland (ed.), *Emergencies and Disorder in the European Empires after 1945*, London

Hristidis 1967: Hristoforos Hristidis (Damonides), *Κυπριακό και ελληνοτουρκικά* (The Cyprus Question and Greek Turkish [Relations]), Athens

Hristodoulou 1987: Miltiadis Hristodoulou, *Η πορεία μιας εποχής. Η Ελλάδα, η κυπριακή ηγεσία και το Κυπριακό πρόβλημα* (The Course of an Era. Greece, the Cypriot Leadership and the Cyprus Question), Athens

Iatrides 1968: John O.Iatrides, *Balkan Triangle: Birth and Decline across Ideological Boundaries*, the Hague

Ioannides 1991: Christos P. Ioannides, *In Turkey's Image: The Transformation of Occupied Cyprus into a Turkish Province*, New York

Karpat 1975: Kemal Karpat (ed.), *Turkey's Foreign Policy in Transition 1950-1974*, Leiden

Kelling 1990: George Horton Kelling, *Countdown to Rebellion: British Policy in Cyprus, 1939-1955*, New York-Westport-London

Kent 1994: John Kent, 'The Egyptian Base and the Defence of the

Middle East, 1945-54' in Holland (ed.) 1994, 45-65

Kitromilides 1979: Paschalis Kitromilides, 'The Dialectic of Intolerance: Ideological Dimensions of Ethnic Conflict ', *Journal of the Hellenic Diaspora*, VI.4 (1979), 5-30

_____ 1981: Paschalis Kitromilides, «Το ιδεολογικό πλαίσιο της πολιτικής ζωής της Κύπρου: κριτική θεώρηση» (The Ideological Framework of Political Life in Cyprus: A Critical Review), in Tenekides-Kranidiotis (eds.) 1981, 449-471

_____ 1990a: Paschalis Kitromilides, '"Imagined Communities" and the Origins of the National Question in the Balkans', in M. Blinkhorn-T. Veremis (ed., reprint from special issue of the *European History Quarterly*, 19[1989]), 1990, 23-66

_____ 1990b: Paschalis Kitromilides, 'Greek Irredentism in Asia Minor and Cyprus', *Middle Eastern Studies*, 26.1 (1990), 3-17

Kondis 1991: Basil Kondis, 'Greek National Claims at the Paris Peace Conference of 1946', *Balkan Studies*, 32.2 (1991), 309-324

Konidaris 1964: Gerasimos Konidaris, «Ιστορικαί αναμνήσεις από την προετοιμασίαν του αγώνος της Κύπρου» (Historical Reminiscences from the Preparation of the Struggle for Cyprus), *Parnassos*, VI.2 (1964), 251-258

Kranidiotis 1981: Nikos Kranidiotis, *Δύσκολα χρόνια. Κύπρος 1950-1960* (Difficult Years. Cyprus 1950-1960), Athens

Kyriakides 1968: Stanley Kyriakides, *Cyprus: Constitutionalism and Crisis Government*, Philadelphia

Kyrou 1955: Alexis Kyrou, *Ελληνική εξωτερική πολιτική* (Greek Foreign Policy), Athens 1955, 1984

_____ 1972: Alexis Kyrou, *Όνειρα και πραγματικότης. Σαραντανέντε χρόνια διπλωματικής ζωής* (Dreams and Reality. Forty Five Years of a Diplomat's Life), Athens

Kyrris 1977: Costas Kyrris, *Peaceful Co-existence in Cyprus under British Rule (1878-1959) and after Independence: An Outline*, Nicosia

Landau 1974: Jacob M.Landau, *Radical Politics in Modern Turkey*, Leiden

_____ 1981: Jacob M.Landau, *Pan-Turkism in Turkey: A Study of Irredentism*, London

Linardatos I 1977: Spiros Linardatos, *Από τον εμφύλιο στη χούντα* (From Civil War to the Junta), vol. I: *1949-1952*, Athens

Linardatos II 1978: Spiros Linardatos, *Από τον εμφύλιο στη χούντα* (From Civil War to the Junta), vol. II: *1952-1955*, Athens

Loizidis 1980: Savvas Loizidis, *Άτυχη Κύπρος. Πώς έζησα τους πόθους και τους καημούς της, 1910-1980* (Unfortunate Cyprus. How I Lived its Aspirations and Yearnings, 1910-1980), Athens

Louis 1984: William Roger Louis, *The British Empire in the Middle East 1945-1951: Arab Nationalism, the United States, and Postwar Imperialism*, Oxford

Lucas 1990: Scott Lucas, 'The Path to Suez: Britain and the Struggle for the Middle East, 1953-56', in Deighton (ed.) 1990, 253-272

Markezinis 1994: Spyridon V. Markezinis, *Σύγχρονη πολιτική ιστορία της*

308 *Sources*

Ελλάδος (1936-1975) (Contemporary Political History of Greece),
Athens

Mavratsas 1996: Caesar Mavratsas, 'Approaches to Nationalism: Basic
Theoretical Considerations in the Study in the Study of the Greek-
Cypriot Case and a Historical Overview', *Journal of the Hellenic
Diaspora*, 22.1 (1996), 77-102

Mayes 1981: Stanley Mayes: *Makarios: A Biography*, London

Mihalopoulos 1982: Dimitris Mihalopoulos, 'The 1950 Plebiscite in
Cyprus', *Hellenic Review of International Relations*, 2.2 (1981-1982),
569-579

_____ 1989: Dimitris Mihalopoulos, *Ελλάδα και Τουρκία 1950-1959. Η
χαμένη προσέγγιση* (Greece and Turkey 1950-1959. The Lost Rapprochement), Athens

Nachmani 1987: Amikam Nachmani, *Israel, Turkey and Greece: Uneasy
Relations in the East Mediterranean*, London

Nea Estia LVI: *Nea Estia* (literary periodical), Christmas 1954 (Homage
to Cyprus), LVI (659), Athens

Nicholas 1971: H.G.Nicholas, *The United Nations as a Political Institution*,
4th edition, Oxford

Ovendale 1988: Ritchie Ovendale, 'Egypt and the Suez Base Agreement', in Young (ed.) 1988, 135-154

Papageorgiou 1984: Spyros Papageorgiou, *ΑΚΕΛ, το άλλο ΚΚΕ* (AKEL,
the Other KKE), Athens

Papaioannou 1988: Ezekias Papaioannou, *Ενθυμήσεις από τη ζωή μου*
(Reminiscences from My Life), Nicosia

Pipinelis 1959: Panayotis Pipinelis, *Η διαχείρισις του Κυπριακού ζητήματος
κατά τα τελευταία έτη* (The Handling of the Cyprus Question during
the Last Years), Athens

Pollis 1973: Adamantia Pollis, 'Intergroup Conflict and British Colonial Policy: The Case of Cyrpus', *Comparative Politics*, 5 (1973), 575-
599

Reddaway 1986: John Reddaway, *Burdened with Cyprus: The British Connection*, London

Seferis *Diary* II: Giorgos Seferis, *Πολιτικό ημερολόγιο* (Political Diary),
vol. II, 1945-1947, 1949, 1952 (edited by Alexandros Xydis), Athens, 1985

_____ *Meres* VI: Giorgos Seferis, *Μέρες* (Days), vol. VI, 20 April 1951-4
August 1956 (edited by Panayotis Mermingas), Athens, 1986

Servas I 1985: Ploutis Servas, *Κυπριακό: Ευθύνες* (The Cyprus Question:
Responsibilities), vol. I, Athens

_____ 1989: Ploutis Servas, *Ένα άλλο μνημόσυνο* (An Other Commemo-
ration), Nicosia

Shaw 1991: Malcolm N.Shaw, *International Law*, 3rd edition, Cambridge

Sked-Cook 1984: Alan Sked and Chris Cook, *Post-War Britain: A Political History*, 2nd edition, London

Stefanidis 1991: Ioannis Stefanidis, 'The Cyprus Question, 1949-1952:
British Attitude, American Reactions and Greek Dilemmas', *Byzan-*

tine and Modern Greek Studies, 15 (1991), 212-267

Stephens 1966: Robert Stephens, *Cyprus: A Place of Arms*, London-New York 1966

Sulzberger 1969: Cyrus Sulzberger, *A Long Row of Candles: Memories and Diaries, 1934-1954*, London

Svolopoulos 1985: Constantine Svolopoulos, 'The Lausanne Peace Treaty and the Cyprus Problem', *Greece and Great Britain During World War I*, Institute for Balkan Studies-King's College, Thessaloniki, 1985

Tenekides-Kranidiotis (eds.) 1981: Georgios Tenekides and Yannos Kranidiotis (eds.), *Κύπρος: Ιστορία, προβλήματα και αγώνες του λαού της* (Cyprus: History, Problems and Struggles of its People), Athens

Terlexis 1971: Pantazis Terlexis, *Διπλωματία και πολιτική του Κυπριακού. Ανατομία ενός λάθους* (Diplomacy and Politics of the Cyprus Question. Anatomy of a Mistake), Athens

Vàli 1971: Ferenc A. Vàli, *Bridge across the Bosporus: The Foreign Policy of Turkey*, Baltimore and London

Vlahos 1980: Angelos Vlahos, *Δέκα χρόνια Κυπριακού* (Ten Years of the Cyprus Question), Athens

Xydis 1966: Stephen Xydis, 'Toward 'Toil and Moil' in Cyprus', *The Middle East Journal*, 20.1 (1966), 1-19

_____ 1967: Stephen Xydis, *Cyprus: Conflict and Conciliation, 1954-1967*, Columbus, Ohio

_____ 1968: Stephen Xydis, 'The UN General Assembly as an Instrument of Greek Policy: Cyprus, 1954-58', *Journal of Conflict Resolution*, 12.2 (1968), 141-158

Young 1988: John Young (ed.), *The Foreign Policy of Churchill's Peacetime Administration, 1951-1955*, Leicester

INDEX